The Cahokia Mounds

Classics in Southeastern Archaeology
Stephen Williams, Series Editor

Publication of this work has been supported in part by the
Dan Josselyn Memorial Fund

The Cahokia Mounds

WARREN K. MOOREHEAD

Edited and with an Introduction by John E. Kelly

THE UNIVERSITY OF ALABAMA PRESS
Tuscaloosa and London

The three works by Warren K. Moorehead (including sections by Jay L. B.
Taylor, Morris M. Leighton, and Frank C. Baker) reproduced by facsimile in
this volume were published originally as the following University of Illinois
Bulletins, University of Illinois, Urbana: Portions of *The Cahokia Mounds: A
Preliminary Paper* XIX, no. 35 (April 24, 1922); portions of *The Cahokia Mounds:
Part I, A Report of Progress*, and *Part II, Some Geological Aspects* XXI, no. 6 (October 8, 1923); and *The Cahokia Mounds* XXVI, no. 4 (September 25, 1928, copyright © 1929).

1 2 3 4 5 6 7 8 9 • 08 07 06 05 04 03 02 01 00

Cover design by Robin McDonald

∞

The paper on which this book is printed meets the minimum requirements of
American National Standard for Information Science–Permanence of Paper
for Printed Library Materials, ANSI Z39.48–1984.

Library of Congress Cataloging-in-Publication Data

Moorehead, Warren King, 1866–1939.
    The Cahokia Mounds / Warren K. Moorehead; edited and with an
    introduction by John E. Kelly.
        p. cm. — (Classics in southeastern archaeology)
        Includes bibliographical references and index.
        ISBN 0-8173-1010-X (alk. paper)
        1. Cahokia Mounds State Historic Park (Ill.)   I. Kelly, John Edward.
    II. Title. III. Series.

    E78.I3 M66 2000
    977.3`89—dc21   99-047252

British Library Cataloguing-in-Publication Data available

Contents

Figures and Plates   vii

Acknowledgments   xv

Note on This Edition   xvii

Introduction by John E. Kelly   1

     References   49

The Cahokia Mounds: A Preliminary Paper (1922)   59

The Cahokia Mounds: Part I, A Report of Progress and
     Part II, Some Geological Aspects (1923)   97

The Cahokia Mounds (1929)   189

Plates   369

     Key to Plates and Figure Numbers   370

Index   427

Figures and Plates

FIGURES

Painting of Monks Mound in 1876   xviii

Introduction

1. Newspaper headlines   12
2. Cahokia Mounds Historic Site-National Historic Landmark boundaries   *facing page* 12
3. Advertisement for trolley car rides to Monks Mound, ca. 1900   13
4. Ramey mural of Monks Mound   15
5. Warren King Moorehead meeting with the Rameys   19
6. First page of flier, "Help Save The Cahokia Mounds"   20
7. Letter from Fred Ramey showing letterhead and map, December 1921   23
8. Location of Moorehead's investigations at Cahokia, 1921, 1922, and 1927   26
9. Cahokia site chronology   34
10. Location of Moorehead's investigations in the American Bottom, 1922, 1923   35
11. Augering into the Harding Mound, 1927   37
12. William Seever's 1896 map of the Mitchell site   40
13. Grid layout at the Harding Mound, 1927   47

Moorehead 1922

Design on a fragment of pottery   92
[Figures 1–46 are contained within the plates, *following page* 371.]

Moorehead 1923

1. Positions of skeletons in trench cut through mounds   112

2. Ground plan of trench in James Ramey Mound   115
3. Plan of circular trench, etc., in James Ramey Mound   116
4. Diagram of Tusant Jondro Mound   121
5. Field plan of the Jondro Mound   122
6. Mound on bluffs east of St. Louis   127
7. Large polished celt or hatchet   138
8. Map showing the location of the Cahokia Group   159
9. Sketch of west face of trench, James Ramey Mound   168
10. Sketch of chimney section, James Ramey Mound   170
11. Arrangement of materials in the east face, James
    Ramey Mound   172
12. Sketch of irregular contacts between layers of fine
    material in mounds   174
13. Sketch showing arrangement of materials in
    Albert Kunnemann Mound   176
14. Sketch of structure of materials in north face, Sam
    Chucallo Mound   178
15. Sketch of structure of materials in south face, Sam
    Chicalo [sic] Mound   179

Moorehead 1929

1.   Reproduction of the map drawn by J. J. R. Patrick
        about 1880   facing page 204
[1a.]   Design on a fragment of pottery   227
2–7.   [Same as 1–6 in Moorehead 1923]   starting on page 231
8.   Contour lines, survey of Mound No. 66   facing page 268
9.   Cross section of Mound No. 66 at major axis facing page 269
10–18. [Same as 7–15 in Moorehead 1923] starting on page 285
19.   Cross section of Mound No. I, Havana group   347
20.   Ground plan and cross section of Mound No. 5, Havana,
        Illinois   348
21.   Ground plan of interments and objects in Mound
        No. 6, Havana group   357

Following Page 371
PLATES FROM MOOREHEAD'S WORKS

[I]   [from 1922 volume] Fig. 1.—Reproduction of the map
      drawn by J. J. R. Patrick about 1880.
I   Cross section of Kunnemann Mound a short distance north of
      the center.

II   Fig. 1.—East view of Monks Mound. Fig. 2.—North view of Monks Mound.

III   Fig. 1.—Monks Mound as it appeared at the time of Putnam's visit. Fig.   2.—Dr. Patrick's restoration of Monks Mound.

IV   The Red Mound south of Monks Mound.

V   View of the Fox Mound and another mound located south of Monks Mound.

VI   One of the smaller mounds of the group, north of Monks Mound.

VII   Fig. 1.—A large pond near the Kunnemann Mound. Fig. 2— The face of the trench of the Kunnemann Mound at a height of 25 feet. Fig. 3.—Trench in the Kunnemann Mound.

VIII   The altar of baked clay in the Kunnemann Mound.

IX   Skeleton of Cahokia Indian in the Edwards Mound.

X   Fragments of pottery, James Ramey Mound, No. 33.

[XI]   [From 1922 volume] Fragments of pottery from the Cahokia mounds, collected by Dr. George Higgins.

XI   Fragments of pottery from the village site located on the Wells and Tippetts farms.

[XII]   [From 1922 volume] Fig. 21, 22, 23, 24, 25.—Designs on pottery fragments from Cahokia. Fig. 26.—Head of a bird in white and red. Fig. 27.—Head of bird. Fig. 28.—Forearm and hand. Figures 27 and 28 show the beginnings of sculpture in clay.

XII   Fragments of pottery from village site on the Ramey, Wells, and Tippetts farms.

[XIII] [From 1922 volume] Figs. 29, 30, 31, 32.—Designs on pottery fragments from Cahokia.

XIII   The Cahokia type of arrowheads.

XIV   Fig. 1.—The hollowed bone awl. Fig. 2.—A slender, broken drill. Fig. 3.—Cahokia type arrowheads. All found in the field opposite Monks Mound.

XV   Fig. 1.—Pottery bird effigy. Found south of Monks Mound. Fig. 2.—Agricultural implements found north of the Merrell Mound.

XVI   Fig. 1.—Hand and forearm in clay. Fig. 2.—Effigy in clay. Fig. 3.—Ornament in red stone. Fig. 4.—Stone pipe. Fig. 5.—Effigy in clay. Fig. 6.—Engraved stone. Fig. 7.—Stone pipe. Fig. 8.—Cutting tool (hatchet).

XVII   Figs. 1, 2, 3.—Burial pots with skeleton No. 12, Mound No. 20; 2, 3, characteristic Cahokia forms, especially 3. (A363, a, b, c.) Fig. 4.—Small pot with skeleton No. 9, a child (A304). Fig. 5.—

Small crucible-like pot from burned basin, Sawmill Mound (A305). Fig. 6.—Burial pot with skeleton No. 11, Sawmill Mound (A306).

XVIII   Fig. 1.—A vessel of considerable size, probably a salt pan, Wells-Tippetts Village Site (A355). Figs. 2–4.—Grooved stones of quartzite-like sandstone, possibly sinew stones (A356), Ramey Village Site. Fig. 5.—Grooved stone of quartzite-like sandstone, from burned basin 100 yards south of Sawmill Mound (A357).

XIX   Figs. 1–6.—Types of decorated pottery. Wells-Tippetts Village Site (A313).

XX   Figs. 1–9.—Fragments of pottery. Wells-Tippetts Village Site, 1 to 3 $^1/_2$ ft. below surface (A313). Fig. 10.—Peculiarly decorated pottery fragment, Ramey Village Site (A314). Figs. 5, 6 are common Cahokia designs.

[XXI]   [From 1923 volume] Monk's Mound viewed from the southeast, showing the left foreground the terrace or apron.

XXI   Fig. 1.—Pottery fragment, James Ramey Mound, depth of 23 feet (A310). Figs. 2–8.—Ramey Village Site, types of pottery design (A312).

[XXII]   [From 1923 volume] Map of Cahokia Mound Group. Based on map of J. J. R. Patrick, 1880. Camp sites and burial sites are indicated, showing result of 1921–22 field work.

XXII   Decorated pottery from the James Ramey Mound. Figs. 1–3.—Near surface (A307). Fig. 4.—Depth of 19ft. (A309). Figs. 5, 6.—Depth of 15 ft. (A309). Fig. 7.—Depth of 23 ft. (A310). Fig. 2.—Engraved sandstone (A311).

XXIII   Fig. 1.—Shell gorget with skeleton No. 11, Sawmill Mound (A321). Fig. 2.—Shell effigy, Sawmill Mound, made from shell of fresh water mussel (A322). Fig. 3.—Nose or ear ornament made from shell of freshwater mussel (*Elliptio dilatatus*) James Ramey Mound (A323). Fig. 4.—Clay bird's-head effigy, Wells-Tippetts Village Site, 3 ft. deep (A324). Figs. 5, 6.—Clay bird's-head effigies, James Ramey Mound, 16–23 feet below surface (A325). Fig. 7.—Clay mammal-head effigy, Sawmill Mound (A326). Fig. 8.—Portion of clay pot or ornament (A327). Fig. 9.—Ornament on rim of pot (A328). Figs. 8, 9.—From James Ramey Mound.

XXIV   Figs. 2, 4, 9, 12.—Shell beads made from marine conch (*Busycon*) (A329). Figs. 5, 6.—Shell beads made from fresh water mussels (A330). Figs. I, II.—Shell ornaments from marine *Busycon* (A331). Figs. 7, 8, 10, 20.—Shell ornaments made from fresh water mussels (A332). Figs. 13, 15, 17.—Shells and central axis of marine conch, *Busycon perversa* (A333). Fig. 16.—Marine conch, *Busycon carica* (A442). Fig. 19.—Ornament made of side of *Busycon* shell (A334). Fig. 14.—Marine shell, *Strombus Pugilis alatus* (A334). Fig. 18.—Marine olive shell, *Oliva literata* (A336). All from James Ramey Mound, between 8 and 23 feet below surface.

XXV   Figs. 1, 2.—Awl and celt made of deer bone (A337, A338) Wells-Tippetts Village Site. Figs. 3, 7.—Deer bone awls, James Ramey Mound, 8 feet deep (A339). Fig. 4.—Bone awl with skeleton No. 39, Pittsburg Lake (A340). Figs. 5, 6.—Bone awls (A341, A342). From Judge Sullivan's Mound, 10 ft. below surface. Fig. 8.—Bone knife with skeleton No. 11, Sawmill Mound (A343). Fig. 9.—Part of breast bone of Virginia deer, Ramey Village Site (A344). Fig. 10.—Awl made from heel (calceneous bone) of deer (*Odocoileus virginianus*) found with skeleton No. 18 (Mounds 19, 20, 21) (A345). Fig. 11.—Pathologic leg bone of deer, from Ramey Village Site (A346). Fig. 12.—Foot bone of Wapiti with deeply incised lines, James Ramey Mound (A347). Fig. 13.—Lower jaw of Virginia deer used as a chisel or gouge, Sawmill Mound (A348).

XXVI   Fig. 1.—Flint or chert knife of fine workmanship; James Ramey Mound, 12 feet deep, near stake 125 (A358). Fig. 3.—Shouldered hoe. Figs. 2, 4.—Spades, of flint or chert, from field southwest of Monks Mound (A359, A360). Fig. 5.—Spade of flint or chert; James Ramey Mound, west side, 17 feet deep (A361).

XXVII   Pottery discs perforated and unperforated, are common in the mounds and on the surface. Attention is directed to the peculiar design on Fig. 3. Fragments such as Fig. 1, with a rude circle and cross lines are frequently found. Fig. 1.—Pottery fragment with oval design; Sawmill Mound, 3 feet deep (A315). Fig. 2.—Pottery disc, James Ramey Mound, 15 feet deep (A316). Fig. 3.—Fragment with peculiar design; Stockyards Village Site (A317). Fig. 4.—Pottery disc, James Ramey Mound, 12 feet deep (A318). Fig. 5.—Perforated clay disc, Wells-Tippetts Village Site (A319). Fig. 6.—Perforated disc of fine-grained sandstone, Ramey Village Site (A320).

XXVIII   Fig. 1.—Flint knife, broken; James Ramey Mound, 8 feet deep (A349). Fig. 2.—Fine-pointed needle of bone, with skeleton No. 30; Mounds 19, 20, 21 (A350). Figs. 3–5.—Bone awls, Wells-Tippetts Village Site (A351). Figs. 6–8.—Flint arrow points, James Ramey Mound, 17 feet deep (A352). Figs. 9, 10.—Flint war arrow points. Wells-Tippetts Village Site (A353). Fig. 11.—Flint spearhead, James Ramey Mound, 17 feet deep (A354).

XXIX   Fig. 1.—Digging trench in Sawmill Mound. Fig. 2.—Skeleton No. 11, Sawmill Mound (A302).

XXX   Fig. 1.—Skeleton No. 12, from Mound No. 20 (A485). Fig. 2.—Circle in James Ramey Mound.

XXXI   Fig. 1.—Trench in James Ramey Mound (No. 33). Note altar in center foreground at trowel. Fig. 2.—Skeletons in position, Mound No. 20. Fig. 3.—General view of circles in James Ramey Mound.

XXXII   Fig. 1.—Bone awls and needles. Figs. 2–6.—Mussel shells (*Lampsilis ventricosa*); W. J. Seever collection. (¼ natural size.) Fig. 7.—Hematite axe. Fig. 8.—Grooved axe; Monticello Seminary collection. Fig. 9—Celt of porphyritic rock, Wells-Tippetts Village Site (A362).

XXXIII   Figs. 1–5.—Five pipes, several of them effigies, from the Monticello Seminary collection. Figs. 6, 7.—Stone effigies; Monticello Seminary collection. Fig. 8.—Large effigy pipe; W. J. Seever collection.

XXXIV   Fig. 1.—string of shell beads cut from busycon conch. Fig. 2.—Marine conch shell, *Busycon carica*. Fig. 3.—Marine conch shell, *Busycon perversa*. (¼ natural size.) Monticello Seminary collection. Fig. 4.—Arrowhead of quartz, unusual workmanship. Found on the surface of Monks Mound.

XXXV   Characteristic Cahokia motifs from the James Ramey Mound.

XXXVI   The discoidal, or chunkee stone, found on the face of a skeleton in Section 15-C of Mound No. 66.

XXXVII   Mound No. 66. Property of the Baltimore & Ohio Railroad Company.

XXXVIII   Cross section of Mound No. 66 at Station 35, major axis.

XXXIX   The Powell Mound, from Taylor's photograph.

XL   Jar with serpent motif. Mound No. 6, Neteler.

XLI   Jar from the Neteler Mound, No. 6.

XLII   Four copper hatchets.

XLIII   Illustrating six bear tusks, two of which are split; three small copper hatchets and spearhead of agate-like flint from the Neteler Mound.

XLIV   Necklace of split bear tusks, Skeleton 6, Mound No. 6, Neteler.

XLV   Copper head-band and portions of two human jaws cut into ornaments, Mound No. 6, Neteler.

XLVI   View of some skeletons *in situ* in the mound owned by Dr. Don F. Dickson, Lewistown, Illinois, also accompanying objects.

XLVII   Skeleton and objects in position.

XLVIII   Objects from the log tombs near Liverpool.

XLIX Bone knife inserted in a grizzly bear tusk. Found in the long tomb, Liverpool, Illinois.

L Field map of Dickson's Cemetery.

Acknowledgments

A ny attempt to understand the history of archaeology cannot be accomplished without the much needed assistance and perceptiveness of those colleagues also engaged in this endeavor. The author would like to thank the following individuals who provided suggestions on the Introduction as well as their respective institutions where many of the documents are presently curated: Dr. James Bradley, Director of the R. S. Peabody Museum at Andover Academy; Professor Douglas Brewer, Director of the Natural History Museum at the University of Illinois; Dr. Thomas Emerson, Director of the Illinois Transportation Program and Laboratory of Anthropology at the University of Illinois; William Iseminger, Site Archaeologist at Cahokia Mounds Historic Site; and Dr. Bradley Lepper of the Ohio Historical Society.

Other institutions that provided access to their archives and collections include the National Anthropological Archives of the Smithsonian Institution, the University of Michigan Museum of Anthropology, and the Illinois State Museum. Dr. Hal Hassen of the Illinois Department of Natural Resources directed me toward the Illinois State Archives. Professor James Brown of Northwestern University, Scott Bruton of the University of Oklahoma, Professor Melvin Fowler of the University of Wisconsin at Milwaukee, Professor Robert Hall of the University of Illinois at Chicago, and Lucretia Kelly of Washington University have all provided helpful suggestions and comments.

I also cannot thank enough the late Dr. James B. Griffin, Dean of North American Archaeology, for the insights he shared with me on Moorehead. I would like to acknowledge Paul Chucalo, his sister Zorina Lane, and the late Marie Fingerhut for their historical perspective on Moorehead. Professors George Milner of Pennsylvania State University and James Stoltman of the University of Wisconsin provided extensive comments on the content and organization that helped immensely.

To Dr. Stephen Williams, emeritus historian of archaeology, I extend my gratitude for his critical reading of the various drafts. Steve has provided numerous comments, suggestions, and extremely useful criticisms of this introduction. Nearly a decade ago Steve provided some of the initial direction that has lead me into some of the archives and literature that I have pursued in my attempt to understand the overall context of Moorehead's involvement at Cahokia.

Lastly, I would like to thank especially Judith Knight of The University of Alabama Press for the opportunity to reprint Moorehead's volumes on Cahokia as part of the Classics in Southeastern Archaeology series and Professors Janet Keller, Chair, and Timothy Pauketat of the Department of Anthropology at the University of Illinois for their support in pursuing this project.

Note on This Edition

This edition reproduces the 1922, 1923, and 1929 University of Illinois Bulletins on the Cahokia Mounds by Warren K. Moorehead, without the bibliographies from the 1922 and 1923 volumes.

The plates in the original 1922, 1923, and 1929 bulletins were placed at the end of each volume. The 1929 volume included the plates from the previous two volumes, plus some new plates. To avoid duplication, this edition reproduces the plates from the 1929 volume, along with a few plates that were included in the 1922 and 1923 volumes but omitted in the 1929 volume.

The captions in the 1922 and 1923 volumes differ slightly from the captions reproduced herein from the 1929 volume. Also, the plate and figure numbers differ in the three volumes; for example, a photograph of Fox Mound is Plate V in the 1929 volume, Plate XIX in the 1923 volume, and Plate VI (Figure 8) in the 1922 volume. Because this edition uses the 1929 numbering, a "Key to Plate and Figure Numbers" is included at the front of the plates section and can be used to find the plates referred to in the text for the 1922 and 1923 volumes. In the 1922 volume, the text refers only to figure numbers.

The line drawings within text (intratext, numbered figures in the 1923 and 1929 volumes) are reproduced as they were in the original volumes.

The 1929 volume originally contained six foldout figures (figs. 1, 8, 9, 19, 20, 21) which have been included herein, but not all of them as foldouts.

Monks Mound as it was in 1876. Painted by Miss A. R. Brooks, Monticello Seminary, 1924, after careful study of previous views 1870–1900. (Frontispiece from Moorehead 1929)

The Cahokia Mounds

Introduction

John E. Kelly

Nearly one hundred mounds distributed over a five-square-mile area of the Mississippi floodplain constitute the large Mississippian site complex of Cahokia. Although located within eight miles of metropolitan St. Louis, Missouri, the Cahokia site has managed to survive much of the ravages of modern development. Within the last two hundred years Cahokia has attracted much attention from travelers, archaeologists, and other scientists. One of the many individuals attracted to the Cahokia Mounds in the early part of the twentieth century was Warren King Moorehead. The results of his investigations at Cahokia and a number of nearby sites were published in a series of three reports through the University of Illinois. In later correspondence with Frank C. Baker, Moorehead (1936) indicated that the notes were left at the University of Illinois.

The first two Moorehead volumes published in 1922 and 1923 succinctly summarized his fieldwork and his efforts to demonstrate the human construction of the mounds that form part of the large Cahokia site. The results of a third season at a number of sites outside Cahokia were not published until after the fourth and final season was completed in 1927. The last of three volumes, published in 1929 (in the September 25, 1928, bulletin), included the work of the first two seasons along with a description of the 1923 and 1927 field seasons. The reports contain a description of each mound, site, or location examined. Occasional maps show some of the more relevant profiles, and each report contains a map of Cahokia with the various mounds numbered following John J. R. Patrick's initial numbering sequence.

At the end of each report is a set of plates that show the various excavations and some of the artifacts recovered. Occasionally Moorehead relied on specialists such as zoologists, chemists, and geologists for the analysis of certain materials. Of particular importance was the work of Morris Leighton, a geologist with the Illinois Geological Survey at the University of Illinois. His field study of the mound profiles described in the 1923 and 1929 reports laid to rest any notion that the mounds were natural features. Once Leighton's initial results were known, it was then possible for the state to purchase a portion of the Cahokia site.

Moorehead's reports were not only a source documenting the prehistoric construction of the Cahokia Mounds by Native Americans but also the only substantive publication on the site for over four decades. More important, they are a tribute to his participation in the successful preservation of a small section of Cahokia as a state park in 1925 (Figure 2). As a result of his initial efforts and those of the local citizens, the Cahokia Mounds State Historic Site presently contains nearly 50 percent of the site. Today Cahokia has achieved the prestigious status as a UNESCO World Heritage Site, something no one probably could have envisioned 75 years ago. It was then a very different time and place. Nonetheless, the concerns of those involved in the preservation endeavor were no less important than the challenges that face us today.

This introduction essentially provides the context behind Moorehead's work, especially the purchase of the mounds at Cahokia. His reports, as with many of his earlier publications, are largely descriptive and not analytic. Although Moorehead understood the concepts of stratigraphy, his interest, as with many others before him, was the artifacts. Thus, although more rigorous and systematic techniques were being employed at the time, Moorehead continued to use large horse-drawn scrapers and human labor to remove mound fill.

The techniques Moorehead used at Cahokia in 1921 were the same ones he used 30 years earlier in the excavations at the Hopewell group in Ohio. Although some profile and plan maps of his Cahokia excavations were completed, most of the work was not mapped. In looking at the broader picture of the Eastern Woodlands, the differences observed in the cultural materials recovered were more apt to be related to geography than stratigraphy. A decade later others had begun to establish a chronology that placed much of what was being discovered in some type of culture-historical framework.

The following introductory discussion is divided into several parts: The first part describes Moorehead and his background in archaeology. Then I discuss the antecedents to the preservation of Cahokia and the initial efforts. Next, I examine the context of the four seasons of excavation at Cahokia and the surrounding environs with respect to the three reports reprinted herein. Finally, I conclude with an epilogue discussing other work done at Cahokia and a summary.

WARREN KING MOOREHEAD, ARCHAEOLOGIST*

Warren King Moorehead was born to Helen King and Dr. William G. Moorehead, an American Presbyterian minister, in Sienna, Italy, in 1866. The family returned in 1870 to Xenia, Ohio, where the elder Dr. Moorehead was affiliated with the theological seminary. Their return to America ironically coincided with the removal of the large Cemetery Mound in East St. Louis (Kelly 1994) and one year after the final removal of the St. Louis mound group's last vestige, Big Mound. The young Moorehead developed an early interest in archaeology as a result of collecting numerous artifacts in the vicinity of his Ohio home.

In 1884 Moorehead entered Denison College at Granville, Ohio, for a brief two years. Although he never graduated, he was later awarded an honorary Sc.D. from Denison in 1930. Other honorary degrees granted included an M.A. from Dartmouth in 1901 and in 1927 an Sc.D. from Oglethorpe University in Atlanta, Georgia. At the time he entered college, anthropology and archaeology were not being taught. It was not until a few years later that educational institutions began to offer these subjects as courses of study. In fact, during the fall of 1892 Moorehead taught a series of lectures on American Anthropology at Ohio State University, the first at this institution.

Moorehead's early interest in fieldwork in archaeology was stimulated during his enrollment at Denison College. While there, he was within a short distance of the Flint Ridge chert sources, which he visited on numerous occasions; and on one occasion he left school with spade and lunch in hand to dig into a nearby mound (Moorehead diary, April 27, 1885). Throughout the 1880s he undertook excavations in Ohio on his own, including work at Fort Ancient in 1889. His efforts at this earthwork resulted in the creation of a state park, one of the first of its kind. Not only did Moorehead collect, excavate, and sell artifacts, he also exhibited his finds to the public. His displays at the Cincinnati Centennial Exposition of 1888 attracted the attention of Dr. Thomas Wilson, Curator in the United States National Museum of

---

* This biography is derived from Byers's (1939) obituary in the American Anthropologist; the biographical sketch in the Warren K. Moorehead collection's synopsis at the Ohio Historical Society; and some early information presented by Moorehead in the *Field Diary of an Archaeological Collector* (Moorehead 1902).

the Smithsonian Institution. Wilson was the successor in the National Museum to Charles Rau and continued Rau's tradition of artifact classification.

Wilson arranged to have Moorehead join him in Washington as an assistant at the Smithsonian between 1888 and 1890, where Moorehead studied his own collections under Wilson. While at the Smithsonian, Moorehead also assisted in some of the fieldwork in the Washington, D.C., area. By the end of his brief tenure at the Smithsonian, Moorehead had been made a fellow in the American Association for the Advancement of Science. Three years later he assumed the role of Secretary of Section H (Anthropology) for this association. The contacts that he made in Washington and his involvement in this prestigious organization of scientists were to benefit him throughout his life.

After his museum work with Wilson, he traveled to the Dakotas in 1890 where he reported on the Sioux uprising, the Ghost Dance, and the Messianic movement for the *Illustrated American* magazine. His sympathies with the Sioux shortly before Wounded Knee resulted in the military removing him from the area. His interest in Native Americans led to his appointment as a member of the Board of Indian Commissioners by Theodore Roosevelt in 1909—a position he held for 24 years.

Moorehead was a prolific writer, describing, in various venues, much of what he did and found in the field. His publication record was initiated as early as 1884. He not only was an author but also served as editor of such early outlets for the archaeological enthusiast as *The Archaeologist*. This pattern of public dissemination persisted until his death. His works continued to be artifact oriented and descriptive and thus were in much the same line as many of his contemporaries and predecessors. These writings simply described the work that was done and were profusely illustrated with the recovered artifacts.

Because of his earlier field experience in Ohio, Moorehead was selected as a field assistant in 1891 by Frederic Ward Putnam of Harvard University to lead the World's Columbian Exposition's expedition to southwestern Ohio. Here he undertook excavations at several sites including the famous Hopewell site. The overwhelming quantities of chert, copper, shell, obsidian, bone, and clay artifacts, when placed on exhibit at Chicago in 1892, "attracted the attention of thousands of visitors at the Exposition" (Moorehead 1922b:80). He then led an expedition sponsored by the Peabody Museum at Harvard, the American Museum of Natural History, and the Smithsonian Institution to cliff dwellings in the San Juan valley of New Mexico.

Upon returning from the Southwest in late 1892, he married Evelyn Ludwig. His work then took him to Chicago where he was involved in setting up the Hopewell archaeological exhibit at the Columbian Exposition. From 1894 to 1897, he served as Curator of the Museum of Ohio State University and the Ohio Archaeological and Historical Society. After this brief period of museum work, he returned to the field again to conduct investigations in the Southwest at places such as Chaco Canyon and the La Plata and Salt River valleys for Robert Singleton Peabody of Philadelphia, who was a nephew of George Peabody and a longtime collector of Indian artifacts. Between Moorehead's trips to the Southwest he conducted work along the Ohio river. In 1901, Peabody founded the Department of Archaeology at Phillips Academy, Andover, Massachusetts, whereupon Moorehead became the curator. Peabody's son Charles served as director until 1924, when he resigned and Moorehead assumed the position. Moorehead held the directorship until his retirement in 1938.

During his tenure at Phillips Academy, he worked extensively in the eastern United States, including the area around Andover, in Maine, and in the Connecticut and Susquehanna River valleys. In the Southeast, he investigated a large Mississippian site at the Mouth of the Wabash (Murphy) site, as well as sites near Hopkinsville, Kentucky, in the Tennessee-Cumberland region. Later he spent three years (1925–1927) at the famous Etowah Mounds in northern Georgia. Some earlier work was also spent west of the Mississippi river in the Arkansas River valley and in the Ozarks of southwest Missouri where he met the archaeological enthusiast and surveyor Jay L. B. Taylor. Much of his work in the Southeast was coeval with that of Clarence Bloomfield Moore, who seemingly explored every river valley in the Southeast. Moorehead, on the other hand, appeared to bounce from one part of the eastern United States to the next. I suspect this behavior was based on the contacts he had made over the years.

Of importance here is the work he conducted at Cahokia and nearby sites in the American Bottom during the 1920s from his base in Andover and his significant role in the preservation of the Cahokia Mounds. His fieldwork at Cahokia began in the fall of 1921 and was part of the local effort to preserve the mounds as a state park. He continued his investigations at Cahokia the following year. In 1923 he expanded his explorations to several outlying sites. By 1925 a portion of the Cahokia site had been purchased as a state park. Moorehead returned in 1927 to work on the Harding and some other smaller mounds at Cahokia outside the new park. Although his fieldwork ended at Cahokia, he pursued work that extended up the Illinois River valley to the north, and he continued to be instrumental in promoting the importance of the Cahokia site until his death in January 1939.

As research into the history of archaeology at Cahokia progresses, it is slowly becoming clear how Warren King Moorehead became involved with the Cahokia Mounds. In part, this event can be traced to a sense of urgency precipitated by developers pressuring the owners to sell their lands for the construction of factories. It is important to realize that the Industrial Revolution impacted the region, with the Metro-East area in Illinois emerging as a major rail center and industrial locality with numerous steel mills and other manufacturing enterprises.

As early as 1910, Moorehead presented a speech on Cahokia to the Illinois State Historical Society (Moorehead 1912). His investigations were instrumental in inspiring the state officials to purchase the central portion of the site for a state park. The extensive nature of his excavations and the subsequent publications of his work at Cahokia and other sites in the American Bottom also provided important insights into the prehistoric occupations of this region.

In many respects Moorehead represented the last of a generation of archaeologists whose efforts were focused on the collection of artifacts with minimal contextual information. Other individuals, including his colleague at the R. S. Peabody, Alfred Vincent Kidder, had already begun to establish more rigorous field methods accompanied by a more systematic analysis of the artifactual materials recovered. Institutions were also evolving with the appearance of Departments of Anthropology, especially graduate programs that served to train a new generation of archaeologists. These new approaches and institutions emerged during Moorehead's career as an archaeologist. Indeed, individuals such as Frederic W. Putnam, who had initially hired Moorehead, had already instilled some of these methods in his workers and colleagues. By the time Moorehead died, the Midwestern Taxonomic system was in place providing some of the basic elements of archaeological classification. Thus Moorehead's work at Cahokia and the surrounding region was not one that generated new methods and analysis; what he produced in his publications were a series of guidebooks to those areas investigated, especially the mounds that have undergone a minimal amount of study since his presence. When Moorehead's information on the specific locations is connected with the materials collected, we have some useful insights into Cahokia that can be pursued in greater detail.

THE PRESERVATION OF CAHOKIA: ANTECEDENTS

The Mississippian mounds at Cahokia and other locations throughout the St. Louis metropolitan area were erected between A.D. 1050 and 1350. Many of these edifices were once the earthen substructures on which ritual activities were established or the abodes of the chiefs and ritual specialists were constructed; other mounds capped the tombs of the chiefs and their kin. Each mound group had its own unique history. The seemingly sudden abandonment of Cahokia, sometime during the fourteenth century, as perhaps the last center in the region, left a series of barren earthen monuments. These vacant centers and their buried secrets remained as a tribute to the human activity that once dominated the surrounding landscape (Williams 1990).

The appearance of an alien society of Euro-Americans, some three hundred years later, brought with it a combined sense of curiosity, ignorance, and the rapid ability to destroy the monuments of the past. French missionaries, explorers, soldiers, and farmers melded well with the landscape and the indigenous people that were here to greet them. The earthen monuments were skillfully rendered on the maps (see Fowler 1997) by French cartographers such as Collot (1826) and Finiels (1989) some 200 years ago. Their portrayal of the mounds on these maps were readily identifiable landmarks linking some of the pathways between communities such as Bellfontaine, Cahokia, St. Louis, and Florissant. Although the mounds were depicted, there was little discussion in the literature about what they represented. A label, "anciens tombe aux des sauvages," on Finiels's map was printed as "Indian Ancient Tombs" on Collot's map and placed adjacent to the Pulcher group.

The battle between the different European powers for the western lands along the Mississippi River eventually gave way in 1783 to a new American nation. Many of the Americans, educated in the Anglo-Saxon tradition of the Eastern establishment, brought with them new perspectives on the earthen monuments dispersed across the landscape of the American Bottom and uplands of St. Louis. At the end of the eighteenth and beginning of the nineteenth century the mound-builder myth had fully emerged. Seasoned veterans, such as George Rogers

Clark, however, relied on the thoughts and words of the indigenous peoples such as the Kaskaskia chief Baptiste DuCoigne, who indicated that the mounds were the palaces of his forefathers. The oral traditions of native peoples, whose ancestors were in some small way involved in mound construction, were carefully concealed, and alternative explanations embedded in the religious tenets of Americans, such as Noah Webster and others, were espoused. These views were reinforced by the perception of existing native peoples as simply "savages." Ironically, in the minds or words of those proponents of the mound-builder myth, it was these "savages" who drove the highly civilized mound-builders off the face of the earth. The identities of the mythical and mystical mound-builders were many including: Phoenicians, Carthaginians, and of course the proverbial "Lost tribes of Israel."

Significant publicity regarding the mounds in the St. Louis region did not emerge until after the 1811 publication of a series of articles in the *Louisiana Gazette* written by Henry Marie Brackenridge describing the mounds in St. Louis, East St. Louis, and Cahokia. Fortunately, an accurate map of the St. Louis group was also prepared by T. R. Peale and Thomas Say as part of the Stephen Long expedition up the Missouri in 1819 (Peale 1862). In fact an earlier map of the region in 1816 showed the numerous mounds in the groups of Cahokia and East St. Louis (Milner 1998:Fig. 1.1). By 1869 the last mound in the St. Louis group had been destroyed with the infamous razing of the Big Mound (cf. Williams and Goggin 1956; Marshall 1992).

It was during this period of the early nineteenth century that numerous outsiders, such as Charles Alexander LaSueur (1820) and Paul Wilhelm, the Duke of Württemberg (1823), visited St. Louis and the different mound groups in the city and also at outlying sites. These individuals provided interesting glimpses, verbally and visually, of the mounds. Hence, St. Louis became known as "Mound City," especially during the years prior to the Civil War. Outsiders, such as the prominent Knickerbocker Charles Hoffman (1835) in 1834 and also editorials in the local papers by Thomas Hart Benton as early as 1820 urged that the St. Louis Mounds be preserved as a park.

Because of the considerable attention paid to the mounds, three perspectives emerged with regard to the origin of these earthworks. A number of authors popularized the idea that the mounds, especially those in the Midwest, were built by an earlier group known as the "Mound Builders," who were unrelated to the Native Americans

(Silverberg 1968; Williams 1991). The second perspective, of course, was that these monuments were the efforts of the Native Americans. Within the scientific circles of educated St. Louisans, a debate raged regarding the mounds and their origins. Although considerable attention had been paid to the mound-builder myth on a national level, a third perspective emerged locally that posited that the "hills of earth" were instead natural features. Beginning as early as the 1830s, individuals such as John Russell (1831) of Bluffs, Illinois, and many scientists, especially geologists Amos Worthern (1866), and later N. M. Fenneman (1911) and A. R. Crook (1914, 1915, 1916, and 1922b), were of the opinion that the mounds in this area were indeed *natural* phenomena such as geological outliers of glacial drift. It was this latter perspective in particular that partly contributed to the destruction of the "Big Mound" in St. Louis, although the city of St. Louis did make an attempt to purchase the mound and have it preserved as a park. Unfortunately, such preservation efforts were not successful.

Members of the St. Louis Academy of Science in the 1860s, debated the Big Mound's origin (Anonymous 1860:700–701; 1868:565–569). Nevertheless, it was not until the Big Mound was destroyed and its human construction confirmed in the process that the error in their explanation was realized. This understanding led in 1876 to the formation of a Mound Survey Committee within the Academy to investigate the mounds especially in Southeast Missouri and also in the immediate area. Despite much evidence to the contrary, many geologists afterwards continued to perceive the mounds as natural features (Fenneman 1911; Crook 1915). Because they were indeed men of science, their views, in part, slowed the impetus to purchase and protect the mounds at Cahokia.

The loss of the St. Louis group was mirrored across the river in Illinois where a similar fate awaited the East St. Louis group (Kelly 1994), although recent investigations indicate the basal portions of some of these mounds are still intact, as are a number of low platforms. The remaining groups, Cahokia, Mitchell, Emerald, and Pulcher, because of their rural setting, remained largely extant. The Belleville dentist, Dr. John J. R. Patrick, upon his return from the Civil War, took it upon himself to map the mounds in St. Clair County. This resulted in the preparation of maps not only of the Cahokia group but those in East St. Louis, Fairmont City, and the "Snyder Groupe," known today as Pulcher.

THE PRESERVATION OF CAHOKIA: INITIAL EFFORTS

With the destruction of the St. Louis and most of the East St. Louis Mounds by the 1870s, concerns centering on the preservation of the Cahokia Mounds grew and were stimulated by individuals such as Dr. John Francis Snyder in the late nineteenth century. Snyder was an important figure in Illinois archaeology at the time (Connolly 1962; Fowler 1962). He spent his early years at the "Square Mound" farm, an earlier reference to the Pulcher site (Kelly 1993) and had developed an interest in archaeology while growing up in Belleville, Illinois, located 11 miles southeast of the Cahokia site. Although trained as a physician, his avocational interest was archaeology. A founding member of the Illinois State Historical Society in 1899, Snyder "delivered an impassioned plea at the first meeting of the Illinois State Historical Society, January 6, 1900, for the preservation of Illinois antiquities and the granting of state aid to insure their adequate investigation" (Connolly 1962:19).

Perhaps stimulated by individuals such as William McAdams (1882) and John Snyder, who surveyed the Cahokia group in 1882 for Thomas's mound survey, persons at the Bureau of Ethnology (later the Bureau of American Ethnology) in Washington, D.C., were aroused by the importance of Cahokia and the need to preserve it. For example, in a letter to Cyrus Thomas, Henry W. Henshaw (John Wesley Powell's linguistic coordinator in the Smithsonian Institution's Bureau of Ethnology) requested more information on the Cahokia mound: "We have finally settled down upon this as on the whole the most important single mound or locality for preservation. The Major [Powell] now wishes to know as nearly as possible how much land about the mound it is desirable to preserve" (Henshaw 1888).

Henshaw's letter also includes a request for an estimate for the cost of purchase. The landowner's daughter, Priscilla Ramey, asked a price of $100,000 for the Cahokia (Monks) Mound and adjacent land. This cost information was contained in a letter sent by John Nicholas Brown of Providence, Rhode Island, to Major Powell of the Bureau of Ethnology. Mr. Brown's response to this offer was: "This price seems to me preposterous" (Brown 1890). He basically urged that this was a matter for Congress to undertake, especially as part of the public domain. It is still unclear how far this matter went; however Congress never did purchase the mounds.

Since 1860, Thomas Ramey was the owner of Monks Mound, the

largest monument, and an adjoining 260 acres, and he had worked to preserve the mounds, including placing restrictions on excavation (Moorehead 1921d). Ramey also served in the Illinois General Assembly in the 1890s. During his tenure as a legislator, he attempted to have the Cahokia Mounds established as a State Park; however, his efforts were thwarted by an upstate Chicago legislator who later in 1913 remarked that his "district needs parks for live people and the guys in that mound are all dead ones" (Iseminger 1980:6).

Upon the death of Ramey in 1899 (Anonymous 1899) and later his wife in 1908, a renewed interest in preserving the mounds was set into motion when it was realized that the estate was to be partitioned and sold. The concern was that, if the heirs did not purchase the property, it would be bought by an East St. Louis brewery that would convert the property into a Sunday resort and beer garden and possibly "honeycomb the great structure with vaults for storing the products of the brewery" (Anonymous 1909:20). Clark McAdams (1907), the son of the noted, archaeologist, William McAdams, reported that David I. Bushnell, Sr., a St. Louis businessman and collector of Indian artifacts, offered to buy Monks Mound for $10,000; however, the asking price was tenfold.

The years between Thomas Ramey's death and Moorehead's involvement at the Cahokia Mounds (1900 to 1920) was one of intense local interest in Cahokia's preservation. It must also have been one of considerable frustration. Newspaper accounts continued to portray the mounds in odd and bizarre fashion (Figure 1). In an earlier article, entitled "The Great Turtle Mound" (Bryan 1901), the author indicated this should be the real name for Monks Mound's because that is what the builders intended the mound to represent. One could also take affordable trips along the suburban rail lines to Cahokia (Figure 3).

In honor of the Louisiana Purchase and St. Louis's emergence as "the Gateway to the West," St. Louis hosted the World's Fair in 1904. Numerous ethnological exhibits involving "natives" were represented at the Fair along with archaeological exhibits (Bruton 1992). And many archaeological dignitaries who visited the Fair also made a trip to Cahokia (Anonymous 1929). In 1901, prior to the construction of exhibits and buildings in St. Louis's Forest Park, David I. Bushnell, Jr., excavated several mounds. He published the results, as well as maps of the various mound groups including Cahokia, in a short article (Bushnell 1904).

St. Louis Daily Globe-Democrat, Sunday Morning, July 18 1909.

WHERE HUMAN BEINGS WERE SACRIFICED WITHIN SIGHT OF ST. LOUIS

EVIDENCES OF BLOODY RITES IN THE WORSHIP OF THE SUN GOD ON CAHOKIA MOUND, THE GREAT MONUMENT OF A LOST RACE WHICH IT IS NOW PROPOSED TO MAKE THE CENTRAL FEATURE OF A STATE PARK

Fig. 1. Newspaper headlines, *St. Louis Daily Globe-Democrat*, Sunday morning, July 18, 1909 (courtesy of Cahokia Mounds State Historic Site Archives)

The President of the Illinois State Historical Society, Clark E. Carr, visited Cahokia in 1909 and discussed some of the options for preserving the mounds, such as making the site into a state park or including it within the East St. Louis park district. He also appointed a committee on archaeology and decided that the secretary of the Society should "call attention of the State Park Commission to the Great Cahokia Mound. . . . and that the suggestion be made that such historic spots or sites . . . not suitable for State parks be marked in some manner" (Anonymous 1909:25). The directors of the society also instructed the secretary and editor to bring to the attention of the Illinois Park Commission the need to preserve Monks Mound. The Commission was at this time in the process of preserving other areas, such as the Starved Rock Historic site.

Finally, Illinois Congressman William A. Rodenberg was urged by a resolution of the East St. Louis Schubert club to introduce a bill that designated the mounds as a National Park (Anonymous 1910:92). The Schubert club's resolution was prompted by a similar request in April 1910 on the part of the Federation of Women's clubs convention in Granite City, endorsed by all the women's clubs in the state of Illinois

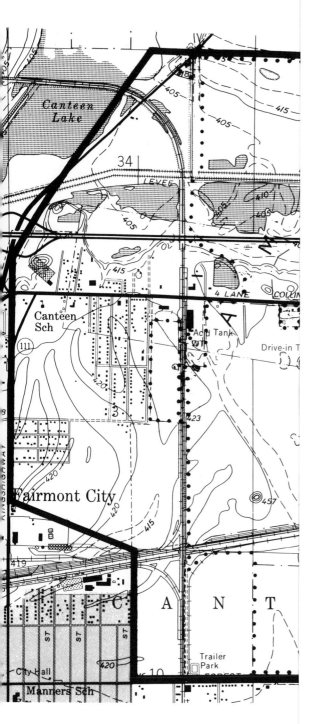

Fig. 2. Cahokia Mounds Historic Site–National
Cahokia Mounds State Historic Site limits (Base
courtesy of Cahokia Mounds State Historic Site

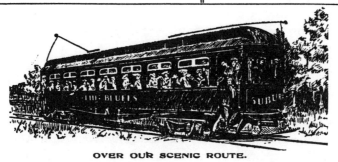

Fig. 3. Advertisement for trolley car rides to Monks Mound, ca. 1900
(courtesy of Central Mississippi Valley Archaeological Research Institute)

(Anonymous 1910:93). In addition to pushing their congressional representative for national recognition of Cahokia, the Illinois State Historical Society continued their statewide effort with the Honorable Norman G. Flagg also introducing in the 1910 legislature a bill calling for the legislature to appoint five commissioners "to investigate the historic importance of the Cahokia mound; to ascertain its adaptability for the purpose of a State park, and ascertain the price for which the State can purchase the property" (Anonymous 1910:93). Overall, this preservation movement may have had its legislative roots in the 1906 Antiquities Act of the United States Congress that was directed at the destruction of Southwestern sites by pothunters.

Also in 1910, Moorehead (1912) spoke before the Illinois State Historical Society and made reference to the proposal by the "Street Railway lines" to remove "the Cahokia Mound" to fill in the low areas on the floodplain. This speech appears to have been Moorehead's earliest involvement with the site and its preservation.

In 1911 the "Monks of Cahokia," a secret organization of business and professional men, was formed in order to work toward the preservation of Monks Mound (Flagg 1912:384). One of the members was John Francis Snyder, who lived at some distance in Virginia, Illinois. The members would secretly gather atop Monks Mound in hooded Monks' robes and perform certain rituals (Anonymous 1913b). Afterward they would gather at Schmidt's Mound Park, later known as the

Mounds Club, a quarter of a mile east of Monks Mound. A year later in 1912 the group made their first public appearance in the Madison County Centennial celebration parade. At the end of this parade, in a place of honor, came a "mammoth painting of the Cahokia Mound" (Flagg 1912:385) (Figure 4).

The concerns, such as those expressed by Moorehead in his 1910 speech before the Illinois State Historical Society, regarding development in what was predominately a rural landscape can be readily related to the emergence of St. Louis as one of the hubs of industrialization. Transportation networks of rail lines and river traffic were critical to the economic growth of the St. Louis region. The main source of infrastructure growth in the nineteenth and early twentieth century was the railroads. Unfortunately the railroads were also responsible for the removal of the Big Mound in St. Louis in 1869 and the Great Mound at the Mitchell in 1876 (Howland 1877). Thus contemporary construction in the area can be seen in a 1916 map that includes plans to extend a railroad spur across a portion of the Cahokia site (see Fowler 1997:Figure 3.6), which may have precipitated subsequent legislation for Cahokia's preservation. Once the automobile was introduced, the construction of highways then served as the single most important impetus to development and subsequent destruction of sites.

Nevertheless, preservation efforts slowly began in March of 1913, when a bill was introduced by a local state representative, Norman G. Flagg, from the 47th district in Moro, Illinois, north of Edwardsville (Anonymous 1913a). This bill requesting $250,000 for the purchase of 200 acres of the Cahokia Mounds site failed to pass. The failure in part resulted in the formation and incorporation of the Cahokia Mound Association (CMA) the following year in March 1914. Its president was the famous collector and pharmacist, Dr. Henry M. Whelpley; Representative Flagg was the Vice-president; and an anatomist from Washington University, Dr. Robert J. Terry, served as Secretary-Treasurer.

The other CMA board members included R. D. Griffin from the Board of Education in St. Louis and F. W. Shipley, a professor at Washington University. By 1915 they had enlisted 84 members. The at-large membership consisted of the mayors of Alton, Belleville, East St. Louis, and the President of the Board of Trade of Alton (Anonymous 1914). Most of the members, however, were local landowners such as the Ramey brothers—Fred, Jesse, and James; George Merrell; and F. B. Harding. George Higgins, a druggist and local collector from St.

Fig. 4. Ramey mural of Monks Mound, carried as a banner in 1912 Madison County Centennial Parade (1967 photograph courtesy of Melvin Fowler, Cahokia Mounds State Historic Site Archives)

Louis, was a member as was Moorehead. Moorehead had often corresponded with Snyder and thus was probably kept well abreast of the developments in Illinois.

Of great concern to the Mound Association members was Alja Robinson Crook's (1914) brief note on the natural origins of Monks Mound in *Science*, a perspective that he reiterated at Geological Society of America meetings (Crook 1915). Crook, a geologist and at that time curator of the Illinois State Museum (Thompson 1988:24), had based his conclusions on the results of 25 borings placed in the north side of Monks Mound. The notion that many if not all the mounds were natural phenomena had been debated earlier by members of the St. Louis Academy of Science, such as the geologists Worthen and Gates in the nineteenth century, and by Fenneman (1911) in the twentieth century.

Furthermore, as was discussed earlier, this premise of natural origin contributed in part to the razing of the "Big Mound" in St. Louis. The idea that these piles of earth were natural was also one of the reasons many of the legislators refused to be involved with the purchase of the mounds. Oddly enough, Crook favored the preservation of Monks Mound, simply as an unusual geological feature. Although David I. Bushnell, Jr., responded to Crook, as did Snyder (1917) at a later date, their arguments were to no avail because another bill to purchase the mounds, introduced in March 1915, again failed. After this defeat, the Cahokia Mound Association appears to have become inactive, and it remained that way until October 1933 when it was dissolved.

The urgency to preserve the mounds appears to have subsided until after World War I, when real estate prices began to rise, causing developers to become interested in the mounds. With the formation of the National Research Council (NRC) in 1916 as a war-time measure and its Division of Anthropology and Psychology, a Committee on State Archaeology was created in 1920 under the initial chair of Roland Dixon of Harvard and later Clark Wissler of the American Museum of Natural History (Wissler 1922). Although the documentation for their involvement in Cahokia has not been fully researched, members of this committee must have visited the site by 1920, if not sooner. By late 1920, Crook of the State Museum had met Wissler (1921a), who later wrote about inaugurating an Illinois survey through Crook's institution.

Early in 1921, Moorehead had also met with Wissler and discussed with him "the survey and exploration of the great Cahokia group"

Classics in Southeastern Archaeology

(Moorehead 1921b). Wissler informed Moorehead that this was in the hands of the State of Illinois. Moorehead (1921a) wrote Crook indicating the R. S. Peabody Museum was "much interested in a thorough exploration of the Cahokia group covering the next six or eight years." He further indicated that it needed to be studied in detail since it was different from the Tennessee Cumberland and Ohio cultures. He went on to offer his services without salary, just expenses. He assured Crook that the "bulk of the specimens would remain in the state where they properly belong" (Moorehead 1921a). Crook accepted Moorehead's offer to participate.

Moorehead also corresponded with Berthold Laufer of the Chicago Field Museum, who was a member of the National Research Council's Committee on State Surveys, regarding this same matter. In a subsequent letter from Wissler (1921b) to Crook, he noted Moorehead's interest and urged Crook to consider him since his institution has "a considerable fund of money that can be devoted to archaeological research," and Crook agreed. Nevertheless, at this point there was no discussion of the site's preservation. As described earlier, Moorehead's initial interest in Cahokia was one centered around research, especially the manner in which Cahokia differed from sites in Ohio and the Tennessee-Cumberland region.

What may have turned Moorehead's attention toward the site's preservation was a January 1921 *Alton Telegraph* newspaper article (Anonymous 1921). The article highlighted a protest raised by certain citizens in Alton and Edwardsville regarding the establishment of six state memorial parks in Illinois commemorating the sacrifice for democracy in World War I of Illinois boys. No site in the southern part of the state had been selected, although the aforementioned citizens urged that Monks Mound be made a Memorial Park. The following month the "Friends of Our Native Landscape" wrote Crook for information on the Cahokia site since they were trying to include the preservation of Cahokia and Monks Mound in a report to one of the legislators supporting a State Parks bill (Smith 1921).

In Moorehead's Annual Report for 1921 to the Board of Trustees at Phillips Academy he indicated that during the spring he had "consulted with members of the National Research Council [NRC], Mr. Willoughby of Harvard [Peabody Museum], and scientists in Washington, New York, and Chicago. They had formed a committee to deal with the Cahokia problem." In fact it appears that the NRC and other committees had visited Cahokia urging its preservation but did little to impress the owners (Moorehead 1921f). The problem of preservation with no support was also alluded to in Moorehead's meeting with the owners in June 1921 (Figure 5), where it was discussed how they had protected the mounds at heavy expense for the last ten years and were "rather weary of scientists who have come to them and urged continued protection, but contribute no money toward upkeep, etc." (Moorehead 1921d:2).

It was then thought that someone familiar with field conditions in the Mississippi valley should visit the owners. Crook (1921a) wrote Jesse Ramey, one of the site's owners, on behalf of Moorehead and indicated any archaeological work would arouse interest in the site and would help the state purchase the mounds. In Moorehead's June 1921 meeting with the owners at Cahokia, it was clear that there was imminent danger of the property being sold to realtors for development; already factories and railroads were within a mile of Monks Mound.

The various owners preferred to have the state purchase their properties as part of a State park, and this preference was again reinforced by Moorehead's meeting with different organizations locally including Congressman Rodenberg. Some of the owners had prevented excavations for nearly 35 years, and it was necessary, of course, for Moorehead to obtain permission for any excavations. The excavations were especially critical if they were to convince the legislature that the mounds were of human construction and that they contained objects of value. This 1921 visit in essence focused Moorehead's attention on the preservation of the mounds.

Upon returning to the R. S. Peabody Museum (until very recently the R. S. Peabody Foundation for Archaeology) at Phillips Academy, Moorehead requested permission to initiate investigations at Cahokia in the fall of 1921. William Henny Holmes of the Smithsonian Institution and Roland Dixon of the Peabody Museum at Harvard both wrote Moorehead encouraging him to "take charge of the work" (Moorehead 1921d:3). He also received support from Clark Wissler of the National Research Council. Moorehead's basic purpose was "to inaugurate a movement to preserve these mounds," which ultimately had to be done through the state legislature via the voters who could best be reached by way of the newspapers. Moorehead (n.d.), outlined four steps to reach this goal:

1) The first was "to secure the permission from the owners for limited explorations."

Fig. 5. Warren King Moorehead (on the right) meeting with the Rameys, with Monks Mound in the background, ca. June 1921 (courtesy of Ohio Historical Society)

2) The second was "to interest the press in telling the story of Cahokia to the people of Illinois and Missouri."
3) The third was "to secure funds from all sources for the exploration."
4) And the fourth was "to persuade some central institution to take over the work for the future."

By August 1921 he had prepared a flier entitled "Help Save the Cahokia Mounds" (Figure 6) telling of the mounds, their importance, the urgency of the situation, and requesting financial support. A similar flier had been produced by the Cahokia Mounds Association in 1914. Moorehead also contacted numerous newspapers regarding providing this same information along with the notice of the impending investigations. Articles appeared not only in the St. Louis papers but also over the wire service in Chicago, New York, Boston, Kansas City, Washington (D.C.), Newport News, Portland (Maine), and Huntington (West Virginia). He also lectured to different civic organizations such as the Rotary and the Daughters of the American Revolution and received support from them.

Funding for this ambitious endeavor came from several sources.

══════Help Save══════
The Cahokia Mounds

Andover, Mass., August 1921

The First National Bank of East St. Louis, Illinois, has kindly agreed to receive checks for the Cahokia Fund.

Men of Illinois should be especially interested in explorations of these mounds, located as they are in your own state. It is proposed to send one of the largest exhibits of specimens to your State Museum at Springfield, and another collection to the Field Museum at Chicago. Without cooperation of Illinois citizens we shall not be able to carry on our researches to the extent desired.

W. K. MOOREHEAD.

For several years it has been rumored that the famous Cahokia group of mounds might be destroyed. Originally sixty-eight in number, there still remain sixty-four of these tumuli, nearly all of which are in a good state of preservation.

I visited these mounds a short time ago and held consultations with the several owners. I also walked over all the tumuli and the village site and made a careful inspection. While in the region conferences were held with prominent citizens of East St. Louis, Illinois, and Dr. H. M. Whelpley and others in St. Louis. The rotary Club of East St. Louis held a meeting at which the question of preservation of these mounds was discussed at some length. Interviews appeared in the public press of the region.

I found widespread interest in both Illinois and Missouri among the intelligent citizens, even as there is interest on the part of all scientists, for the safeguarding of these mounds.

When it was proposed that someone familiar with Mound Builder culture, mound exploration, etc., make a special attempt to explore and preserve the Cahokia group, the subject was taken up with the leading museums and prominent archaeologists of this country. The gentlemen named in the list have either by letter or through personal interviews, endorsed my plan: — Prof. Wm. H. Holmes of the Smithsonian; Dr. Clark Wissler, Chairman of the Committee on State Archaeological Surveys of the National Research Council; Dr. A. R. Crook, Chief, State Museum Division, Springfield, Ill.; Dr. Roland B. Dixon, Peabody Mu-

Fig. 6. First page of flier, "Help Save The Cahokia Mounds," circulated by Moorehead, August 1921 (courtesy of Cahokia Mounds State Historic Site Archives)

There was, however, concern in the St. Louis area about whether Moorehead would be able to raise the necessary money locally because numerous supporters, particularly in St. Louis, were upset about an archaeological expedition to South America by Edgar Lee Hewitt in which he returned unfortunately with "ordinary stones and rubbish" (Moorehead 1921d:3; see also Moorehead 1921c, 1921e).

First, Moorehead attempted to raise funds through the aforementioned circular by establishing a "Cahokia Fund" at the First National Bank in East St. Louis. An amount for Cahokia preservation totaling $3,300 was raised, including $1,800 from individual and museum donations and $1,500 from his own institution. Eventually the University of Illinois Board of Trustees at the urging of their president, David Kinley, an Andover graduate, passed a resolution providing an additional $1,500 for Cahokia. This resolution not only supported the work but also provided for the curation of materials at the Museum of Natural History on the University of Illinois campus. This project was to be done in conjunction with the Illinois State Museum under its director A. R. Crook. Plans were also made for the University of Illinois to assume responsibility for the work in subsequent years.

THE 1921 FIELD SEASON

Moorehead's archaeological investigations began on September 13, 1921, and lasted nearly two months. He was assisted by Clinton Cowen, a civil engineer and a former Ohio highway commissioner. Cowen had attended Denison College with Moorehead, and both had worked together collecting and excavating while they were in college (Moorehead 1902). This association continued until Cowen's death in 1923 with Moorehead often relying on his friend for his surveying skills. Moorehead's crew consisted of four individuals who had worked with him in New England and several ex-servicemen from the immediate area of the site. William J. Seever, a collector from St. Louis, also assisted him and was undoubtedly an important source of information about the previous investigations of Patrick, McAdams, and others. Seever had provided Moorehead with a list of other sites, especially those with mounds and cemeteries, in the region that might be tested.

Generally, Moorehead stayed at the Planters Hotel in St. Louis and commuted to the site. As represented on his letterhead (Figure 7), his "headquarters" were considered to be the Ramey's farm, specifically Mound 48, which Fred Ramey (1921) referred to as the Castle Mound.

Marie Fingerhut, the daughter of Albert Kunnemann, recalled in an interview (Reinhart 1992) that her family would feed Moorehead's crew at noon. She was also taken by the fact that every time a burial was excavated, Moorehead would kneel and pray!

The first excavations were conducted into the Kunnemann Mound, the third largest in the Cahokia group. After Kunnemann, seven other mounds at the site were tested (Table 1, Figure 8). These included Schmidt's (Smith's) Mound in October; then the Edwards Mounds (Nos. 24 and 25); the Jesse Ramey Mound (No. 56); and finally the mound (No. 64) between the Baltimore and Ohio Railroad (B&O) tracks. Two other mounds south of highway 40 were also tested; however, it is unclear as to which two these were.

In addition to the mound excavations, Moorehead attempted to locate the prehistoric cemetery northeast of Monks Mound that William McAdams and others had investigated in the 1880s. With the assistance of Seever and McAdams's son Clark, Moorehead excavated a number of trenches 600 feet northeast of Monks Mound. They located a burned floor and a single burial. They also located another burned floor near the large borrow pit south of Monks Mound.

The Kunnemann Mound excavations were the most important of his Cahokia investigations. A sixty-foot-wide trench into the previously disturbed north side of the mound (Fowler 1997; Pauketat 1993) clearly settled the question that the mounds were man-made. In addition to the materials recovered, three burned floors and a clay altar or hearth were uncovered. The burned floors were often referred to by Moorehead as "dance floors." Excavations at the other mounds also served to reinforce their artificial nature.

Despite the short field season, the results were encouraging, and they made arrangements to return the following year. The results of the first season were published by the University of Illinois as a preliminary report (Moorehead 1922a). This publication emphasized the necessity for preserving the Cahokia Mounds (see also report to Phillips Academy trustees 1921g:5).

The report and the occasional calling card placed in with the material recovered currently provide the only notes or information on these excavations. Little doubt exists that notes were indeed taken, because Moorehead quotes from them in his report and because cross-section paper for making maps was purchased according to the extant vouchers. Unfortunately, the original field notes and maps remain at large.

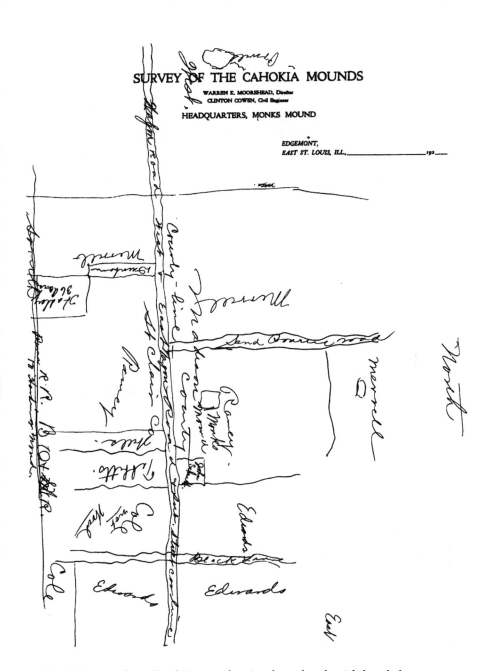

Fig. 7. Letter from Fred Ramey showing letterhead, with hand-drawn map of Cahokia site, December 1921 (© Robert S. Peabody Museum of Archaeology, Phillips Academy, Andover, Massachusetts. All rights reserved.)

Table 1. Summary of Moorehead's Investigations at Cahokia Mounds in 1921, 1922, and 1927

AREA INVESTIGATED	YEAR	NATURE OF WORK	REFERENCE
Kunnemann Md (No. 11)*	21	Excavation; stages, hearth	M 22:18-20; M 29:34-36, 133-134
Smith's (Schmidt's) Mds (Nos. 30-31)	21	Excavation; lots of debris	M 22:20-21; M 29:36-37
Jesse Ramey Md No. 56	21	Excavation 65 foot N-S trench; test pits; augers	M 22:22; M 29:37-38
Edwards Mds No. 24 (No. 25)	21	Excavation; burial	M 22:21-22; M 29:37
Edwards Mds No. 25 (No. 26)	21	Excavation; scales of copper	M 22:21-22; M 29:37
Ramey Md No. 48	21	headquarters; augered; aka Castle Md	M 22:18; M 29:33-34
Md between RR tracks, Mound 64	21	Tested; nothing recovered	M 22:22; M29:38, 83-84
Two mds south side of Collinsville Rd (Nos. 52-53)	21	Tested; lots of pottery; gumbo; no burials	M 22:23; M29:32,38
Village area 600 ft NE of Monks Md	21	Excavation; scattered burials, area of McAdams excavations	M 22:23-24
Village area 1/4 mi south of Monks Md along lake (BP)	21	Excavation; adjacent to borrow pit; burned floors	M 22:24; M 29:23, 28
Three mds (Nos. 32-34) north of Smith's	21	Surface collection; much fine pottery and numerous effigy heads	M 22:24; M 29:29
Sawmill Md No. 39	22	Excavations; burials on south side of slope	M 23:14-17; M 29:38-41, 136
Mound 82 (Md. 77)	22	Excavations; circular hearth with galena; referred to as Md 77 in 1929	M 23:14-15; M 29:40
Mound 80 (Md. 75)	22	Excavations; 50 ft. long, 6 ft. wide trench with lots of village debris	M 23:16; M 29: 41
Mound 75 (Md. 50)	22	Excavations; much burned clay with reed impressions; referred to as Md 50	M 23:39: M 29:31-32

Mound 19	22	Excavations; burial	M 23:17-19; M 29:41-44
Mound 20	22	Excavations; most of burials on south slope	M 23:17-19; M 29:41-44
Mound 21	22	Excavations	M 23:17-19; M 29:41-44
James Ramey No. 33	22	Excavations; 100 ft. N-S trench 35 ft. wide; circular structures beneath md.	M 23:19-27; M 29:44-51, 125-133
Temple Md No. 32	22	Excavations; platform md with spiral pit	M 23:19, 24-25; M 29:46, 49
Jondro Md No. 83 (No. 78)	22	Excavations; burials; referred to as Mound 86 in 1929 report	M 23:27-29; M 29: 51-52
Mound 14	22	Excavations; mostly gumbo; located in channel scar	M 23:31; M 29: 55
Mackie Md No. 84 (No. 79)	22	Excavations; mostly gumbo; located in channel scar; referred to as Md 79 in	M 23:31; M 29: 55
Harding Md No. 66	22	Excavations; N-S trench; an estimated 140 burials present	M 23:34-35; M 29:65-80
Mrs. Tippetts' Md No. 61	22	Excavations	M 23:35-36; M 29:58
Kruger Bone Bank	22	Excavations; 16 burials	M 23:34; M 29:58
Wells'-Tippetts' Village Site	22	Excavations; area 100-200 yds south of Md 51	M 23:39; M 29: 31-32
Village west of Md 19	22	Excavations; numerous broken hoes and galena	M 23:17
Merrell Tract (Stolle lease)	22	Excavations; 1500-2500 ft. west of Monks Md	M 23:38; M 29: 31
Ponds (Borrow Pits)	22	Excavations	M 23:41-42
Mound 65	27	Test holes	M 29: 76, 81-83
Two low mounds west of Md 66 (Nos. 82-83)	27	Test trench; north-south and four foot wide through both mounds	M 29: 84-85
Monks Mound	?	Augered	M 29: 15-22, 137-139

*-mound numbers in parentheses refer to current md. no. see Fowler 1997

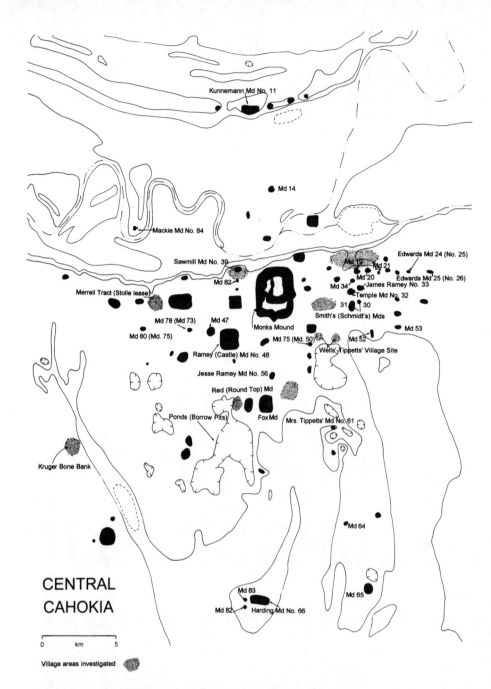

Fig. 8. Location of Moorehead's investigations at Cahokia during 1921, 1922, and 1927 (courtesy of Central Mississippi Valley Archaeological Research Institute)

Classics in Southeastern Archaeology

In later correspondence with James B. Griffin, Moorehead indicated the notes were left at the University of Illinois.

The materials recovered from Moorehead's 1921 testing of eight mounds and several residential areas just described were originally to be curated at the Illinois State Museum. However, because the University of Illinois had contributed substantial funds to the project, it was eventually decided that the State Museum would only retain materials from the Schmidt and Kunnemann Mounds and the Ramey village site. In addition to these excavated lots, other materials were present in the State Museum collection representing what we assume were surface collections from specific mounds and areas of the site (Kelly et al. 1996).

By the end of the season Dr. A. R. Crook (1921b), Chief of the Illinois State Museum noted that "14 small boxes of fragments of pottery, human skeletons, other bones and Indian utensils were secured and are now in the State Museum." In each of the Illinois State Museum containers, which were probably cigar boxes, Moorehead had apparently placed his calling card. On each card, scrawled in pencil, was some provenance information. Recent research at the museum revealed that along with each sample was a four-by-six-inch carbon copy piece of paper with typed information on the expedition, and in many instances, the same notation visible on the accompanying calling card was transferred in pencil to the paper. It is not known precisely when these materials were accessioned, catalogued, and labeled, but an occasional typed card was found indicating that Thorne Deuel, the new museum director, had inspected that particular sample.

Apparently at some point the materials were placed in "dead" storage in the Centennial building in Springfield and were discovered in the 1960s when the museum moved to its new facility. Robert Hall (personal communication 1995) had borrowed some of the material for research, and one of his students conducted refiring and drilling and cutting on one of the sherds.

Crook (1922a), a geologist, stated personally that "the material do not amount to much, but of course I may be mistaken." In general, I suspect that most people including Moorehead were expecting quantities of large and unique artifacts to be recovered from a site such as Cahokia. Such expectations were probably the same ones St. Louisans had earlier when Edgar Lee Hewitt returned from Central America. Nevertheless, the lack of any unique specimens for the Illinois State

Museum was perhaps a moot point since the University of Illinois was to be given the preponderance of the recovered materials.

President David Kinley (1921) of the University of Illinois instructed Frank Collins Baker, a zoologist and curator at the university's Museum of Natural History, to arrange with Crook to have the specimens examined and selected for the university's collection. In Baker's (1921) subsequent correspondence with Crook, he inquired "whether it [the material] can be carried in a suit case or whether it must be shipped." Instead, arrangements were made to ship all the materials to Urbana and sort them there. The shipment consisted of seven large boxes. And as noted by Baker (1922),

> In the division of the material . . . it was deemed best not to break the sets from the different mounds, but to keep the material from each mound intact, thus preserving the continuity of material from each location and adding to its scientific and research value. . . . three mounds are represented in the University lot, the Edwards and the Alton, and a mound near the Schmidt mound. The State Museum has the Schmidt mound, the Kenneman [sic] mound, and the Ramey village site. The material from the Edwards mound is quite the greatest in bulk and also one of the most interesting. Some other general things are included from the surface and other places.
>
> The collection well illustrates the character of the ethnologic material contained in these mounds, and may prove of great future value in determining the character, both ecological and geological, which other students give to these interesting mounds.

It is unclear what the "Alton" Mound referred to above is. A small collection of materials from the Schmidt Mound are also presently curated in the Department of Anthropology at Washington University in St. Louis.

At the University of Illinois, Baker carefully catalogued and labeled all the materials coming from the field. After they were accessioned and catalogued, a label was made for each material class. Apparently none of Moorehead's original cards with notes were retained. Eventually a number of exhibits were designed to display the materials at the university's Museum of Natural History.

The collection at the University of Illinois was briefly examined by the author several years ago as part of a systematic study of certain materials in it. Although this assortment of materials lacks the detailed provenance, it does provide some information for future reference.

George Higgins provided Moorehead with another collection of unprovenanced material from Cahokia at this time. These materials are in the R. S. Peabody Museum collections at Phillips Academy.

By the end of the year (1921) the American Anthropological Association (AAA) had met and passed a resolution urging the preservation of the Cahokia Mounds. Since Moorehead's ongoing work with the New England survey was under control, Moorehead felt it his duty to continue with the work at Cahokia. Phillips Academy would release him for six weeks in the spring and again in the fall of 1922. The University of Illinois would fund the work, and Phillips Academy would provide for Moorehead's salary. Moorehead viewed this venture as a five-year project and even suggested Gerard Fowke as a possible field director.

Fowke, incidentally, was another Ohio valley archaeologist, who Moorehead (1902) initially met at the 1888 Cincinnati Centennial exposition. Like Moorehead, Fowke had conducted archaeological work in a number of different locales throughout his career. Unlike Moorehead, who became established at the R. S. Peabody, Fowke was affiliated with numerous institutions. In the St. Louis area, he had worked in Missouri some 20 years earlier for the Missouri Historical Society and again for William H. Holmes of the Smithsonian Institution.

While at the Missouri Historical Society, Fowke investigated the Montezuma Mounds in the Illinois river valley and even trenched one of the mounds in the Kunnemann group (Fowke 1906). However, Moorehead (1921f:3) also points out that "his personal likes and dislikes are such that he might not be able to keep the various interests harmonized" as Moorehead had. The purpose in continuing the fieldwork was to keep the public interest aroused because the legislature did not meet again until January 1923.

While the initial work at Cahokia in 1921 lasted only six weeks, a considerable amount was accomplished. First and foremost, Moorehead was able to demonstrate the artificial nature of the mounds to a point that even Crook (1922b) concurred with most of the data, and another geologist, Morris Leighton, was able to confirm this both in the field and in the lab. Second, this first season established the foundation for subsequent fieldwork at Cahokia in 1922 and again in 1927 and at several outlying sites in 1922 and 1923. Finally, Moorehead's efforts also greatly increased the interest of the general public, and he was able to establish an excellent rapport with the local landowners.

One final footnote to the 1921 season was the fact that it included aerial photographs taken of the site by Lieutenants Harold R. Wells and Ashley C. McKinley of the War Department's Army Air Service during the winter of 1921 and 1922. These were done at the request of David I. Bushnell, Jr., who was also present in the St. Louis area on behalf of the Smithsonian Institution and who was conducting "a reconnaissance of the remarkable mound groups in the vicinity of the great Cahokia Mound" (Bushnell 1922:92).

Bushnell (1904), a St. Louisan and son of the collector, David I. Bushnell, Sr., had prepared an initial summary of work on the different groups in 1904 while he was Assistant in Archaeology at the Peabody Museum, Harvard University. Bushnell's 1921 work, including the subsequent aerial photographs, augmented the original 1904 study. It should be noted that these were the first aerial photographs of any archaeological site in the New World (Fowler 1997; Hall 1968). Moorehead (1922c), when he heard Bushnell was in the area, was extremely upset, especially because Bushnell had not come to visit him.

THE 1922 FIELD SEASON

Alja R. Crook, the geologist, had seen aerial photographs when he attended a meeting in Chattanooga, Tennessee, during the fall of 1921 and thought they would help interpret the origins of the mounds at Cahokia (Hall 1968:76). After his return to Springfield, he spent several months contacting people in the War Department in an attempt to arrange for a flight to obtain photographs, but he was unsuccessful. In February of 1922, Crook learned of the Wells-McKinley aerials, which were thought by some to be of little use because of their poor quality. Eventually, Crook's efforts were successful through contacts he made when he was involved with a reception for the army's General John J. Pershing as part of Lincoln's birthday celebration in Springfield.

Correspondence with Pershing's aide-de-camp shows that Crook's request for a fly-over was granted, and in April 1922, Lt. G. W. Goddard, an army aerial photographer and a pioneer in aerial photography, accompanied by Lt. H. K. Ramey, made a flight that resulted in numerous aerial photographs of the site. (To the best of my knowledge, Lt. Ramey was unrelated to the Rameys who owned Monks Mound.) Some of the photographs were published by Crook (1922b) in his article on the origins of Monks Mound. Although they were not used to interpret any specific features at the time, these photographs, along with those made by Col. Dache Reeves in 1933, were important in identifying the palisade that surrounds central Cahokia (Anderson 1969) and were an integral part of identifying Moorehead's 1921 excavations into the Jesse Ramey Mound and the Edwards Mounds (Fowler 1997:78). None of Moorehead's reports mention these aerial photographs of Cahokia.

The 1922 field season began in March and continued until the beginning of May. It again resumed in September, finishing in October. All materials from this work were turned over to the University of Illinois Museum of Natural History, where they were exhibited and subsequently curated. Moorehead's crew, under the supervision of William J. Seever, tested several low mounds and the adjoining areas. The methods he employed were clearly tied into his objective of determining the extent of the village deposits and whether burials occurred near the surface. To detect bones and other cultural objects, he used $3^1/_2$- to $4^1/_2$-foot-long rods, the presumed prototype for the "Fulton County walking stick," which was a type of long metal probe popular in the Dickson Mounds area in the 1920s and 30s used to locate burials.

Areas between 11 mounds were probed. They included the area between Mounds 23 and 43, east and west; Mounds 20 and 62, north and south; Mounds 19, 20, and 21, where burials were encountered; the south slope of Mound 39 (Sawmill Mound) and Mound 82 (the small mound to the south), where in both instances human remains were encountered. The field crew also "prospected" two low mounds (Nos. 47 and 73?) to the west of Mound 48 (Castle Mound) (Moorehead 1923:16). Based on these results, excavations into fourteen mounds were then conducted during the spring and fall field seasons (Figure 8). In most cases this entailed long, often-wide trenches through the centers. At other times the trenches extended beyond the mounds into the aboriginal residential areas. At least two major village areas were extensively tested, one west of the Merrell Mound and the other southeast of Monks Mound and south of Mound 51, known as the Wells-Tippetts site. Finally, one non-mound cemetery area, the Kruger Bone Bank, was also investigated.

One of the problems encountered during the course of the fieldwork was the hoards of visitors. To deal with this problem, Moorehead's field crew would shift investigations to other areas and then return at a later time. In some instances it was necessary to collapse the walls and partially backfill the trenches. This peculiar method made it more difficult for anyone not involved in the excavation to remove materials, although by no means did it really prevent them from doing so.

The mound investigations west of Monks Mound occurred at the Sawmill Mound (No. 39) and its small companion, Mound 82 to the south. Eight burials were encountered on the south slope of the Sawmill mound. The associated ceramic vessels and a fenestrated shell gorget of the Cruciform genre as classified by Brian and Phillips (1996) are indicative of a Sand Prairie phase component. Moorehead's trenches that extended beneath the Sawmill Mound encountered an extensive village deposit three feet deep, below that mound. Here Moorehead (1923:15) noted, "black pottery predominated, and a few red fragments were observed." Materials examined in the University of Illinois collections indeed do suggest an intense pre-mound Stirling phase component.

A large, circular clay hearth was uncovered during the excavation into Mound 82. This finding suggests that this small earthen edifice was a substructure mound. Again, the materials recovered appear to be affiliated with the Sand Prairie phase occupation in this area of Cahokia (Kelly et al. 1995).

Mound 80 (actually Mound 75 [Fowler 1997]), approximately 2,500 feet to the southwest of Sawmill, contained "a large number of potsherds, bones, burned clay, and village site material" (Moorehead 1923:16). The two low mounds (Nos. 47 and 73) between Mound 80 and Mound 48 were also "prospected" by Seever and a crew of men. These two mounds form the southern edge of the West Plaza.

The mounds trenched by Moorehead's fieldworkers east of Monks Mound included mounds 19, 20, 21, 32, and 33 (the James Ramey Mound). These mounds form the northwest corner of the East Plaza (see Kelly et al. 1996). An east-west trench, approximately 250 feet long, extended from Mound 19, on the west, into Mound 21 on the east. Mortuary remains were recovered from the slopes of Mounds 19 and 20. Apparently their work extended beyond this area to the west, where at a distance of 150 feet, they recovered at a depth of 3 feet numerous hoe and spade fragments of a reddish (burned Mill Creek) chert. Fifteen feet beyond this area they found a mass of pulverized galena lying in ashes.

The most extensive excavations occurred at the important James Ramey Mound. This large conical mound at one time measured 38 feet in height before having its upper 15 feet removed. A north-south trench, 100 feet long, 45 feet wide at the top, and 23 feet deep was placed into this mound. The depth of the trench was such that it was necessary to narrow it to 35 feet at the base. Because of the crowds, the excavations were temporarily halted until Moorehead could return the following fall, at which time the fieldworkers expanded the trench another 10 feet to the west. During the course of their excavations, they uncovered and mapped two circular structures, the first features to be described and mapped at Cahokia or in the American Bottom. Several hearths were also mapped, and several old surfaces within the mound were identified as burned floors.

Clinton Cowen, who took notes during the course of the excavations, provided a number of profiles for the James Ramey mound (Moorehead 1923:10, Fig. 9-11). Geologist Morris Leighton described in detail the various strata in this mound, removing all doubt that the mounds were indeed a result of human endeavor (Leighton 1923). Leighton also provided descriptions of profiles from the Albert Kunnemann Mound (no. 16); the Sawmill Mound (no. 39); and the Sam Chucallo [sic] Mound in Fairmont City. Finally, four borings were made into Monks Mound. He suggested that the nucleus of Monks Mound might indeed be natural, but he urged caution, especially with regard to the scientific value of borings when contrasted with data from open trenches. Cores can provide a useful starting point in the investigation of mounds; however, as Leighton noted, ultimately a larger area must be examined to properly interpret these cores (see Reed et al. 1968 as an example).

The materials from the James Ramey Mound were described as part of Robert W. Wagner's (1959) master's thesis at the Department of Anthropology, University of Illinois. Moorehead had collected the materials in rough stratigraphic units of variable thickness (mostly four foot, but in one instance eight foot). "The various artifacts found . . . were kept in cigar boxes according to the levels at which they occurred" (Moorehead 1923:24). By employing these units in conjunction with Griffin's (1949) ceramic types and the current Cahokia sequence (Figure 9), we can assign the upper portion of the mound to the Moorehead phase, and the lower part appears to be affiliated with the Stirling phase. This result coincides with a similar dating for Mound 34 to the northwest and, in general, for most of the material in this part of the site. Of interest is Moorehead's observation that the lower part of the mound contained a thin red ware different from the ceramics elsewhere in the

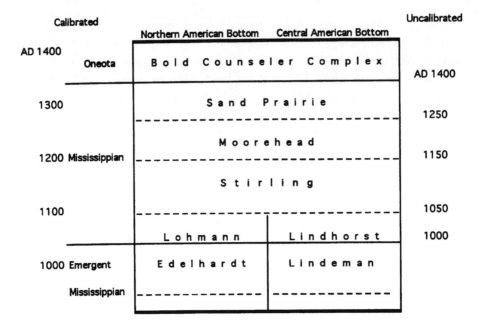

Calibrated		Northern American Bottom	Central American Bottom	Uncalibrated
AD 1400				
	Oneota	B o l d C o u n s e l e r C o m p l e x		AD 1400
1300		S a n d P r a i r i e		1250
		M o o r e h e a d		
1200	Mississippian			1150
		S t i r l i n g		
1100				1050
		L o h m a n n	L i n d h o r s t	1000
1000	Emergent	E d e l h a r d t	L i n d e m a n	
	Mississippian			

Fig. 9. Late prehistoric chronology of Cahokia site (sources: **Hall** 1991 and Kelly 1990)

mound. These sherds were found in the area 15 to 20 feet below the mound summit.

Mound 32, which adjoins the James Ramey Mound on the southwest, had a 14-by-8-foot trench placed in its summit during the fall. Because of this mound's flat-topped, rectilinear configuration, it was named the Temple Mound. It measured approximately 17 feet in height. As in the James Ramey Mound, considerable amounts of Moorehead and Stirling phase ceramics were also encountered.

The mounds investigated north of Monks Mound, Mounds 14 and 84 (the Mackie Mound), were located in the abandoned Mississippi channel of the Edelhardt meander and floodplain of Cahokia Creek. Both were composed of gumbo clay and contained little debris.

Farther west, Moorehead's investigations included the Kruger Bone Bank and the Jondro Mound, number 83 (Figure 10). The Kruger Bone Bank mortuary area, north of the Roach Mound group, was situated on a low sandy ridge along a slough to the west. A total of 16 burials was recovered, most within 20 inches of the surface, although some extended to a depth of 3 feet. The Jondro Mound was farther west, located south of the Powell group. Seever trenched it and recovered a

Fig. 10. Location of Moorehead's investigations in the American Bottom during 1922 and 1923 (based on Bushnell 1921:Fig. 99, courtesy of Central Mississippi Valley Archaeological Research Institute)

number of burials but little else.

South of Monks Mound the remaining mounds to be examined included numbers 75, 61 (Mrs. Tippetts' Mound), and 66 (the Harding or Rattlesnake Mound). Materials in Mound 75 (actually Mound 50 [Fowler 1997]) were restricted to a considerable amount of burned clay with reed and stick impressions (Moorehead 1923:39).

Mrs. Tippetts' Mound, located adjacent to two borrow areas, had two test pits placed in this oval mound with little material recovered. Like many of the other mounds, it was composed of gumbo.

The Harding Mound is perhaps one of the largest mounds next to

Monks Mound. It was a long, linear, ridge-topped mound, approximately 550 feet long, 125 feet wide, and 40 feet high. Several pits were placed in the mound 12 to 17 feet deep, revealing some stratigraphy but little debris. The mound was also augured to a depth of 22 feet with 7-inch-diameter cores obtained (Figure 11). Moorehead recommended that the mound be tunneled. He later returned to the Harding Mound in the spring of 1927 for more in-depth excavations.

In addition to testing the aforementioned mounds, one of Moorehead's objectives was to determine the extent of Cahokia's "village area." In the fall of that year he tested the area between the Merrell Mound (No. 42) and Mound 44 west of Monks Mound and recovered materials between one and four feet in depth that indicated to him that the area was heavily populated. This settlement pattern extended one quarter mile farther west to what appears to be the area between Mounds 45 and 46. Based on materials housed at the University of Illinois, his excavations also extended into Mound 43 and its base.

Other village areas examined or identified included the Wells-Tippetts village site. His investigations were focused on the area 100 to 200 yards south of the Persimmon Mound (No. 51) and the intervening low mounds, 55, 74, and 75. The testing, conducted during the fall, revealed "village debris . . . as heavy as any point on the Ramey lands" (Moorehead 1923:39).

Unlike the first season (1921) when his investigations were restricted to Cahokia, in later seasons Moorehead's work extended well into other parts of the American Bottom, where a number of other mounds were trenched and sites tested (Figure 10). The western mound, Sam Chucallo [sic], in the Fairmont City group, was trenched, uncovering ten burials, seven of which were on a "burnt bench" one foot above the base. The mound was primarily gumbo; its edges had been partially disturbed by railroad construction on the west, a house and garage on the south, a street on the east, and by trolley tracks on the north. This mound still exists today, where it has been protected by Sam Chucalo's son Paul. Paul's older sister, Zorina, was a young girl of eight during Moorehead's excavations. She was present at the time and was assigned the task of guarding the human remains placed in a nearby garage. Although the remains were cordoned off, one visitor, "an archaeologist from Washington University" in St. Louis, attempted to bribe her with a candy bar in order to view the remains.

On the bluffs to the southeast of Cahokia, Seever trenched Sullivan's Mound in an area known as Signal Hill. A large depression with a num-

Fig. 11. Augering into the Harding Mound, 1927 (courtesy of Cahokia Mounds State Historic Site Photographic Archives)

Introduction

ber of pits was delineated beneath this mound; however, except for a cranium depicted in profile of the mound (Moorehead 1923a:Fig. 6), no skeletal material was found.

On the floodplain west of Sullivan's mound, Moorehead arranged to excavate at the Pittsburg Lake cemetery that had been uncovered a number of years earlier when Louisiana Boulevard was being constructed. The earlier excavations by H. M. Braun had uncovered 30 to 40 individuals with some 51 pottery vessels. Moorehead arranged for excavations on two acres. In an area 20 by 25 feet he uncovered 13 skeletons with eleven vessels. His description of these vessels suggests a Sand Prairie phase affiliation because he refers to them as being similar to those of the Middle South, that is, Tennessee-Cumberland. The exact location of this cemetery is still unknown.

Finally, as part of his attempt to determine the extent of the village area along Cahokia Creek, Moorehead conducted excavations in East St. Louis. He indicates in his report that materials were recovered from test pits along Cahokia Creek near the Stockyards. The materials recovered are indicative of a Stirling phase occupation and an earlier Emergent Mississippian component (Kelly 1994). He also alludes to excavations conducted in the backyards of residences in East St. Louis with archaeological materials found to depths of 20 and 36 inches (Moorehead 1929b:26). His observation on the presence of such materials in the backyards of residences at these depths between 20 and 36 inches has been recently verified (Kelly 1994).

In general the 1922 investigations at Cahokia were the most extensive that Moorehead undertook and were published by the University of Illinois the following year (Moorehead 1923). A complete copy of the text, excluding plates and bibliography that also appear in the 1929 report, is included here in facsimile form. He was able to integrate into his investigations the work of geologists, anatomists to examine human remains, and other specialists. The ashes from one of the hearths in the James Ramey Mound were sent to a chemist who supplied a chemical assay of the ash. This analysis represents the first use of a specialist in the work at Cahokia.

THE 1923 FIELD SEASON

With the impending legislative session in January of 1923, over 20 editors and publishers of newspapers in St. Clair, Madison, and Bond Counties met to provide support for the bill that was being introduced

(Anonymous 1923). The legislation proposed the purchase of 200 acres for $250,000 to create a state park. In estimating the possible value of the mounds, Moorehead (1923c) suggested that the legislature purchase 30 of the mounds for $238,000, letting the adjoining areas go until additional funds were available. By the time the bill was finalized, it allotted $50,000 for 144 acres. This amount was far less than what the owners expected. In fact, Moorehead (1923b:3) felt that real estate people interested in selling the land for development had influenced the legislators and compromised the bill's intent.

Field investigations during the 1923 season were again conducted by Moorehead under the auspices of the University of Illinois. A complete copy of the report of this work, except for the bibliography and plates that also appear in the 1929 report, is included in this edition. The work was restricted to three sites outside of Cahokia. The first to be investigated was the Mitchell group located seven miles north of Cahokia. Moorehead's examination of the Mitchell group was initiated in March and, in general, was kept secret at the landowner's request. Although Bushnell (1904) had published a detailed map and description of the group, Seever provided Moorehead with a map (Figure 12) he had prepared in November 1896, some eight years earlier.

Bushnell's own map may well have been based on Seever's survey, because he knew Seever through the Missouri Historical Society. Moorehead used Bushnell's designations in identifying the different mounds, but made notes on Seever's map. Four of the mounds were tested with few significant results. To reduce costs, an auger was employed in investigating two of the mounds. Porter (1974) later, while excavating at Mitchell, recovered a "catsup" bottle with Moorehead's signature scribbled on an enclosed piece of paper from an auger hole in Mound E. Archaeologists have often commented on the true contents of the bottle, since this was the period of prohibition.

Apparently a portion of Mound A (also referred to by McAdams as the Great Mound at Mitchell), which was mostly destroyed in 1876 (Howland 1877), remained between the railroad tracks. Excavations placed by Moorehead between the tracks uncovered two burials on a sand platform. Six projectile points were located with the burials, and a few sherds indicative of a Moorehead phase affiliation (Kelly 2000b) were recovered. According to the notes on the map, Moorehead also tested the Hoefken Mound located south of the Mitchell group and Long Lake.

After the Mitchell excavations, his investigations shifted northward

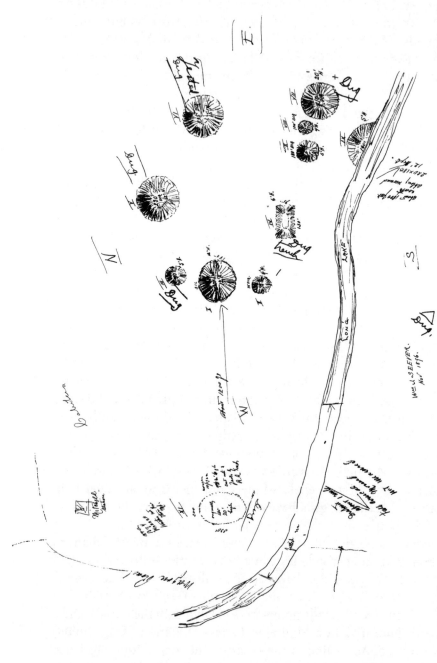

Fig. 12. William Seever's 1896 map of the Mitchell site with notations on Moorehead's 1923 investigations (© Robert S. Peabody Museum of Archaeology, Phillips Academy, Andover, Massachusetts. All rights reserved.)

to the mound group near Wood River, known today as Grassy Lake (Kelly 2000a). Five of the eleven mounds in the group were subject to excavation. The mound on the Frank Smith property contained burials including a Late Woodland (Sponemann phase) vessel and some copper-stained soil. Other ceramic materials recovered from elsewhere on the site indicated the presence of several components, including all of the major periods from Early Woodland to late Mississippian. Substantial quantities of lithic materials were collected, some of which are part of the aforementioned components, as well as several even earlier Archaic occupations.

A small sample of materials curated at the University of Illinois includes a label referencing a collection from the surface of the Aluminum Ore Company Mound in April 1923. This mound is designated as part of the Lohmann site. None of Moorehead's publications include a discussion of this site. Except for a Middle Woodland sherd, the materials are indicative of a Mississippian, Lohmann phase, affiliation. With the exception of the celt cache recovered from beneath this mound in 1943 (Harn 1971; Esarey and Pauketat 1992), this artifact is the only material recovered from the mound.

The remaining site investigated in 1923 was the Emerald Mound group, in the upland Silver Creek drainage 15 miles east southeast of Cahokia (Koldehoff et al. 1993). In his publication, Moorehead referred to this site as the Stock Mound, which included the largest mound and two smaller mounds to the east. In the curated materials at the University of Illinois, another lot refers to the mounds $3^1/_2$ miles northeast of Lebanon, which is presumably the Emerald group, although the actual distance is 2 miles. The small sample of artifacts recovered from the mounds tested are indicative of a late Emergent Mississippian occupation and a later Moorehead phase component (Kelly 1999).

The results of the 1923 investigations were not published until 1929 when the final report was completed (Moorehead 1929b). Although investigations were scheduled for 1924 and the publication's front cover refers to a 1924 season, no work was conducted until 1927. The 1924 season was supposed to have been the last season at Cahokia for Moorehead and the University of Illinois. Apparently the focus of the these investigations was to be the tunneling of Monks Mound (Taylor 1927[?]), for which President Kinley was considering an appropriation of $15,000. This suggestion actually resurfaced again in 1929 when Moorehead's field assistant, Taylor (1929) submitted a budget for the proposed tunneling. The implementation of the tunnel excavations into Monks Mound fortunately never materialized.

During the course of his investigations in 1921 and 1922, Moorehead had worked on a much larger area of the Cahokia site than was eventually proposed for purchase by the State of Illinois. As discussed earlier, the proposed 200-acre area for purchase was reduced considerably by the legislature to an appropriation of $50,000 for the purchase of Monks Mound and a smaller area of 144 acres (Anonymous 1925). The bill was passed in 1924. The Rameys, whose land was being purchased, refused the state's offer, and it was necessary for the state to condemn the land. In June of 1925, a jury awarded the Rameys $52,000 for the 144 acres. The Rameys then appealed to the Illinois State Supreme Court but subsequently withdrew the appeal and accepted the settlement.

In 1926 the state began laying out the park, including a road that extended into the south side. Later that year, the state park was opened. Meanwhile, Moorehead continued to lobby for the purchase of other mounds. In particular, he urged that the Powell Mound was of utmost importance. Alas, it was destroyed as we will soon see. In an editorial in Addison Throop's *East St. Louis Call* in May 1924, Moorehead chided the citizens of Illinois for the tragic developments occurring at the mounds. He stated that there is "obviously . . . something abnormal in the brain of either man or woman who prefers to see this heritage of the ages destroyed and two or three bungalows or a filling station or 'hot dog stands' erected in its place" (Moorehead 1924). Unfortunately, little has changed since then.

THE 1927 FIELD SEASON

Although plans existed for another season in 1924, Moorehead instead focused his work in 1924 on mounds and sites in the Natchez, Mississippi, area. The 1925 through 1927 seasons were then spent at the large Mississippian site of Etowah in north Georgia. By the time Moorehead returned to Cahokia in April 1927, the park was open. The final field season was conducted between April and June 1927. The excavations were actually directed by Jay L. B. Taylor, who had worked earlier for Moorehead in Missouri. The focus was on the Harding (or Rattlesnake) mound and three other nearby mounds, which had been acquired earlier by the B&O Railroad. The Harding Mound is a long, narrow ridge-topped mound that marks the southern limits of the site as defined by the mounds. Moorehead had briefly tested this mound in 1922 and had recommended that it be tunneled. Taylor's 1927 work entailed the placement of a north-south trench through the center. He laid out a grid and, as in the earlier excavations, began to remove the mound using a team of horses and a slip. He reached a depth of 23 feet before his work was halted when one of the landowners would not let them cross his land with the team. They then resorted to using the large augers to determine the mound's depth and construction (Figure 11).

Taylor's description of his work on the various mounds was issued in 1929 and is reprinted here. Additional maps related to this specific work were located at the University of Michigan's Museum of Anthropology (Pauketat and Barker 2000). The materials recovered from the slope of the Harding Mound include early Lohmann and Sand Prairie phase ceramics. One of the sherds is Oneota (Kelly 1999b). Early Lohmann phase ceramics were also collected from the small mound west of the Harding Mound.

Moorehead's Final Report (1929b) was basically a compilation of the previous reports published in 1922 and 1923 of the 1921 and 1922 investigations and the work from the last two field seasons, 1923 and 1927. A complete copy of Moorehead's final report, including plates and bibliography, appears in facsimile in this volume. Please note that the bibliography is arranged in chronological order by publication date in the original, and we have retained the original rather than modifying it into a standard bibliographic format for this edition. For nearly four decades this 1929 volume represented the only significant publication on Cahokia, although various articles and an occasional thesis appeared. The momentum Moorehead initially started at Cahokia and the surrounding region in the 1920s essentially dwindled after the 1927 archaeological investigations. A. R. Kelly, a recent Harvard Ph.D., arrived at the University of Illinois in 1930 and was immediately thrust into the position of salvaging the Powell Mound in 1930 and 1931. By 1933 Kelly was en route to Georgia and the Macon Plateau site, so in essence no sustained research emerged from his brief presence. After Kelly, any investigations at Cahokia were restricted to private lands and were either conducted by amateurs such as Paul Titterington (1938) and Gregory Perino (Grimm 1949) or were of a salvage nature in which a mound was hurriedly excavated before the construction of a subdivision as Harriet Smith did in 1942 (Smith 1942, 1969); or a motel, as Dr. Preston Holder of Washington University did in 1955 (Fowler

1997:27); or a discount store in the heart of Cahokia as Dr. Joseph Caldwell of the Illinois State Museum did in 1959 (Fowler 1997:27–28). The only systematic research at Cahokia and several nearby sites was conducted in the early 1950s by James B. Griffin and Albert Spaulding of the University of Michigan Museum of Anthropology (Griffin and Spaulding 1951).

A new momentum returned to Cahokia archaeology in 1960, largely because of the efforts of individuals, such as Professors Charles J. Bareis, Melvin L. Fowler, Robert L. Hall, James W. Porter, and Warren Wittry, who were involved in the highway salvage excavations at Cahokia and the American Bottom. Numerous theses have been produced as a result of this early salvage work, as well as the other more recent investigations (for a summary see Hall 1991). Since these salvage excavations of the 1960s, a considerable amount of research has been conducted at Cahokia and the surrounding region, including the Cahokia research initiated by Professor Melvin L. Fowler (1997:35–39) in 1966. By the end of this century a number of edited reports and volumes and at least five monographs have been produced on Cahokia, including Melvin Fowler's (1989) atlas and its subsequent revision (1997), which incorporates a considerable amount of Moorehead's information. Nonetheless, Moorehead's publications stand as a major tribute to his work at Cahokia, especially in his efforts to have the site preserved.

THE CAHOKIA EPILOGUE

Although no additional work was conducted at Cahokia by Moorehead, a review of his correspondence indicates that he was kept abreast of the various developments at the site. An opportunity to return to St. Louis was provided by a Conference on Midwestern Archaeology sponsored by the NRC's Committee on State Archaeological Survey and held in St. Louis in May 1929. In Moorehead's remarks during the dinner addresses, he noted three questions generally asked by the public: Where did the Indians originate? How old is the mound? And the one that most concerned them: Who was paying for this work? (Moorehead 1929a:97) C'est le vie. In many respects his participation at this conference provides some additional perspective on his work. One of the items that Moorehead (1929a:98) emphasized in his address to the conference was that "we deal too much with the mere materials of archaeology and are apt to forget the human interest side. Consider the Indian men and women themselves for a moment."

From this brief statement Moorehead (1929a:98) expounds on the contributions of various Native Americans from "Sa-cah-gah-wea" to the nearly one third of the Indians who were fit for military service, who fought in World War I. He in fact notes that the efforts to preserve Cahokia were dedicated to the memory of Native peoples. The various addresses like the one Moorehead presented on Saturday evening were broadcast over the air waves of KMOX (Dunlap 1929:4), thus reaching an even larger audience.

Although Monks Mound had been purchased, a major concern was the fate of the Powell Mound, which was one of the largest mounds in the Cahokia group. Efforts were underway by the state to purchase this mound that marked the western limits of greater Cahokia. The state had made an offer to purchase the Powell Mound and a lane leading to it. The Powells, however, wanted to sell both the mound and the adjoining tract. From an archaeological and preservation standpoint, the purchase of both mound and land would have been great. In the meantime, the Powell brothers had a standing offer to pay $3,000 to any institution that would remove the mound. This price was based on what it would cost them to have it removed so that a nearby swamp could be filled and the area beneath the mound farmed.

Addison J. Throop, an East St. Louis newspaper editor and avid collector, contacted Moorehead regarding the destruction of one of the smaller mounds in the group in October 1929. Certainly the situation must have been tense. In December 1930 the act of razing the Powell Mound began. It was the most devastating incident ever to occur at Cahokia, only comparable to the removal of the Big Mound in St. Louis and the Cemetery Mound in East St. Louis 60 years earlier. This unfortunate incident began in response to rumors that the state was about to condemn the land. The Powell's began secretly to remove the north side of the mound with a steam shovel. This activity remained out of sight of the public for nearly seven days, before their friend, an amateur archaeologist and radiologist, Dr. Paul F. Titterington, was made aware of the situation. He contacted Dr. Arthur R. Kelly at the University of Illinois who appeared four days later and began recording information and recovering materials, along with Dr. W. C. McKern of the Milwaukee Public Museum, Thorne Deuel of the Illinois State Museum, and Professor Fay-Cooper Cole of the University of Chicago, as the mound was inexorably destroyed.

The materials recovered from the large Powell Mound were briefly described in a series of short articles in the transactions of the Illinois

Academy of Science in 1934. A more lengthy description has been provided by Ahler and DePuydt (1987), who suggest that this mound dates to the Lohmann and Stirling phases. More important, however, were the ceramic materials associated with the smaller Powell Mound No. 2. They included ceramics from beneath this mound as well as those from intrusive burials. A. R. Kelly (1933) recognized a difference in the two assemblages and proposed that the earlier materials be called the "pure village site" culture, whereas the later ceramics were designated the "Bean pot-duck effigy" culture. Griffin (1941, 1949) later revised the terms for these two assemblages as the Old Village (now the Stirling phase) and Trappist (now Moorehead and Sand Prairie phases) foci. The latter mortuary assemblage from the Powell Mound No. 2 can be readily identified as Moorehead phase.

The area within the park had remained the same size until 1963 when the state purchased additional property, presumably as a result of the salvage work being conducted by a strong-willed group of archaeologists, which included Charles J. Bareis, James W. Porter, and Warren Wittry. Although the state currently owns a large area of the site, much of it remains to be acquired.

SUMMARY

The field of archaeology is composed of individuals who, in general, attempt to understand the past through the study of the materials and documents left behind. As a subset of society, the profession contains a range of individuals with different roles, capabilities, and of course, personalities. Some are excellent administrators, and others are astute academicians, well suited to the study, analysis, and interpretation of artifacts. There are those whose fieldwork is impeccable, and others who are less thorough and careful. As much as we classify, we are, certainly, subject to being placed in one of the aforementioned categories.

Warren King Moorehead was assuredly one of those unique individuals who had a passion for doing archaeology. In many respects, he was a promoter of archaeology and appears to have maintained excellent rapport with the public, press, and the amateurs. Although he conducted a considerable amount of fieldwork and gathered an extraordinary amount of material, his expertise was not that of a careful excavator or analyst. Much of what he did was rooted in his upbringing as a young archaeologist in the late nineteenth century. This period was a time of transition and growth in the discipline, a time that saw in some instances the union of museums with the newly established departments of anthropology of which archaeology in the New World was part. This wedding effectively linked the "mound-builders" to the ethnographic present.

Moorehead's excavations at Cahokia left much to be desired. He continued to use techniques that he had employed nearly 40 years earlier, although he was fully aware of more controlled methods, such as laying out a grid in Jacob's Cavern in 1904 with Charles Peabody and Jay L. B. Taylor. The method of establishing a grid was followed again when Taylor returned to assist Moorehead in his excavations of the Harding Mound (Figure 13).

Nonetheless, Moorehead's work at the site had an impact. The major benefit, of course, was the preservation of 144 acres as a state park. In some respects, however, the new park served as a recreational infrastructure that attracted development and building of subdivisions, racetracks, bars, brothels, and golf courses in the decades to come. Nonetheless, the park was a start. Moorehead's inability to do more on the preservation side, particularly for a site as unique as Cahokia, is unfortunate because of the low priority often and still assigned by politics and society to historic properties.

The momentum for preservation that local people had generated

Fig. 13. Grid layout at the Harding Mound, 1927 (courtesy of Cahokia Mounds State Historic Site Photographic Archives)

prior to Moorehead's involvement waned. Such localized efforts did not occur again until the 1970s when the Cahokia Mounds Museum Society was established. This society was created by local avocational and professional archaeologists to support the site and construct a new museum. The preservation problems faced by Moorehead 60 years ago continue to haunt us today. Despite state and federal laws, it is incumbent upon us to reestablish those grass-roots efforts again for the preservation of the remaining mounds and sites in the region.

In the end, Moorehead's most compelling contribution at Cahokia was his efforts to preserve the mounds. To achieve this goal, he conducted some of the most extensive excavations at the site to demonstrate the artificial nature of their construction. Furthermore, Moorehead attempted to integrate other specialists into the project. Although his work in the field and subsequent reports lacked analytical detail, the artifacts recovered can still be a useful body of data providing valuable insights into certain areas of the site yet to be examined (see Kelly et al. 1996).

References

Ahler, Steve, and Peter DePuydt
   1987   *A Report on the 1931 Powell Mound Excavations, Madison County, Illinois.* Reports of Investigations No. 43. Illinois State Museum, Springfield.

Anderson, James P.
   1969   A Cahokia Palisade Sequence. In *Explorations into Cahokia Archaeology*, edited by Melvin L. Fowler. *Illinois Archaeological Survey Bulletin* 7:89–99. University of Illinois, Urbana.

Anonymous
   1860   *The Transactions of the Academy of Science of St. Louis.* Vol. I, 1856–1860. St. Louis.
   1868   *The Transactions of the Academy of Science of St. Louis.* Vol. II, 1861–1868. St. Louis.
   1891   A Munificent Gift. *Weekly Advocate*, May 1.
   1899   Monk's Mound. Owner of the Celebrated Reminder of a Prehistoric Age Died Monday Afternoon. *Weekly Advocate*, June 30.
   1909   *Transactions of the of the Illinois Historical Society for the Year 1909.* Springfield.
   1910   The Great Cahokia Mound Again. *Journal of the Illinois State Historical Society* 3(2):92–93.
   1913a   Bill to Purchase Monks' Mound Introduced in the Legislature. *Daily Journal, East St. Louis,* March 30:2.
   1913b   Mysterious Black-Robed Figures Flit over Monk's Mound. *Belleville Daily Advocate*, June 21:4.
   1914   Directors' Meetings. *Transactions of the of the Illinois Historical Society for the Year 1913.* Springfield.
   1921   Wants Monks Mound to be Memorial Park. *Alton Evening Telegraph*, January 18:1.
   1923   20 Illinois State Editors Plan State Park in Cahokia Mound Region: Assurance of Legislature's Support of Project Announced at Meeting. *St. Louis Globe Democrat*, January 10.
   1925   Monks Mound Land Valued at $52,110.00: Jury Fixes Value at Higher Sum Than was Appropriated for Purpose by Legislature—$500 an Acre Value of Monk [sic] Mound Site. *Belleville Daily Advocate*, June 4.

1929   Report of the Conference on Midwestern Archaeology, Held in St. Louis, Missouri, May 18, 1929. *Bulletin of the National Research Council* No. 74. National Research Council of the National Academy of Science, Washington, D.C.

Baker, Frank C.
1921   Letter to Dr. A. R. Crook, December 19. University of Illinois, Department of Anthropology files, Urbana.
1922   Letter to President David Kinley, February 3. University of Illinois, Department of Anthropology files, Urbana.

Brackenridge, Henry Marie
1811   *The Missouri Gazette.* (St. Louis) January 9.

Brain, Jeffrey P., and Philip Phillips
1996   *Shell Gorgets: Styles of the Late Prehistoric and Protohistoric Southeast.* Peabody Museum Press, Peabody Museum of Archaeology and Ethnology. Cambridge, Mass.

Brown, James, and John E. Kelly
2000   Cahokia and the Southeastern Ceremonial Complex. In *Mounds, Modoc, and Mesoamerica: Papers in Honor of Melvin L. Fowler,* edited by Steven R. Ahler. Illinois State Museum, Scientific Papers, Springfield.

Brown, John Nicholas
1890   Letter to Major J. W. Powell, Providence, R.I., February 25. Smithsonian Institution, Bureau of Ethnology, Washington, D.C. On file Smithsonian Institution, National Anthropological Archives, MS 2400.

Bruton, Scott A.
1992   The Rise of the St. Louis Scientific Community, 1869–1913. Honor's Thesis, Department of History, Washington University, St. Louis, Missouri.

Bryan, W. S.
1901   The Great Turtle Mound. Newspaper article on file at the Missouri Historical Society.

Bushnell, David I., Jr.
1904   *The Cahokia and Surrounding Mound Groups.* Papers of the Peabody Museum of American Archaeology and Ethnology (1904–1913) Vol. 3, No. 1:3–20. Harvard University, Cambridge.
1922   Archaeological Reconnaissance of the Cahokia and Related Mound Groups. Explorations and Field Work of the Smithsonian Institution in 1921. *Smithsonian Miscellaneous Collections* 72(15):92–105. Washington.

Byers, Douglas S.
1939   Warren King Moorehead. *American Anthropologist* 41:286–294.

Collot, Georges-Victor
1826   *A Journey in North America.* 2 vols. Arthur Bertrand, Paris.

Connolly, Phyllis E.
1962   A Biographical Essay. In *John Francis Snyder: Selected Writings,* ed-

ited by Clyde C. Walton, pp. 3–24. Illinois State Historical Society, Springfield.

Crook, A. R.

1914   Cahokia or Monks Mound not of Artificial Origin. In Discussion and Correspondence, *Science* 40(1026):312.

1915   Origin of Monks Mound. *Bulletin of the Geological Society of America* 26:74–75.

1916   The Composition and Origin of Monks Mound. *Transactions of the Illinois Academy of Science* 9:82–84. Springfield.

1921a   Letter to Mr. Jesse Ramey, June 21. Illinois State Archives, Illinois Department of Conservation, Parks and Memorials file, Springfield.

1921b   Letter to Dr. Clark Wissler, November 18. Illinois State Archives, Illinois Department of Conservation, Parks and Memorials file, Springfield.

1922a   Letter to Mr. Frank C. Baker, January 18. University of Illinois, Department of Anthropology files, Urbana.

1922b   The Origin of the Cahokia Mounds. *Bulletin of the Illinois State Museum.* Springfield.

Dunlap, Knight

1929   Preface. Report of the Conference on Midwestern Archaeology, Held in St. Louis, Missouri, May 18, 1929. *Bulletin of the National Research Council* No. 74:3–4. National Research Council of the National Academy of Science, Washington, D.C.

Esarey, Duane, and Timothy R. Pauketat

1992   The Lohmann Site: An Early Mississippian Center in the American Bottom. *American Bottom Archaeology FAI-270 Site Reports* Vol. 25. University of Illinois Press, Urbana.

Fenneman, N. M.

1911   Geology and Mineral Resources of the St. Louis Quadrangle Missouri-Illinois. *U.S. Geological Survey Bulletin* No. 438. Department of the Interior, Washington, D.C.

Finiels, Nicolas de

1989   *An Account of Upper Louisiana,* edited by C. J. Ekberg and W. E. Foley. University of Missouri Press, Columbia.

Flagg, Norman G.

1912   The Madison County Centennial Celebration. *Journal of the Illinois State Historical Society* 5(3):382–385.

Fowke, Gerard

1906   Illinois Mounds. *The Commerce Monthly,* pp. 26–27.

Fowler, Melvin L.

1962   Pioneer Archaeologist: John Francis Snyder, An Appraisal. In *John Francis Snyder: Selected Writings,* edited by Clyde C. Walton, pp. 181–189. Illinois State Historical Society, Springfield.

1989   *The Cahokia Atlas: A Historical Atlas of Cahokia Archaeology.* Studies in Illinois Archaeology No. 6. Illinois Historic Preservation Agency, Springfield.

1997   *The Cahokia Atlas: A Historical Atlas of Cahokia Archaeology.* Revised Edition. University of Illinois Urbana-Champaign Department of Anthropology, Studies in Archaeology No. 2. Illinois Transportation Archaeological Research Program. Urbana.

Griffin, James B.
1941   Report on Pottery from the St. Louis Area. *The Missouri Archaeologist* 7(2):1–17.
1949   The Cahokia Ceramic Complexes. *Proceedings of the Fifth Plains Conference for Archaeology*, pp. 44–58. Notebook No. 1 of the Laboratory of Anthropology, University of Nebraska, Lincoln.

Griffin, James B., and Albert Spaulding
1951   The Central Mississippi Valley Archaeological Survey, Season 1950: A Preliminary Report. *Journal of the Illinois State Archaeological Society* 1(3):74–81.

Grimm, Robert E.
1949   *Cahokia Brought to Life: An Artifactual Story of America's Greatest Monument.* The Greater St. Louis Archaeological Society. Wellington Printing Company.

Hall, Robert L.
1968   The Goddard-Ramey Cahokia Flight: A Pioneering Aerial Photographic Survey. *The Wisconsin Archaeologist* 49(2):75–79.
1991   Cahokia Identity and Interaction Models of Cahokia Mississippian. In *Cahokia and the Hinterlands: Middle Mississippian Cultures of the Midwest*, edited by Thomas E. Emerson and R. Barry Lewis, pp. 3–34. University of Illinois Press, Urbana.

Harn, Alan
1971   *An Archaeological Survey of the American Bottoms and Wood River Terrace.* Reports of Investigations No. 21, Pt. 1. Illinois State Museum, Springfield.

Henshaw, H. W.
1888   Letter to Professor Thomas, May 25. Smithsonian Institution, Bureau of Ethnology, Washington, D.C. On file Smithsonian Institution, National Anthropological Archives, MS 2400.

Hoffman, Charles
1835   *A Winter in the West.* Harper, New York.

Howland, Henry R.
1877   Recent Archaeological Discoveries in the American Bottom. *Buffalo Society of Natural History, Bulletin* 3(5):204–211.

Iseminger, William R.
1980   How Cahokia Mounds Became a State Historic Site. *Historic Illinois* 2(6):6–7.

Kelly, Arthur R.
1933   Some Problems of Recent Cahokia Archaeology. *Transactions of the Illinois State Academy of Science* 25(4):101–103. Springfield.

Kelly, John E.
  1990   The Emergence of Mississippian Culture in the American Bottom Region. In *The Mississippian Emergence*, edited by Bruce Smith, pp. 113–152. Smithsonian Institution Press, Washington, D.C.
  1993   The Pulcher Site: An Archaeological and Historical Overview. *Illinois Archaeology* 5:434–451.
  1994   The Archaeology of the East St. Louis Mound Center: Past and Present. *Illinois Archaeology* 6:1–57.
  1999a   Notes of Moorehead's 1922–23 Investigations Outside Cahokia.
  1999b   Notes of Moorehead's 1922–27 Investigations at the Harding Mound.
  2000a   The Grassy Lake Site: An Historical and Archaeological Overview. In *Mounds, Modoc, and Mesoamerica: Papers in Honor of Melvin L. Fowler*, edited by Steven R. Ahler. Illinois State Museum, Scientific Papers, Springfield.
  2000b   The Mitchell Mound Center: Then and Now. To be published in Papers in Honor of Howard Dalton Winters, edited by Anne-Marie Cantwell and Lawrence A. Conrad.
Kelly, John E., Kenneth Keller, and Jennifer Fee
  1996   The 1921 Moorehead Excavations at Cahokia. Report submitted to the Cahokia Mounds Museum Society.
Kinley, David
  1921   Letter to Mr. F. C. Baker, December 17. University of Illinois, Department of Anthropology files, Urbana.
Koldehoff, Brad, Timothy R. Pauketat, and John E. Kelly
  1993   The Emerald Site and the Mississippian Occupation of the Central Silver Creek Valley. *Illinois Archaeology* 5:331–343.
Leighton, Morris M.
  1923   The Cahokia Mounds: Part II, The Geological Aspects of Some of the Cahokia (Illinois) Mounds. *University of Illinois Bulletin* XXI(6).
McAdams, Clark
  1907   The Archaeology of Illinois. *Transactions of the Illinois State Historical Society for 1907*, pp. 35–47. Springfield.
McAdams, William
  1882   Letter to Prof. Cyrus Thomas, Dec. 28. Smithsonian Institution, Bureau of Ethnology. On file Smithsonian Institution, National Anthropological Archives, MS 2400.
Marshall, John
  1992   The St. Louis Mound Group: Historical Accounts and Pictorial Depictions. *The Missouri Archaeologist* 53:43–79.
Milner, George R.
  1998   *The Cahokia Chiefdom*. Smithsonian Institution Press.
Moorehead, Warren K.
  n.d.   Statement with Reference to the Cahokia Mounds. Illinois State

Archives, Illinois Department of Conservation, Parks and Memorials file, Springfield.

1902 *Field Diary of an Archaeological Collector.* R. S. Peabody Museum, Andover, Mass.

1912 Archaeology of the Mississippi Valley (Synopsis of Professor Warren K. Moorehead's Lecture). *Transactions of the Illinois State Historical Society for the Year 1910,* pp. 184–185. Publication No. 15, Illinois State Historical Library.

1921a Letter to A. R. Crook, Esq., January 14. Illinois State Archives, Illinois Department of Conservation, Parks and Memorials file, Springfield.

1921b Letter to Dr. Berthold Laufer, January 21. Illinois State Archives, Illinois Department of Conservation, Parks and Memorials file, Springfield.

1921c Letter to Doctor A. R. Crook, May 20. Illinois State Archives, Illinois Department of Conservation, Parks and Memorials file, Springfield.

1921d Letter to Doctor Charles Peabody, July 1. Ohio Historical Society, MSS 106, Box 63.

1921e Letter to Doctor Charles Peabody, August 1. Ohio Historical Society, MSS 106, Box 63.

1921f Letter to Doctor Charles Peabody, November 9. Ohio Historical Society, MSS 106, Box 63.

1921g Report of the Curator of the Museum and Field Director of New England Work. To the Trustees of Phillips Academy, Andover, Mass. Ohio Historical Society, MSS 106, Box 63.

1922a The Cahokia Mounds: A Preliminary Report. *University of Illinois Bulletin* XIX(35).

1922b The Hopewell Mound Group of Ohio. *Field Museum of Natural History, Publication 211, Anthropological Series* 6(5). Chicago.

1922c Letter to Doctor Charles Peabody, November 18. Ohio Historical Society, MSS 106, Box 63.

1922d Preservation of the Cahokia Mounds. *The Wisconsin Archaeologist* 1(1):25–27.

1923a The Cahokia Mounds: Part I, A Report of Progress by Warren K. Moorehead, and Part II, Some Geological Aspects by Morris M. Leighton. *University of Illinois Bulletin* XXI(6).

1923b Letter to Professor James H. Ropes, October 31. Ohio Historical Society, MSS 106, Box 67.

1923c A New Plan for the Cahokia State Park; and A New Estimate of Cost of Mounds. American Hotel, St. Louis, March 29. Ohio Historical Society, MSS 106, Box 65.

1924 Cahokia—A Tragedy. *East Side Call,* May 24, 1924. East St. Louis.

1929a Address in Part III: Addresses at the Dinner Following the Conference Sessions, Together with Additional Radio Addresses. In Report of the Conference on Midwestern Archaeology, Held in St. Louis, Missouri, May 18. *Bulletin of the National Research Council* No. 74:97–98. National Research Council of the National Academy of Science, Washington, D.C.

1929b The Cahokia Mounds: Part I, Explorations of 1922, 1923, 1924, and 1927. *University of Illinois Bulletin* XXI(4): 7–106.

1936 Letter to Professor Frank C. Baker, August 25. University of Illinois, Department of Anthropology.

Pauketat, Timothy R.

1993 *Temples for Cahokia Lords: Preston Holder's 1955–1956 Excavations of Kunnemann Mound.* Museum of Anthropology Memoir 26, University of Michigan, Ann Arbor.

Pauketat, Timothy R., and Alex Barker

2000 Mounds 65 and 66 at Cahokia: Additional Details on the 1927 Excavations. In *Mounds, Modoc, and Mesoamerica: Papers in Honor of Melvin L. Fowler,* edited by Steven R. Ahler. Illinois State Museum, Scientific Papers, Springfield.

Peale, T. R.

1862 Ancient Mounds at St. Louis, Missouri, in 1819. *Annual Report of the Smithsonian Institution 1861,* pp. 386–391. Washington, D.C.

Porter, James W.

1974 *Cahokia Archaeology as Viewed from the Mitchell Site: A Satellite Community at 1150–1200.* Ph.D. dissertation, University of Wisconsin. University Microfilms, Ann Arbor, Mich.

Ramey, Fred

1921 Letter to Prof. W. K. Moorehead. On file at R. S. Peabody Museum, Phillips Academy, Andover, Mass.

Reed, Nelson, John W. Bennett, and James W. Porter

1968 Solid Core Drilling of Monks Mound: Technique and Findings. *American Antiquity* 33(2):137–148.

Reinhardt, Dianne

1992 Remembrances of Warren King Moorehead's Visit to Cahokia: An Interview with Marie Fingerhut. Manuscript on file at the Powell Archaeological Research Center.

Russell, John

1831 Western Antiquities. *Illinois Monthly Magazine,* March.

Silverberg, Robert

1968 *Mound Builders of Ancient America: The Archaeology of a Myth.* New York Graphic Society, Greenwich, Connecticut.

Smith, Harriet M.

1942 Excavation of the Murdock Mound of the Cahokia Group. *Journal of the Illinois State Archaeological Society* 1(1):13–18.

1969 The Murdock Mound. In *Explorations into Cahokia Archaeology,* edited by Melvin L. Fowler. *Illinois Archaeological Survey Bulletin* 7:48–88. University of Illinois, Urbana.

Smith, Jesse L.
  1921   Letter to Professor A. R. Crook, February 21. Illinois State Archives, Illinois Department of Conservation, Parks and Memorials file, Springfield.
Snyder, John Francis
  1917   The Great Cahokia Mound. *Illinois State Historical Society Journal* 10:256–259. Springfield.
Taylor, Jay L. B.
  1927(?) The Proposed Tunnel through Monks Mound. University of Illinois, Department of Anthropology files. Urbana.
  1929   Prospect Tunnel Monks Mound. Ohio Historical Society, MSS 106, Box 80.
Thompson, Milton D.
  1988   *The Illinois State Museum: Historical Sketches and Memoirs.* Illinois State Museum Society, Springfield.
Throop, Addison, J.
  1928   *The Mound Builders of Illinois.* Call Printing Co., East St. Louis, Illinois.
Titterington, Paul F.
  1938   *The Cahokia Mound Group and its Village Site Material.* St. Louis, Missouri.
Wagner, Robert W.
  1959   *An Analysis of the Material Culture of the James Ramey Mound.* Master's thesis, Department of Anthropology, University of Illinois at Champaign-Urbana.
Wilhelm, Friedrich Paul
  1822–24 *Travels in North America.* Translated by W. Robert Nitske, edited by Savoie Lottinville. University of Oklahoma Press, Norman.
Williams, Stephen
  1990   The Vacant Quarter and Other Late Events in the Lower Valley. In *Towns and Temples Along the Mississippi*, edited by David H. Dye and Cheryl Anne Cox, pp. 170–180. University of Alabama Press, Tuscaloosa.
  1991   *Fantastic Archaeology: The Wild Side of North American Prehistory.* University of Pennsylvania Press, Philadelphia.
Williams, Stephen, and John M. Goggin
  1956   The Long-nosed God Mask in Eastern United States. *The Missouri Archaeologist* 18(3):1–72.
Wissler, Clark
  1921a   Letter to Doctor Crook, January 10. Illinois State Archives, Illinois Department of Conservation, Parks and Memorials file, Springfield.
  1921b   Letter to Doctor Crook, February 4. Illinois State Archives, Illinois Department of Conservation, Parks and Memorials file, Springfield.

1922   Notes on State Archaeological Surveys. *American Anthropologist* 24:233.

Worthern, A. H.

1866   *Geological Survey of Illinois*, vol. 1, Illinois Geological Survey, Urbana.

The Cahokia Mounds

A Preliminary Paper

1922

Warren K. Moorehead

TABLE OF CONTENTS

Preface 6

Introduction.. 7
    The View from Monks Mound... 9
    The Village Site.. 11

Description of the Mounds and of Recent Explorations............ 13
    The Largest Mound. Monks or Cahokia............................ 13
    The Ramey Mound.. 18
    The Kunnemann Mound.. 18
    Smith's Mound.. 20
    The Edward's Mounds.. 21
    The Jesse Ramey Mound.. 22
    Other Mounds Tested.. 22
    Conclusions on the Excavations.. 23
    Exploration of the Village Site.. 23

Utensils and Implements from Cahokia...................................... 25
    Notes upon a Collection Secured from the Surface.......... 29
    The Pottery from Cahokia.. 30
    Caches at Cahokia.. 31
    Use of Copper at Cahokia.. 31

Conclusions.. 35
    Possibility of Important Discoveries.................................. 36
    Preservation of the Group.. 37
    Resolution by American Anthropological Association........ 39

Cahokia Bibliography.. 40

PREFACE

It is a pleasure to thank those who contributed toward the Cahokia explorations of September-October, 1921. The President and Trustees of the University of Illinois have my gratitude for their liberal appropriation. Doctor A. R. Crook, Chief, Illinois State Museum Division, also contributed generously and I desire to express appreciation. The Trustees of Phillips Academy made an advance appropriation and financed the preliminary work, for which I thank them. As the museums and societies had already made their budgets for 1921, it became necessary to appeal to individuals. A grand total of $4800 was raised, of which the University of Illinois, the State Museum of Illinois and Phillips Academy, Andover, Massachusetts, gave $3,050. I hereby express sincere thanks to the following contributors:

Illinois Historical Society.........................Springfield, Ill.
American Museum of Natural History............New York, N. Y.
Davenport Academy of Sciences..................Davenport, Iowa
John H. Beebe .... Boston
E. W. Payne .... Springfield, Ill.
W. T. Bush .... New York, N. Y.
W. F. Chandler .... Fresno, California
East St. Louis Traction Company................East St. Louis, Ill.
C. L. Hutchinson .... Chicago
Dr. O. L. Schmidt .... Chicago
Chicago Historical Society .... Chicago
Willard V. King ....New York, N. Y.
M. C. Long ....Kansas City, Mo.
The Newark Museum Association....................Newark, N. J.
The Charleston Museum .... Charleston, S. C.
F. P. Hills ....Delaware, Ohio
G. C. Fraser .... Morristown, N. J.
Joseph Pulitzer, Jr. ....St. Louis
Victor L. Lawson .... Chicago
Major Albert A. Sprague .... Chicago
Mr. and Mrs. Isaac Sprague.................Wellesley Hills, Mass.
John B. Stetson, Jr. ....Elkins Park, Pa.
Judge Edward Lindsey .... Warren, Pa.
Miss Lucy L. W. Wilson.........................Philadelphia, Pa.

It is thought best not to expand our list by including everyone who gave towards our explorations, but appreciation of their kindness is hereby expressed.

To the owners we are all greatly indebted. Without their cooperation and permission to explore, it would have been impossible to carry on our observations. The Ramey and Merrell families have my especial thanks; also Messrs. Edwards, Smith, Cole, Tippetts, Powell and Harding. To Mr. Kunnemann and other tenants of the properties, and Major Merrell (in charge of the ex-service men's camp) we were much indebted. All of the owners, both men and women, fully appreciate the importance of Cahokia and were and are willing to give a full measure of aid in any movement leading up to the preservation of these monuments.

INTRODUCTION

One stands upon the summit of the largest Cahokia mound and looks across the famous American Bottoms. He is one hundred feet above the plain and his vision is, therefore, not impaired since there are few buildings nearby, and trees not numerous save far to the south. Both the site and the view are conducive to reflection on the past and one's mind harks back to the days of Brackenridge, Flagg, and Featherstonehaugh—for these men saw Cahokia at its best. Fortunate indeed is it that these pioneers in Cahokia archeology gave us clear word pictures of conditions then, for while practically all of the tumuli remain, their external contour is altered. And after these pioneers came Rau, McAdams, Patrick, Putnam, Bushnell, and others who mapped and described the mounds as they saw them in the years 1874 to 1905.

Notwithstanding the preëminence of Cahokia over all other mound-groups in the United States there appears to have been little attempt at either study or exploration. Indeed, the several gentlemen who visited the mounds between the years 1874 and 1905 contented themselves with brief descriptions. The longest published account is the paper by Mr. D. I. Bushnell, Jr.*

Mr. W. W. McAdams, who was curator of the State Museum at Springfield, and Dr. J. J. R. Patrick seem to have excavated to a considerable extent in the cemetery northeast of the largest mound, yet I am unable to find any detailed record of their observations.

After reading all the references to Cahokia I consulted with witnesses who were present during McAdams' explorations and also with persons living in the vicinity who had more or less knowledge of conditions at Cahokia during the past fifty years. After one has examined the assembled evidence, both written and spoken, it is not difficult to explain the lack of thorough exploration of these famous mounds.

Most attention seems to have been concentrated on the largest tumulus locally known as Monks Mound. In fact, nearly all the descriptions center in this ranking structure. Mr. Thomas Ramey, the father of the present eight Ramey heirs, was probably the first owner of Cahokia property to manifest a real interest in the preservation of the mounds. This does not indicate, permit me to hasten

*Peabody Museum Report; 20 pages, 7 figures, and 5 plates.

to explain, that other owners today do not appreciate the importance of the group. On the contrary, the statement refers to the past—a period from about 1868 to 1890. Altho Ramey employed some coal miners from Collinsville and ran a short tunnel into the mound, and also permitted one or two excavations in mounds south of Monks, yet on the whole, he was adverse to excavations. From the time of his death until the summer of 1921 his heirs, the Misses and Messrs. Ramey, have refused permission to those who sought to excavate. This also applies to Mr. George B. Merrell and his family and the other owners. Numbers of persons visited the mounds with a view to exploration the past thirty years and several collectors in the neighborhood also sought to dig. We thus have the explanation, it seems to me, of the general impression that the owners were adverse to an examination of the mounds. As a result of many conversations with these owners I am prepared to state that they are not and have not been adverse to scientific research at Cahokia, but they think that such should be part of a definite plan which will culminate in the preservation of the area in a state or national park.

There is even a more potent reason why the mounds have not been examined. The undertaking would be very expensive. Until recent years no museum or institution could spend larger sums of money in American archeology excepting perhaps in Central and South America. Undoubtedly it would require years to properly explore Cahokia. A large force of labor would be required. Mr. Ramey, Sr., once desired to ascertain the cost of certain explorations, and requested an engineer to estimate the cost of two tunnels at right angles through the base of Monks Mound. Even in the days when labor was much cheaper, work could not be done short of $15,000. We trenched the Kunnemann mound through to the center, employing twenty men and using five teams and our expense was $600. It will thus be observed that without great outlay of both time and money an exploration of Cahokia would be impossible. These two factors explain why Cahokia is, today, practically unexplored.

In the light of modern archeological science, it is fortunate that Cahokia has not been explored. We should render all the owners a full meed of praise since they have protected these mounds at considerable expense for many years. Some forty-two acres are lost to cultivation. That is, on the several estates mounds not available for agriculture cover forty-two acres. Aside from taxes there are charges for drainage, roads, etc. This together with the loss of revenue from forty-two acres during the past twenty years amounts to many thousands of dollars.

THE VIEW FROM MONKS MOUND

We are again standing on the summit of this remarkable pyramid. Six miles to the west we clearly observe the great city of St. Louis. Four miles in the same direction is East St. Louis. A scant two miles west, northwest and southwest we see the encroaching factories and railway yards. The charm of the Great Plain, the primitive simplicity and beauty of the American Bottoms as observed by Brackenridge, Ford, and Featherstonehaugh is of the past. Yet looking directly south over the Merrell, Ramey, Tippett and Wells estates we note that there has not been so great a change. True, many of the mounds have been cultivated until the original contour is somewhat marred. Yet it would be no very great undertaking to restore them to the pyramidal and conical form. About the shores of the lake and in the woods and even beyond the railway, two-thirds of a mile south where is located the great Harding pyramid, are nearly a score of mounds in practically the same condition as they were a century ago. Eliminating a few mounds in the edge of East St. Louis here to the south and also to the north across Cahokia creek we have spread before us a great possibility (and we hope probability) of a state park.

Brackenridge's description, written in 1811 and published in 1814, has been so frequently quoted it is unnecessary to repeat it here. He observed as did Flagg a great number of artifacts strewn over the surface and that there were many small elevations which have probably since disappeared. What impressed him, as well as the others of those early days, was not only the charm and mystery of the mounds themselves but their pleasant location in the Great Plain and that this plain was not entirely a prairie but broken here and there by clumps of heavy vegetation and ponds of water.

It requires no stretch of imagination to those familiar with American archeology to catch the point of view of these early visitors to the Cahokia group. After reading their accounts carefully, it is not difficult for one, from the top of the great mound, to reconstruct the past. One eliminates the factories, the macadam road and the cities. And having done this we will surrender the pen to Mr. Flagg,* since his account has been less frequently published than those of others.

"The view from the southern extremity of the mound, which is free from trees and underbrush, is extremely beautiful. Away to the south sweeps off the broad river-bottom, at this place about seven miles in width, its waving surface variegated by all the magnificant hues of the summer flora of the prairies. At intervals, from the deep herbage is flung back the flashing sheen of a silvery lake to the oblique sunlight; while dense groves of the crab-apple and other indigenous wild fruits are sprinkled about like islets in the verdant sea. To the left, at a distance of three or four miles, stretches away the long line of bluffs, now presenting a surface marked and rounded by groups of mounds, and now wooded to their summits, while a glimpse at times may be caught of the humble farmhouses at their base. On the right meanders the Cantine Creek, which gives the name to the group of mounds, betraying at intervals its bright surface through the belt of forest by which it is margined. In this direction, far away in blue distance, rising through the mist and forest, may be caught a glimpse of the spires and cupolas of the city, glancing gayly in the rich summer sun. The base of the mound is circled upon every side by lesser elevations of every form and at various distances. Of these, some lie in the heart of the extensive maize-fields, which constitute the farm of the proprietor of the principal mound, presenting a beautiful exhibition of light and shade, shrouded as they are in the dark, twinkling leaves. The most remarkable are two standing directly opposite the southern extremity of the principal one, at a distance of some hundred yards, in close proximity to each other and which never fail to arrest the eye. There are also several large square mounds covered with forest along the margin of the creek to the right, and groups are caught rising from the declivities of the distant bluffs.

"Upon the western side of Monk Mound, at a distance of several yards from the summit, is a well some eighty or ninety feet in depth; the water of which would be agreeable enough were not the presence of sulphur, in some of its modifications, so palpable. This well penetrates the heart of the mound, yet, from its depth, cannot reach lower than the level of the surrounding plain. I learned, upon inquiry, that when this well was excavated, several fragments of pottery, of decayed ears of corn, and other articles, were thrown up from a depth of sixty-five feet; proof incontestible of the artificial structure of the mound. The associations, when drinking the water of this well, united with its peculiar flavour, are not of the most exquisite character, when we reflect that the precious fluid has probably filtrated, part of it, at least, through the contents of a sepulchre."

Aside from the mounds the depressions or ponds and the village site are quite important. From our vantage point we note that while certain of the mounds are clustered together, others are at a considerable distance apart. In these level spots lying between the mounds is a village site. Indications of Indian habitation were most

*The Far West, Vol. I, pages 166, 167, 1838.

numerous northwest of Monks Mound, about the pyramid owned by Mr. Smith, 400 yards east and south across the fields to the line of timber. It is impossible at present writing to give the actual extent of the village. Although we spent two months at Cahokia with a large crew it can be truthfully affirmed that our observations are just begun.

THE VILLAGE SITE

Where we excavated at various points in the village site, we found disturbed ground at depths ranging from one to four feet. Northeast of the dominant mound the debris appears to be the thickest, yet all over the area south of the state highway pottery fragments, chips, and flint arrowheads may be found from the surface to a depth of one foot. More than a thousand broken artifacts and pottery were secured by us from our test pits. In our preliminary examination there were extensive areas of land which we were unable to test. These should be carefully inspected during the coming season and next year.

One of these, which we did not see, should be here noted. In the Twelfth Annual Report of the Bureau of American Ethnology pp. 133-134, Dr. Cyrus Thomas describes the work of McAdams and Patrick on the banks of the old channel of Canteen creek—the southern branch of Cahokia creek. He states:

"It is worthy of note that nearly all the relics found at the Cahokia group of mounds have been taken from the low ground between the mounds. The remarkable find of pottery, implements, and shells made by Mr. McAdams in the winter of 1881 was in the low land a short distance from the northeast corner of the great mound. The articles were nearly all taken from a square rod of ground. This has been to some extent Dr. Patrick's experience in making his fine collection of pottery.

"The real burial place of the builders of the Cahokia mounds probably is yet to be discovered.

"The bank of Cahokia creek during the occupation of the mounds was evidently more to the south than its present line along the eastern part of the group. The old bank is still plainly visible. The low land between this old bank and the creek is now covered with forest trees. All along this bank, which forms the edge of the plateau on which the mounds stand, are abundant evidences of occupation in remote times. In digging 2 or 3 feet at almost any point along this bank indications of fireplaces are found, with numerous river shells, broken pottery, and kitchen refuse. As all the arable ground about the mound has been in cultivation many years, it is quite possible that some of the burial places, which are usually quite shallow, have been destroyed, as pieces of human bones are very common in the plowed fields."

Since, as stated, barely sufficient has been done to make sure of the presence of a large village site, further comment on it at this time is unnecessary. Subsequently in this report we shall quote Dr. Rau upon pottery and agricultural implements found at Cahokia fifty years ago.

DESCRIPTION OF THE MOUNDS AND OF RECENT EXPLORATIONS

The best and most complete map of the Cahokia group I have observed is the result of a survey made by County Surveyor Hilgard under the direction of Dr. J. J. R. Patrick assisted by B. J. Van Court of O'Fallon, Ill., and Wm. J. Seever of St. Louis. The work was done about 1880 and the original map owned by the Missouri Historical Society was loaned us. We made a copy which is herewith reproduced (Fig. 1). The plot of the mounds presented in the 12th Annual Report of the Bureau of Ethnology (Plan VI.) (opposite page 134) apparently reproduces Hilgard's map.

A model was prepared for the Peabody Museum at Harvard by Mr. D. I. Bushnell, Jr. A small model has been made by Doctor George B. Higgins of St. Louis and left with the Ramey family. Doctor Higgins does not claim that his model is accurate, but it shows the location of the principal mounds

Reference to our map will indicate that the majority of the mounds are west, south or east of Monks Mound. There are a few on the north side of Cahokia Creek. The larger tumuli occupy the center of the group east and west, but not the center north and south. Probably the low lands lying along Cahokia Creek interfered with mound construction. Seven of the rectangular mounds or pyramids are almost in a straight line east and west. Today many of the mounds shown in the original map by Mr. Hilgard, also on Bushnell's model and Thomas' map, appear externally as ovals rather than pyramids. This is due to farming operations. It will therefore be necessary for us to compare and check up very carefully all descriptions by observers in the past with measurements and descriptions to be made in the future. Manifestly the survey of 1875 is accurate and if Mr. Hilgard or Mr. Patrick drew a certain mound as a pyramid and today it appears as an oval or oblong mound, it should be classified as a pyramid. The steep conical mounds do not seem to have been altered as much as the larger pyramids.

THE LARGEST MOUND. MONKS OR CAHOKIA.

This has for many years been called Monks Mound (Figs. 3, 4) because of the presence of the Trappists during a short period between 1808-1813. It would seem to the writer that we should call the entire group of tumuli the Cahokia group and that the larger mounds should be named in honor of the many owners rather than numbered. Whether the largest mound should be called Cahokia or Monks can be determined later. Most persons refer to all of them as the Cahokia group, and to designate one mound as the Cahokia Mound seems rather confusing. For the present, or at least in this report, we shall refer to the largest one as Monks Mound.

It is much washed and weather-worn at the present time, and has lost a great deal of its original charm. In fact if one should compare the various views taken twenty or thirty years ago of the mound with a photograph of it today, one would scarcely imagine the two to represent the same structure.

The truncated pyramid effect was observed by all the early visitors. It is necessary to make use of their descriptions in order to reconstruct the mound as it was.

Professor Putnam was in close touch with Doctor Patrick and others and in the 12th Annual Report of the Peabody Museum he presents the following observations.

"*Cahokia Mound.* In company with several gentlemen from St. Louis, I had the good fortune in September last (1879) to visit the largest mound within the limits of the United States. * * * While there is not the slightest evidence that the Cahokias of the time of LaSalle were builders of this, or of other mounds in the vicinity, it is a gratification to be able to perpetuate the name of an extinct tribe of American Indians in connection with this monument of an unknown American Nation, rather than that of a religious order of foreign origin.

"Situated in the midst of a group of about sixty other mounds, of more than ordinary size, several in the vicinity being from 30 to 60 feet in height, and of various forms, Cahokia Mound, rising by four platforms, or terraces, to a height of about one hundred feet, and covering an area of over twelve acres, holds a relation to the other tumuli of the Mississippi Valley similar to that of the Great Pyramid of Egypt to the other monuments of the Valley of the Nile.

"I am glad to be able to state that Dr. J. J. R. Patrick, a careful and zealous archeologist, residing in the vicinity of this interesting monument has, with the assistance of other gentlemen, not only made a survey of the whole group of which Cahokia is the prominent figure, but has also prepared two accurate models of the mound itself; copies of which have been promised to the Museum.

"One of these models (Fig. 5) represents the mound as it now appears, with its once level platform and even slopes gullied, washed and worn away; and the other (Fig. 6) is in the form of a restoration, showing the mound as it probably existed before the plough of the white man had destroyed its even sides and hard platforms, and thus given nature a foothold for her destructive agencies. The projecting portion (A) from the apron (B) points nearly due south.

*Twelfth Annual Report, Peabody Museum of American Archeology, pages 470-475, 1880.

"Probably this immense tumulus was not erected primarily as a burial mound, though such may prove to be the case. From the present evidence it seems more likely that it was made in order to obtain an elevated site for some particular purpose; presumably an important public building. One fact, however, which I observed, indicated that a great length of time was occupied in its construction, and that its several level platforms may have been the sites of many lodges, which, possibly, may have been placed upon such artificial elevations in order to avoid the malaria of a district, the settlement of which in former, as in recent times, was likely due to the prolific and easily cultivated soil; or, more likely, for the purpose of protection from enemies. The fact to which I allude, is that everywhere in the gullies, and over the broken surface of the mound, mixed with the earth of which it is composed, are quantities of broken vessels of clay, flint chips, arrowheads, charcoal, bones of animals, etc., apparently the refuse of a numerous people; of course it is possible that these remains, so unlike the homogeneous structure of an ordinary mound, may be the simple refuse of numerous feasts that may have taken place on the mound at various times during its construction. The first interpretation, however, is as well borne out as any other from our present knowledge of this mound; the structure and object of which cannot be fully understood until a thorough examination has been made, and while such an examination is desirable, it is to be hoped that this important and imposing monument will never meet the fate which Col. Foster, under a false impression* due to a confusion of names and places, mourns as having already occurred.

"McAdams spent a great deal of time at the group and studied the largest mound in some detail which he describes in his volume, 'Records of Ancient Races in the Mississippi Valley. St. Louis, 1887.' "

McAdams gives a general account of the mounds in central and southern Illinois in his book. It is unfortunate he did not make more complete observations as his opportunities were unexcelled. The collections made by him are somewhat scattered, yet it may be possible, through some research, to identify considerable of the material.

His observation are:

"The form of the Cahokia Mound is a parallelogram, with straight sides, the longer of which are north and south. It is about one hundred feet in height.

"On the southern end, some 30 feet above the base, is a terrace or apron, containing near two acres of ground.

"On the western side, and some thirty feet above the first terrace, is a second one of somewhat less extent.

"The top of the mound is flat and divided into two parts, the northern end being some 4 or 5 feet higher than the southern portion. The summit contains about an acre and a half.**

"Near the middle of the first terrace, at the base of the mound, is a projecting point, apparently the remains of a graded pathway to ascend from the plain to the terrace. The west side of the mound below the second terrace is very irregular, and

*The destruction of "Big Mound" on the opposite side of the river, within the city limits of St. Louis, probably led Col. Foster into error.

**See Plate IV, Figs. 5 and 6, from Putnam's report, previously quoted.

forms projecting knobs, separated by deep ravines, probably the result of rain-storms; to the northwest corner of the base of the structure there seems to be a small mound attached, in exact imitation of the small mounds attached to the base of the pryamids of Egypt as well as those of Mexico.

"The remaining sides of the structure are quite straight and but little defaced by the hand of time.

"About the sides of the mound are still growing several forest trees, one of which is an elm several centuries old.

"As the size of the Cahokia Mound has been given variously we applied to Mr. B. J. VanCourt, a practical surveyor living in the vicinity, at O'Fallen, and whom we knew had made a regular survey of the mound. Mr. VanCourt sent us the following:

" 'In my survey I did not follow the irregularities of the mound, but made straight lines enclosing the base. The largest axis is from north to south and is 998 feet, the shortest from east to west is 721 feet. The height of the mound is 99 feet. The base of the structure covers 16 acres, 2 roods and 3 perches of ground.'

"The summit and lower terrace of the Cahokia Mound has been plowed a few times. Brackenridge who visited the mound in 1811, says that the monks used the lower terrace for a kitchen garden, and also had the summit of the structure sown in wheat. The great pyramid has not been materially changed, however, and doubtless presents the same outlines to-day as at the time of the discovery of this continent by Columbus.

"Since some doubts have been expressed as to the artificial origin of this structure we were much interested to ascertain what could be learned in this respect by examination. On the top of the pyramid are the remains of a house, said to have been commenced by the monks, but afterwards added to and finished as a comfortable residence for the family of a man named Hill, an enterprising settler who owned the mound and a large body of land adjoining. Beneath this house is a deep unwalled cellar. A section down the side of the cellar to the depth of ten feet is very plainly revealed a deposit of various kinds of earth without stratification. The principal part of this deposit was the black humus or mould, so common in the bottom and forming the principal soil, very sticky when wet and breaking into cubical blocks when dry. Here and there, as if thrown promiscuously among the black mould, is a bunch of yellow clay, or sand, or marly loess, these bunches being about such size as a man could easily carry.

"Similar sections can be seen up the old road made by Hill to ascend to his residence.

"On the second terrace is a well (He republishes Flagg's account of it).

"About midway, on the north side, or face of the pyramid, and elevated 25 or 30 feet above the base, in a small depression, stands a pine tree, singularly enough, since this tree is not found in the forests in this locality. There was a story rife among the early settlers that this tree stood at the mouth of an opening or gallery into the interior of the mounds. To ascertain the truth of this matter, Mr. Thomas Ramey, the present owner of the mound, commenced a tunnel at this tree and excavated about ninety (90) feet towards the centre of the mound. When fifteen feet from the entrance to the tunnel a piece of lead ore was discovered, but no other object of interest was found. The deposits penetrated by the tunnel are very plainly shown to be the same as seen in the cellar mentioned above."

Mr. Bushnell, as previously stated, gives us our best account of the group. His measurements of Monks Mound are north and south, 1,080 ft., east and west 710 ft., with a height of 100 ft. The Ramey family tells me that they have understood the height to be 104 ft. The differences in the dimensions are easily explainable. There is a long or gentle slope or "feather" edge at the base of the mound, on all sides. One observor might differ 30 to 50 ft. from another investigator as to where the mound actually began. A new survey of the entire group is scarcely necessary, but it would be well to remeasure Monks Mound.

A question arose some years ago with reference to whether Monks mound was built by man or a natural formation. None of the archeologists ever doubted the artificiality of the large mound, but the statement that it might be natural seems to have affected the legislature and that was one of the reasons why the bill to make a state park at Cahokia failed of passage. The evidences of Hill's well, previously cited, and Ramey tunnel, together with the presence of pottery fragments and bones which were apparent last fall in the gulley six or eight ft. in depth in the lower terrace, are sufficient to prove that the mound is the work of human hands. The brief statement that broken pottery was found at the depth of 60 or 65 ft. is significant.

Some light is shed on this question by another observer who talked with the first owner nearly eighty years ago:

"At this time it is the possession of the mechanic named Hill, who has built a home at the top, around which we saw abundance of Indian corn, pumpkins, tomatoes, etc., for the soil of which it consists is the rich black mould taken from the surface below which is extremely fertile. Mr. Hill laid the foundation of his dwelling upon an eminence he found on the summit of his elevated territory, and upon digging into it found large human bones, with Indian pottery, some axes and tomahawks, from whence it would appear that this mound not only contained a sepulchret at its base, but has been used for the same purpose in aftertimes at the summit." *

Until the mound is tunnelled or trenched, one can not draw positive conclusions as to the purpose of construction, but it is my opinion that it was a long time in the building and that it probably began as a repository for the dead. That is, certain burials were made, as in the case of the large mound of the Hopewell group, Ohio, and other small mounds added as burials were made. Finally

*Excursion through the slave States. G. W. Featherstonehaugh, F. R. S. London, 1844, pp. 264 to 272.

the structure became so large that the natives made it into a pyramid, added the upper terraces and used the top as a place of residence. This is mere opinion and may be not verified by exploration.

THE RAMEY MOUND

Across the state highway, a little southwest from the ranking mound, is a large pyramid over 27 ft. in height on the summit of which is the residence constructed by Mr. Thomas Ramey. Instead of numbering this mound, we gave it the name Ramey Mound. Mr. Bushnell gives the elevation as 25 ft. dimensions of base 200x180 ft. We did not measure this but Mr. Fred Ramey and his brother ran lines and state that the base of the mound is 425 feet square. On the summit it is 250 feet east and west and 225 feet north and south. Possibly Mr. Bushnell refers to the mound just west of the Ramey residence as that one corresponds more nearly with his measurements. Our headquarters were in the farm house on top of this structure. We looked it over carefully and believe that the mound covers interments.

The personal equation is a large factor in archeological researches. It will be impossible to give the reasons why we believe the Ramey Mound to contain many burials. It is merely a matter of opinion. It certainly should be explored.

THE KUNNEMANN MOUND

About half a mile directly north of Monks site, on the land of Mr. George Merrell is a large mound. Mr. Merrell's tenant, Mr. A. Kunnemann has resided on the tract for over twenty-five years and we named the structure for him. Originally the tumulus was about 400 feet diameter and conical—not a pyramid as has been recorded on one of the maps. Twenty years ago fifteen to sixteen feet of the summit was removed and a trench run in from the north side some 90 feet in order that earth to build a dyke along Canteen creek might be obtained. Thus the mound had been seriously damaged. We wished to test one of the larger structures, and as this one offered unusual facilities, we began work Sept. 16th. Witnesses present during the previous work were questioned and all agreed that the mound was conical or "pointed" as Mr. Kunnemann expressed it. The present diameter of the top is 75 by 56 feet. The sides are about twenty-five percent slope. Restoring this same ratio of slope to the top would give fifteen to sixteen feet more elevation, as stated. We found the base near the center to be thirty-five feet below the present flattened summit. Therefore, the tumulus was originally not below 50, or more than 51 feet in altitude. This would make it the third mound of the whole group in height, but not in cubic contents.

Some two weeks were spent upon Kunnemann's Mound. When we stopped work we were near the center and had excavated some 80 feet beyond the point reached by the dyke builders (Figs. 11, 12). No skeletons were discovered, but in the earth were great quantities of flint chips, broken pottery, animal bones and other refuse scooped up by the natives when they took the earth from about their cabins to build the mound.

As we had before us a nearly straight wall thirty-five feet in height, we were able to study the mound construction.

It was found that the mound (that is, the portion we excavated) rested upon a heavy layer of clear sand. Test pits sunk in this sand indicated that it was natural, had not been deposited by man. The lowest part of the mound is ordinary mixed earth and not stratified. About eight feet above the sand, or base, is dark earth in which are many broken artifacts. Above this, some five or six feet of yellowish loam, then a rather distinct decayed vegetation layer running across the face of our fifty foot trench. This is rather thin and even; then several feet of darker soil, but not gumbo, and above this the heaviest layer of decayed vegetation, in some spots about half an inch in thickness. Yellow loam containing some sand extends fully ten feet above. In this and the layer below, the "dumps" or basketfuls of earth are noted. That is, natives carried the earth in loads varying from a trifle over a peck to a half bushel or more. Just below the summit is a four to five feet layer of heavy, compact gumbo (Fig. 2).

All these lines and strata are more or less even, that is level, indicating that the people did not first build a small conical mound and gradually increase the size. Apparently, they decided to construct a large tumulus, built up layers of somewhat different soil, and placed the heavy gumbo some distance from the apex.

After the work had progressed some days and when we were at a point north of the center, and where the mound was originally about forty-one feet high, we found a heavy layer of burned earth.

This was almost floor-like in character. It was followed for a distance of thirty-five feet east and west, but was considerably narrower north and south. In the northern edge of this floor, eighteen feet above the base and eight feet below the present summit, we uncovered a circular, altar-like burned basin. It is shown in Fig. 13. Half of this had been broken off, whether by the Indians or the dyke builders, we do not know. The latter state that they observed no burned basin. It was empty, but consisted of ordinary clay, hard burned. It was about a yard in diameter, ten or twelve inches deep and surrounded by a well defined, broad rim somewhat elevated. Extending in all directions beyond (save north) was the level, burned floor referred to. Why this altar should be nearly half-way above the base, we are unable to state. All the Ohio mound altars lie upon the base line.

When we had dug to near the center of the mound we observed a burned area extending most of the distance across the face of our wall. It was sometimes nearly two feet thick. There was also a light sand stratum, some twenty feet above the base line, which extended some thirty-eight feet east and west.

Near the center and twenty-seven feet from the base, Mr. Eldridge found the head of a frog effigy pipe and numerous fragments of fine pottery. Various large, flat shell beads were also discovered from time to time. Pottery fragments were secured by the hundreds.

Why no burials were found in the north half of Kunnemann's Mound, we do not know. Possibly they will be found in the southern or eastern portions of the structure. The mound should be completed, but as stated on page 8, we did not feel justified in continuing operations. Some fragments of human bones were mingled with the village-site debris, but they were not burials.

SMITH'S MOUND

It lies just back of Mr. Smith's hotel, a quarter mile east of Monks Mound. This is a pyramid with flattened summit. On the east side is an extensive platform, or elevation. While this to one's eye does not appear to be over five feet in altitude, yet on examination we found that burnt stone, pottery sherds and refuse extended to a depth of over seven feet. There was also a layer of burnt ear that that depth. Rising about 80 ft. above the platform is the long pyramid owned by Mr. Smith and whose name we gave to it. The southern edge has been much disturbed, and measurements were not made by us. Mr. Smith kindly agreed to the removal of a large dance-pavilion located on the summit in order that we might run an 80 ft. trench through. We decided to wait until some future time, but we did make two large excavations in the platform.

No one seems to have excavated a terrace, or "apron" leading up to one of the larger mounds. This apron is 115 ft. E. and W. x 120 ft. N. and S. in extent and about 5 ft. high. The field notes are herewith condensed as follows:

Oct. 3rd, 1921. Began a long trench at the extreme eastern end of Smith's platform. Ran due west, keeping on the base line. This trench extended fifty-five feet. Fourteen men completed the trench in two days. After proceeding west for 35 ft. we sank a test pit 10 ft. 5 in. deep. Disturbed earth, charcoal and small pottery sherds were found at 7 ft. 3 ins. depth. At the 55 ft. stake another 10 ft. deep pit was excavated and the bottom of disturbed area reached at 7 ft. 8 ins. Pottery and animal bones found. During the course of excavation half a bushel of broken artifacts were found, some of the pottery being of superior workmanship. What was more interesting, we discovered lumps of burnt clay containing impressions of the reeds or rushes of which the cabins were built.

Nearer the base of Smith's pyramid by means of team and scraper we excavated a pit some thirty feet long and eight feet deep. The same formation noted in the hand-dug trench was apparent. This was a hard burned layer, or floor, near the base line.

Dr. Higgins dug a small mushroom cellar in the north end of Smith's Mound. He secured a number of artifacts. Whether it is a burial structure or merely for houses or ceremonial lodges, can not be determined until a wide trench is carried through the structure.

The Edwards' Mounds

About a quarter of a mile directly east from Smith's Mound are four small tumuli north of the Collinsville road and on the land of Mr. Edwards. The largest of these is not over 9 ft. in height. We explored the two mounds lying about half way between the turnpike and Canteen creek. In the one to the west was found the skeleton shown in Fig. 14. This was at a depth of 4 ft. and was extended and all the bones present and in position. There were some flint chips and two or three flint knives near the head, also some large fragments of broken pottery. The base of the mound was about a foot below the present surface. A trench some 60 ft. in length and 20 ft. wide was run through the structure. The soil was filled with broken pottery.

East of this, distant about 400 ft. is another mound about 7 ft. in height. We dug a trench through the center and sunk eight or ten test pits, finding no burials but discovered scales of copper on the base line. About one-third of this mound remains to be explored next year.

THE JESSE RAMEY MOUND

This is about 20 ft. in height at the present time, the base diameter some 300 ft. It is the second mound directly south of Monks. It is not quite clear whether this was originally an oblong mound or of the pyramid type since it has been cultivated for many years. Some twenty-five men were employed in the work and a trench 65 ft. in length was extended from near the base on the south side to a line some distance from the center. This trench was excavated to an average depth of 10 ft. Then test pits were sunk and post augers used. Five or 6 ft. farther down (a total depth of 14 to 16 ft.) we came upon rather soft, dark earth quite different from the clay and gumbo of which most of the mounds were composed. It resembled the earth found about burials in the several mounds of the Hopewell group. There were a few scales of copper, and some fragments of highly finished pottery. The pottery was above the average found on the surface or in the village site. That is, the fragments recovered indicate the finer pottery such as accompanies burials.

This mound was trenched late in October and being the end of our season we filled the excavation. While it can not be confidently confirmed, yet it is the opinion of the author that the Jesse Ramey Mound is a burial structure and should be thoroughly explored.

OTHER MOUNDS TESTED

Between the Pennsylvania and Baltimore and Ohio railroad tracks is a little triangle of land over which there was a dispute as to ownership. Mr. Cole now owns it. Here was a large mound of which the Baltimore & Ohio construction crew removed two-thirds. A stone pipe, said to represent an eagle and some 20 inches in length, was found in this mound, in the late 50's. We dug eight or ten test pits in the structure but found very little. We do not recommend exploration.

On the south side of the Collinsville road are the lands of Mr. Tippett, Mr. Cole, and Mr. Wells. Two mounds were tested superficially. Both are composed of gumbo and while there was much broken pottery, no burials were encountered.

CONCLUSIONS ON THE EXCAVATIONS

Although we employed a very large crew, we were a short time at Cahokia. The area of Indian occupation covers at least 1,000 acres. It will therefore be observed that it would be impossible for any corps of explorers to do work which might be considered thorough in less than five or six seasons. It is the writer's opinion that about ten years are necessary to a thorough understanding of the Cahokia culture.

Our purpose was to test some of the mounds both large and small and first learn the construction and also ascertain whether burials were general in the mounds. With the exception of the smaller Edwards Mound, none of them were thoroughly explored by us. Technically, we can not affirm that the others are not burial mounds, since they were not dug out entirely. Briefly, our limited explorations would indicate that excepting the Jesse Ramey Mound, and Kunnemann Mound, the other mounds examined were house sites. The Kunnemann Mound is more or less of a mystery since being cone shape there would not be room for more than one very small lodge on the summit. If there are burials, they remain in the unexplored two-thirds.

Mr. W. J. Seever, who was present during McAdams' excavations and dug somewhat himself, thinks that the views of Putnam and others correct to the effect that there are one or two cemeteries which have not been found and that these are in addition to presumable burials in the larger mounds. We hope to do more thorough work in the seasons of 1922 and 1923. It is proposed to put several men testing the plain in various directions for the cemetery and concentrate another body of workers either on Smith's Mound or one of the flat pyramids to the west or south of Monks.

The excavations indicate that the village was well established and populous at the time the mounds were constructed. This is proved by the great quantities of broken artifacts, which lay about the ground near the houses and were scooped up with the earth.

EXPLORATION OF THE VILLAGE SITE

About 600 ft. north-east of Monks Mound, McAdams is said to have found the pottery and skeletons. Both of his sons, as well as Mr. Seever and one or two other witnesses, visited the scene of our operations and indicated where Mr. McAdams had dug. On page 57 of his volume he says that he secured 100 urns, pots or bottles from the cemetery near the base of Monks Mound. Some of these were painted. In plates 1 and 2 in his pamphlet entitled "Antiquities of Cahokia or Monk's Mound" (Edwardsville, 1883) he illustrates a number of these and other objects from the Cahokia village site.

He says "there were also the paint pots and dishes holding the colors, together with the little bone paddle for mixing, and other implements of the aboriginal artist." It is unfortunate that such an exhibit could not have been kept intact and preserved in the State Museum.

For a number of days we excavated at the McAdams site and also for a radius of 300 yds. east and north-east. Some of the trenches were 50 ft. in length. Broken human skeletons were found scattered here and there, probably where Mr. McAdams had made finds. We discovered one flex burial accompanied by half of a bowl. There was another partial burial a few feet to the west. The ground about it was much disturbed. Above both burials was a layer of hard baked, red earth some 2 ft. from the surface. The disturbed earth extended from 3 to as much as 5 ft. in depth. During the course of operations in the village site, numbers of fragments of galena, portions of Busycon shells, arrowheads, hammerstones and other material in common use among the Indians were discovered.

When excavating by means of test pits, with a view of studying the character and extent of the village site, we found a number of level, clay burned floors varying from 20 to 30 ft. in diameter. Three or four of these had been disturbed by the plow, others somewhat deeper were well preserved. One near the shore of the lake, a quarter of a mile south of Monks Mound, was composed of ordinary clay, burned quite hard and some 20x25 ft. in diameter. Whether these are the floors of wigwams or houses, we do not know. They seem rather small for dance floors or assembly places. There may be many more of them revealed by future explorations. No more refuse occurred on these floors than elsewhere on the village site.

Just north of Smith's Mound are three mounds which have been cultivated until the edges overlap. About the bases of these the village site material seems to be most numerous. We are of the opinion that this part of the site should be quite thoroughly examined, since we dug up several pottery heads of birds, etc. all of exceptional form and finish.

UTENSILS AND IMPLEMENTS FROM CAHOKIA

It will be necessary to visit several museums and also inspect some of the larger private collections within one-hundred miles of Cahokia in order to make studies and comparisons of the various artifacts found at this famous place. This will require considerable time but it will be possible to identify a great deal of Cahokia material. From the collection in the Missouri Historical Society and the large exhibits owned by E. W. Payne, Esq., of Springfield, Doctor H. M. Whelpley, and Doctor George B. Higgins of St. Louis, the Ramey heirs, William Waters, Esq., of Godfrey, Illinois, and one or two persons in Edwardsville, an idea of prevailing Cahokia forms may be obtained. These were inspected by the writer somewhat superficially, yet it can be stated that there are in the chipped implements (if not in the ceramic art) what might be called the Cahokia types. That is, the Cahokia people lived for such a length of time that they established their own localized art. The details of this can be worked out later when all collections are more carefully studied.

On the objects or artifacts themselves I find little or nothing has been published save by Doctor Charles Rau, formerly Curator in the Smithsonian Institution. He presented a study on pottery and other observations on agricultural flint implements in the Smithsonian reports. The descriptions follow herewith.

"That the fabrication of earthenware was once carried to a great extent among the Indians, is shown by the great number of sherds which lie scattered over the sites of their former villages and on their camping places; but they are, perhaps, nowhere in this country more numerous than in the "American Bottom," a strip of land which extends about one hundred miles along the Mississippi, in Illinois, and is bounded by the present bank of that river and its former eastern confine, indicated by a range of picturesque wooded hills and ridges, commonly called the "Bluffs." This bottom, which is on an average six miles wide and very fertile, was formerly the seat of a numerous indigenous population, and abounds in tumular works, cemeteries, and other memorials of the subdued race. Among the lesser relics left by the former occupants may be counted the remnants of broken vessels, which occur very abundantly in various places of this region. These fragments are, however, mostly small; and, according to my experience, entire vessels are not found on the surface, but frequently in the ancient mounds and cemeteries, where they have been deposited with the dead as receptacles for food, to serve on their journey to the happy land of spirits.

"About six years ago, while living in the west, I was much gratified by the discovery of a place in the American Bottom where the manufacture of earthenware was evidently carried on by the Indians. The locality to which I allude is the left bank of the Cahokia creek,* at the northern extremity of Illinoistown, opposite St. Louis. At the point just mentioned the bank of the creek is somewhat high and steep, leaving only a small space for a path along the water. When I passed there for the first time, I noticed, scattered over the slope or protruding from the ground, a great many pieces of pottery of much larger size than I had ever seen before, some being of the size of a man's hand, and others considerably larger; and, upon examination, I found that they consisted of a grayish clay mixed with pounded shells. A great number of old shells of the *unio*, a bivalve which inhabits the creek, were lying about, and their position induced me to believe that they had been brought there by human agency rather than by the overflowing of the creek. My curiosity being excited, I continued my investigation, and discovered at the upper part of the bank an old fosse, or digging, of some length and depth, and overgrown with stramonium or jimson weed; and upon entering this excavation, I saw near its bottom a layer of clay, identical in appearance with that which composed the fragments of pottery. The excavation had unmistakably been dug for the purpose of obtaining the clay, and I became now convinced beyond doubt that the fabrication of earthen vessels had been carried on by the aborigines at this very spot. All the requisites for manufacturing vessels were on hand; the layer of clay furnished the chief ingredient, and the creek not only supplied the water for moistening the clay, but harbored also the mollusks whose valves were used in tempering it. Wood abounded in the neighborhood. All these facts being ascertained, it was easy to account for the occurrence of the large fragments. Whenever pottery is made, some of the articles will crack during the process of burning, and this will happen more frequently when the method employed in that operation is of a rude and primitive character, as it doubtless was in the present case. The sherds found at this place may, therefore, with safety be considered as the remnants of vessels that were spoiled while in the fire, and thrown aside as objects unfit for use.

"I did not succeed in finding the traces of a kiln or fireplace, and it is probable that the vessels were merely baked in an open fire, of which all vestiges have been swept away long ago. The occurrence of the broken pottery was confined to a comparatively small area along the bank, a space not exceeding fifty paces in length, as far as I can recollect. They were most numerous in the proximity of the old digging, and at that place quite a number of them were taken out of the creek into which they had fallen from the bank. Farther up the creek I saw another excavation in the bank, of much smaller dimensions, and likewise dug for obtaining clay. Among the shells and sherds I noticed many flints which had obviously been fashioned to serve as cutting implements; they were perhaps, used in tracing the ornamental lines on the vessels or in smoothing their surfaces.

"I did not find a single complete vessel at this place, but a great variety of fragments, the shape of which enabled me to determine the outline of the utensils of which they originally formed parts. This was not a very difficult matter, especially in cases when portions of the rim remained. The rim, it will be seen, is formed into a lip and turned over, in order to facilitate suspension; sometimes, however, it is cut off abruptly. Some of the vessels—more especially the smaller ones—were provided with ears, others had the outer rim set with conical projections or studs, both for

*This creek runs in a southwardly direction through Madison county and a part of St. Clair county, and empties into the Mississippi, four miles below St. Louis, near the old French village of Cahokia.

convenience and ornament; and a few of the fragments exhibit very neatly indented or notched rims. In size these vessels varied considerably; some measured only a few inches through the middle, while the largest ones, to judge from the curvature of the rims, must have exceeded *two feet in diameter*. The bottom of the vessels mostly seems to have been rounded or convex. I found not a single flat bottom-piece. This, however, may be merely accidental, considering that flat-bottomed vessels were made by the Indians. The appearance of the fragments indicates that the earthenware was originally tolerably well burned, and the fracture exhibits in many instances a reddish color. But, as the art of glazing was unknown to the manufacturers, it is no wonder that the sherds, after having been imbedded for many years in the humid ground, or exposed to rain and the alternate action of a burning sun and a severe cold, are now somewhat brittle and fragile; yet, even when new, this aboriginal earthenware must have been much inferior in compactness and hardness to the ordinary kind of European or American crockery.

"The thickness of the fragments varies from one-eighth to three-eighths of an inch, according to the size of the vessels, the largest being also the strongest in material. But in each piece the thickness is uniform in a remarkable degree; the rims are perfectly circular, and the general regularity displayed in the workmanship of these vessels renders it almost difficult to believe that the manufacturers were unacquainted with the use of the potter's wheel. Such, however, was the case. I have already mentioned that the clay used in the fabrication of this earthenware is mixed with coarsely pulverized unio-shells from the creek; only a few of the smaller bowls or vases seem to consist of pure clay. The vessels were covered on the outside, and some even on both sides, with a thick coating of paint, either of a black, dark brown, or beautiful red color, and in some fragments the latter still retains its original brightness. Only *one* color, however, was used in the painting of each article. It is evident that the coloring preceded the process of baking, and the surfaces thus coated are smooth and shining, the paint replacing to a certain extent the enamel produced by glazing."*

Doctor Rau comments as follows on "A deposit of Agricultural Flint Implements in Southern Illinois:"

"I was, therefore, much interested in the recent discovery of a large *deposit* of such implements at East St. Louis, (formerly Illinoistown), in St. Clair county, Illinois, a place situated directly opposite the city of St. Louis, in the so-called "American Bottom," which forms a fertile plain extending for a considerable distance along the Mississippi shore in Illinois. This region, I must state, is very rich in Indian remains of various descriptions,**but particularly interesting on account of numerous artificial mounds, among which the celebrated truncated pyramid called Cahokia Mound, or Monk's Mound, is by far the most conspicuous, reminding the beholder of those gigantic structures in the valley of the Nile, which the rulers of Egypt have left to posterity as tokens of their power and their pride.

"The particulars of the discovery to which I alluded were communicated to me by Dr. John J. R. Patrick, of Belleville, Illinois, a gentleman to whom I am greatly indebted for long-continued co-operation in my pursuits relative to the subject of

*I possess a small food vase of this shape, which was taken out of an old Indian grave on the "Bluffs," near French village, six or seven miles east of Illinoistown. It was, perhaps, made at the very place which I have described.
**Smithsonian Report, 1866, pp. 346 to 350.

American antiquities. As soon as Dr. Patrick heard of the discovery he hastened to East St. Louis, for the purpose of ascertaining on the spot all details concerning the occurrence of those flint tools; and in order to obtain still more minute information, he afterwards repeatedly revisited the place of discovery which is about 14 miles distant from Belleville, and can be reached after a short ride, the latter place being connected by railroad with East St. Louis. The removal of ground in extending a street disclosed the existence of the deposit, and Dr. Patrick derived all facts concerning it character from Mr. Sullivan, the contractor of the street work, who was present when the tools were exhumed, and therefore can be considered as a reliable authority. The results of my informant's inquiries, communicated in various letters addressed to me, are contained in the following account:

"In the early part of December, 1868, some laborers, while engaged in grading an extension of Sixth street in East St. Louis, came upon a deposit of Indian relics, consisting of flint tools, all of the hoe and shovel type, and of small fossil marine shells, partly pierced, and in quantity about equal to the contents of a bushel. Close by were found several boulders of flint and greenstone, weighing from 15 to 30 pounds each, and many fragments of flint. The soil in the immediate neighborhood is composed of black loam, overlying a stratum of a sandy character, and the deposit which occurred in the latter, was covered with from 18 to 24 inches of the black earth, bearing a luxuriant turf on its surface. According to the contractor's statement, the flint tools, the shells, and the boulders were deposited in three separate holes dug out in the sand, but not more than a food apart from each other, and placed like the corners of a triangle. To use his language, the implements formed a "nest" by themselves, and so did the shells, and likewise the boulders. The flint tools, however, instead of being packed close together, like the shells and the boulders, were arranged with some regularity, overlapping each other or standing edgewise, and covering a circular space. The whole deposit did not extend more than seven or eight feet on either side. The contractor neglected to count the implements, but he thinks there were from 70 to 75 in all; some 50 hoes and about 20 shovels. No other stone articles, such as arrow and spear-heads, tomahawks, etc., had been deposited with the agricultural implements. The latter were soon taken away by persons from the place, attracted by the novelty of the occurrence, and it is to be regretted that many, if not most of them, have fallen into the hands of individuals who are unable to appreciate their value. But this is usually the case when discoveries of similar character are made. Dr. Patrick examined upwards of 20 of the flint implements, and found that none of them had been used, as they had not received the slightest polish on the cutting edge.

"The place of discovery lies about a mile and a half, or still further, from the Mississippi, on elevated ground, and above ordinary high-water mark; but formerly before the bed of the river was narrowed by the dike connecting the Illinois shore with Bloody Island, the distance cannot have been more than half a mile. The spot is situated nearly midway between two mounds, half a mile apart from each other. One of them was formerly used as a graveyard by the French of the neighborhood, and the other serves as the substructure for a dwelling-house.

"Several of the agricultural implements found at East St. Louis are now in my possession. Their material is a yellowish-brown variety of the flint to which I already referred. In shape they correspond with the tools of the same class previously described by me; most of the shovels, however, instead of having the end opposite the cutting part worked into a rounded edge, terminate in a more or less acute angle. The edges of all are chipped with the utmost regularity, and exhibit not the slightest wear, which proves that the implements were in a perfectly new condition when buried in the ground.*

"The fossil shells of marine origin are all small univalves, and belong almost entirely to the genus *Melampus*. Of nearly 300 specimens sent to me by Dr. Patrick, 19 only represent other genera, namely, *Columbella, Marginella, Conus,* and *Bulla*. All have a decayed and chalky appearance. They were probably obtained in the neighborhood, and obviously destined for ornamental purposes. This may be inferred from the fact that a number of the *Melampus* shells are pierced with one hole in the lower part, which was sufficient for stringing them, as the connecting thread could easily be passed through the natural aperture of the shell. On close examination, I found that these shells had been reduced, by grinding, to greater thinness at the place of perforation, in order to facilitate the process of piercing.

"The boulders, which formed a part of the deposit, were probably designated for the manufacture of implements. A piece of one of the boulders was sent to me for examination. It is a compact diorite, the material of which many ground articles of the North American Indians, such as tomahawks, chisels, pestles, &c., are made."**

NOTES UPON A COLLECTION SECURED FROM THE SURFACE

The Messrs. Ramey have accumulated more than 1,200 various objects found on the surface of the village site and the mounds the past thirty years. Omitting detailed descriptions, considerable can be learned from inspecting material found within a distance of one-half mile from Monks mound. In the chipped objects the triangular arrow point predominates. The drills, or perforators, are very slender and rather short. There are not many scrapers. There are over eight-hundred flint objects in the collection and while these have not been accurately divided, it is safe to assume that nearly 80% are of the peculiar Cahokia triangular form. There are a number of discoidals or bicaves and one fine disc composed of rose quartz. Several of the more interesting objects were photographed and are presented in Figs. 39 to 46. Attention is called to the sandstone tablet about 3⅜ inches in diameter on which a peculiar lattice-like design has been carved (Fig. 44). There are several effigies in pottery. The Cahokia people frequently made a little base, slightly curved, of clay, adding to same the head of a bird. These should not be confused with handles to pottery. There is an excellent example of this in the Ramey collection. It is painted red on the back and is shown in Fig. 37.

*Some years ago I discovered near East St. Louis the traces of an Indian pottery, described in the Smithsonian report for 1866.
**Smithsonian Report, 1868, pp. 402, 404.

Mr. James Ramey found a cache of several rough, notched hoes and spades all composed of limestone. Among them was a rough axe 10¾ ins. long, and nearly 5 ins. in width. There was also a large, flat stone which was covered with various grooves and depressions due to grinding other stones upon its surface, and a few hammer-stones. These have been carefully preserved and probably are the working tools of some aboriginal lapidary.

There are a few specimens of hematite in the collection and a remarkable bone awl, or perforator, made from the bill of some large bird (Fig. 34). It is about 3 ins. in length, carefully hollowed out and perforated. Certain peculiar forms in flint occur, such as the square, or angular, knife-scraper type.

The Ramey collection would indicate the correctness of previous observations to the effect that fixed types have developed at Cahokia.

THE POTTERY FROM CAHOKIA

We confine our brief description to fragmentary pottery, since we have not yet positively identified the perfect vessels and bowls found by McAdams and others. The fragments indicate that black, brown, red and combination of red and white are the favorite colors employed by the pottery maker. Figs. 15 to 32 present a number of fragments. The handles are quite interesting, some of them portraying the forearm and hand, the fingers usually clenched against the palm (Fig. 15). Other handles are round and pointed. The third form of handle, shown in Fig. 17, is sharply grooved on the upper surface and rounded on the lower.

Eliminating the common bowls and pottery which appear to be of the same forms as elsewhere in the Mississippi valley, the distinctive Cahokia types are shown in the figures. The large fragment Fig. 20 is a most favored design and also occurs farther south. Figs. 16 and 18 are characteristically Cahokia. Both are in red and both contain small, depressed squares. In these may have been inserted thin squares of shell. Of this we are not certain.

Mr. W. E. Myer, who is familiar with pottery from the south and middle Mississippi valley, examined the Cahokia fragments and concurs in the opinion that they indicate not only a highly developed ceramic art but specialized art, that the people had developed certain designs and motifs which do not occur outside of the Cahokia area. It is too soon for us to form positive conclusions and these few observations are based upon a hasty examination of some hundreds of fragments.

When perfect vessels are discovered with burials in the cemetery or in the mounds, we shall be able then to present proper classification and study of the ceramic art of the Cahokia people.

CACHES AT CAHOKIA

A number of caches have been discovered from time to time, one with several bicaves or discoidal stones was found by a tenant and is now in the possession of Mr. Payne. Another was composed of unusually large *Busycon* sea shells. Two or three of these are in the collection at Edwardsville. One of Mr. Merrell's tenants last spring discovered several large agricultural implements compactly placed together near the surface. A large quantity, said to exceed a bushel, of the black, perforated shell beads ½ to 1½ inches in diameter were found with some burials in the bluffs a few miles directly east of the largest mound.

There is a low mound on Mr. Merrell's land some 300 yds. due west from Kunnemann's sites. At the present time this is not over one or two ft. in elevation. Mr. Seever informs me that large numbers of unfinished celts, many of them of considerable size, were here discovered and that he secured and distributed something like 100 of these objects the past twenty-five years. The fields have been searched by persons desiring specimens for nearly one-hundred years and thousands of objects have been found and carried away. One of the most interesting of the fixed types is the so-called Cahokia type of arrowhead, the name having been given by Doctor H. M. Whelpley. I present several of them in Fig. 33 from Doctor George B. Higgins' collection. Not many were found by us as we spent very little time in surface hunting. The characteristic feature is the notch in the base. This occurs in hundreds of specimens of all practically the same form.

USE OF COPPER AT CAHOKIA

The only detailed reference to copper from the Cahokia region was written by Doctor Howland many years ago. This has never been reprinted and should be inserted here.*

*From Bulletin of the Buffalo Society of Natural Sciences.   Recent Archeological Discoveries in the American Bottom, by Henry R. Howland.   March 2, 1877.

"Prior to the destruction of the St. Louis "Big Mound," in 1870, no articles of copper had been found in the vicinity; in leveling that mound two "spoon-shaped" copper implements were discovered, and in the possession of Dr. J. J. R. Patrick, of Belleville, Ill., is a nugget of native copper, which was found in a large mound at East St. Louis. The mound from which the articles now under consideration were taken was one of that second group of the American Bottom system to which I have alluded. Some twelve miles north of East St. Louis, a sluggish creek or slough with high banks, called Long Lake, joins Cahokia Creek, and on its banks, near the point of junction, stands a group of some thirteen or fourteen mounds, circled around a square temple mound of moderate height. At the western border of this group, and close to Mitchell Station, stood originally three conical mounds of considerable size, which were first cut into some years since in laying the tracks of the Chicago and Alton Railroad. On the twentieth of January, 1876, acting upon a chance intimation in a St. Louis morning paper, I visited this group, and found that the largest of these three mounds was being removed to furnish material for building a road dike across Long Lake, replacing an old bridge. The work was already far advanced, but in its progress some singular discoveries had been made. The mound was originally about twenty-seven feet high, and measured one hundred and twenty feet in diameter at the base, but the various assaults which from time to time had been made upon it for similar purposes had materially altered its proportions, the surface workings having reduced its height some ten feet, though I could not learn that in these early openings anything of especial interest had been discovered.

"During the present excavations, however, the workmen found, at a height of four or five feet above the base of the mound, a deposit of human bones from six to eight feet in width, and averaging some eight inches in thickness, which stretched across the mound from east to west as though the remains had been gathered together and buried in a trench. On this level, scattered about within an area of six or eight feet square, and perhaps twenty feet from the south-easterly side of the mound, were discovered a number of valuable relics, together with a large quantity of matting in which many of them had been enveloped. The archaeological zeal of the Celtic mind was, however, not adequate to the preservation of this matting, and, unfortunately, most of it, together with the bones, had been carted off and re-interred in the ditch. I was able to secure several small fragments, which show a coarse, vegetable cane-like fibre, simply woven without twisting, the flat strands measuring about one-eighth of an inch in width.

"Among the many curious articles carefully wrapped in these mattings, and here buried, were found a number of small tortoise shells formed of copper, which, being unique, are worthy of special attention. Of these I obtained three specimens, the rest having been scattered.

"They are made of beaten copper scarcely more than one sixty-fourth of an inch thickness, the larger and more perfect one measuring two and one-eighth inches in length and 13-16 inches in height. Their shape is remarkably true and perfect, showing a central ridge from end to end, produced by pressure from the under surface. A narrow flange or rim, about $5\frac{1}{2}12$ inch in width, is neatly turned at the base, and over the entire outer surface the curious markings peculiar to the tortoise shell are carefully produced by indentation—the entire workmanship evincing a delicate skill, of which we have never before found traces in any discovered remains of the arts of the

the Mound Builders.   Each of these tortoise shells would seem to have originally been covered with several wrappings of a very singular character,
and one still adheres to its original envelope, presenting a peculiar mummified
appearance.   Closely fitting over the outer surface of the copper shell is, first,
a woven cloth of a vegetable fibre, similar in its general character to the outer
matting above described, but of a stronger and better preserved fibre, apparently
more like that which forms the woven coating of the Davenport axes.*   This is covered
in turn with a softer, finer fabric, now of a dark-brown color, formed of twisted strands,
laid or matted closely together, though apparently not woven.   The material of
which these strands are formed proves, under microscopic examination, to be animal
hair.   This fact is of singular interest, as it is believed that this is the only instance in
which any such fabric has been discovered in connection with relics of the mound
builders.   A careful examination would seem to show the material to be rabbit's
hair, in a perfect state of preservation, though none but short hairs are found and most
of these are without either tip or base, though occasionally, as shown in the plate,
the tips are found, as also the parts towards the base of the hairs, showing several rows
of cells.

"Overlying this singular fabric and adhering quite closely to it is a dark colored
layer, which under the microscope is shown to consist of a membraneous substance with
numerous pores and distinct cellular structure (nuclei not visible), and would seem
unquestionably to be an animal cuticle, a conclusion which is confirmed by the opinion
of the eminent botanist Sir Josep Hooker, who has examined the specimen.   The
pores are apparently gland openings, and the dark line shows a rent in the cuticle.

"This layer seems also very carefully and smoothly shaped, and is covered in
turn with a final coating of small dark iridescent scales which probably owe their
color to carbonization, as they show in the spectroscope traces of carbon.   They appear
however, on microscopic examination to be the remains of a layer of non-striated muscular fibre with connecting tissue, possibly from the intestines or bladder of some animal,
this having originally served as an outer wrapping for these carefully treasured objects.

"Next in point of interest are two specimens (also believed to be unique in their
character) of the lower jaw of the deer in both of which the forward part or that containing the teeth is ensaced in a thin covering of copper, which extends over the teeth,
and over this copper sheathing are the same mummy-like wrappings which I have
already described, though in one specimen the coarse vegetable fibre-cloth is lacking,
and the case is primarily formed of the fine, soft, matted fabric of animal hair which
in the others forms the second coating.   In both, these wrappings are skillfully made
to form a close-fitting and symmetrical case.   They measure about two and a half
inches from the end of the teeth to the point where the bone is cut off, and the copper
sheathing reaches to within half an inch of this, while a hole is bored from side to side
through the back of each jaw, as though the articles had been worn suspended from the
neck for totems or as badges of authority.

"Three curious implements which were found were in the shape of two flat circular discs of uniform size, 2 3-16 inches in diameter, united by a central shaft, and in
general appearance not unlike a narrow spool or thread reel, each having a circular
hole through the center ¾ inch in diameter.   These were made of bone, and having

*Prof. Asa Gray, on a hurried examination of this matting, expresses the opinion
that it is made of a bark fibre (not bast), possibly from the fibrous bark of Thuja.

been polished very smoothly were neatly coated with beaten copper. This is also true of a slender pointed rod of wood 8¾ inches long, which was skillfully covered with a thin copper sheathing extending over its entire length. A number of pieces of very thin wood (of which I secured eight specimens), were also found, which were about 3 inches long, probably about 2¼ inches across at the widest point and very carefully shaped, being rounded at the base and running to a point at the top where they were perforated for convenience in stringing or fastening them together. The striking peculiarity of these thin plates of wood, as of the other objects just mentioned, is that they show evidence of having once been coated with thin copper, many fragments of which still adhere to their surfaces. It is as difficult to conjecture the use of these articles as of a series of five flat copper rods, measuring 3⅛ inches in length and pointed at one end, placed edge to edge and fastened together with flat bands probably of the same material.

"Close at hand were one or two rude weapons of stone. Of one a fragment only was preserved, the other was a double-pointed spear head, a foot long, made of light-colored chert and precisely similar to those made by the North American Indians. With them was found a bundle of eight copper rods or needles from fourteen to eighteen inches in length, all in one bundle, wrapped together with matting. In addition to these, several awls and needles of various sizes made of bone were discovered, and with them a considerable quantity of beads made from the column of Busycon shells; two of those which I obtained measure respectively 2 1-8 and 4 inches in length, are slightly curved in shape and perforated from end to end. Not less curious is a necklace or circlet of twenty flat crescent-shaped ornaments of shell, each some three inches long and pierced at one end for the cord or thong which fastened them together.

"A day or two later, in digging on the northwest side of the mound, the workmen found near its base a mass of bones indicating another trench burial; but the only relics found with these remains were numerous sea shells of the species *Busycon perversum*, which must have been brought from the Gulf of Mexico, concerning which it is worthy of note that the crowns or tops of the shells are missing, having apparently been cut off in each instance at about the same angle, indicating that one part or the the other was made to serve some useful purpose in the economy of this strange people. In one very large specimen which I secured, the whorl or column of the shell had been cut away and the edges smoothly ground, forming a scoop-shaped implement about a foot in length."

CONCLUSIONS

No definite observations as to age, cultures, or people can be offered the reader at this time. Our work is but begun. However, it seems to be generally accepted by all observers that Cahokia is strictly pre-historic, since later Indians seem to know nothing concerning its builders.

When Marquette, LaSalle or Hennepin visited the region, they certainly would have stopped at so large a settlement as Cahokia had it then been occupied. That La Salle and Hennepin went to the Illinois villages, more than a hundred miles north-east seems to indicate that Cahokia in 1670 to 1680 was uninhabited. Dr. J. Owen Dorsey made a special study of Siouan tribes. In the Third Annual Report of the Bureau of Ethnology (Washington, 1884), he refers to a tradition that the Omahas once dwelt at a place near the present city of St. Louis. Also, that there was a "high mountain" on this peninsula. Mr. Gerard Fowke has given the subject considerable attention and published in Bulletin Thirty-Seven of the Bureau of American Ethnology (pp. 6 and 7) his observations which are as follows:

"The continuous and extensive changes of channel in the Missouri river, and the Mississippi below their junction deprive us of any certainty as to the location of the "peninsula" referred to in the Siouan legend. The narrators naturally would have applied the name "Missouri" to the whole river; that is to say, they would have regarded what we now call the Missouri as the principal stream, because they lived on it, and the Mississippi above the junction as a tributary. So we may not have to go to "The northern part of Saint Louis county" to find the place the tradition calls for.

"There is strong evidence that within a comparatively recent period the stream crossed abruptly from the Missouri to the Illinois bluffs then back to the Missouri side, in a space of a few miles above and below the present levee. Horseshoe and Pittsburg lakes are remains of this former channel. The mounds of the Cahokia group correspond in form and situation with mounds which formerly existed on the site of Saint Louis, and they are not at all of the same type as those nearest them in Illinois—an indication that when built they were all on the western side of the Mississippi, or according to aboriginal ideas, of the Missouri, river. Thus it is quite probable, providing we admit the essential truth of the Omaha tradition, that this is the "peninsula" to which reference is made, and that in the term "high mountain" we find the linguistic successor of "high mound"—in other words, the towering artificial structure called the Great Cahokia Mound. There is no other locality near the mouth of the Missouri which accords with the description given by Dorsey, certainly no "high mountain," so it is safe to assume that the Siouan tribes were settled for a time on an extensive bottom in front of the present city, with the Mississippi river on the north, east, and south. They may have constructed the small burial mounds found in the county and westward; and when, in their renewed migration, they reached a region where flat rocks were abundant and earth hard to dig, may have evolved the stone vaults.

"As no mention is made in the legend of contact with an unrelated tribe, either at that time or afterward, the Mound builders had no doubt abandoned the site before the advent of the Sioux; otherwise we should certainly have heard of them."

POSSIBILITY OF IMPORTANT DISCOVERIES

In the large, low depression or pond, south of the largest mound occur great quantities of village site debris. One of the survey members collected a peck of broken pottery, chips, arrowheads and burnt stone several hundred feet from the shore. As the bottom of the pond is below the depth at which village site material has been found, it is difficult to account for the presence of so much fragmentary material. It is not claimed that the ancient Cahokia people lived on pile dwellings over the water, but it seems advisable to make a thorough examination of the bottom of this and other ponds.

The original diameter of many of the mounds can be ascertained by trenching in from the present feather edge. Scales of copper, the finding of a broken copper serpent, and some fragments of copper indicating repoussé work, point to the possibility of copper being in general use. The copper plates found in Dunklin County, Missouri, and described by Mr. Fowke in Bulletin 37 of the Bureau of American Ethnology report, present a characteristic Cahokia

Design on a fragment of pottery.

design. A fragment of pottery is illustrated in the figure above. On this is the same symbolic bird-head-eye design present on all the copper plates. This design was generally used at Cahokia.

An inspection of the fragments of pottery furnished evidence of the remarkable development of the ceramic art and it is to be hoped that perfect vessels will be secured for study.

The relationship of Cahokia to other mound groups in the region is important and has as yet received no attention. The range of possibility for archeological work of importance at Cahokia seems almost limitless. The place certainly merits detailed and intensive study on the part of some observer for many years to come.

PRESERVATION OF THE GROUP

The chief purpose of the writer's visit to Cahokia the past year was to arouse interest on the part of the public in the preservation of these famous mounds. They could be explored subsequently provided they were protected by the state or the nation, or some wealthy individual. Obviously, they could not be explored satisfactorily if the tracts were sold for commercial purposes and factories erected, as has been suggested. During this present year, the owners assure us the tumuli may be considered safe, yet it is probable that should the state decline to purchase, some if not all of the mounds may become lost to posterity. East St. Louis is rapidly growing and extending its streets, buildings and factories toward the east. A railroad has already been constructed within a mile and a half of some of the largest mounds. Real estate values are increasing and the owners may be forced to sell these properties, since the land is now too valuable to be longer used for agricultural purposes.

Various statements to the effect that the land owners placed a high valuation on their properties, or that the largest mound was to be destroyed by steam shovels and the earth used to make fills across the American Bottoms, have been in circulation. After consultation with certain members of the National Research Council and prominent archeologists it was thought best to make a preliminary investigation. We now know that the owners do not seek more than the ordinary real estate value of their lands, and to such they are entitled. We are also aware that some years of exploration at Cahokia are necessary. It is for the citizens of the state of Illinois to inaugurate and carry to successful termination a movement having for its purpose the preservation of these remarkable monuments. In brief, a state park of 1,000 acres would safeguard for all time these tumuli.* The writer was informed that there were

*Or, even 500 acres would include the chief monuments.

several proposals to make parks of certain areas of bluffs along the Mississippi. From a little below Alton to above Quincy there are many miles of picturesque bluffs which might be secured at any time, and these are in no danger of destruction. This is mentioned particularly, because several men of prominence stated to the writer that they were interested in any state park project provided it was to be located in their particular neighborhood. They did not fully appreciate that Cahokia may be lost irrevocably; other sites cannot be destroyed. Persons really familiar with the situation believe there should be concentrated action by men's and women's clubs, educational institutions and all organizations in order that the bill to be introduced next winter may be certain of passage through the legislature. Wisconsin, Ohio, New York, New Mexico and other states have made parks of their prehistoric monuments. Unfortunately, there are many citizens who do not realize that there is great danger of the Cahokia lands being sold for commercial purposes. While the writer was at Cahokia there was a tentative proposition involving nearly $800,000 made to a certain group of owners. Their patriotism and high regard for the mounds lead them to defer action.

The parks in Ohio—Serpent Mound, Fort Ancient and the great works at Newark—are visited by thousands of persons each summer and are practically self supporting. The great expanse of rich soil lying about the mounds of Cahokia, when leased, would bring in sufficient revenue to take charge of the overhead expense. Many appeals have been made through pamphlets and memorials to the state officials of Illinois on the part of intelligent citizens of that commonwealth and elsewhere. Far back in 1836, Mr. Edmund Flagg, a very intelligent traveler, lamented the fact that some of the St. Louis mounds had been destroyed. He offers this suggestion: "The ancient tumuli could, at no considerable expense, have been enclosed, ornamented with shrubbery and walks and flowers, and thus preserved for coming generations. . . . . . The practical utility of which they are available appears the only circumstance which has attracted attention to them. One has already become a public reservoir, and measures are in progress for applying the larger mound to a similar use, the first being insufficient for the growth of the city." Flagg's plea might well be transferred to Cahokia at the present time. People come from remote sections of the United States to see the Cahokia mounds. While we were at work last year a Scotchman and an Englishman, touring America, visited the group. The mounds preserved in a state park would be a continual reminder to coming generations of the strange and interesting life of our prehistoric Indians. To destroy them and erect on the spot where they once stood unsightly factories is nothing short of sacrilege, and we of today would be subject to severe censure. Future generations would say of us, even as has been said of Easau of long ago, that we sold our priceless heritage of the ages for a mess of pottage.

RESOLUTION PASSED BY THE AMERICAN ANTHROPOLOGICAL ASSO-
CIATION AT THE ANNUAL MEETING IN BROOKLYN, N. Y.,
DEC. 29, 1921.

Since it has come to our knowledge that steps are now being taken by citizens of the State of Illinois to preserve the large and unique group of pre-historic earth-works near East St. Louis, we desire to express our hearty approval of these efforts and our sincere wishes for the success of the undertaking. Not only do we regard the preservation and restoration of this group as urgent, but it is also highly desirable that an early survey of the whole site be made to reveal the culture of the builders and their place in the pre-historic life of the Mississippi valley.

ALFRED V. KIDDER, Secretary

NOTE

For the benefit of any readers unfamilar with the work of the American Anthropological Association, it is well to state that the men and women comprising it represent all the leading museums, research institutions, and many of the colleges of the entire United States. Nearly all persons engaged in the study of the American Indian both past and present belong to this organization.

The Cahokia Mounds

1923

Part I
A Report of Progress on the
Exploration of the Cahokia Group

Warren K. Moorehead

Part II
The Geological Aspects of Some
of the Cahokia (Illinois) Mounds

Morris M. Leighton

TABLE OF CONTENTS

Part I

Introduction... 9

Explorations in the Spring of 1922........................ 12

Descriptions of the Mounds Investigated................... 14

    The Sawmill Mound, No. 39......................... 14

    Mounds 19, 20, and 21............................. 17

    The James Ramey Mound, No. 33..................... 19

    The Jondro Mound, No. 83.......................... 27

    Sam Chucallo Mound............................... 29

    Pittsburg Lake Cemetery........................... 30

    Mounds 14 and 84................................. 31

    Sullivan's Mounds................................. 32

    The Kruger Bone Bank............................. 34

    The Harding Mound, No. 66........................ 34

    Mrs. Tippetts' Mound, No. 61...................... 35

    The Mitchell Mounds.............................. 36

    The Collinsville-Edgemont Bluffs.................. 37

Village Site Observations................................. 38

    The Wells'-Tippetts' Village Site.................. 39

    The Stock Yards Site.............................. 39

    Testing the Bottoms of the Ponds.................. 41

Previous Work and Collections Relating to the Cahokia Group.. 43

    Dr. Patrick...................................... 43

    Specimens from Cahokia........................... 44

Observations on the Season's Work........................ 47

    The Immensity of Cahokia......................... 49

Notes on Cahokia Skeletons, by Dr. R. J. Terry........... 51

Cahokia Bibliography..................................... 53

Part II

Letter of Transmittal.................................... 59

Introduction... 61

    The Problem...................................... 61

    Acknowledgments................................. 61

    Former Opinions of Geologists....................... 62

General Description of the Mounds........................ 67

    Number, Size, and Shape............................ 67

    Monks Mound...................................... 68

    Arrangement of the Mounds......................... 68

The Geological Setting of the Mounds..................... 71

    Topographic Position............................... 71

    The Alluvial Filling............................... 72

    Remnants of the Original Glacial Filling............... 73

    Post-Glacial Conditions............................ 75

    Bearing Upon the Age and Origin of the Mounds........ 76

Constitution of the Mounds.............................. 77

    The James Ramey Mound, No. 33.................... 77

    The Albert Kunnemann Mound, No. 16................ 86

    The Sam Chucallo Mound........................... 87

    The Sawmill Mound, No. 39......................... 89

    Auger Borings on Monks Mound..................... 89

    Comparison with the Materials of the East Valley Bluff... 92

Summary of the Evidence and Conclusions................. 95

Part I

A REPORT OF PROGRESS ON THE EXPLORATION OF THE CAHOKIA GROUP

BY

WARREN K. MOOREHEAD

Curator, Department of Archeology, Phillips Academy, Andover, Mass.
Director, Archeological Survey of the Cahokia Region
for the University of Illinois

INTRODUCTION

In the spring of 1922 and again during the fall of the same year, researches were continued at the Cahokia Mounds. It was due to the Trustees and the President of the University of Illinois that these additional researches were made possible. Two generous appropriations were made by the University. All artifacts and specimens found are in the Museum of Natural History at Urbana, and are on exhibition in the Hall of Ethnology. I desire to express full appreciation of the cooperation and kindness of President David Kinley, Curator Frank C. Baker, Mr. F. W. De Wolf, and Dr. M. M. Leighton. Dr. Leighton made observations upon the geological features of Cahokia and his report appears in Part II.

Continuing the same spirit manifested last year, the owners permitted excavations upon their several properties. In some places large pits were excavated, but for the most part the holes were rather small. Extensive testing was projected in various directions and some damage to crops resulted. In the case of Mound 33—which we called the James Ramey Mound—two acres of wheat were destroyed, and as the pit was left open until fall, the corn crop on that tract could not be planted. Thus four acres of crops were destroyed on this one mound. The general testing of the village site extending over the lands owned by George Merrell, Esq., interfered somewhat with planting, yet Mr. Merrell and his tenants, Mr. Henry Stolle, Mr. Wm. Johnson, and Mr. Louis Recklein, did not object to our work. Mr. F. B. Harding gave consent for us to put down our long testing augers in the Harding mound. I desire to thank the Ramey family for their assistance to the survey and unlimited permissions to explore; also Mr. Merrell and all his tenants. Mrs. Wm. Tippetts, Mr. J. H. Edwards, Mr. Ernest Cole, and others permitted many testings on their lands, and Mr. Rufus Wells and his tenant, Mr. Udell Allen, allowed us to work out large pits in the heavy village site south of the National Highway.

Mr. A. J. Throop and Mr. W. E. Herrington took us on several trips to see sites and owners and rendered the survey assistance, for which we are grateful. Mr. Otto Kruger and Mr. Chas. Jondro allowed series of large pits to be dug in their fields. Judge J. D. Sullivan permitted the men to excavate the two mounds located near his residence at Signal Hill, and the National Stock Yards Company let us excavate on Cahokia Creek in the busiest section of East St. Louis. The survey wishes to thank all these persons.

Thomas H. English, a graduate student in the University of Wisconsin, made researches in the library and furnished additional Cahokia tiles. Hon. W. E. Myer, of Carthage, Tenn., an authority on southern pottery, studied our collections. We appreciate their co-operation.

I am especially indebted to Clinton Cowen, Esq., of Cincinnati, engineer of the survey, and to William J. Seever, Esq., of Webster Groves, Mo., for long and arduous labors in the field. Mr. Cowen redrew the Patrick-Van Court Map, inserted sites omitted by the first surveyors and made our cross-sections. Dr. R. J. Terry of Washington University, St. Louis, undertook a study of the skeletal material; Mr. H. M. Whelpley of St. Louis gave us the benefit of his wide experience in archeological matters; Dr. O. L. Schmidt, President of the Illinois Historical Society, did us many favors. Miss Adele R. Brooks of Monticello Seminary, Godfrey, Illinois, came to the mounds and painted two pictures of the mounds when they were covered by a blanket of brilliant sumac. The principal of Monticello, Miss Congdon, permitted us to study and photograph the Cahokia objects in the Seminary collection. And there were many others who aided us in various ways to whom we express full appreciation.

This report will be confined, chiefly, to a narration of excavations and observations. Yet since the preliminary report is out of print and there is a constant demand for copies, a few of the pages in it are published herein, with some changes.

The plates of specimens in the collection of the Museum of Natural History of the University of Illinois, were made by Mr. A. G. Eldredge, Director of the University Photographic Laboratory. All other photographs, excepting those of the Seever collection, and two by Mr. Gordon Servant, were made by the author.

The numbers following the descriptions of figures on some of the plates indicate the catalog numbers of the Division of Archeology, Museum of Natural History. All of these specimens are on exhibition in the new Hall of Ethnology.

EXPLORATIONS IN THE SPRING OF 1922

The second survey began operations early in March, 1922. During the winter the writer had seen Cahokia again and at the annual meeting of the American Anthropological Association, consulted with other archeologists as to the Cahokia problem. When visiting museums the writer made special efforts to obtain the point of view of field men and investigators as to the best method of procedure in the investigations.

Previous to our arrival, Mr. William J. Seever was authorized to employ men to test lesser elevations, or low mounds, and the area between. He made use of several long, narrow, steel rods from 3½ to 4½ feet in length, and as the ground was very soft at that time of the year, these probes were of great assistance in locating the bones and objects. In case the point of a rod strikes some object the workmen carefully prod all around, get its direction, and size. The soil of the American Bottoms is free from stone and so far as the survey was able to determine all stones—even pebbles—seem to have been brought in by Indians. This view is confirmed by the owners and tenants. For a number of days, the men probed the area lying between Mounds 23 and 43 east and west, and 20 and 62 north and south. Mounds 19, 20, and 21 on the map at the time of the Patricks' visits seem to have been distinct and separate. Now, due to cultivation, the edges overlap. The probes indicated burials in these low mounds, and also on the southern slope of Mound 39, and in Mound 82. The probing was stopped and several trenches were run through the edge of Mound 39, and subsequently a large pit was sunk in the center.

It was thought best to do general prospecting and by this means secure accurate information as to the extent of the village site, and whether there were burials near the surface.

It became necessary to change the working crew from one part of the field to another since large numbers of visitors came from adjacent towns, and particularly from both St. Louis and East St. Louis. Naturally, the survey did not wish to offend any of these people, yet spectators interfered with research work, and frequently specimens disappeared. It may interest readers to know a little of the plan followed. After working a few days in one spot, and when the "gallery" became too large, the trenches were caved in, and the men moved to some other portion of the field, a mile or more distant. It was generally known when skeletons were discovered, and such finds always brought numerous visitors. On return to their homes, these persons invariably told their friends, and larger numbers would come out to the scene of exploration the next day. Finding no skeletons in sight, and the members of the survey nowhere to be seen, they would naturally conclude that either work was abandoned, or the excavators had moved to some distant point. By this plan we were able to carry on proper reseach.

DESCRIPTIONS OF THE MOUNDS INVESTIGATED

THE SAWMILL MOUND, No. 39

Reference to the large map in the back of this report will indicate that on Rameys' land (northwest from the barn) is Mound No. 39, which is designated by local people as the Sawmill Mound. It is, as near as we could determine without actual survey, 240 feet by 240 feet in extent, a square mound, with level summit. South of it 600 feet is a large oval mound, No. 41, 25 feet high. The original form may have been either pyramidal or oval. No one knows. We think a long, low platform existed between the Sawmill Mound and the one to the south. On the north side of the Sawmill Mound (39) is the old bed of Cahokia Creek, and on that side the mound appears to be 18 or 19 feet high, whereas to the south there is a more gradual slope. To the eye the mound does not appear to be over 7 or 8 feet high when one looks northward. Probably a low mound (82) adjoined it.

The name was given long ago, since sometime between 1850 and 1860 a mill boiler exploded, killing twelve to fifteen men, who were buried in a small mound south of the turnpike, probably Mound 78, or possibly No. 47. This circumstance should be remembered in case some future explorers find well preserved skeletons with traces of wooden coffins about them.

It is not necessary to present a map of the burials along the southern slope of the Sawmill Mound (39). Extending in a somewhat irregular row, or line, for about 30 feet east and west, eight were found, and numbered 4 to 11. The first four of these burials were headed north, the next three south, and No. 11, northeast. Nos. 4, 5, and 6 lay in black soil at a depth of about 30 inches. The surrounding area for a distance of several hundred feet was tested carefully and disturbed ground extended down for a depth of as much as 3 feet, indicating an extensive village site. Black pottery predominated, and a few red fragments were observed.

Just south of No. 39 is a small mound (82), on the slope of which, down 2 feet, was discovered a small bowl-like mass of hard, burnt clay. Altho broken somewhat, it appeared to be circular in form, about 20 inches in diameter, or 36 inches around the curvature. No complete measurement could be made, yet the rim was well defined. In the cavity, where the base should have been, was a large lump of galena blackened by fire, also some pulverized galena. The lump weighed fully 8 pounds and the powdered galena was about a quart in quantity. There was a pottery bowl, 7 or 8 inches in diameter, and 3 inches high, with this deposit, and a shallow dish very flat, like a plate, of rather thick clay, also an oval stone on which were distinct markings or lines (Pl. II, Fig. 5). There were several ordinary hammer stones, and a small jar, almost crucible like. This is dark brown, well made, stands about 4 inches in height, and the base is unusually thick and heavy. The jar is shown in Fig. 5, Pl. I.

The work continued along the southern slope of Mound 39, and with skeleton No. 9, a young person, was a small toy vessel, about 2 inches in diameter, near the head (Pl. I, Fig. 4). At the right of skeleton No. 8 was a blackened bone object, probably an awl; also an entire deer jaw bone, in the point of which had been cut a groove, thus forming a small chisel or gouge. On the east side of this mound we ran a trench 35 feet in length, and 5 feet deep, but no burials were encountered. A pit was sunk in the center, 14x15 feet. This was dug down 16 feet, then the post augers put down 3½ to 4 feet farther. In the extreme base was found a heavy wet clay. The mound was stratified as follows:—

Mixed earth - - - - 4 feet	Dark streak - - - 3 inches
Dark earth - - - 10 inches	Yellow earth - - - 1 foot
Yellow earth - - - - 2 feet	Mixed earth - - - - 2 feet
Dark streak - - - 4 inches	Dark earth - - - - 3 feet
Yellow earth - - - 18 inches	

The layers in the Sawmill Mound were not even; in the northwest corner they radiated from a cone formation—

dipping to the southeast or east. Yet when we were down about 10 feet they appeared to be more horizontal. On the south side of the trench was a heavy black layer.

Some fragments of pottery (Pl. XI, Fig. 1) also chips and spalls were found scattered throughout the structure. A peculiar clay effigy of a mammal head, an awl cut from the lower jaw of a deer (Pl. IX, Fig. 13), and a rare shell effigy cut from a river mussel, were also found in this mound (see Pl. VII, Figs. 2, 7). The auger borings in the south side of the pit showed heavy blue clay, along with the gray.

While some workmen sank the pit, others continued searching for burials. They found a number of disturbed burials, or rather fragmentary ones, much broken. These were scattered throughout the soil 2½ to 4½ feet in depth and without regularity. Probably Dr. Patrick or Mr. McAdams had dug here, since the soil seemed soft and disturbed. Below all the burials we sank test pits several feet in depth.

Skeleton No. 11 lay extended head northeast (Pl. XIII, Fig. 2). It was quite well preserved. An ordinary jar lay near the right hand, and a bowl near the left knee (Pl. I, Fig. 6). A shell gorget and a bone knife were also found with this skeleton (Pl. VII, Fig. 1; Pl. IX, Fig. 8).

While part of the men were working under the writer's direction, Mr. Seever took a crew and prospected two low mounds west of No. 48. In Mound 80 he ran a trench about 6 feet in width, and 50 in length, finding a large number of potsherds, bones, and burnt clay, and village site material. He also went more than a mile up Canteen Creek and prospected both sides of the stream for a distance of half a mile. The drainage canal system inaugurated by the County Commissioners sometime ago has so changed conditions that it was impossible for him to make further observations. He says, "I find that the old bottom lands of Cahokia and Canteen creeks have been filled in by wash in flood time from 5 to 10 feet, thus obliterating some low mounds that were in existence, and covered up the deposits mentioned as having been seen by Charles Rau in the '60's."

MOUNDS 19, 20, AND 21

Probing the lesser mounds indicated burials north of Mound 33, and reference to the large map will indicate that there are seven mounds in a line east and west. Three of these, Nos. 19, 20, and 21, are so near together that the edges overlap. This is probably due to cultivation of the soil. The original heights of these structures are unknown, but we assume that No. 20 was the largest. No. 19 is at present about 5 feet in height, 20 about 4 feet, and 21 is about 3 feet in altitude. Most of the burials were in No. 20, or on the slope of it. Skeleton No. 12 was found on the southern slope of No. 19 at a depth of about 3 feet, and was fairly well preserved. The right leg had been much elevated and we found the tibia and femur at least a foot above the rest of the body; yet it had not been disturbed by the plow, and this curious form of burial must have been intentional.

At the head of this skeleton were four pots shown in Pl. XIV, Fig. 1: first the bowl, next the jar, then a dish in which a fine, dipper-like object was placed. This is decorated with sun symbols and has a long, slender, projecting handle. The right arm of the skeleton was in normal position to the elbow, but the ulna and radius lay across the abdomen, and the left leg was bent at the knee. All of this pottery was perfect, but there was nothing else in the grave. (Pl. I, Figs. 1-3). Skeleton 33 was doubled up, the knees being drawn up to the abdomen. There was disturbed earth just east of it, and a detached skull 2 feet north. Numerous test pits showed several fragmentary human skeletons, and much village site debris.

About 150 feet from the west end of our trench, at the depth of 3 feet, were many fragments of spades and hoes, or digging tools of reddish chert. Why these were all broken we do not know. There were enough fragments to comprise 15 or 20 of the tools, and about them were ashes, and burnt earth. Fifteen feet beyond was a mass of pulverized galena lying in ashes.

Our total trench was extended a distance of over 250 feet from the center of Mound 19 well into No. 21. Much village site material occurred through the soil and extended in places as deep as 7 feet. Naturally, the greatest depths at which village site debris occurred were near the highest parts of the mounds. Plate XV, Fig. 2, shows the position of two skeletons. The burial in the foreground had a vessel at the head; the skull rested upon a small sea shell and there were traces of pigment (in small lumps) near the face. Between burials 21 and 22 was found an

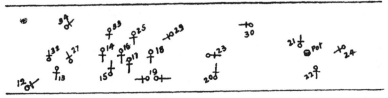

Fig. 1—Position of skeletons in trench cut through mounds 19, 20, 21.

ordinary cooking pot, lying 5 feet from the nearest skeleton. With three or four of the other skeletons we found ordinary clay dishes or bowls usually placed by the head. None of the skeletons were well preserved altho two or three were taken out fairly entire and loaned to Dr. A. J. Terry of the Medical Department of Washington University. It is not necessary to record all the depths of the skeletons; they varied from 2½ feet to 6½ feet, and save one or two were all extended. Eight of them lay with the heads to the north, 3 with the heads to the east, 2 with the heads west, 5 with the heads south, and others northwest and southeast (Text Fig. 1). Whether pottery originally placed by the natives had been removed by McAdams, Patrick, or others, we do not know. It is possible that no pottery was placed with these interments, except such as we recovered. Assuming that such statement is correct, about one-third of the burials were accompanied by vessels or pottery. Two-thirds were without pottery. The exception is with No. 12 which was accompanied by four vessels as has been stated. A fine needle was found with skeleton No. 30 (Pl. XIII, Fig. 2) and an awl made from the heel of a deer with skeleton No. 18 (Pl. IX, Fig. 10).

Dr. F. S. Smith, of Nevada, Iowa, was present during the removal of these skeletons, and attempted to make some observations on the remains, as they lay in the ground. He made no measurements and his notes are mere field suggestions.

No. 16. Female.

No. 18. Probably female, decayed, and therefore sex uncertain.

No. 20. Young woman 18 to 25 years.

No. 21. Female; pelvis very light, the brim typical form. Antero-posterior diameter about 4½ inches. The iliac crest very thin and the roughened crest for attachment of muscles not well developed. All long bones small and delicate. The femora typical form and meeting of the lower leg at the usual angle for women.

"It is impossible to make any accurate measurements but the thin light bones, and typical size and form of the clavicles all point to the above numbered skeletons as being females."

All the interments appear to be on the same level or base line, and were probably village rather than mound burials. That most of them appear to be women is interesting, as usually both sexes are found in the cemeteries.

The James Ramey Mound, No. 33

Spring Operations.—It was decided to select a large tumulus and examine as much of it as possible. This structure adjoined a pyramid or "temple mound" and both seemed to occupy a central position in ancient Cahokia times.

There was originally a deep depression between Mounds 33 and 34, so the Rameys informed me, which had been filled in by dragging the earth from the summit of the mound down the steep slopes into this depression. The mound was conical originally, and according to all witnesses probably 15 feet higher than at the time of our exploration. This would give it a height of 38 feet. The adjoining mound to the west, No. 32, is a temple or pyramid structure with flattened summit, and is so shown in the maps and old records. No. 33 was supposed to be a burial structure, since it came to a "point", and local tradition is persistent in so describing this tumulus.

Testing elsewhere was deferred and fourteen men were put to work on the north side at the lowest slope. We began at a point which appeared to the eye to be 4 or 5 feet above the general surface, yet we had gone down over 7 feet before we found the base line. Our trench extended to the south.

When Professor F. C. Baker of the University of Illinois came to visit our survey, on the 3rd of April, we had run the trench 30 feet south in the mound. The face of the trench, or south wall, was 12 feet high. The width of the pit was 27 feet east and west. A number of marine shells, a few bone awls, and the usual broken pottery and animal bones were found. While Professor Baker was present we sank a number of pits with the post augers and brought up bones from the lower layers or bottom. These bones were observed to be of brownish green color. Later, during the research in this mound, the same peculiarity was observed, and all bones below the 18 foot level were coated and discolored. Chemical analysis will determine the nature of this action, which has seldom been observed in other mounds. On the 7th of April the trench wall, being nearly 15 feet in height, became dangerous and the earth caved in frequently. It was therefore sloped down by the men and four teams were put to work scraping the earth out and depositing it on the slopes to the north and south. Teams and scrapers were continued at work until about the 22nd of April when we again resorted to hand work to complete the trench.

Our total area excavated was about 100 feet north and south, and 35 feet east and west. Some area was lost since it became necessary to slope the walls (23 feet high) to prevent injury to our men. East and west, on top, the opening was about 45 feet—the base line narrower, as stated. In text Fig. 9, Part II, is shown a cross section made by Dr. Leighton. The scale indicates the thickness of the strata.

For some two weeks the men dug until the base line was exposed. On the west side of the trench opposite stakes 110 to 130 were a number of post holes 3 to 5 inches in diameter. The posts had decayed but traces of wood remained. There had been no fire at this point. The holes appeared to be part of a large circular edifice or wigwam, and were found at a depth of about 14 feet from the summit. Lying near one of them was a long double

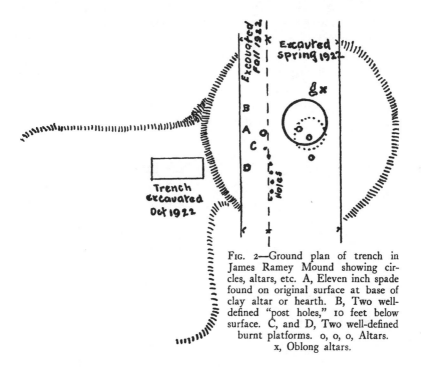

Fig. 2—Ground plan of trench in James Ramey Mound showing circles, altars, etc. A, Eleven inch spade found on original surface at base of clay altar or hearth. B, Two well-defined "post holes," 10 feet below surface. C, and D, Two well-defined burnt platforms. o, o, o, Altars. x, Oblong altars.

pointed flint knife which is shown in Plate X, Fig. 1. In the center of the cut was found the circular trench, and the circular post holes, and the altars or basins shown in text figures 2 and 3. These lay upon the base line about 23 feet from the summit.

Nothing just like these circles and basins have been previously found in mounds so far as the writer is aware. That is, there have been more perfect altars, and post holes arranged in circular form but not all of them in one place. Pl. XV, Fig. 1 shows the excavation, the circles being in the foreground; Pl. XV, Fig. 3 the two circles and depressions in the distance; and Pl. XIV, Fig. 2 a close view of the depressions or altars and the two circles. As the holes would not show clearly in a negative, corn stalk stubs were inserted to bring into sharper relief the holes. The men carefully hand troweled the entire space for a distance of 25 feet. In the center were two burnt basins or depressions which were filled with ashes.

Mr. Cowen has called them altars in his drawing, and they may be such. They vary from 17 to 26 inches in diameter and the depressions were four to seven inches in depth. They were not burned hard as are the Ohio altars. The one south of the circle contained nothing.

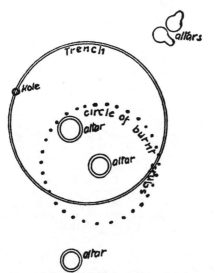

FIG. 3.—Plan of circular trench, altars, etc., in James Ramey Mound.

North of the circle were two shown near the top in Fig. 2, and these were of different form, rather shallow, and three-fourths circular. Instead of the circle being complete, the depression in one was extended to the east and in the other to the north. When uncovered, they were not unlike crude pans in appearance, the handles being rather short and the cavity in them not as deep as in the main body of the depression.

The trench was about 3 inches wide and 20 feet in diameter. It was nearly a true circle (Text Fig. 3). To form it the Indians dug out the earth to a depth of several inches and then filled it with dark soil so that the contrast was unmistakable. There was nothing in this trench—

not even ashes or charcoal. From the center of the sun symbol and extending south was a circle of post holes 2 to 3 inches in diameter. Probably saplings had been inserted and then the primitive wigwam burned, as there were great quantities of charred stubs and charcoal. In the center of this wigwam circle was a burnt basin and to the north-west lay another. Ashes from these two depressions were taken by Mr. Alfred C. Carr and analyzed for Mr. V. C. Turner of the Scullin Steel Company by Mr. L. Z. Slater.

"I enclose herewith complete qualitative and quantitative analysis of the samples you gave me. You will note there is a large quantity of silica. We could not account for this until the specimens were examined under a microscope and then it was found that small quantities of clay or sand had been washed down into and between the fibres of the specimens. It was impossible to take these off and therefore we have assumed that the silica was the particles which adhered to the fibre, together with part of the iron and alumina. The phosphoric acid, calcium carbonate, and magnesium carbonate, together with some of the alumina led us to assume that specimen must have been bone at one time, at least it could not have been wood-ash or charcoal.

"There was also another interesting discovery and that is that under fire test there is a trace of lithium. This leads us to believe that there was tobacco present among the bones and clay, as this lithium is always present in tobacco and it is hardly possible that it would be in any other substance that was placed in the receptacle where the samples were found."

V. C. Turner

"Following is the analysis of sample taken from James Ramey Mound:—

Silica (Si) 62.10
Iron and alumina (Ir & Al)........................25.15
   mostly oil 203
Phosphoric acid (P205)................................. .49
Calcium carbonate ($CaCO_3$)............................10.55
Magnesium carbonate ($MgCO_3$).................... 1.66

———————
99.95

Fire test shows trace of Lithium."

L. Z. Slater

Through an area of 25 feet, having as a center the altars, was a floor not very hard burnt, and yet beyond question a level surface on which fires had been built.

Sections of gas pipe were screwed together and with these the men were able to test to a depth of 15 or 20 feet with the augers. They thoroly tested the mound to the east and south of these circles. It was then thought that possibly there might be burials in the structure and that the altars and sun symbols occupied the center portion of the mound area. However, no burials could be discovered.

The various artifacts found during the course of exploration were kept in cigar boxes according to the levels at which they occurred. There was no particular difference in material to be noted except, possibly, the best pottery—that is the red ware and the sherds indicating thin, well made vessels—was found from 15 to 20 feet below the surface. Near the bottom there appeared to be more village site material, and at about 10 feet from the summit the preponderance of fragments indicating ordinary cooking vessels. Types of pottery fragments are shown on Plates V and VI.

Numerous photographs were taken at various stages of the work. About the 1st of May the walls were thrown in, and with the consent of the owners the mound was abandoned until fall. When we left, the excavation had the appearance of a crater about 100 feet in length, 60 feet in width, and 12 feet deep in the center.

September-October Operations.—On arrival at the James Ramey Mound in the fall of 1922, altho but four months had elapsed since the abandonment of the work in the spring, we noted that vegetation had sprung up in the depression. Visitors had attempted to dig, but fortunately we had left the mound in such shape that they could do no damage.

It was decided to work toward the west and extend the trench in that direction. Text figure 11 presents the total work done on the mound. When we completed operations the latter part of October, the total area excavated was 120 feet north and south and about 55 feet east and west. As the Temple Mound, No. 32, adjoined this structure, a deep pit was sunk to the bottom of that mound. The pit was about 25 feet from the western edge of our trench and was 14x8 feet in diameter at the bottom. This is shown in Fig. 2. While the teams lowered the mound to the bottom, the men sank the pit mentioned, and found the base line down about 17 feet. It was not thought necessary to excavate the space between the west wall of No. 33 and this pit, altho the augers were put down at many points. The usual village site debris extended clear to the bottom, but on the base line was a very heavy deposit of dark soil and ashes a few inches in thickness and here we observed much more village site material than in the other mound. It would appear that the Temple Mound was erected over a site occupied by a wigwam, for the mound was built directly on this part of the village site and none of the refuse had been cleaned up. Some thirty 7-inch auger holes were put to the bottom of No. 32, and decayed bones, burnt earth, etc., were found at several points. It might be advisable to trench this mound at some future time.

On October 12th but one team was retained and a party of sixteen men dug out the remainder of Mound 33 by hand. Another of these burnt basins was found near stake 130. This was about 20 inches in diameter and about 5 or 6 inches deep and was filled with charcoal. The west side of our trench, being somewhat beyond the center of the mound, was not over 19 feet in height. Stratification was not as well marked as observed last spring. There was a good deal of gumbo in the west wall and it was not necessary to slope the bank very much. A thin layer of pure sand about half an inch in thickness, which we had traced continuously from the north side of the old trench, extended in the mound but seemed to disappear a little south of the center.

The large post holes observed last spring in the west side of our trench did not continue regularly. Several more were observed but there was no special regularity and we therefore concluded that they did not represent a circular dwelling.

During the course of sinking the trench, part of a human femur some 6 inches in length, a vertebra, and two teeth were found, but there were no burials. Near stake 120, at a depth of 17 feet, was found a large flint spade about a foot in length. This is shown in Fig. 5, on Plate X. Nothing very important was found during the course of exploration save that a heavy layer of charcoal, in which was bark, extended to the south and south-west between stakes 130 and 140. When we ceased operations this layer continued in the walls, but as we had already spent a great deal of money on this mound the pit was not enlarged.

There was an even, burnt floor, and covered by a thin layer of white ash and above that large pieces of charcoal and charred wood. We estimated this layer to be some 3 feet above the base of the mound. At several points on the burnt floor were small, flat stones, irregularly shaped and apparently limestone, which had been subjected to heat. There were also many calcareous clay concretions. This platform or burnt floor with accompanying ashes and charcoal, we hand trowelled for a distance of nearly 20 feet. It still continued in the wall of our trench toward the southwest when we ceased work.

Conclusions on James Ramey Mound.—The circles have been called sun symbols, tho they may not be such, but that is our opinion. What led the Indians to construct such a mound, we do not know. It is often difficult for us to appreciate the aboriginal point of view. That certain ceremonies were here enacted we may believe, but the nature of these still remains a mystery.

A few notable objects found in the James Ramey Mound are shown on the plates. Two clay discs on Pl. XI, Figs 2, 4. Peculiar pottery designs on Pl. VII, Figs. 8, 9. Two bird head effigies on same plate, Figs. 5, 6. Two good bone awls on Pl. IX, Figs. 3, 7. A peculiarly cut foot bone of wapiti or American elk is shown in Fig. 12, on Pl. IX. A very finely-cut and decorated gorget shell of the spike river mussel *(Elliptio dilatatus)*, with evenly notched edges, probably used as a nose or ear ornament, is shown in Fig. 3, on Pl. VII. It was found at a depth of 20 feet, near stake 110. Broken projectile points and arrow heads are figured at 1, 6-8, 11, on Pl. XII. Marine mollusks, beads, and ornaments are shown on Pl. VIII. Most of the Cahokia beads are flat and not cylindrical.

THE JONDRO MOUND, No. 83

This was not put on the map which we inserted in our previous report (Vol. 19, No. 35, University of Illinois publications). In fact, Patrick, Van Court, and the other surveyors seem to have left out a number of small mounds. It lies nearly a mile and a half west of Monks, and is almost circular, being 140 ft. x 130 ft. A diagram is shown of it in Text Fig. 4. The surface is rather irregular and we

FIG. 4—Diagram of Tusant Jondro Mound. Sec. 34, Twp. Edgemont, St. Clair Co. Position of burials is indicated, the first burial being 75 feet from north edge of mound.

supposed originally the mound was conical and that it had been worked down during cultivation in the field, but the owner, Mr. Tusant Jondro, informs us that while his father had a garden on one side and he set out an orchard, the eastern half had never been cultivated. Therefore the structure, which now varies from four to six feet in elevation, could not have been much higher than at present. It might have served a double purpose, that is, for burials and later as an elevation on which wigwams were set.

Mr. Wm. J. Seever had charge of the work, and spent some time running a trench north and south through the entire mound, and another trench from the south end of the mound, northwest for 20 feet. He found twenty-four burials, and enough detached burials, or rather bodies so decayed that only a portion of skeletons were observed, to account for sixteen or seventeen more. In the north half of the mound there are probably many more burials. Mr. Jondro states that his father uncovered burials during the operations incident to tree planting or gardening. The cross section in Fig. 4 shows that at the north end there was an original mound 4 feet high, composed of buckshot gumbo. This was extremely hard digging, and nothing was found

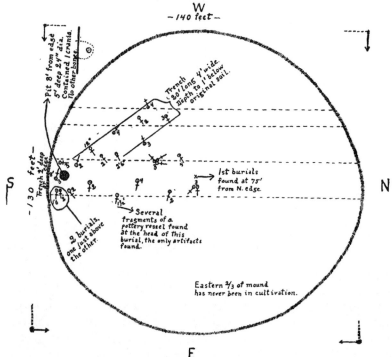

FIG. 5—Field plan of the Jondro Mound.

therein. In fact, in our excavations, survey members never found burials or much village site debris in gumbo soil, except the Chucallo Mound and this was not all gumbo.

The skeletons were headed in various directions, and no uniformity as to points of the compass was observed by the Indians. Excepting one skeleton noted on the map, no objects accompanied any of the burials (Text Fig. 5). Not enough pottery fragments were found with this burial to enable restoration. Every skeleton was badly decayed; in many instances it was impossible to remove even one-third of a femur or tibia.

About 200 feet north of the mound is a sunken depression from which earth and gumbo were taken for this mound; a similar one lies 175 feet south of the mound.

Sam Chucallo Mound

This is the last of the several tumuli in the corporate limits of East St. Louis and is not on the original map. It lies on the edge of a deep depression where the earth has been removed by the Pennsylvania Railway to make a filling. Cahokia Creek is 100 yards to the north. The distance from Sam's Mound to Monks Mound is something over 3 miles. The Pennsylvania excavation removed the western edge of the mound, up to where it was about 4 feet in height. The owner did not wish a large group of men to be put to work so he and another man were employed to dig a trench some 70 feet in length, 10 feet deep, and 8 feet in width (March-April, 1922). The mound was of very heavy gumbo, and unpromising. Very little village site material occurred save now and then a hammer stone and animal bones. A large flint spade was taken from the 7 foot level, somewhat east of the center of the mound. At the 9 foot level, near the center, Sam discovered a skeleton surrounded by a dome shaped mass of very black gumbo. The soil on either side and above this mass was somewhat lighter. Dr. M. M. Leighton of the University of Illinois was present when part of this skeleton was uncovered. After Dr. Leighton departed, the workmen uncovered 7 other skeletons lying on a little burnt bench about a foot above the bottom of the mound, or 9 feet from the surface. This find was made just west of the skeleton mentioned. Above the burials one could clearly observe a small mound of tough gumbo perhaps 4 feet in height. Apparently the burials were covered by this, and the rest of the mound added afterwards. A brick building (the residence of the owner) to the south somewhat disturbed the southern edge of the mound. In making the street a little of the east edge was removed, and the trolley tracks are flanked by a low bank on the north side of the mound. It is, therefore, difficult to give accurate measurements but we judge the mound to have been about 150 by 120 feet in diameter.

The seven skeletons referred to were bunched burials, all crushed by the heavy gumbo and many of the bones powdered so that they appeared like sawdust. This form of decay had not previously been observed, and several boxes full of disintegrated bones were taken for preservation. There were no objects with the burials. Undermining the bank to the south brought into view the feet of two more skeletons—better preserved and not bunched burials. Altho badly broken, as stated, the bones seemed unusually heavy. However, the owner did not wish explorations continued, and we were compelled to suspend work. We hope to complete work on this mound at some future time.

PITTSBURG LAKE CEMETERY

On the shores of Pittsburg Lake, about 6 miles southeast of Cahokia, a large cemetery was discovered when a new automobile road, known as the Louisiana Boulevard, was constructed a few years ago. Mr. H. Braun was present when the teams and scrapers at work on the boulevard uncovered the remains. He states there were 30 or 40 burials and he secured some 51 pottery vessels.

To ascertain whether this cemetery was of the Cahokia culture, we visited the site, paid the owner for two acres of wheat and began testing. We found a total of 13 skeletons in a space some 20 by 25 feet. With them were 11 pottery vessels, 6 of which were whole. The cemetery was thoroly trenched by us for several days, 6 workmen being employed, but we could discover no other interments.

The skeletons (save one) were badly decayed, due to the character of the soil, and most of them were near the surface. Our field notes are as follows:

Skeleton 38. Head south. Extended. Depth 3 ft.
Skeleton 39. Bowl, set with rim upwards.
Skeleton 40. Two pots. A detached skull. 3 awls were laid across a wide dish. Head south. Dish against the jar 2 inches from jar. One foot from surface. Well preserved. Body extended on back. Bone arrow point on face.

Skeleton 40. Depth 3 ft. Head east, and badly crushed.

Skeleton 41. Skeleton south. Decayed and broken, 24 ins. from surface.

Skeleton 42. Red pot with decayed skeleton. Pot in dish. Effigy head broken off. Some red paint. 20 in. down.

Skeleton 43. Small pot by head of a child. Very badly decayed. 18 in. down.

Skeleton 44. Young person, 2 pots. Head north. Badly decayed. Down 18 in.

Skeleton 46. 5 feet deep. Legs drawn up. 2 photos. No objects.

In several instances, near the head of the body was a large flat stone set in the grave. There were several of these, and they were smaller than the stone slabs forming the well known box graves of the middle South. Mr. Braun stated that this peculiarity was observed in many of the burials destroyed by the road construction crew. All pottery found was typical of the middle South, and did not exhibit any of the Cahokia decorations. A bone awl found with skeleton No. 39 is figured at 4 on Pl. IX.

MOUNDS 14 AND 84

Except the Kunnemann Mound, none lying north of Cahokia Creek had been examined by us. Therefore, in April, we trenched two of them.

NUMBER 14.—The field notes state, "About one-third mile north of Monks is a mound lying between old Cahokia and the present drainage canal. Years ago a road through the swamp passed along the crest of this structure. There is a sunken depression in the center of this mound from end to end. Dimensions, north and south 180 feet, east and west 110 feet. About 5 feet high. Composed of heavy gumbo. Very hard digging. Put 8 men to work. Sunk 10 pits each 4 feet deep; also used post augers for 3½ feet. A few pieces of stone, no pottery; some broken bones."

MACKIE MOUND, No. 84.—This is about 1¼ miles west of Monks Mound and is on the bank of old Cahokia Creek. It is covered by a heavy oak grove, has never been plowed, and is about 130 feet north and south and 10 feet high. It is surrounded on three sides by a swamp and

there is a long low platform, or apron, extending about 150
feet to the east. This platform varies from 3 to 5 feet high.
A trench was extended a distance of about 30 feet in the
mound down to within a few feet of the base line, then the
post augers brought into service. Numbers of pits were
sunk 3 or 4 feet in depth. With the exception of a few
scales of flint or chert and one pottery fragment, absolutely
nothing was found. The mound was composed of the
hardest kind of buckshot gumbo, with no sign of stratification. It is clear that no village existed at the point from
whence the earth was taken to build this mound, as there
are no broken artifacts to be observed in the soil.

SULLIVAN'S MOUNDS

Persons frequently called our attention to two mounds
on Signal Hill. These command a view of the American
Bottoms and in an air line are some four miles south of
the largest tumulus—Monks. We secured permission to
excavate from Judge J. D. Sullivan, both structures being
in his yard. The largest one when viewed and measured
from its base, is a low conical mound, 10 feet in height,
some 90 feet in diameter, nearly circular at the base line,
very symmetrical in the contour line, not differing, when
viewed from the slope on which it is erected, from similar
ones in the Cahokia Mound region (Text Fig. 6). Excavations of a trench some 6 feet wide through the east and
west axis, carried down to and below its base, revealed,
however, a very unusual mound construction or building.
Instead of beginning upon the original surface and upbuilding from there, as they usually did, the builders of
this tumulus reversed the procedure, by excavating a bowl-
like depression apparently the diameter or size of the
structure afterwards to be erected. This excavation, rather
uneven on the floor line, a few inches in depth at its outer
edges, increasing in depth until at or near the center, it
attained a maximum depth of 18 inches. Into this bowl-
like depression, numerous oval and circular pits were dug,
in depth from 2 or 3 to 18 inches; in diameter from 12
inches, to the largest encountered, of 5 feet 2 inches. Nine

of these pits were located in the floor of the trench (with traces of others on outer sides of the trench) ; these were thoroly "cleaned out", and accompanied clearly definite strata of white or gray ashes, mixed with charcoal, in very dark and loose loamy soil, numerous pieces of broken pottery or earthenware, some animal and bird bones, quantities of small irregular broken stones showing discoloration from heat, one battered and broken grooved granite axe, several defective celts, hammer stones, and unio shells mingled with the dark colored earth of the pits.

From one pit were taken two highly specialized bone implements some 4 in. long (Pl. IX, Figs. 5, 6). From

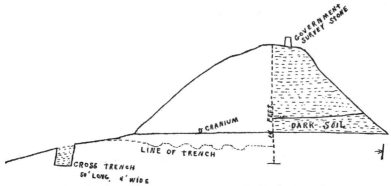

Fig. 6—Mound on bluffs east of East St. Louis, on Judge Sullivan's land. Excavated Oct. 5, 6, 9, 10, 1922.

another, two perforated bone beads, and from another a fragment of quartz crystal, and a small specimen of worked hematite.

Apparently, the entire floor or bowl-like depression of this structure contains similar pits or depressions, since edges of others were noted in the trench.

The loess formation, of which these uplands largely consist, being of an almost bright yellow color, the least discoloration or excavation therein, and subsequent filling in of foreign material is instantly and plainly discernable and easily followed.

Seemingly these pits had been used either as hearth, or for purposes of cremation. Then the bowl-like depression was filled in with a dark soil or earth to the original surface and on top of this the mound was erected, the latter being a mixture of light and dark colored earths.

Directly east of this mound some 250 feet was a smaller tumulus removed some years since during the erection of a residence. Numerous pottery fragments were taken therefrom, and an entire pot or vase; it could not be ascertained if there were any human remains.

THE KRUGER BONE BANK

At the point marked burial and village site on the map near the lower left hand corner, is a long low ridge flanking a depression in which, in former times, there was considerable water. Old residents state that before the present drainage system was inaugurated, there were many fish in this depression, and that it was connected with the pond to the east.

Along the sandy ridge burials had been made by Indians, and both Mr. Kruger and the owner who preceded him had dug up skeletons. He permitted excavations and about a dozen men sank test pits here for two days. None of the burials were more than 3 feet in depth, and most of them within 20 inches of the surface. There were fragmentary skeletons indicating disturbances. Doctor James Terry of Washington University took one or two of the best ones to the medical school for observation. The rest were left in the ground. We did not excavate the entire area as the burials were accompanied by no objects and did not appear to be of special importance. Some 16 bodies were found.

It is well to remark in passing that these scattered burials and little cemeteries are found throughout the entire Cahokia area.

THE HARDING MOUND, No. 66

This is one of the finest mounds of the entire group. It is about 550 feet in length, and at the base line about 125 feet north and south. It stands out very prominently, and appears to the eye at least 40 feet in height, altho it may be less. At several points pits were dug by hand to a depth of 12 to 17 feet. In the bottoms of these pits the augers were put down to a depth of 22 feet. That is as far as it is possible to test with the augers. Seven inch cores were obtained from these testings, and studied. The mound appears to be stratified, but there was little village site debris to be found at the different levels.

Our auger testing was rather unsatisfactory, and we were not able to determine whether the mound contained interments. On a structure so long and narrow, it does not seem possible that wigwams would be placed. In the event of its use for house sites, the dwellings would be of restricted diameter, and placed in a long row. Such arrangement is unusual in Indian villages.

This mound has never been cultivated and is well preserved. Explorations by means of tunnels have been suggested. Such a procedure would not injure the contour, and its character could thus be determined if a tunnel were extended through the long diameter, and in addition several cross section tunnels at various points. This structure is one of the same form as the Powell Mound, but of shorter base. Like the Powell Mound its long axis lies east and west, and that similarity has given rise to various conjectures on the part of observers.

Mrs. Tippetts' Mound, No. 61

This is an oval mound located between the two ponds on land owned by Mrs. William Tippetts. Externally it is rather promising, and as it is shaped not unlike altar mounds of the Ohio Valley, the survey decided to test it. Much to our surprise we found it composed of exceedingly heavy, black gumbo. Two pits were sunk and by means of the augers we tested to the base, a distance of 20 feet. Very little in the way of material was encountered. The mound appeared to be unstratified. The ground was so hard it required the united efforts of six strong workmen to put down six auger holes in three days time. The structure is placed on the "reserved list" for future exploration. Gumbo can be more easily excavated in February or March, as after winter rains and snow it is soft.

THE MITCHELL MOUNDS

Several observers, who have visited the Cahokia region in past years, have included the group of mounds at Mitchell Station under the general descriptions applying to Cahokia. Whether these mounds are culturely a part of Cahokia itself can be determined by exploration. Since copper and other forms similar to finds made in the Ohio mounds and along the Illinois river were discovered at the time the Chicago and Alton Railroad cut through one of the mounds (about 1871), it is suggested that the Mitchell group of mounds may have been erected by another tribe. In the Illinois valley itself platform or monitor pipes, copper ear bobs, and copper hatchets and plates have been found, and the mouth of the Illinois river is not more than thirty-five miles from the Cahokia group. It should be remembered that these observations are based on specimens in private or public collections secured during the course of superficial explorations on the part of workers who left us neither field notes nor photographs.

Owners of the Mitchell mounds have given consent for exploration of one or two of the structures next March, and the survey looks forward with anticipation to this work. After its completion we will be able to determine the relationship of the builders of the Mitchell group to those of Cahokia.

Dr. J. F. Snyder of Virginia, Illinois, in his various papers (see bibliography) has given us some light on prehistoric Indian occupation of the State. Granting full credit to Dr. Snyder and all others, one is justified in the assertion that we know little concerning aboriginal inhabitants of the great State. Inspection of the many collections seems to indicate that we have at least three, and possibly four, tribes or cultures of stone age times, yet nothing definite can be ascertained until thoro explorations and studies are undertaken. Beyond question Illinois offers one of the most attractive fields in the United States for research work. Its primitive people may have been affected by contact with, or knowledge of, the Plains Tribes. The relationship between bands of Indians living in the northern part of the state along the lake to those of the Illinois valley; whether the Indians living along the Wabash are of the same stock as those from the Illinois River region, and the lake front; or the cultural status of those occupying the extreme southern portion of Illinois— all these and many other questions are of the greatest importance and one is free to affirm that our present reliable information is so meager that we are unable to formulate even preliminary observations.

The Collinsville-Edgemont Bluffs

Flanking the east side of the American Bottoms are the high bluffs frequently referred to. McAdams, Patrick, and others seem to have secured most of their better specimen (pipes, bicaves, and long chipped objects) from graves, small mounds, or sites on these promontories. Local collectors affirm that the entire range of high-land flanking the river from Alton to Cairo is one vast, ancient cemetery. Mr. E. W. Payne, whose agents have collected extensively in that region, estimate that thousands of various implements, ornaments, and utensils have here been gathered. Skeletons are plowed up every spring and fall. A thoro investigation of the remains on these bluffs should be made at some future time.

VILLAGE SITE OBSERVATIONS

On our large map are several areas marked "Village Site." Readers should not conclude that wigwams existed merely at those places. Such markings indicate that at certain points we dug pits and found the indications of occupation extended several feet into the ground. We believe that all the area was occupied except a space south of the National road. This is bounded on the west by tumuli 68 and 70, on the south by 66 and 65, on the east by 64 and 62, and on the north by 77. We did not test very extensively in this area but where we did so, little was found.

The land lying west of Sand Prairie Road belongs to George Merrell, Esq., and for nearly half a mile, until Mr. Recklein's property is reached, is leased by Mr. Stolle. Throughout this land, from 1500 to 2500 feet west of Monks Mound, we found indications of a heavily populated village. Varying from 12 inches to 4 feet in depths, the soil was disturbed, and the usual pottery fragments, bones of animals, ashes, unio shells, hammer stones, spalls, etc., were present. The Stolle land was tested in October. We then examined properties to the south, owned by Mrs. Tippetts, Mr. Wells, and Mr. Cole. Beyond Stolle's land, to the west of the Recklein land, the Village Site continued for more than a quarter of a mile, and is said to extend through the property owned by Mrs. Thomas. She was one of the very few persons in the Cahokia region who would not permit us to excavate. Her workmen, however, said that pottery vessels and bones were dug up when they sank post holes. We have proved, by continued testing, that the village extended from over a third of a mile northeast of Monks Mound to the edge of Mrs. Thomas' land, all of which parallels Cahokia Creek. This is a total extent of over a mile and a half. Just how far north of Cahokia Creek the village existed, we do not know, but we presume about a quarter of a mile.

THE WELLS'-TIPPETTS' VILLAGE SITE

The tests on the Ramey heirs' lands, so far as village sites are concerned, were completed last year. Plates II, IV, V, VI, IX, and XI illustrate different artifacts from the Ramey Village Site. Fig. 6 on Pl. 5 is decidedly Algonquin. Numbers of specimens containing this decoration were found. When our pottery collection is larger we may be able to shed some light on the mingling of forms and designs, a few of which do not appear to be southern.

This fall, the survey did not sink additional pits, but on Mrs. Tippetts' estate, south of Monks, and on the adjoining property owned by Mr. Cole, and Mr. Wells, much work was done. Mr. Allen had leased land of Mr. Wells and he permitted us to work extensively with 8 or 10 men on an area lying 100 to 200 yards south of Mound 51. Here the village debris was as heavy as at any point on the Ramey lands. There were several low mounds (74, 75, and 55). In No. 75 much burnt clay was discovered, also lumps in which were impressions of reeds and sticks,—doubtless the walls of dwellings.

Stone celts, bone awls, arrow points, and beads were found in the Wells site. Some of these are figured on Plates II, IV, VII, IX, XI, XII, and XVI. On Pl. X, a shouldered hoe and two spades from field southwest of Monks Mound, are figured (Figs. 2-4).

THE STOCK YARDS SITE

In the Smithsonian Report for 1866 (pp. 346-350), Dr. Charles Rau presents the first description of pottery from the Cahokia region. His observations were quoted in our preliminary report[1] and need not be repeated here.

We visited lower Cahokia Creek, and found it very difficult to conduct field operations. In Rau's time, East St. Louis was a small place, and the stock yards not extensive. Today, the buildings, pens, tracks, streets, etc., comprising that great industry, must cover at least 500 acres. We were able to discover but one open tract, and

[1]*University of Illinois Bulletin*, Volume 19, No. 35, pp. 25-27.

that bordered Cahokia Creek, and was at the end of a short thorofare called Bogard Street, and some 300 yards west of St. Clair Avenue. Here was an acre and a half of land upon which no buildings had been erected. The creek bank is some 12 or 15 feet in height. The place had been used as a city dump, and it was necessary to remove debris before original surface was reached. We could not identify the clay bank to which Rau referred, but did find thick pottery, and one or two sections of bowls which appeared to be unfinished. A piece of pottery with peculiar design, resembling in outline a large beetle or water bug, is shown on Pl. XI, Fig. 3.

Observations were rather unsatisfactory. In 1866 the creek water was clear; there were unio shells present; also one could walk along the foot of the bank for a considerable distance. Rau had no trouble in locating the clay deposit from which the women secured material for pottery making. Much of the creek bed is filled with sewage, waste, chemicals from the factories and stock yards, and the bank is now sloping.

Probably at the time of his observations he was able to select the best section for study. We assume that this was up the creek from where we worked. It is proposed next year to send two men from Monks Mound westward along either bank of Cahokia Creek, and test all places not yet covered by buildings. The old bed east of the corporate limits of East St. Louis is now filled with vegetation. Probably as late as 1875, work could have been satisfactorily carried on along the creek, for a distance of about 4 miles; now most traces of Indian occupation have been obliterated.

We see no reason to doubt that the entire southern bank of Cahokia was occupied by the ancient people. From the fartherest eastern extent of the village site, down Cahokia Creek to the Stock-yards site is about six miles.

In last spring's report we estimated the territory covered by cabins or wigwams to be 1000 acres. How far back from the creek, both north and south, habitations extended, we do not know, but we assume variations in width due to the configuration of the site, ponds, etc., interfering. Actual testing proves above 1,000 acres of occupation. If the creek bank was inhabited through the present site of East St. Louis, the total should be given at 2000 and possibly 2500 acres.

The extent of the prehistoric village located at the great group of stone ruins in New Mexico, known as the Chaco, has not been stated. So far as the writer's observations extend, he neither knows of, nor has read concerning any village equal in extent to that at Cahokia. And the more we excavate, the more area we include in our estimates.

TESTING THE BOTTOMS OF THE PONDS

The presence of chipped objects and pottery fragments in the muck in the several ponds surrounding the Cahokia Group gave rise to the suggestion that possibly (but not probably) the Indians built houses on piles over the water. Four men were put to work in October testing the bottom of two or three of these depressions. A dredging apparatus similar to oyster tongs was made, and the workmen lowered the tongs from a flat bottomed boat, and continued dredging for about two days. Where the water was shallow, they waded and made use of an ordinary garden rake. The result of the test was not satisfactory. The bottom is rather smooth, not irregular, and slippery. While numbers of artifacts were brought up, the tongs slipped over others. Our work was not completed but we came to the conclusion that there is not sufficient material to indicate that Indians had built dwellings over the water, and furthermore, in a dry season such as last Fall, there would not be sufficient water to afford protection. Two of the large depressions were dry, and the survey was able to test them with augers and shovels. Little material was secured.

The Ramey brothers claim that when they were boys, two of these ponds contained water throughout the year, were deeper, and such fish as crappie, bass, and buffalo were taken frequently. A more careful search, extending over a greater length of time, might give different results, but at the present writing, we are of the opinion that artifacts were either lost or thrown in the ponds by the Indians.

PREVIOUS WORK AND COLLECTIONS RELATING TO THE CAHOKIA GROUP

DR. PATRICK

Dr. A. J. R. Patrick, Belleville, Illinois, was one of the pioneers in Cahokia work. The survey called on his widow, who is now Mrs. John Bauman. She showed us some field notes written by Dr. Patrick, in 1877. November 18, of that year, he visited Monks Mound, and did some exploring in the vicinity. Again, on April 7, 1878, April 6, 1879, and May 11 and 12, 1879, Dr. Patrick dug in numbers of places along Cahokia Creek, and in the low mounds. His observations, for the most part, were confined to burials, within 4 feet of the surface, since he used a slender, steel rod, by means of which he sounded for bones, pottery, or stone. This method of testing has been employed for many years by collectors, and others, and is possible when soil is free from stone. The rods will not penetrate hard gumbo, but in the late winter, or early spring, the rods penetrate easily to a depth of 4 feet. One is able to distinguish by feeling with these rods stone from pottery, bone or decayed wood from layers or sections of hard earth. The use of the rod in the Mississippi Valley burial places, (where the soil is favorable) has been so extensive that a large percentage of all burials near the surface have been reached. Most of the large collections of pottery vessels were secured in the manner described.

Dr. Patrick, in the field notes, states that in a small mound east of Monks, he found a floor of clay. In the center there was a depression, or basin. On the slopes of mounds and in one or two low mounds he found some effigy pottery, portraying frog, deer, bear, fish, and duck, but unfortunately, he does not give us the numbers and we cannot identify the mounds he explored. In one of his notes, he does not think the large mounds were used for burial places. He suggests the theory that they were made in order that dwellings might be elevated above the plain. He considered the ponds as artificial. On April 6, 1879, he found a skeleton and pottery, also a skull, which he calls No. 3, accompanied by a copper plate. Mrs. John Bauman says this plate was sent to the Smithsonian Institution. A letter from Dr. Neil M. Judd, Curator of Archeology, informs the writer that he cannot locate the copper specimen in the Smithsonian collections.

Mrs. Bauman has in her possession several field maps, and a profile survey of the group. She says that the first survey was executed Nov. 5, 1876, and that the profile survey was made July 5, 1879, and that Louis Gainer Kahn, a surveyor, either made this survey, or assisted on it. She thinks there were several surveys, more or less thoro, made of the Cahokia mounds in the period between 1870 and 1888.

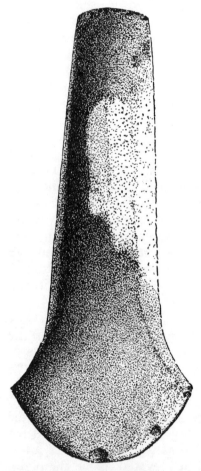

FIG. 7—Large polished celt or hatchet in Peabody Museum. Half natural size.

SPECIMENS FROM CAHOKIA

After considerable investigation we were able to trace the location of a number of Cahokia objects. Most of these were found many years ago and the exact circumstances of discovery are not available. The interesting local collection on exhibition in the museum of Monticello Seminary, Godfrey, Illinois, was made by William McAdams probably 25 to as far back as 40 years ago. Some of the objects in this collection appear to have been in the hands of other owners for some time.

The largest private collection of material from Indiana, Illinois, Kentucky, and Missouri is that owned by E. W. Paine of Springfield, Illinois. Mr. Payne has many objects from mounds, graves, and the surface of the Cahokia district and a radius of 10 miles about it. His collection is packed away and it is impossible to secure photographs or descriptions.

In the Peabody Museum is a large polished celt, or hatchet. This is shown in Text Fig. 7. This was chipped from very fine, highly colored flint—dark brown and yellow, with a suggestion of pink in the coloring. The specimen was then carefully ground and polished until all depressions made by flaking were removed. Mr. Charles C. Willoughby, Director, called my attention to this specimen. The catalog stated that it was secured from Monks Mound about 1873. This was six years prior to Professor Putnam's visit to the mounds.

Fig. 8, Plate XVI, shows a very large axe 12x17 inches, weight 17 pounds. It was found near the Kunnemann Mound. There is a low mound just west of the Kunnemann, No. 12, from which a large number of large unfinished celts have been secured. Mr. Seever obtained a number of these for the Missouri Historical Society collection years ago. The small hematite axe (Pl. XVI, Fig. 7) was also found near the Kunnemann Mound, on the surface.

Plate XVII, Figs. 1-5 show five pipes, three of which are effigies. No. 1 is a large frog effigy pipe from a grave on the bluffs east of Cahokia. No. 2 is a human effigy pipe found near Cahokia. No. 5 is a pipe of sandstone, from the region, exact locality not given. No. 3, a clay pipe from a grave near Cahokia. No. 4 is probably a bird effigy, altho the workmanship is not very good.

Plate XVII, Fig. 8 is a sandstone effigy pipe, large. Shown ⅓ size. Found with a burial in the cemetery on the bluffs between the two sugar loaf mounds, known as Group 3, Madison County, Illinois. William J. Seever collection.

Plate XVII, Figs. 6, 7, show two stone idols from the Monticello Seminary collection. Number 7 is of fluorspar and about 12 inches high. It was found on the bluffs directly east of Cahokia. Number 6 is of red material, almost pipestone, is about 18 inches high, exceedingly well made and came from a small mound, one of the Cahokia Group, on the Caseyville Road, St. Clair County, Illinois. Unfortunately the number of the mound is not given.

Plate XVIII. Two sea shells and a string of shell beads. The string of shell beads (Fig. 1) and the shell vessel (Fig. 2) were taken from the Mitchell Mound at the time it was destroyed by the Chicago and Alton R. R. in the winter of 1876. The shell (Fig. 3) shown for comparison, was found in a mound in Jersey County. They are shown ¼ size.

Plate XVI, Figs. 2-6. Shell spoons and bone awls (Fig. 1) from cemeteries south and west of Cahokia. Collection of William J. Seever. Broken unio shells with scalloped edges have frequently been found by the survey and were identical with those shown in this picture.

Plate XVIII, Fig. 4. Attention is called to this remarkable art-object. It portrays the height of efficiency in flint-chipping. Found by Mr. Barth, a tenant of the Rameys, south of Monks Mound, in December, 1921, on the surface. Shown full size.

OBSERVATIONS ON THE SEASON'S WORK

Comparison of the map presented in this bulletin with that published in our preliminary paper (Vol. XIX, No. 35) will indicate that we have added many more mounds, the last one being No. 84. We have also included burial places and such areas of village site as were excavated. In addition to these 84 mounds there is one lying in the edge of East St. Louis, those of East St. Louis which were destroyed, mounds south of East St. Louis, those about Horseshoe Lake, and Mitchell. Including these, together with the mounds on the bluffs in the vicinity of Edgemont and Collinsville, there must have been a grand total of at least 125 mounds within 10 miles of the dominant structure known as Monks. At some future time all of these will be mapped and then we shall know the exact number.

The work of the past two seasons would indicate that some of the mounds are older than others. This is not made as a definite statement but such is our opinion. It is based on that fact that such tumuli as Nos. 84, 66, 61, and 39 contain very few pottery fragments, bones or broken stone. Other mounds such as Nos. 33, 32, 30 (which is really a part of 31), 76, and 11 (Kunnemann), on excavation were found to be composed of earth taken from a populous village site. The mounds in which very little material occurred were chiefly composed of black gumbo. An exception should be noted in the case of No. 66 (the Harding Mound), which was tested so superficially that even preliminary observations are scarcely in order.

It must be remembered that our augers took out cores from 6 to 7 inches in diameter, and altho they were frequently put down, yet the area these cores represent is but a minute portion of the structure as a whole. In the case of a trench or pit much more satisfactory observations are possible, yet pits in the large mounds are expensive and trenches even more so. Hence the use of augers as these would determine whether a mound was stratified. Obviously, augers might penetrate within a foot of either a burial or an altar containing objects, or a deposit of artifacts, and we would not know that such existed in the mound unless the auger cores when brought up included either bones or some other objects. Hence, construed technically, a mound may not be said to be properly tested if we depend on the auger cores for our information. It seemed to us, however, in view of the number of times these augers penetrated to the bases of mounds, that were burials or deposits of objects numerous they would have been encountered in some of the borings.

Since none of the very large mounds, notably 57, 60, 48, 5, 58, 41, and 42, were examined, it is possible that the interments are in these or in No. 38 (Monks). It is a question whether these largest ones could be tested by means of the augers. Probably tunnels will be necessary.

Considering that some of the mounds contain much refuse material scattered through the earth and others almost none, it would seem that two explanations might be offered. First, that the earth was taken from spaces on which had stood no cabins. Second, that these mounds were among the first constructed and when the village population was restricted. The fact that much material is found in mounds in which gumbo does not predominate might indicate that the natives did not place their cabins or wigwams on gumbo soil at that particular time, yet we do find a great deal of surface indication directly south of the largest mound, where gumbo soil predominates. Our explorations have not progressed sufficiently to determine positively this and other questions with any degree of finality, yet what little light we have been able to shed on the past would indicate that certain mounds were built before there was much population at Cahokia. Furthermore, it does not seem possible that all the mounds would have been constructed within a few years. There must have been a gradual, more or less systematic mound construction epoch covering a considerable length of time and quite likely several generations.

The soil around Mrs. Tippett's Mound (61) is mostly gumbo; the village site indications are not heavy, but several hundred yards north, where there is less gumbo, the village was thickly populated. It does not seem likely that the Indians would go any distance to secure the earth for the construction of No. 61. It would be more convenient to obtain it from points nearby and the two depressions marked "lakes" on the map probably represent the places from which earth was taken for 61 and 62, and probably for other mounds. A similar argument would apply to No. 84 located in an unfavorable spot for a village site, but it would not apply to others of the mounds. It will require a very careful study and comparison, as well as more research in the way of excavation, to determine these points. Whether it will be possible in the future to assign dates is quite problematical. Certainly the pits and trenches are sufficiently extensive to have brought to light objects of European manufacture had the Cahokia people lived here during the historic period. We are safe in assuming that the Cahokia Mounds are prehistoric, for not one single tool, weapon, ornament, or vessel of white man's make has been taken from any one of our hundreds of pits.

THE IMMENSITY OF CAHOKIA

After three seasons of exploration and considerable study, that which impresses one most is the immensity of Cahokia. That there is no mound group to compare with it north of Mexico is quite obvious. As the survey continues and extends its operations it becomes more and more evident that it will require considerable time and a great deal of work in order to secure sufficient data and specimens to reconstruct the ancient life of the Cahokia builders. One might not go far afield if he claimed that notwithstanding the amount of actual digging—there has been considerable—that the survey has but begun the real exploration of this place. Beyond question, the population was extensive—how numerous, we do not know, but certainly many thousands of Indians lived hereabout. According to the funeral customs of all mound building tribes previously studied elsewhere in the United States, the most artistic and valuable objects were placed with the dead. That the survey has unearthed so little material is not to the writer discouraging, neither does it tend to imply that such material did not exist. On the contrary it is quite evident that we have not investigated the tombs in which the ranking personages of Cahokia were interred. Continued research will bring them to light.

NOTES ON CAHOKIA SKELETONS

By Dr. R. J. Terry

Washington University, St. Louis, Mo.

Skeleton No. 28. Cemetery in mounds 19, 20, 21. Skull, most of the vertebrae and ribs, parts of the sternum, fragments of scapulae, clavicles, right humerus, parts of both radii and ulnae, some hand bones, fragments of hip bones, both femora and right tibia, parts of both fibulae, some bones of the feet. Skeleton was found two feet beneath the surface; extended, head to the east, face upward. A univalve shell was found beneath the chin; five rough flints around the neck; a piece of sandstone marked with two straight grooves on opposite surfaces, a small bone spatula, pieces of ochre, and soft red hematite upon the chest. The bones are fragile, very dry, and porous. The cranium lacks the basioccipital and sphenoid; is symmetrical, broad, and high. Marked occipital taurus, tendency toward keeling of vertex; beginning closure of sagittal suture. Teeth much worn; incisors lost; lower molars all shed. Glabello-occipital length 16.8 cm.; greatest breadth 14.2 cm.; height 12.3 cm.; bigoniac breadth of mandible 9.8 cm. Clavicles slender, curved, right measures 14.7 cm.; right humerus, maximum length 30.7 cm.; right radius 24.1 cm.; right femur, maximum length 42.6 cm. Shape of shaft prismatic: platymeria marked. Right tibia presents shape of shaft No. 5 (Hrdlicka) length 34.5 cm. (medial malleolus lost); platycnaemy marked; retroversion of head slight.

Skeleton No. 29. Cranium large, broad and high; not well enough preserved to give trustworthy measurements. Marked asymmetry apparently post-mortem; vertex reaches highest point at obelion; sagittal suture closed. Slight keeling of vertex. Occipital taurus prominent. Bigoniac breadth 10.8 cm.; teeth much worn; shovel-shaped incisors; left lower canine, three ridged. Right clavicle slender, curved, length 15.8 cm. Humeri perforated; left large, right medium. Left humerus maximum length 32.1 cm.

Femora moderately platymeric; shape cylindrical to prismatic. Right bone maximum length 45.8 cm.; tibiae show pathological enlargement in diameters of shafts; head of left bone roughened, marked retroversion in right and obscure facet at lower anterior margin. All of the bones are very brittle and dry. A male skeleton.

Skeleton No. 1 consists of only a cranial fragment including face and frontal bone, left parietal and temporal. Very dry and fragile. Apparently a high cranium. Slight tendency to keeling. Dental alveoli all present; wisdom teeth not erupted: incisors and canines present lateral ridges.

Skeleton No. 100. Skull only, taken from cemetery at Pittsburg Lake. Well preserved. Glabello-occipital length 17.4 cm.; greatest breadth 13.6 cm.; height 19.4 cm. No tendency to keeling. No occipital taurus. Sagittal suture open; coronal obliterated inferiorly. Chin pointed, bigoniac breadth 8.8 cm.; teeth much worn. Evidently the skull of a woman.

The skulls excepting No. 100 have the highest point of the vertex about the obelion with a steep slant to the glabella. This head form is also strikingly marked in an endocranial cast that was obtained by lifting away the fragile bones of the cranium from the hard mass of gumbo which completely filled the cranial cavity. A plaster replica of this earth cast has been made and will be the subject of future study.

PART II

THE GEOLOGICAL ASPECTS OF SOME OF THE CAHOKIA (ILLINOIS) MOUNDS

BY

MORRIS M. LEIGHTON

Illinois Geological Survey

State Geological Survey Division
March 1, 1923

Dr. David Kinley
   President, University of Illinois

Dear President Kinley:

The accompanying report on a geological investigation of Cahokia mounds by Dr. M. M. Leighton, undertaken at your suggestion, is transmitted for your information and for publication if desired.

The interest attaching to the mounds, and particularly the movement to include them in a state park, made it desirable to supplement the archeological investigations of Dr. W. K. Moorehead with those of a specialist in surficial geology, in order that all possible light might be thrown on the origin of the mounds. While there has been a decided difference of opinion, and casual consideration of the problem would lead a geologist to assume, tentatively, that the mounds are natural remnants of an alluvial terrace which has been mostly removed by erosion, the careful scrutiny of the excavations, supplemented by systematic auger borings and study of the oxidation and leaching of the materials in the mounds and under the surrounding flood plain, makes it clear that the mounds so far investigated are artificial rather than natural. Others which have not been studied may prove to be natural, but I am not justified in expressing an opinion in advance.

The careful observations and deductions by Dr. Leighton supplemented by my own less extensive studies may lead to a conclusion harmonious with that of Dr. Moorehead. I am glad to transmit the results of Dr. Leighton's efforts and to express the hope that the State may acquire and preserve these interesting and significant relics of a settlement and civilization in Illinois far back of anything recorded in the history of man.

Very respectfully yours,

F. W. DeWolf, *Chief*
State Geological Survey

INTRODUCTION

THE PROBLEM

For many years there has been a difference of opinion as to whether the group of mounds northeast of East St. Louis, on the American Bottom of the Mississippi River, has had a natural mode of origin, or whether they represent the work of mound-builders. Monks Mound has been pointed out by some as being the largest Indian Mound in North America, if not in the world, while others have insisted that it is natural.

In September, 1921, excavations were started in the smaller mounds by Professor Warren K. Moorehead, Archeologist, of Andover, Massachusetts, and continued for two months under the joint auspices of the University of Illinois and the Illinois State Museum Division. The following spring and fall of 1922, the exploratory work was assumed entirely by the University.

The excavations afforded an excellent opportunity for a geologic examination of the materials composing the mounds, and in this work the State Geological Survey Division cooperated. The writer was requested to undertake the geological work. Five visits of about two days each were made at advantageous times for inspection, and the data for the following report were collected.

ACKNOWLEDGMENTS

The writer wishes to express his sincere thanks to the Ramey family, owners of Monks Mound and other mounds; to Mr. Schmidt, owner of the Schmidt Mound, and to Mr. Kunnemann, owner of the Kunnemann Mound, for the privileges they extended and their hearty spirit of cooperation; to Professor Warren K. Moorehead for his contribution of men for certain manual labor necessary to the study; to Curator Frank C. Baker, of the Museum of Natural History, University of Illinois, for his identification of fossil shells found in the mounds and the east bluffs; and to Professor W. S. Bayley of the Department of Geology, University of Illinois, for his identification of certain rock materials. The writer also acknowledges his indebtedness and gratitude to F. W. De-Wolf, Chief of the Illinois Geological Survey, who by his discussions and suggestions contributed scientifically to the success of the study.

FORMER OPINIONS OF GEOLOGISTS REGARDING THE ORIGIN OF THE MOUNDS

In searching the literature for opinions regarding the origin of the mounds, the writer has been careful to select those of geologists, rather than those of archeologists, inasmuch as the supreme motive of the former is to critically study and properly interpret land forms and the materials of the earth, while the archeologists are interested primarily in the physical, mental, and social characteristics and activities of pre-historic man.

The Views of G. W. Featherstonhaugh, F.R.S., F.G.S.—During his travels in 1834 and 1835 from Washington, D. C., to the frontier of Mexico, the English geologist, G. W. Featherstonhaugh, visited the Cahokia mounds, and gave his account in his book, "Excursions in the Slave States," Vol. I, 1844, pp. 266-270. Featherstonhaugh evidently did not doubt the human origin of the mounds, for he offered no suggestions to the contrary and definitely states that "the soil of which the mound consists is the rich black mould taken from the surface below. . . ." (p. 268).

The Views of Professor A. H. Worthen.—As early as 1866, the natural theory of the origin of the mounds received the support of a no less reputable geologist than Professor A. H. Worthen, Director of the Geological Survey of Illinois. Professor Worthen, in Volume I of the Geological Survey of Illinois, page 314, considered the mounds as "proof" that the Mississippi Valley had been filled to a height of 50 or 60 feet above its present level and that this was "in part removed by subsequent erosion during the period of elevation and drainage that succeeded the drift epoch." Artificial exposures in the large mound in the upper part of the city of St. Louis, now destroyed, were examined by him, and these showed about 15 feet of common chocolate brown drift clay at the base, overlaid by 30 feet or more of "the ash colored marly sands of the loess, the line of separation between the two deposits remaining as distinct and well defined as they usually are in good artificial sections in the railroad cuts through these deposits."

From this he inferred that the "mounds are not artificial elevations .... but, on the contrary, they are simply outliers of loess and drift, that have remained as originally deposited, while the surrounding contemporaneous strata are swept away by denuding forces."

It seems pertinent to call attention to the fact that the science of Glacial Geology was scarcely beyond its embryonic state at this time, and but little more could be claimed for the sciences of Physiography and Sedimentation.

The Views of William McAdams.—William McAdams, a teacher and careful observer of natural science, including geological phenomena, regarded Monks Mound (called by him Cahokia Mound) as of artificial origin. In his pamphlet, "Antiquities of Cahokia, or Monk's Mound in Madison County, Illinois," Edwardsville, Illinois, 1883, pages 2-3, he says:

"Since some doubts have been expressed as to the artificial origin of this structure we were much interested to ascertain what could be learned in this respect by examination. On the top of the pyramid are the remains of a house, said to have been commenced by the monks, but afterwards added to and finished as a comfortable residence for the family of a man named Hill, an enterprising settler who owned the mound and a large body of land adjoining. Beneath this house is a deep unwalled cellar. A section down the side of the cellar to the depth of ten feet very plainly revealed a deposit of various kinds of earth without stratification. The principal part of this deposit was the black humus or mould, so common in the bottom and forming the principal soil, very sticky when wet and breaking into cubical blocks when dry. Here and there, as if thrown promiscuously among the black mould, is a bunch of yellow clay, or sand, or marly loess, these bunches being about such size as a man could easily carry.

"Similar sections can be seen up the old road made by Hill to ascend to his residence.

"About midway, on the north side, or face of the pyramid, and elevated 25 or 30 feet above the base, in a small depression, stands a pine tree, singularly enough, since this tree is not found in the forests in this locality. There was a story rife among the early settlers that this tree stood at the mouth of an opening or gallery into the interior of the mounds. To ascertain the truth of this matter, Mr. Thomas Ramey, the present owner of the mound, commenced a tunnel at this tree and excavated about ninety (90) feet towards the center of the mound. When fifteen feet from the entrance to the tunnel a piece of lead ore was discovered, but no other object of interest was found. The deposits penetrated by the tunnel are very plainly shown to be the same as seen in the cellar mentioned above."

Mr. McAdams republished a paragraph from Edmund Flagg's book on "The Far West," 1838, p. 167, regarding an old well on the Mound. Flagg's description reads:

"Upon the western side of Monk Mound, at a distance of several yards from the summit, is a well some eighty or ninety feet in depth; the water of which would be agreeable enough were not the presence of sulfur, in some of its modifications, so palpable. This well penetrates the heart of the mound, yet, from its depth, cannot reach lower than the level of the surrounding plain. I learned, upon inquiry, that when this well was excavated, several fragments of pottery, of decayed ears of corn, and other articles, were thrown up from a depth of sixty-five feet; proof incontestible of the artificial structure of the mound."

The Views of Doctor N. M. Fenneman.—Doctor N. M. Fenneman of the University of Cincinnati believes that the valley was much aggraded in the Wisconsin epoch, but that this filling has not been entirely removed, there being remnants left within the cut-offs of the meanders which were later eroded, dissected, and narrowed "by the meander of the main stream and its tributaries until mounds were produced.[1] Among those," he continues, "was the great natural hill which was subsequently modified by man and is now the partly artificial Monks Mound.

"The partly artificial character of Monks Mound is evident from its form. That it is in part a natural feature, is seen by its structure. Sand is found neatly inter-stratified with loam at an altitude of about 455 feet, or 35 feet above its base. To this height, at least, the mound is natural and as there is sufficient other evidence that the valley was

[1]*Physiograyhy of the St. Louis Area*, Ill. State Geol. Survey Bull. 12, 1909, pp. 62, 63.

filled in the Wisconsin epoch to at least that height, the original mound may be regarded as a remnant of the alluvial formation of that time. Its base was probably narrowed artificially by the removal of material which was carried to the top. In this way also the conspicuous abruptness of its slopes was probably produced. No natural stratification has yet been found more than 35 feet above its base and therefore, for aught that is now known, more than half its height may be artificial. There is therefore no reason at present to deny to Monks Mound the distinction claimed for it of being the largest artificial mound of its kind in the world. The time of its building and the people by whom it was built are unknown.

"The many other mounds within a mile or two of Monks Mound had the same origin. Several of the larger ones have been similarly altered artificially. The low ones of gentle slope and less definite outline are believed to be in their natural forms.

A later statement[1] reads: "To a height of 35 feet above its base the material of Monks Mound shows assortment and stratification, which is evidently natural. Above that height it affords no structural evidence bearing on the question whether it is of natural or artificial origin; but the form plainly indicates the work of man, and not of geologic processes. It is highly probable that the mound in its natural condition was much lower and broader than at present, and was of rounded, almost drumloidal form, similar to the smaller ones of the group which now surround it. By cutting down its margin to the level of the surrounding plain its builders obtained material to raise the mound to perhaps two or three times its former height without making excavations beneath the level of the plain and without carrying material from the bluffs, 2½ miles distant. There is no evidence that material was obtained by either of these latter means."

The Views of Doctor A. R. Crook.—At the Philadelphia meeting of the Geological Society of America, December 29-31, 1914, Doctor A. R. Crook, Chief of the State Museum Division, presented a paper on the "Origin of Monks Mound," based upon 25 borings made in the north face of the mound, and upon an examination of the surrounding mounds and the valley bluffs two miles away. Quoting from an abstract of this paper which appears in Volume 26, 1915, of the Society, pages 74, 75, he says:

"Twenty-five borings were made in the north and most abrupt side. 1. They showed different strata at different elevations. 2. These strata agree with similar elevations in the other mounds and with

[1]*Geology and Mineral Resources of the St. Louis Quadrangle*, U. S. Geological Survey Bull. 438, 1911, p. 12.

soil from the bluff two miles away. 3. Fossil hackberry seeds *(Celtis occidentalis)* and such gastropods as *Pyramidula, Succinea, Helicina,* and *Physa* are found in beds. 4. A study of the physiography of the mounds makes clear that they occur along the divide between streams, and that their arrangement and individual forms are characteristic of the remnants of stream cutting.

"Chemical and mineralogical study of the soil, as well as paleontological and physiographical investigations, indicate that the mounds are the remnants of the glacial and alluvial deposits which at one time filled the valley of the Mississippi River in this region.

"It may be well to inquire if all so-called mounds in the Mississippi Valley are not natural topographic forms."

Doctor Crook held to the same view in subsequent papers[1] until May, 1922, when he published a bulletin on "The Origin of the Cahokia Mounds" under the auspices of the Illinois State Museum. In this bulletin, which was written following a field conference between him and the present writer when several of the mounds were excellently exposed for study, he inclines strongly towards the artificial theory of origin and has since definitely expressed himself in favor of that theory.[2]

[1]"The Composition and Origin of Monk's Mound," *Trans. Ill. Acad. of Sci.,* Vol. 9, 1916, pp. 82-84; Additional Note on Monks Mound, *Bull. Geol. Soc. Amer.,* Vol. 29, 1918, pp. 80, 81.

[2]Remarks before the Section of Geology and Geography, Illinois Academy of Science, Galesburg meeting, 1923.

GENERAL DESCRIPTION OF THE MOUNDS

Our chief concern in this connection will be to fix our attention upon those points which are of significance in the question of the origin of the mounds. The reader whose interest carries him into archeological questions and interpretations is referred to (1) Part I of the present volume, (2) a preliminary paper on the Cahokia Mounds by Warren K. Moorehead, and (3) the bibliography at the end of Part I. If, on the other hand, the reader is interested in a brief summary of the geologic evidences and conclusions he is referred to the summary statement at the close of this paper. The discussion which now follows is a rather detailed treatment of the geologic aspects of the mounds so far as they have been examined.

Number, Size, and Shape

Some eighty mounds have been mapped within a radius of about 1½ miles, and more widely scattered mounds are to be found in adjacent territory. Monks Mound dominates them all. It stands about 100 feet high above the plain, and the longer side of its rectangular base is about 1000 feet and its shorter side about 700 feet. An inspection of the map, Plate XXII, will show approximately the comparative sizes in ground plan of the rest of the important mounds. The smallest mounds are mere swells of the surface and are not shown on the map. In shape the mounds range from pyramidal forms, with nearly rectangular bases, to elongate ovoid and conical forms. Rain-wash and farming have modified some of the pyramidal mounds and given them sub-rectangular to sub-oval basal outlines. Some are flat-topped and, as in No. 48, have sufficient summit area for a residence site. Practically all of the mounds which are large enough to attract attention have a distinct artificiality in their regularity of form and steepness of slope (Plates XIX, XX). They lack the irregularity in ground plan and the wide range in summit area so characteristic of erosional remnants and they show no meander scars at their bases or on their slopes. They are but little sculptured by slope-wash—Monks Mound the most of all—which speaks for their recency geologically, altho they may be rather ancient historically. Some of the larger mounds, those about 30 or 35 feet high in the vicinity of Monks Mound, show some accordance of level.

MONKS MOUND

Monks Mound has some peculiarities of form worth noting, which were faithfully described by McAdams:[1]

"On the southern end, some 30 feet above the base is a terrace or apron, containing nearly two acres of ground (Plate XXI). On the western side, and some thirty feet above the first terrace, is a second one of somewhat less extent. The top of the mound is flat and divided into two parts, the northern end being some 4 or 5 feet higher than the southern portion. The summit contains about an acre and a half. Near the middle of the first terrace, at the base of the mound, is a projecting point, apparently the remains of a graded pathway to ascend from the plain to the terrace. The west side of the mound below the second terrace is very irregular, and forms projecting knobs, separated by deep ravines, probably the result of rain-storms. . . . The remaining sides of the structure are quite straight and but little defaced by the hand of time."

It should be added that on the north side, there are projecting spurs, 50 to 100 feet long and 30 to 50 feet high. Some have horizontal summits, while others are sloping and have the form of approaches. This is the most abrupt side and some gullying has no doubt taken place. On the east side there is some evidence of creep of considerable masses of material and deposition at the base of the mound of material washed down from above.

The present writer's impression of the form of this huge mound with its platforms and approaches is in harmony with that of Dr. Fenneman, that it "plainly indicates the work of man and not of geologic processes."[2]

ARRANGEMENT OF THE MOUNDS

There are certain significant points regarding the arrangement of the mounds. (1) The elongate mounds are, in

[1]*Records of Ancient Races in the Mississippi Valley*, St. Louis, 1887.
[2]*Geology and Mineral Resources of the St. Louis Quadrangle*, U. S. Geological Survey Bull. 348, 1911, p. 12.

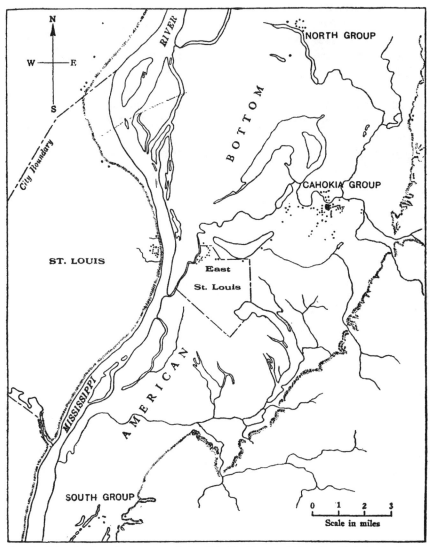

FIG. 8—Map showing the location of the Cahokia Group. (After David I. Bushnell, Jr., Smithsonian Institution)

most instances, oriented with respect to the cardinal points of the compass, either north-south or east-west. (2) Some have a striking alignment, as for example, Nos. 19 to 26 and 6 to 11 (see Plate XXII), and this alignment as well as their orientation carries the aspect much more of the human mode of origin than by ordinary physiographic processes: (3) The grouping of the mounds on the American Bottom is shown in Fig. 8. This grouping, as well as the alignment and elongation, is not in harmony with the theory of terrace remnants or any other physiographic origin to which they can tenably be referred.

THE GEOLOGICAL SETTING OF THE MOUNDS

Topographic Position

The American Bottom.—The Cahokia Mounds are situated upon the great flood-plan of the Mississippi River, known as the great American Bottom, some four miles northeast of the center of East St. Louis (Fig. 8). The mounds offer the only relief possessed by this extensive flat except the valley bluffs which bound it. Before the artificial levees were built, large portions of the flood-plain were subject to the highest floods, but so far as the writer could learn there has been no time in the history of the settlement by white man that all of it was under flood-waters. Even today, with the artificial levees, the flood-waters back up into some of the abandoned channels previously occupied by the Mississippi River, as for example the old channel now followed by Cahokia Creek, in its wanderings across the plain.

The highest known flood-level of the Mississippi River at St. Louis was in 1844,[1] when the waters rose 7.58 feet above the city directrix, reaching an altitude of 420.31 feet above sea-level. According to the topographic map of the St. Louis quadrangle, published by the U. S. Geological Survey, involving the site of the Cahokia Mounds, there are considerable areas above the 420-foot level along the foot of the east valley wall and in the vicinity of Granite City. Monks Mound and a few others nearby are on a slight swell a little above 420 feet, but the surface surrounding most of the others appears to be somewhat under that level. Hence, it is thought that many of the mounds were surrounded by this flood. The flood of 1903, 2 or 3 feet below that of 1844, reached and covered the low sags in the vicinity of the mounds.

The valley has a maximum width of about 12 miles just north of Granite City and a minimum of 3¾ miles south of the village of Cahokia. In the latitude of the mounds it is about 9½ miles wide. The valley flat is

[1]Woodward's *The Saint Louis Bridge*, G. C. Jones and Co., Publishers, St. Louis, 1881, p. 2.

traversed by many old channels—former courses of the Mississippi River—showing that many shiftings have taken place in recent geological times, and the existence of ox-bow lakes in several of these indicate an occupancy so recent geologically that they have not yet been filled. Besides the distinct abandoned channels, faint sags apparently represent earlier channels.

The East Valley Wall.—The east valley wall rises from 150 to 200 feet above the valley flat. It is generally a distinct bluff, notably steep in spite of the weak resistance of the Coal Measures shale and Pleistocene clays of which it is chiefly composed, and surprisingly steep when the width of the valley is considered. This has an important bearing upon the activity of the Mississippi River, making it clear that this great stream frequently shifts its course, geologically speaking, striking the valley wall here and there and preventing weathering, slope-wash, and creep from making the slope gentle.

THE ALLUVIAL FILLING

Thickness and Characteristics.—The filling of the valley is considerable; the bedrock floor lies deep. The upper 10 to 12 feet is mud and clay, beneath which is 50 to 100 feet of sand with subordinate beds or lenses of clay and gravel, and gravel and boulders at the base.[1] The position of the bouldery material at the base has a special significance. Great changes in the volume of the stream take place in response to heavy rainfall or rapid melting of snow over the large basin which the river drains, and this greatly modifies the velocity and the stream's transporting power. At St. Louis, the velocity of the Mississippi River has been known to vary from 2¾ miles per hour at low water to 8½ miles per hour at high water, or three-fold. In time of high flood, therefore, the stream scours deeply, probably reaching and abrading the bedrock, making it necessary for the piers of the bridges at St. Louis to be sunk into the rock. When the excavations were made by the engineers

[1]Fenneman, N. M., *The Physiography of the St. Louis Area,* Ill. State Geol. Survey Bull. 12, p. 6, 1909.

for the St. Louis bridge, and the bed-rock was laid bare, the rock surface was found to be smooth and water-worn and to be overlain by the heavier debris of river floods.[1] There have been known instances of scour reaching nearly 100 feet. The larger materials are moved at a slower rate than the smaller, and are the first to be deposited, upon the slackening of the current during the ebb of the flood. Altho the scouring is probably local in the bed of the channel during any one flood, yet in successive floods all points along the channel may become affected.

The Age of the Alluvial Filling.—In view of (1) the scouring action of this great stream along its present channel and the alternate play of scour and fill; (2) the abundant evidence that in the past the stream has had almost every conceivable position on the valley-flat; (3) the lateral shifting of the meanders, cutting on the outside of the curves and filling on the inside; (4) the length of postglacial time having probably been sufficiently long for this great stream working in loose and fine materials to plane the full width of the valley several times, and (5) the gradation from bottom to top of coarse to fine, it would appear that the larger part if not all of the present alluvial filling has been worked over and repeatedly shifted down-stream and that its present position is due to the action of the stream in the Recent epoch. It is in a transitory state of rest; it is the "potential" load of the present stream. Therefore, it seems proper to regard it as chiefly post-glacial in age.

REMNANTS OF THE ORIGINAL GLACIAL FILLING

Inasmuch as this portion of the Mississippi River received glacial drainage from more than 2,000 miles of ice front of the Wisconsin Glacier—from the basin of Illinois River to the Rocky Mountains—it would be expected that the valley here would show evidence of fill, provided it was given more load than it could carry; and since this locality was far from the ice edge, that such a filling would be composed dominantly of fine material; and further, that since the

[1]Woodward, op. cit., page 5.

volume of the glacial waters varied greatly between the
winter and summer seasons, the glacial Mississippi behaved much as the modern Mississippi, only on a much
larger scale; and moreover, that since the suspended load
and bed-load were probably greater, the amount of filling
during the recession of floods would average greater and
the average level of the flood-plain would be higher.

Evidence of such a condition appears to exist chiefly in
the mouths of some of the tributaries,—Canteen Creek and
Prairie du Pont Creek, where alluvial terraces are found,
some of them rising 40 to 60 feet above the Mississippi
valley flat. The material of these terraces, however, is
probably not so much that brought down by the Mississippi
River as that washed down from the uplands and deposited in the back-water of the tributaries due to filling in
the main valley. But in either case they seem to record a
former higher filling in the main valley than now exists,
which is the significant point in this connection.

This period of aggradation was brought to a close by
the melting back of the ice into the basins of the Great
Lakes and Lake Agassiz. From these bodies of water three
great streams of relatively clear water combined and
formed a Mississippi of more constant volume than before.
Just how the amount of this water would compare with the
maximum summer floods which had been coming down the
valley from the glacier before the lakes came into existence
is problematical, for, on the one hand the length of the ice
front was now much less, and on the other the climate was
becoming warmer and the rate of melting greater. An important point to keep in mind tho is this. The waters from
Lake Chicago and its contributary area to the east, the
waters from Lake Superior, and the waters from Lake
Agassiz formed a stream of very large volume, with less
fluctuation than when the drainage came direct from the
ice, and since most of the sediment had been dropped in the
lakes, the outflowing waters were much less loaded.

This condition of flow lasted during the building of
several recessional moraines and a corresponding number

of periods of ice recession,[1] probably resulting in a lowering of the former glacial flood-plain, and probably to a level considerably below the present plain. Indeed, the previous fill may have been entirely swept away and the rock-floor subjected to abrasion, but this cannot be affirmed.

Post-Glacial Conditions

With (1) the melting away of the ice from the basin of Mississippi River, (2) the establishment of the outlet of the Great Lakes by way of St. Lawrence River, (3) the disappearance of Lake Agassiz, and (4) the melting of most of the contributing Alpine glaciers of the Rocky Mountains, the drainage conditions of the Mississippi River assumed approximately their present proportions and variations. Inheriting the low gradient of the preceding epoch, the Mississippi of smaller volume must have built up its flood-plain to its present level.

The widespread distribution of abandoned channels and the absence of any tendency on the part of the present stream to break up into distributaries indicate that the present flood-plain is essentially at grade or some of it is slightly above grade because of the present fairly straight course of the stream. Before the stream assumed its present course, it meandered widely, as the abandoned channels and ox-bow lakes indicate. Under those conditions much of the present flood-plain was formed. With the stream subsequently assuming the present nearly straight course, probably at a time of widespread overflow, its gradient became higher and its transporting power greater, enabling it to develop a narrow flood-plain adjacent to the channel slightly below the rest of the valley flat, thereby reducing for the present the chances and the frequency of widespread flooding other than in the old abandoned channels and adjacent low areas.

[1]Some of the recessional moraines are known to have been built after a re-advance of the ice following an unknown amount of melting back, but the volume of water was doubtless less during the advance of the ice than during the retreat.

BEARING UPON THE AGE AND ORIGIN OF THE
CAHOKIA MOUNDS

(1) The enormous scour and fill of the Mississippi during the rise and ebb of floods; (2) the fact that the stream has shifted to many different positions over the valley flat; (3) the fact that this shifting has been so frequent that abandoned channels of the second or third stages back are not entirely filled before another shift takes place; (4) the absence of any remnants of filling which clearly correspond to the terraces in the mouths of some of the tributaries; and (5) the fact that the mounds do not show the scars of meander curves on their slopes or at their base as they would if they were remnants of a former higher fill,—when we consider these things, it appears doubtful that the mounds are either natural or that they are as old as the present valley flat.

If this conclusion is correct, the mounds themselves should reveal this in their constitution; should have no nuclei of natural origin, and should rest upon alluvial materials as a foundation. We may well give our attention to this phase of the question.

CONSTITUTION OF THE MOUNDS

There was opportunity to study the character and structure of the material in four mounds, and as a matter of record, these will be discussed separately. These mounds were: the James Ramey Mound, No. 33; the Albert Kunnemann Mound, No. 16; the Sam Chucallo Mound; and the Sawmill Mound, No. 39. As will be seen from Plate XXII, these mounds are widely spaced and are fairly representative of the mounds which range in height from 12 to 35 feet. The James Ramey Mound, No. 33, situated a quarter mile east of Monks Mound, was the most thoroly opened and examined in the greatest detail.

THE JAMES RAMEY MOUND, No. 33

This mound was trenched through its center in a north-south direction, nearly to the level of the surrounding valley flat and a fine opportunity was presented for ascertaining the composition, degree of assortment, arrangement of the materials and their relations to the materials of the valley flat.

General Description of the West Face.—In the west face (Fig. 9), Formation 1 is made up chiefly of yellowish sand with balls and irregularly shaped inclusions of dark silt scattered through it. It is unstratified and has the spotted and lumpy appearance of man-made fills. It is cut off abruptly at the south end. Formation 2 is a mixed gray and yellowish silt and sand with scattered charcoal fragments. The upper surface is strongly undulating. At (a) is a reddish brown horizon having every appearance of having been the site of a bonfire. Charcoal fragments occur in the material. Formation 3 is a mixed gray and yellowish silt and sand with included masses such as is shown in the figure. In the north end is a peculiar mixed mass, (c), and a filling in a well-defined cut-out, (b). At (a) is another apparently burned horizon with charcoal fragments associated with it. Formation 4 is a yellowish sand with an abundance of charcoal fragments up to 1½ inches in diam-

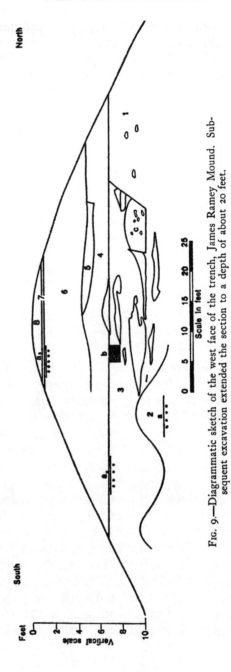

FIG. 9.—Diagrammatic sketch of the west face of the trench, James Ramey Mound. Subsequent excavation extended the section to a depth of about 20 feet.

eter. Formation 5 is finely stratified sand about 8 inches thick—the only clear case of water stratification in the section. It ends bluntly at its northern end and pinches out at its southern. Formation 6 is a fine yellowish sand with bits of charcoal. Formation 7 is a well-defined horizon with an apparent burned horizon at its south end. Formation 8 is a fine grayish yellow sand with some small lumps. Throughout the whole section bones and pottery, artifacts of flint, and angular fragments of travertine and charcoal were found, varyingly oriented. Near the center of the cut a boring was put down with a post-hole digger, and at a depth of about 20 feet from the top of the mound, a fairly large piece of charcoal and a piece of pottery were found. Another boring yielded bones and pottery at a depth of 18 to 19 feet. Regarding the occurrence of human skeletal remains in this and other mounds, the reader is referred to Part I of this publication.

Detailed Description of a Vertical Section in two Dimensions.—A chimney-like section, 3 feet square, was dug in the west face of the main trench and a detailed sketch and description were made of the south and west sides of this section. (Fig. 10.) The description follows:

Thickness
Feet

7. Fine grayish yellow sand, with lumps of gray clay which give a spotted effect; a few small fragments of charcoal up to $\frac{1}{4}$ inch in diameter; the material effervesces to the surface altho it is dark in the upper 3 to 4 inches 2 to 3

6. Interlayered dark and light fine sand and sandy silt, the lower portion with many charcoal fragments, a scattering in the upper part; layers discontinuous and horizontal in the south face, dipping southward in the west face; a few fragments of bones (one a bone of a bird); some fragments of pottery................. $2\frac{1}{4}$

5. Mottled fine silty sand in indefinite layers; a heterogeneous mixture of highly calcareous and slightly calcareous material with no indication of secondary concentration or differential solution; no assorting; a few tiny particles of charcoal........................ $3\frac{3}{4}$

4. Dark clay layer, something like gumbo, with fragments of pottery and charcoal; thickness................ $\frac{3}{4}$

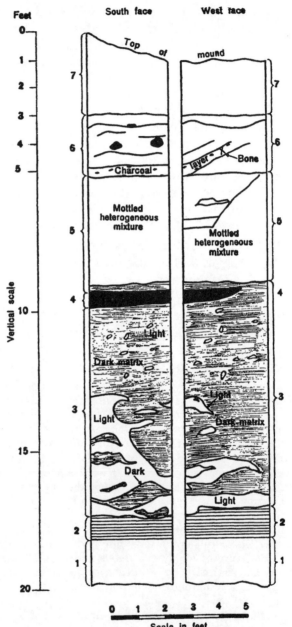

Fig. 10.—Diagrammatic sketch of a chimney section made in the west face of trench, James Ramey Mound.

3. Mostly dark fine sandy silt with light mottling, some brownish clay; irregular lenses and balls of the light colored silt in a dark matrix, and lenses and balls of the dark in the light; the light parts are more calcareous than the dark; a few charcoal and pottery fragments. 5¼

2. Fine stratified silty sand, yellowish gray; calcareous; charcoal fragments mostly minute but two fragments up to 1 inch; layers of sediment thin, numbering 3 or 4 to the inch. These beds fade out to the east, changing upward to mixed material as if the stratified portion were deposited in a local pool in the mound. . .   1

1. Massive dark gray silt, no stratification, scattered specks of charcoal, non-calcareous. 1¾

Special Features of the West Face.—Bones and fragments of pottery were found throughout the vertical section of the mound. In the west face of the trench was found a linear series of holes, about 30 in number in a distance of 23 feet, most of them less than 6 inches in diameter and about 2 feet in depth. Altho they had been completely covered over by at least 9 feet of earth, the holes were only partly filled with dirt. In the bottom of many of them occurred brown decayed bone; a small leg bone of a bird was still preserved. It appeared that originally the holes had been filled with bones before the overlying earth was put on and later the bones decomposed leaving the holes unfilled and a residue of bone material in the bottom. The series trended nearly due north-south and while most of the holes were vertical, a few slanted 10 degrees from the vertical. The full series was not entirely uncovered, for the north end curved slightly west of north into the west face. Such features must be human in their origin.

General Description of the East Face.—A section of the east face is shown in Fig. 11. A-A¹ is a well defined horizontal horizon marked by burned lenses (b) and short stretches of coarse sand (c). The burned lenses are 2½ inches in maximum thickness and up to 3 feet long. They are reddest in the center with charcoal fragments immediately beneath and at the ends. The materials, including the sands, effervesce with acid. Below

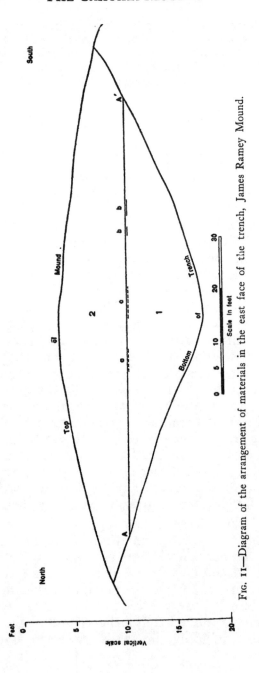

FIG. 11—Diagram of the arrangement of materials in the east face of the trench, James Ramey Mound.

the sharp horizon is Formation 1, a dark, fairly compact silt, irregularly layered and with greenish lenses and some yellow sand layers. In this case the dark is distinctly less calcareous than the light, and charcoal is generally scattered through them. Above the sharp horizon, is Formation 2, a fine sandy silt mottled dark and light, arranged without order in irregular lenses, balls and masses up to 4 inches in diameter. Both the light and the dark are calcareous, and charcoal fragments are scattered through them promiscuously. Bones and fragments of pottery were found from bottom to top of the section. A large marine shell was uncovered near the west end 3 or 4 feet below the surface. Similar shells were found in other parts of the mound, one at a depth of 17 feet.

The mound was about 23 feet high. At a depth of 19½ feet, pottery, bones, and flint were found, some of them on end. The containing matrix was a fine, sandy silt, gray with brownish tinge and slightly calcareous. A fragment of calcareous tufa and a one-inch fragment of charcoal, which clearly exhibited the structure of the original wood were found at the 18-foot level. All of the material, save for a thin lens of finely stratified sand, had the appearance of having been dumped, mixed, and spread by human agencies. It was indeed a motley mixture.

Significant Features Common to Both Sides of the Trench.—(1) The materials are not stratified or assorted like waterlaid sediments, except as above mentioned, tho they have a stratiform arrangement.

(2) The contacts of the various layers are quite irregular in detail, (figure 12), sharp projections of one fitting into the sharp indentations of another. This shows that the surface upon which each layer was spread was irregular in detail altho nearly level, and could not be due to deposition in quiet or slack-water. They are such as would develop from human hands spreading silts and fine sands over a surface previously smoothed artificially but retaining minute irregularities. This is also in harmony with the mixed aspect of the materials.

(3) Some horizons in the mound are reddish brown, with charcoal fragments closely associated. The reddish

color does not appear to be due to natural processes of oxidation in view of the presence of the charcoal, which is reducing in its chemical reaction, and of the promiscuous and limited occurrence of material of reddish color. Its association with charcoal would seem, on the other hand, to point to bonfire oxidation.

(4) Both sides of the trench show a content of bones of several forms of life; shells of gastropods whose habitats vary from terrestrial, fluviatile, and lacustrine of local occurrence to the large ornate marine shells from the Gulf of Mexico; shells which have been shaped or perforated

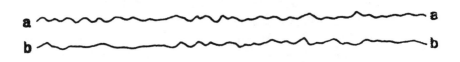

FIG. 12—Diagrammatic sketch of the minutely irregular contacts between the layers of fine material in the mounds.

as ornaments of utility and dress; artifacts of various sorts; flint chips which are at least in part refuse of the Indian stone arts; and travertine fragments apparently derived from local spring deposits. Many of these lack the orientation with the stratiform character of the layers which would be expected if they were alluvial in origin. Such an assemblage of "fossils," such a promiscuous arrangement, and such a complete absence of signs of water attrition is decidedly in agreement with the conception of an artificial mode of origin for this mound.

The Basal Contact of the Mound.—An important question bearing on the origin of the mounds is whether or not the materials of the surrounding plain pass under them. When the trench through Mound No. 33 reached approximately the level of the surface outside of the mound, the writer hoped to ascertain the exact situation by having three pits dug, two of them in the bottom of the trench, near the center of the mound, each 3½ feet square and 4 feet deep, the third outside of the mound,

190 feet east and 137 feet south of the center of the mound, on the valley flat, this pit being 3½ feet square and 3½ feet deep.

The pit outside of the mound exposed:

Thickness
Feet

4. Black soil, no pebbles................................ ½ to 1⅓
        grades into
3. Non-calcareous silt, dirty buff....................... ½
        grades into
2. Non-calcareous silt, yellowish, somewhat mottled, one band somewhat rusty colored, ¾ to 1 inch wide..... 1½
1. Sandy silt, non-calcareous, yellowish, watery.......... 1

All of the latter section looked natural. There was found no pottery, charcoal, bones, flints, shells, lumps, or other material of human derivation, and neither was there any mixing of materials.

The pit nearest the center of the mound showed:

Thickness
Feet

3. Dark gray, sandy silt, slightly effervescent with acid, containing an occasional charcoal fragment......... ¼ to ¾
2. Brownish yellow silt, containing old rootlet channels stained rusty, non-calcareous, limonite, and pellets of $CaCO_3$ up to ¾ inch; no distinct stratification, no charcoal or artifacts here; no sign of disturbance; has every appearance of being a former sub-soil...... 1
1. Fine silty sand, calcareous, scattering of small shells of gastropods, grayish yellow color, some iron oxide spots and streaks, no sign of disturbance................ 2

The second pit beneath the mound, dug 8 feet south and 15 feet west of the center, starting 20 feet below the top, showed:

Thickness
Feet

2. Grayish yellow, fine sandy silt with old root canals stained rusty, very slight effervescence with acid, apparently an old sub-soil................................ 1½
1. Yellowish gray, fine sand, calcareous, after striking water the sand behaved like quicksand................. 2½

These materials were all undisturbed and had every aspect of being natural. They seem to be without question the materials of the flood-plain passing under the mound.

THE ALBERT KUNNEMANN MOUND, No. 16

About ¾ of a mile north of Monks Mound, on the north side of Cahokia Creek, is a large mound known as the Albert Kunnemann Mound. Along a part of the north side of this mound, an excavation was made giving a fairly abrupt face 60 feet long and 30 feet high, the lower 10 to 15 feet being covered. The arrangement of the materials is shown in figure 13. Upon cursory inspection they appear to constitute a stratified deposit, but inasmuch as a de-

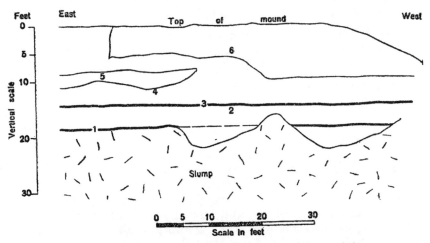

FIG. 13—Diagrammatic sketch showing the arrangement of the materials in the Albert Kunnemann Mound.

tailed examination revealed the structure to merely simulate stratification, the details are deserving of some attention. The appearance of stratification is due to two thin horizontal layers, 1 and 3 in the diagram, about 4 feet apart, the upper one having a position about 14 feet below the top. Layer No. 1 is a dark sandy silt, No. 3 a black soil-like material. No 3 was clearly not a soil in place, however, for the contact with the underlying materials is sharp. At this horizon a large bowl and a burned "altar" were found by Mr. Moorehead in the course of the excavations. Between these layers is No. 2 which is a sand containing broken shells, the spots being due to dark lumps of incoherent sandy silt, which could hardly have been handled by water. Near the east end are oblique black mixed streaks. The sharp irregular contacts of the thin fine layers show that they were not deposited in quiet water but were spread over a level surface, having minute irregularities, by some such agency as man. Horizon (4) is a spotted sand with scattered charcoal, small shells,[1] pottery, bones, and chips of flint. Horizon (5) is a lens in horizon (4) of mixed gray and dark gumbo with charcoal. Its exposed length was about 24 feet, and thickness 2 to 3 feet. Horizon (6) is a mixed dark and gray gumbo-like material showing no stratification. The top of the mound is now flat but it is reported to have originally been some 15 feet higher and to have consummated in a point, the removed material having been scattered over the adjoining fields.

The materials of this mound in their lack of assortment, absence of water stratification, presence of man-made features, mixed materials, and scattering of artifacts are against the natural theory of origin and strongly favor the artificial theory.

THE SAM CHUCALLO MOUND

The Sam Chucallo Mound is situated about 3 miles southwest of Monks Mound and ¼ mile north of Lansdowne Heights at the brink of an old channel.

It is about 100 feet in diameter and 10 to 12 feet high above the surface to the east.

As the result of digging an east-west trench through the mound, 8 feet deep at the maximum, and 40 feet long, it was possible to examine the materials to advantage. The north face of the trench showed a structure as in figure 14. Most of the material is Formation 2, a dark silty clay, the color apparently being due to humus, and mixed in the silty clay are irregular lumps and streaks of gray to dark gumbo which show minute rusty, ramifying canals and

---

[1]The following were identified by Curator F. C. Baker: Gastropods: *Physa gyrina* Say (a common fresh-water shell living in summer-dry ponds), *Vivipara contectoides* W. G. B. (fragments); Pelecypod; *Anodonta grandis* Say (fragment); miscellaneous: shell head of marine conch *(Busycon)*, vertebra of small fish.

imprints of rootlets. The rootlets are almost gone, but such as are found are in these minute canals. Apparently the oxidation of ferrous compounds was favored along these minute canals by the ready access of oxidating ground water. Intimately mixed with the gumbo is some fine sand.

At the base of this motley arrangement of materials is Formation 1, a yellow to grayish-yellow fine sand, the contact being nearly level for most of the distance but sloping and passing beneath the trench at the east and west ends.

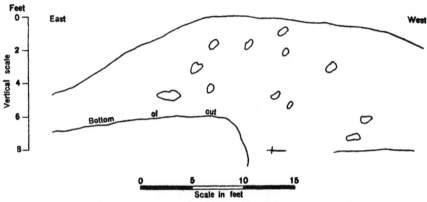

Fig. 14—Diagrammatic sketch of the structure of the materials in the north face of the trench, Sam Chucallo Mound.

Mixed with this sand in heterogeneous fashion are lumps of black soil, and the sand itself is a mixture of calcareous and non-calcareous materials. It contains snail shells,[1] some in fragments, some soft, and some mashed. All of the aspects of this sand layer are unlike those of deposits made by natural agencies and like those made by man.

The south face shows the same sequence and mixing, but the sand layer, No. 1, at the bottom is a little lower than in the north face, and near the center the sand layer is interrupted sharply by gumbo and black silty clay. (See

[1]The following species were identified by Curator F. C. Baker: Gastropods: *Planorbis trivolvis* Say, *Lymnaea palustris* (Müller). *Segmentina armigera* (Say). *Helicodiscus parallelus* (Say). The first three snails live in small ponds which may become wholly or partially dry in summer; the fourth one is a land snail living near water.

Figure 15.) A human skeleton was found just below, at about 8 feet below the summit of the mound. Clearly, after the sand was accumulated there by man, the sand was cut into for burial purposes, and it appears that the overlying material was brought there and dumped, thereby increasing the height of the mound.

THE SAWMILL MOUND, No. 39

A low mound about 1000 feet northwest of Monks Mound, on the south side of Cahokia Creek, was opened for a depth

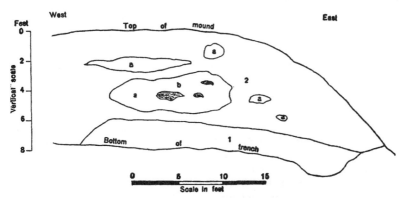

FIG. 15—Diagrammatic sketch of the structure of the materials in the south face of the trench, Sam Chicalo Mound.

somewhat below the ground-water level for wet seasons. About 13 feet was exposed. The upper 3 to 5 feet consist of gumbo material with a few small fragments of charcoal and pottery, and lumps of yellow sandy silt. Below this are yellowish stratified sandy silts, the layers having very irregular contacts, dipping to the east, and showing lumps of dark incoherent silt up to 1½ inches. The materials are somewhat calcareous in spots, but at no particular horizon. The arrangement of the materials has every aspect of being due to human dumping.

AUGER BORINGS ON MONKS MOUND

The size of Monks Mound forbade any extensive exploratory work and hence no decisive evidence was obtained regarding its constitution. Its artificial form, however, invited some investigation to determine the trend of the evidence, and altho it is realized that borings are not conclusive, yet it was felt that they would show something. Three borings were made on the summit and two on the east slope, by means of an auger 1¼ inches in diameter, attached to sections which permitted penetration to a depth of 17½ feet. By digging pits 3 feet deep, the total depth penetrated on the summit was 20½ feet. Samples were laid out in succession and carefully examined and described.

Boring No. 1.—A pit 3 feet deep was dug on the summit near the north end, which showed black soil with charcoal and fragments of pottery at the bottom. The boring was started in the bottom of this pit, and the following materials were revealed:

Thickness Feet

3. Sandy silt, dark, with 1 to 2 inch streaks of fine sand, light gray in color, some of the dark shows mixing with the light,[1] resembling the exposed materials in the smaller mounds...........................   8

Changes to

2. Fine sand, dirty buff, loose; a little ochre-sand........   3
1. Grayish yellow sand, showing a little admixture of dark silt and some thin streaks of light ochre sand, strongly effervescent at 17 feet but not effervescent at the bottom except in spots.............................   6½

Boring No. 2.—About 50 feet south of Boring No. 1 a pit 3 feet deep was dug, all of it being in black soil which contained a few pieces of charcoal. The boring in the bottom of this showed:

Thickness Feet

6. Fine sandy silt, dirty gray, non-calcareous............   9
5. Black clay with a thin streak of fine sand, a piece of charcoal at a depth of 13½ feet from the surface.......   2
4. Fine sand, somewhat silty, moderately calcareous......   4
3. Dark sandy silt, ochre pellets......................   ¼
2. Fine sand, silty...................................   ½
1. Dark clay, like gumbo, with streaks of fine sand.......   1¾

[1]The writer satisfied himself after careful inspection that the mixing was not due to the auger. The relationships of the materials are markedly similar to those found in the exposed mounds.

Boring No. 3.—This boring was made in the bottom of a pit 3 feet deep, about 50 feet south of Boring No. 2, the pit showing dark soil with small chips of brick in the top and charcoal fragments below, changing to dirty silty sand in the bottom. The boring revealed:

Thickness
Feet

3. Fine silty sand, some pellets of limonite and rusty streaks, some trace of charcoal and some evidence of mixing, slightly calcareous at the base.................... 10½
2. Intermixture of dark clay and fine yellow sand, a fragment of charcoal ½ inch in length about 16 feet below the original surface, non-calcareous.............. 5
1. Dark clay, like gumbo; trace of charcoal at depth of 19 feet below the original surface, non-calcareous...... 2

The dark clay and the mixture of materials are similar to that seen in the various human mounds previously described. The presence of charcoal in the lower part of the section as well as in the upper is also indicative that this material has had human associations.

Boring No. 4.—On the east slope due east of Boring No. 1, a pit was dug to a level of 16 feet below the top of the mound at Boring No. 1, and the back edge of the pit was cut back about 4½ feet horizontally from the slope, developing a vertical face 4 feet high. The back face showed a mixture of materials, but whether or not they were in place could not be definitely ascertained. A boring was put down about 3 feet from the natural slope, which showed:

Thickness
Feet

2. Mottled gray and ochre and grayish yellow and black silt, calcareous in spots at a depth of 1 to 3 feet from the top of the boring, non-calcareous below......... 12½
1. Black, tenacious, humus clay, like gumbo, with some suggestion of a gray mixture, non-calcareous........... 5

The mixture of materials, the rather anomalous relation of non-calcareous beneath calcareous without the usual additional evidence of an interval of weathering, and the gumbo-like clay at the base, are indicative of a human mode of origin. The end of the auger reached a level 33½ feet below the top of the mound. It is of course not possible, without trenching or tunneling, to demonstrate that these materials pass into the mound. Even tho the upper part of the boring may be in slump material, the lower part is believed to be deep enough to pass through the slump.

Boring No. 5.—A pit was dug 11 feet lower vertically than the preceding, or 27 feet below the summit of the mound, and a boring was made 3 feet from the outer edge and 3 feet vertically below the slope. The materials found by boring were 16 feet of blue-black clay with thin layers of light gray and ochre-mottled clay, all non-calcareous and without pebbles.

Statement of Conclusions.—Such chance as these borings afford for ascertaining the nature and arrangement of the materials, indicates that they are man-laid. They are at least in line with the evidence offered years ago from the dug well on the west side of the mound and described by Flagg. (See page 64.) Repeating a previous remark, these borings, while made carefully, cannot be regarded as the equivalent in scientific value of open trenches, but it is to be noted that the results are consistent with the artificial form of the mound.

COMPARISON WITH THE MATERIALS OF THE EAST VALLEY BLUFF

Inasmuch as it has been asserted that the materials of the mounds are similar to the materials of the valley bluffs, the writer made a careful examination of the excellent road-cut exposures recently made along the National Highway where it ascends the bluffs directly east of Monks Mound. The deepest cut is at least 25 feet deep and reveals only loess from the foot of the bluff to the top. Judging from the adjacent localities, the loess is a thick mantle concealing the underlying glacial drift and bed-rock, the present grade of the road nowhere being down to the level of the underlying materials.

The loess is loose and friable, floury, gritty, and easily blown. It contains a rather prolific mollusca fauna, the following having been collected, the large species occurring mostly in the lower part:

Polygyra appressa (Say)	*Pupoides marginatus* (Say)
Pyramidula alternata (Say)	*Succinea retusa* Lea
Pyramidula shimekii (Pilsbry)	*Succinea vermeta* Say
Gastrocopta contracta (Say)	*Helicina occulta* Say

From a grayish color in the lower part, the loess grades through yellowish and buff to brownish in the upper part. In places it presents a slight pinkish cast. On the slope it is rarely leached of calcium carbonate more than 4 or 5 feet, and generally less, but below this leached zone it is highly calcareous. Save for a few places where there is a semblance of bedding, stratification is generally lacking. Some sub-spherical concretions are scattered through it, and along horizontal or gently inclined fracture planes there is a limy concentration, the product of the dissolving action of ground water above and precipitation below.

In all of the cuts, there was no such mixture of materials as occur in the excavated mounds; no sign of human disturbance; no content of human implements, flint chips, sea shells, pottery, charcoal fragments, specimens of travertine, burned horizons, bones of animals nor any other evidence of human activity; no content of gumbo lenses or balls or irregular masses; no promiscuous mixing of calcareous and non-calcareous materials. In short, there is no possibility whatsoever of correlating the materials of the bluffs with the layers of the mounds. Some loess may have been secured from the bluff and used with various materials of the Mississippi flood-plain in the building of the mounds, thus accounting for some of the loess fossils reported from the mounds, but the quantity of such material found in the mounds is very small.

In the mouth of Canteen Creek Valley, are terrace remnants with a summit reaching the 480-foot level on the point of a spur where an Indian Mound, 20 feet or more in height, is situated. Many flint chips occur in the soil but no exposure of old alluvial materials could be found. A gulley wash on the south side exposes 7 to 8 feet of fossiliferous buff loess. The terrace has a maximum width of about 300 yards. About ¼ mile farther up the valley is another terrace remnant. On the south side of the creek a 35-foot exposure in the valley wall shows only loess, yellowish in color, with a mottling of gray and buff. Another road-cut, 20 to 25 feet deep, on the north side of Schoenberger Creek, near the interurban tracks, exposes only loess. A new highway cut at Edgemont just north of the cross-roads shows reddish loess with large, sub-spiral snail shells, beneath buff loess.

About one mile southwest of Caseyville, the Pennsylvanian strata make up a considerable portion of the bluff.

SUMMARY OF THE EVIDENCE AND CONCLUSIONS

The present study of the external characteristics and geological setting of the mounds, and of the exposures made in four of them, has yielded the following lines of evidence bearing upon their mode of origin:

1. The summit area of all of the mounds is so limited that this fact alone minimizes the force of the suggestion that they are terrace remnants of a former higher filling of the Mississippi River Valley.

2. Their pyramidal, oval, and circular shapes are not in keeping with the usual irregular outlines of erosion remnants and this, together with their steep uniform slopes, carries the aspect of an artificial mode of origin. They are clearly not sand dunes, kames, eskers, or natural, constructional forms of any sort.

3. The dominant orientation of the elongate mounds with the cardinal points of the compass, and the striking alignment of many of the mounds, are difficult to explain on the basis of the natural theory, and point strongly to their being man-arranged and man-made.

4. The absence of meander scars on the slopes of the mounds or at their base is out of harmony with the idea that they are terrace remnants.

5. A critical consideration of the history of the alluvial filling of the Mississippi River Valley and of the behavior and capacity for work of that master stream, together with the evidences of its great activity and shifting, makes it appear doubtful if any of the original fill is present in the valley, altho such a possibility can hardly be precluded. According to this view, the glacial filling was probably removed by the voluminous waters of Lake Chicago, Lake Duluth, and Lake Agassiz, and the present filling is the result of the "scour and fill" and "cut and fill" processes of the present shifting and oscillatory stream.

6. If the mounds are terrace remnants of a former higher filling, the materials of which they are composed

should show the stratification and assortment of that type of filling. If the filling was glacial till, the materials should be of that character; if eolian, they should be limited in texture to that size which wind can carry; if lacustrine, they should be characteristic of quiet water deposition except near the shore line; if fluvial they should show the texture and structure of materials deposited by running water. The materials of all four mounds examined do not show the characteristics of any of these physiographic agencies. They are stratiform but not stratified; they are mainly of fine materials—silts, fine sands and gumbo— but unassorted, lumps and masses of one kind being intercalated with materials of another kind, and bones, artifacts, flints, travertine fragments, charcoal and pottery being scattered throughout without any suggestion of a mechanical separation or orientation; the contacts of the layers are minutely jagged and not smooth; calcareous materials are mixed heterogenously with non-calcareous materials; salt-water shells from the Gulf of Mexico occur indiscriminately with local fresh-water shells; burned layers occur at various horizons; and a long series of holes with bone refuse in their bottoms was found in one mound. Such mixture, such an arrangement, such a complex association of unusual materials, are characteristic only of man-made mounds.

7. In the mound which was opened down to its base, undisturbed material, characteristic of an old sub-soil zone and similar to natural flood-plain materials was found to underlie the mound. In this case the mound possessed no original nucleus, and if any is present in the other three mounds, which were opened almost to their base, they must be trivial.

In the face of these evidences it is difficult to conclude other than that the mounds which have been thus far exposed are of human origin, and in view of the external features of the others, it seems probable that they are also the product of human activity, the case being less clear for Monks Mound than for any other because of its large size and the possibility of it possessing a considerable nucleus. But it seems fair to say that its artificial form and the evidence derived from auger borings is consistent with the view that a large part of it at least is the work of the mound-builders. Further exploratory work on these mounds will be observed with interest by both the geologist and archeologist.

The Cahokia Mounds

1929

Includes observations printed in Volumes XIX, No. 35, and XXI, No. 6 [the 1922 and 1923 volumes of the *University of Illinois Bulletin*] together with additonal data from subsequent explorations.

Part I
Explorations of 1922, 1923, 1924, and 1927
Warren K. Moorehead

Mound Technique
Jay L. B. Taylor

Part II
Some Geological Aspects
Morris M. Leighton

The Use of Molluscan Shells by the Cahokia Mound Builders
Frank C. Baker

1000   12 28   4117

PREFACE

It has been thought best to include in this report on the investigation and study of the Cahokia Mounds two previous reports which were issued as parts of the University of Illinois Bulletin Series. These are Volume XIX, No. 35, (1922), and Volume XXI, No. 6, (1923). Changes have been made in both texts. In reprinting Bulletin No. 35, certain prefatory remarks are omitted. Particularly does this apply to institutions and individuals who kindly contributed toward the initial exploration, before the University of Illinois assumed responsibility for the work.[1]

There is added the exploration of 1923, and also extensive work on the Harding Mound (No. 66) which was performed between the first of April and August, 1927.

We are particularly indebted to Dr. David Kinley, President of the University of Illinois, the Board of Trustees, and other officials of the University for coöperation and support during these several expeditions. Mr. Frank C. Baker, Curator of the Museum of Natural History of the University of Illinois, has also rendered valuable assistance in the study of artifacts and the identification of shells. We include a paper by him in this report.

The last season's work at Cahokia (1927) was confined to the Harding Mound (No. 66) and the adjacent mound lying to the east (No. 65). Then the survey examined tumuli along the Illinois River near Havana.

Both No. 65 and No. 66, as well as some lesser tumuli, are now owned by the Baltimore & Ohio Railroad and will soon be destroyed. Thanks are due to Mr. H. B. Voorhees and officers of the Railroad who courteously gave the University permission to conduct the exploration of this mound, and acknowledgment is hereby made of their helpfulness. Articles found in the mound are labeled in the University Museum as having been found on the property of the Baltimore & Ohio Railroad.

In previous years the survey was permitted by the heirs of Mr. Thomas Ramey to carry on extensive excavations on their property. The Ramey family owned something more than half of the mounds comprising the main Cahokia group in Madison

---

[1]These were all thanked at some length in the preface.

and St. Clair counties. We are especially indebted to the Misses and Messrs. Ramey for their many kindnesses, coöperation, and good will which they frequently extended to the members of our expedition during those years. Adjoining the Ramey lands to the north, west, and south lie the extensive acres owned by Mr. George R. Merrell of St. Louis. He also permitted research on his property, as did other proprietors: Messrs. J. H. Edwards, John Smith, Ernest Cole, and Mrs. William Tippetts.

It is most fortunate that these explorations were undertaken before the State Park was established, because certain tracts have changed ownership and numbers of buildings of various kinds have been erected along the State Highway, which might interfere with permissions to excavate.

Since the previous reports were published, two of the members of the expeditions have died: Clinton Cowen, Civil Engineer, and Hon. W. E. Myer, an authority on arts of the Southern Indians. Both rendered valuable service at Cahokia.

We especially wish to thank Dr. Morris M. Leighton, Chief of the Illinois Geological Survey, for his studies of the geology of the region, Dr. Harold R. Wanless of the Department of Geology of the University of Illinois, Dr. A. R. Crook, Chief of the State Museum at Springfield; Dr. Otto L. Schmidt, President of the Illinois Historical Society; W. J. Seever, Esq., of Webster Groves, Mo., for generous assistance. Mr. Seever frequently placed his car at our disposal and spent considerable time with the surveys. Others who have rendered much help were A. J. Throop, Esq., of East St. Louis; the late Dr. H. M. Whelpley, of St. Louis; and Dr. R. J. Terry, of Washington University, who kindly made some studies of such osteological material as we were able to preserve.

Dr. Thomas H. English of Emory University, Atlanta, Georgia, has long been a student of Cahokia literature. He revised our bibliography and added a number of titles. We are greatly indebted to Dr. English.

In the explorations along the Illinois River, we were greatly helped by Dr. Don Dickson, who has established a museum a few miles out of Lewistown. All his material was placed at our disposal. Mr. Russell T. Neville made photographs of Dr. Dickson's skeletons, for which we thank him.

Mrs. Anna Neteler of Havana, Mr. L. A. England, and Mr. O. F. Pfetzing, Chairman of the Chautauqua Board, all permitted explorations. We desire to thank them sincerely.

TABLE OF CONTENTS

PART I

PAGE

Historical Setting and General Description 9
    Looking Down from the Summit of Monks Mound in 1927 . . . 13
    Approximate Number of Mounds in the Group 13
    Maps and Descriptions of Cahokia 14
    Monks Mound 15
    Ponds and Depressions 23

The Village Site 25

Exploration of Certain Mounds During the Various
    Seasons 33
    The Kunnemann Mound 34
    Schmidt's Mound 36
    The Edwards Mounds 37
    No. 76, Jesse Ramey Mound 37
    Mound No. 64 38
    The Sawmill Mound, No. 39 38
    Mounds Nos. 19, 20, and 21 41
    The James Ramey Mound, No. 33 44
    The Jondro Mound, No. 83 51
    Sam Chucallo Mound 53
    Pittsburg Lake Cemetery 54
    Mounds Nos. 14 and 84 55
    Sullivan's Mounds 56
    The Kruger Bone Bank 58
    Mrs. Tippetts' Mound, No. 61 58
    The Collinsville-Edgemont Bluffs 58
    The Mitchell Mounds 59
    Wood River Mounds 62
    Mounds at Lebanon, Illinois 64
    Examination of Harding Mound, No. 66 65
    Mound No. 65 81
    Mound No. 64 83
    The Powell Mound 84
    The Two Low Mounds West of No. 66 84

Orientation of the Cahokia Mounds 86

The Use of Copper in the Cahokia Region 90

Notes on Cahokia Skeletons 94

Previous Work and Collections Relating to the
    Cahokia Group 96

Specimens from Cahokia 98

Cahokia Pottery 100

General Observations on the Cahokia Group 101

Part II

	PAGE
Introduction	III
The Problem	III
Acknowledgments	III
Former Opinions of Geologists Regarding the Origin of the Mounds	112
General Description of the Mounds	116
Number, Size, and Shape	116
Monks Mound	117
Arrangement of the Mounds	117
The Geological Setting of the Mounds	120
Topographic Position	120
The Alluvial Filling	121
Remnants of the Original Glacial Filling	122
Post-Glacial Conditions	123
Bearing upon the Age and Origin of the Cahokia Mounds	124
Constitution of the Mounds	125
The James Ramey Mound, No. 33	125
The Albert Kunnemann Mound, No. 16	133
The Sam Chucallo Mound	135
The Sawmill Mound, No. 39	136
Auger Borings on Monks Mound	136
Comparison with the Materials of the East Valley Bluff	139
Summary of the Evidence and Conclusions	142

Appendices

Appendix A—The Use of Molluscan Shells by the Cahokia Mound Builders	147
Fresh Water Mollusca	147
Mussel Shells Probably Obtained Mainly from the Mississippi River	147
Snail Shells	149
Marine Mollusca	150
Comparison with Hopewell Mounds of Ohio	152
Fresh Water Mussels from Mound No. 5	153
Appendix B—Some Researches in the Illinois River Valley Near Havana	155
The Havana Tumuli	155
The Liverpool Group	157
Other Mounds	158
Examination of Mounds	158
General Conclusions	165
Appendix C—The Dickson Mound and the Log Tomb Burials at Liverpool	167
The "Log Tomb" Mounds at Liverpool	168
Appendix D—Cahokia Bibliography	171
Illustrations	178-273

THE CAHOKIA MOUNDS

PART I

EXPLORATIONS OF 1922, 1924, AND 1927

BY

WARREN K. MOOREHEAD

Curator, Department of Archæology, Phillips Academy, Andover, Mass.
Director, Archæological Survey of the Cahokia Region
for the University of Illinois

MOUND TECHNIQUE

BY

JAY L. B. TAYLOR

HISTORICAL SETTING AND GENERAL DESCRIPTION

Flanking the Mississippi River, and extending from the mouth of the Ohio to near Quincy, Illinois, is a long stretch of exceedingly fertile lowland. When the first English-speaking settlers came in and occupied what was formerly French territory, they gave the name American Bottoms to a large tract of land lying across the river from the city of St. Louis. At that time there was no East St. Louis, and the few hamlets, outside of St. Louis proper, near the river on the west bank as well as those towards the southeast, were composed of French inhabitants. The area specified in the term American Bottoms is somewhat indefinite, yet so far as we have been able to ascertain, it was applied to a territory extending from near the mouth of Wood River, where Lewis and Clark had their winter camp in 1804, down to a few miles below where Cahokia Creek joins the Mississippi. Many of the early writers and travellers speak enthusiastically of the natural beauty of this plain. Indeed, its attractive features belong to the past. Certainly in its present appearance it presents little or nothing to arouse sentiment in the breast of any lover of nature or beauty, for, as Kipling would put it, it has become "manhandled."

Researches in the libraries leads one to assume that the earliest French explorers paid no attention to the Cahokia Mounds. Tonti's journal, which was published in London in 1698 and is entitled "an account of de La Salle's last expedition," refers in a number of places to the Indians and their houses, and also to the personal appearance and garments of these people, yet his description is confined to villages along the Illinois River. If the Indians seen by Tonti, La Salle, or others, in the Cahokia region, built mounds or set cabins on mounds, the obvious conclusion is that these careful observers would have referred to that fact. The main village on the Illinois (at the present time the site of Utica, La Salle County) was some two hundred miles north of Cahokia and contained a large population. Yet the evidences of occupation are far less extensive than those left at Cahokia. This is beyond question, and nobody who has examined the full evidence can deny it. Further, this feature has always appeared to the writer to be very significant. Why? Because had the Cahokia group village been inhabited at that time, La Salle or others most certainly would have visited it. They came clear from Quebec to the Illinois village and Cahokia presents a much more extensive settlement. The answer? Quite simple. Our site was not inhabited then and is strictly prehistoric.

Coming down to later times, quite likely some of the members of the Lewis and Clark expedition, during their several months' stay at the mouth of Wood River, may have crossed the American Bottoms and undoubtedly they saw the mounds, yet there appears to be no mention of these monuments in the Lewis and Clark journals.

Reference to the bibliography will indicate that there are not a few writers who visited Cahokia in early times. We should be very grateful to some of these men because the setting today is absolutely different from that presented by Brackenridge, Rau, and others of long ago. The city of East St. Louis has gradually extended and grown until its suburbs include some of the most westerly mounds of the group. Even as late as 1921, at the time of our preliminary inspection, there were few buildings along the State Highway east of the Powell Mounds (which are about two miles directly west of Monks Mound). Within the short space of six years, there has been extensive construction all along the macadam road between this point and the Edwards Mounds, east of Monks Mound. Not only have many bungalows and filling stations been erected, but there are also two large enclosures, the one where patrons of horse-racing assemble, and the other where greyhound races are held throughout the summer and fall seasons.

At the time Dr. Rau, of the Smithsonian Institution, visited Cahokia in 1860, there was no East St. Louis proper, the site was practically undisturbed, and indications of ancient Indian villages covered the ground from a point far up Cahokia and Canteen creeks fully a mile east of Monks Mound, westward over six miles to the junction of Cahokia Creek and the Mississippi. This has since been verified by our many test pits.

During the past century there has been extensive archæological exploration in the territory lying between the Mexican frontier and the St. Lawrence basin. The net result of this work, on the part of many institutions and individuals, is very important, yet I am not aware that it has produced a village six or more miles in extent.

On the east side of the Mississippi this flood plain, already mentioned, varies in width from two to five or six miles. A line of high bluffs ninety to one hundred twenty feet in altitude parallels this plain. From below French Village, the bluffs in early historic times were dotted with mounds and other evidences of Indian occupation. Many of the tumuli have disappeared. Others are more or less effaced, yet a sufficient number remain to afford students a conception of the enormous extent of aboriginal occupation throughout this area. We use the word "enormous" advisedly.

The Cahokia group of mounds lies on either side of a creek of the same name. The most easterly of the tumuli forming this group are approximately one and one-half miles out toward the west from the foot of the Collinsville bluff. An air line from this point to the mouth of the Cahokia Creek would be approximately seven miles in length. Following the contours of the creek the distance might be extended to nine miles.

The dominant monument, around which all the others center, is the great Cahokia Mound. Since we have applied the term "Cahokia Group" to the entire setting, No. 38 on the official map, Fig. 1, will hereafter be known by its local name of Monks Mound.

In the year 1921 we stood on the summit of this eastern pyramid and looked out across the famous American Bottoms. We were one hundred feet above the plain and because at that time there were no buildings or amusement parks nearby, our vision was not impaired. Both the site and the view were conducive to reflection on the past, and one's mind naturally harked back to the days of Brackenridge, Flagg, Rau, and Featherstonhaugh,—for these men saw Cahokia at its best.

Fortunate indeed is it that these pioneers in Cahokia archæology gave us clear word pictures of conditions then, for while practically all of the tumuli remain, their external contour is altered. After these pioneers came McAdams, Patrick, Putnam, Fowke, Bushnell, and others who mapped and described the mounds as they saw them in the years from 1874 to 1905.

Notwithstanding the preëminence of Cahokia over all other mound groups in the United States, there appears to have been little attempt at either study or exploration. Indeed, the several gentlemen who visited the mounds between the years 1874 and 1905 contented themselves with brief descriptions. Previous to 1922 the longest published account is the paper by Mr. D. I. Bushnell, Jr.[1]

Mr. W. W. McAdams, who was curator of the State Museum at Springfield, and Dr. J. J. R. Patrick seem to have excavated to a considerable extent in the cemetery northeast of the largest mound, yet, we are unable to find any detailed record of their observations.

After reading all the references to Cahokia we consulted with witnesses, who were present during McAdams's explorations, and also with persons living in the vicinity who had more or less knowledge of conditions at Cahokia during the past fifty years. After one has examined the assembled evidence, both written and spoken, it is not difficult to explain the reason no prior exploration of these famous mounds was undertaken.

Most attention seems to have been concentrated on Monks Mound. In fact, nearly all the descriptions center on this ranking structure. Mr. Thomas Ramey, the father of the present eight Ramey heirs, was probably the first owner of Cahokia property to manifest a real interest in the preservation of the mounds. This does not indicate that other owners today do not appreciate the importance of the group. On the contrary, our statement refers to the past—a period from about 1868 to 1890. Although Ramey employed some coal miners from Collinsville and ran a short tunnel into the mound, and also permitted one or two excavations in mounds south of Monks, yet on the whole he was adverse to excavations. From the time of his death his heirs, the Misses and Messrs. Ramey, had refused permission to those who sought to excavate. This also applies to Mr. George B. Merrell and his family, and other owners. In view of subsequent events, it would now appear that these owners wished explorations to "lead up to" or culminate in a movement to secure a State Park, which would preserve for all time the Cahokia Mounds. The present state-owned tract of some one hundred forty-three acres is due to the efforts of many persons and societies, but especially to the labors of the University of Illinois expeditions.

There is even a more potent reason why the mounds have not been examined. The undertaking would be very expensive. Until recent years, no museum or institution spent large sums

[1] Peabody Museum Report; 20 pages, 7 figures, and 5 plates.

of money in American archæology excepting, perhaps, in Central and South America. Undoubtedly it would require ten or fifteen years to properly explore the whole Cahokia group and a large force of labor would be required.

Looking Down From the Summit of Monks Mound in 1927

As we have observed, it was only six years ago when we stood upon the summit of that most massive pyramid north of central Mexico. Then one's view was not fully obstructed. Again, in 1927, we occupy the same vantage-point. In all directions, save towards the south, we observed the persistent encroachment of factories, railways, and buildings. Except in the small central area preserved as a State Park, the charm and primitive simplicity of the American Bottoms observed by Bushnell, as late as 1903, are things of the past. It is not our purpose to enter into a lengthy discussion of either the changes at Cahokia or their causes, yet one recommendation seems essential.

In archæological research it is much easier to secure permission for explorations from an institution or single owner rather than from many persons. The reasons are quite obvious. It is understood that the various owners contemplate dividing the Cahokia Mound group into small tracts and selling these to various purchasers. No one questions the right of the owners, but such action will inevitably result in the destruction of many of the mounds. Certainly it will render difficult their exploration. In view of this danger, it might not be inappropriate to here suggest, in the interests of science, that the State of Illinois, through its legislature, be earnestly petitioned to purchase certain tracts lying to the east, west, and south of the State Park. Otherwise, these remarkable tumuli will become lost to both the public and to science forever.

Approximate Number of Mounds in the Group

Our official map (Fig. 1) presents eighty-five tumuli in the Cahokia group proper. The surveys have spent a total of more than sixteen months at Cahokia. Notwithstanding many inspections of the entire plain, we are not prepared to definitely state what should be included under the term Cahokia. One impression is to the effect that the term should be applied to all monu-

ments embraced within a circle seven miles in diameter and
having as its center Monks Mound.   Other observers have
thought that the Cahokia culture extends about nine miles east
and west and fifteen miles north and south.   Inside the seven-
mile circle Mr. Taylor believes that there were originally about
one hundred fifty elevations or mounds.   Indeed the field evidence would indicate that the term Cahokia should include
mounds of the Mitchell group to the north and embrace all
structures lying between Mitchell and the mouth of Cahokia
Creek.   Within such a boundary there must have been, originally, more than two hundred (or possibly three hundred) elevations of mound-like character.   Jay L. B. Taylor, Esq., the
engineer who had charge of the work last year at Cahokia, examined the ground rather carefully and it is his opinion that
there should be a resurvey of the tract before further destruction is caused by real estate development.[2]   It is essential, Mr.
Taylor maintains, that a new and more accurate survey of the
entire group be put into effect.

Mr. Bushnell, in his excellent report, already referred to,
mentions many mound groups in the general region, and also a
number across the Mississippi on the Missouri side, which were
destroyed as St. Louis extended its borders.   One must continually bear in mind, in archæological studies, the extensive
changes which have taken place in Madison and St. Clair counties since Indian times.   Many low elevations now long ago
clearly defined as mounds have disappeared.

When one looks out upon the American Bottoms from the
summit of Monks Mound one observes many elevations, oblong
in form, rather gentle in outline, which were originally either
conical mounds or distinctly pyramidal in form.

Maps and Descriptions of Cahokia

There have been several attempts to map these mounds, but the
most satisfactory result appears to be the survey made by
County Surveyor Hilgard under the direction of Dr. J. J. R.
Patrick, assisted by B. J. Van Court of O'Fallon, Illinois, and
William J. Seever, now a resident of Webster Groves, Missouri.
The work was done about 1880 and the original map, owned by

[2]W. J. Seever, Esq., in a letter Feb. 1, 1928, states that he has been familiar with
Cahokia for forty years and that there must have been nearly three hundred mounds
all told, or over one hundred fifty elevations of all kinds in the central group.

the Missouri Historical Society, was lent us from which our copy[3] was drawn with certain additions of mounds they omitted. The plot of Cahokia presented in the *Twelfth Annual Report of the Bureau of Ethnology* (Plan VI) (opposite page 134) apparently reproduces Hilgard's first map, but includes only sixty-four mounds.

A model of the center of the Cahokia Mound group was prepared for the Peabody Museum at Harvard by Mr. D. I. Bushnell, Jr.

Reference to our map will indicate that the majority of the mounds lie west, south, or east of Monks Mound. There are a few on the north side of Cahokia Creek. The larger tumuli occupy the center of the group east and west, but not the center north and south. Probably the lowlands lying along Cahokia Creek interferred with mound construction. Seven of the rectangular mounds, or pyramids, are so situated that their major axes are nearly east and west. Today many of the mounds shown in the original map by Mr. Hilgard, also on Bushnell's model and Thomas's map, appear externally as ovals rather than pyramids. This is due to farming operations. In case restorations are contemplated, it will be necessary to compare and check up very carefully all descriptions by observers in the past with measurements and descriptions to be made in the future. The survey of 1880 may not be technically accurate, yet if Mr. Hilgard or Mr. Patrick drew a certain mound as a pyramid, and today it appears as an oval or oblong mound, it should be classified as a pyramid.

Those who wish to follow the subject intensively are referred to the numerous titles presented in the bibliography, but particularly to the descriptions presented by Dr. Thomas, Mr. Bushnell, Dr. Snyder, Mr. Flagg, Mr. Brackenridge, and Dr. Crook. We shall not attempt to list in this report the innumerable measurements and descriptions of all these eighty-five mounds. However, as we come to the detailed account of the exploration of certain structures or sections of the village site, approximate measurements will be set forth.

MONKS MOUND
On the Map No. 38 (Fig. 1).

No single ancient monument in this country has been the subject of more frequent mention through a long period of time

[3]Figure 1.

than the famous Monks Mound. I am quite aware that there has been more recent interest in the cultures, or sites, which we have designated by the term Hopewell, Pecos, Chaco, Fort Ancient, or Madisonville. Discussion began with reference to Cahokia more than one hundred years ago. Since it has never been explored, because of its prominence and great size, and, furthermore, in view of the opinion of several geologists that it might be natural, rather than artificial, it is well that we devote considerable space to its description.

We should first consider the question of the artificial origin of Monks Mound. We have always felt that it was a mistake to have injected into the Cahokia situation the question of human origin of these mounds. As will be observed later in this report, shells, pottery fragments, and even one or two ocean shells were found in the bottom of No. 33 (James Ramey Mound) twenty-three feet below the surface.

The fact that Unio and Busycon shells were found practically on the same level in this mound, would preclude the theory advanced by one or two geologists in past years that all such shells were laid down by river action; obviously it would be possible for the fresh water shells to have been so deposited, but the presence of pottery, flint chips, charcoal, and oceanic shells, establishes the human origin of these mounds.

It would seem that the well dug by Hill in the early 1820's is acceptable evidence. Mr. Flagg, in his journal, *The Far West,* Vol. 1, pp. 166-7 (1838) states:

Upon the western side of the Monks Mound, at a distance of several yards from the summit, is a well some eighty or ninety feet in depth; the water of which would be agreeable enough were not the presence of sulphur in some of its modifications so palpable. This well penetrates the heart of the mound, yet, from its depth, cannot reach lower than the level of the surrounding plain. I learned, upon inquiry, that when this well was excavated, several fragments of pottery, of decayed ears of corn, and other articles were thrown up from a depth of sixty-five feet; proof incontestable of the artificial structure of the mound. The associations, when drinking the water of this well, united with its peculiar flavour, are not of the most exquisite character when we reflect that the precious fluid has probably filtrated, part of it, at least, through the contents of a sepulchre.

This narrative was written ninety years ago by an observer who was personally present a short time after the well was dug. Certainly Flagg would gain nothing by exaggeration or falsification. A detailed description, by Dr. Leighton, with reference to the origin of Monks Mound is presented later in this report.

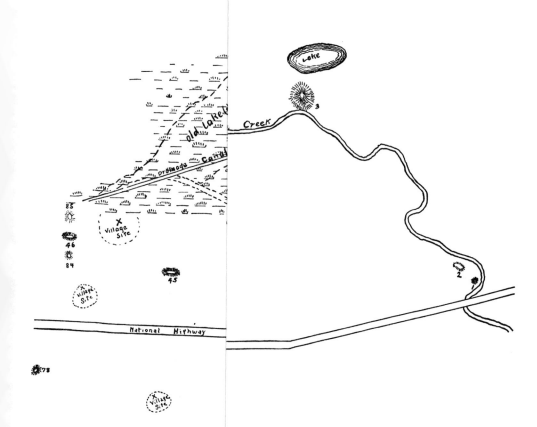

Lake

3

Creek

Old Lake

Drainage Canal

85

46

84

X
Village
Site

45

X
Village
Site

National Highway

78

X
Village
Site

2

X
Village
Site

Burial Site

Dr. A. R. Crook in *The Origin of the Cahokia Mounds,* Bulletin of The Illinois State Museum, Springfield, 1922, states that while he formerly thought these mounds natural, as the result of the work of Moorehead and Leighton he is now convinced of their artificial origin.

Monks Mound was so named because of the presence of that interesting order known as the Trappist monks who lived there for a short period between 1808 and 1813. It is said that malaria was very prevalent, numbers of them died, and according to a letter written to Mr. Bushnell[4] by Father Obrecht, they were recalled to France, yet a few of the monks were buried in the region, and the survey of last year found two white men's skeletons about three feet below the summit of Mound No. 66. There were a few buttons remaining, but nothing to indicate that they were monks. The coffins appeared to have been made of split slabs of wood rather than sawed planks. Mr. Taylor's men reburied the bones midway between the two low mounds southwest of No. 66.

It is well that we devote some space to the observations of other commentators on Monks Mound. Although its character must have changed somewhat, due to erosion between 1820 and 1900, we are all of the opinion that the tumulus has suffered more serious damage the past twenty-five years. Thousands of people, at the time of the St. Louis Exposition, visited it and the publicity due to explorations and newspaper articles between 1922 and 1927 made of the spot a popular resort. The sides of the structure are very much worn, gullies have formed, and photographs taken today exhibit a marked contrast when placed alongside our frontispiece, reconstructed from a photograph and records made in subsequent years. It is respectfully urged upon the Park Commission of the State of Illinois that visitors be confined to one or two paths, and that the various washes and erosions be immediately repaired.

Professor F. W. Putnam of Harvard inspected Monks Mound. Some of his observations are presented in the *Twelfth Annual Report, Peabody Museum of American Archæology,* pp. 470-5, 1880. We present a portion of Putnam's remarks:

Cahokia Mound. In company with several gentlemen from St. Louis, I had the good fortune on September 1st (1879) to visit the largest mound within the limits of the United States. . . . While there is not the slightest

[4]*The Cahokia and Surrounding Mound Groups.* By D. I. Bushnell, Jr. Peabody Museum, p. 9, May, 1904.

evidence that the Cahokias of the time of La Salle were builders of this, or of other mounds in the vicinity, it is a gratification to be able to perpetuate the name of an extinct tribe of American Indians in connection with this monument of an unknown American Nation. . . . .

Situated in the midst of a group of about sixty other mounds, of more than ordinary size, several in the vicinity being from thirty to sixty feet in height, and of various forms, Cahokia Mound, rising by four platforms, or terraces, to a height of about one hundred feet, and covering an area of over twelve acres,[5] holds a relation to the other tumuli of the Mississippi Valley similar to that of the Great Pyramid of Egypt to the other monuments of the valley of the Nile.

I am glad to be able to state that Dr. J. J. R. Patrick, a careful and zealous archæologist, residing in the vicinity of this interesting monument has, with the assistance of other gentlemen, not only made a survey of the whole group of which Cahokia is the prominent figure, but has also prepared two accurate models of the mound itself; copies of which have been promised to the Museum.

One of these models, Plate III (Fig. 1), represents the mound as it now appears, with its once level platform and even slopes gullied, washed, and worn away; and the other (Fig. 2) is in the form of a restoration, showing the mound as it probably existed before the plow of the white man had destroyed its even sides and hard platforms, and thus given nature a foothold for her destructive agencies. The projecting portion (A) from the apron (B) points nearly due south.

Probably this immense tumulus was not erected primarily as a burial mound, though such may prove to be the case. From the present evidence it seems more likely that it was made in order to obtain an elevated site for some particular purpose; presumably an important public building. One fact, however, which I observed, indicated that a great length of time was occupied in its construction, and that its several level platforms may have been the sites of many lodges, which, possibly, may have been placed upon such artificial elevations in order to avoid the malaria of a district, the settlement of which in former, as in recent times, was likely due to the prolific and easily cultivated soil; or, more likely, for the purpose of protection from enemies. The fact, to which I allude, is that everywhere in the gullies, and over the broken surface of the mound, mixed with the earth of which it is composed, are quantities of broken vessels of clay, flint chips, arrowheads, charcoal, bones of animals, etc., apparently the refuse of a numerous people; of course it is possible that these remains, so unlike the homogeneous structure of an ordinary mound, may be the simple refuse of numerous feasts that may have taken place on the mound at various times during its construction. The first interpretation, however, is as well borne out as any other from our present knowledge of this mound; the structure and object of which cannot be fully understood until a thorough examination has been made, and while such an examination is desirable, it is to be hoped that this important and imposing monument will never meet the fate which Colonel Foster, under a false impression[6]

---

[5]Actually over 16 W. K. M.

[6]The destruction of "Big Mound" on the opposite side of the river, within the city limits of St. Louis, probably led Col. Foster into error.

due to a confusion of names and places, mourns as having already occurred.

The various published measurements during all these years differ somewhat as to the length and breadth of this remarkable pyramid. All writers agree that the height is one hundred feet, although the Ramey family claimed that their survey at the time the macadam road was constructed, a few years ago, gave the summit as one hundred four feet above their lawn.

McAdams in *Antiquities of Madison County, Illinois,* states:

As the size of the Cahokia Mound has been given variously we applied to Mr. B. J. Van Court, a practical surveyor living in the vicinity, at O'Fallon, and whom we knew had made a regular survey of the mound. Mr. Van Court sent us the following:

"In my survey I did not follow the irregularities of the mound, but made straight lines enclosing the base. The largest axis is from north to south and is 998 feet, the shortest from east to west is 721 feet. The height of the mound is ninety-nine feet. The base of the structure covers sixteen acres, two roods and three perches of ground."

The summit and lower terrace of the Cahokia Mound have been plowed a few times. Brackenridge, who visited the mound in 1811, says that the monks used the lower terrace for a kitchen garden, and also had the summit of the structure sown in wheat. The great pyramid has not been materially changed, however, and doubtless presents the same outlines today as at the time of the discovery of this continent by Columbus.

Since some doubts have been expressed as to the artificial origin of this structure, we were much interested to ascertain what could be learned in this respect by examination. On the top of the pyramid are the remains of a house, said to have been commenced by the monks, but afterwards added to and finished as a comfortable residence for the family of a man named Hill, an enterprising settler who owned the mound and a large body of land adjoining. Beneath this house is a deep unwalled cellar. In a section down the side of the cellar to the depth of ten feet is very plainly revealed a deposit of various kinds of earth without stratification. The principal part of this deposit was the black humus or mould, so common in the bottom and forming the principal soil, very sticky when wet and breaking into cubical blocks when dry. Here and there, as if thrown promiscuously among the black mould, is a bunch of yellow clay, or sand, or marly loess, these bunches being about such size as a man could easily carry.

Similar sections can be seen up the old road made by Hill to ascend to his residence.

Mr. McAdams reprints the story often related by Mr. Fred Ramey that his father many years ago employed miners from Collinsville and ran a tunnel about ninety feet toward the center of the mound. A fragment of galena was discovered some fifteen feet from the tunnel mouth and there were many small

deposits of the usual masses of different colored earth, indicating that the mound had been constructed by hand. That is,
the construction was similar to that observed in other mounds
of the Cahokia group.

As was previously remarked, Mr. Bushnell's account is the
most satisfactory. With reference to Monks Mound he says:

It is a truncated rectangular pyramid rising to a height of one hundred
feet above the original surface. The dimensions of its base are: from
north to south, 1080 feet, from east to west, 710 feet. The area of base
is about sixteen acres. Viewed from the east it appears regular in form
and three terraces are clearly defined.

In the plan[7] Plate III (Fig. 1) of Cahokia the four terraces and the
point which projects due south from the lowest terrace are clearly represented. The lowest terrace, (B) on plan, is five hundred feet from east to
west and two hundred feet from north to south. From the south face of
that terrace, a point (A) having the appearance of a graded approach,
projects due south for a distance of eighty feet. The western side of this
projection is slightly east of the middle of the mound. The second terrace
(C) is at the present time badly gullied and worn away, which makes it
difficult to ascertain the size of elevation. The next terrace (D) has an
elevation of ninety-seven feet above the original surface. Near the centre
of that terrace, there formerly stood a small conical mound[8] which was
destroyed many years ago when a house was built upon the site. The
fourth terrace (E) is at the present time the most elevated part of the
mound. Its greatest height is one hundred feet above the plain, or three
feet above the third terrace.

The western line of the two upper terraces, extending from north to
south, passes nearly through the centre of the mound. A modern drive-
way, extending from the plain to the summit of the mound, is shown on
the plan. With the exception of the slopes from the lowest terrace—
usually referred to as the "apron"—the sides are deeply gullied; but at the
present time a thick sod covers the greater portion of the surface and will
prevent any further washing away of this famous prehistoric work, unless
it is again attacked by the destructive hand of man.[9]

We have taken the liberty of changing Mr. Bushnell's Fig. 1
to our Fig. 1, Plate III, and also omitting several of his plate
and figure references.

When the famous Hopewell Mound,[10] No. 25, was explored,
it was stated in the report that several observers had presented
different measurements. This is due to the fact that plowing
and rainfall causes all mounds, except those in timber or cov-

[7]Reduced from the plan in the *Twelfth Annual Report of the Peabody Museum,*
p. 472.
[8]Featherstonhaugh. *Excursions through the Slave States,* pp. 66, 67. N. Y. 1844.
[9]Unfortunately the sod is worn away—what Mr. Bushnell feared has come to pass.
[10]*The Hopewell Mound Group of Ohio* by Warren K. Moorehead, Field Museum
of Natural History, Pub. 211, Vol. XI, No. 5.

ered by vegetation, to extend their diameters. The wash down the side forms what is termed the "feather" edge. Therefore one observer may conclude that this "feather" edge extends eight or ten, or even twelve feet from the base of the mound. Another observer will conclude that this gentle slope is due to farming operations, or a dead furrow, and estimate ten or twelve feet less diameter than his predecessor. In a structure as large as Monks Mound it is quite conceivable that at the time of the Hilgard-Patrick-Seever survey of 1880 there was less "feather" edge and the base diameters were from fifteen to thirty feet shorter on all sides save toward the west.

The records state that both the monks and the mechanic, Hill, occupied the summit and the terrace. When Hill laid the foundation of his house, according to the statement of Featherstonhaugh (see bibliography), Mr. Hill dug further and found human bones, Indian pottery, axes, and other objects. Whether these were in Indian graves or deposited in a small mound built on the summit of Monks, does not appear in the narrative.

To explore Monks Mound would be an exceedingly expensive, as well as hazardous, undertaking. In the James Ramey Mound (No. 33) although the walls were slightly over twenty-three feet in height, serious cave-ins occurred and the men were sometimes in danger. One cannot conceive of a trench in artificial earth with walls one hundred four feet in height. It is therefore suggested, since the mound belongs to the State, and both speculation and interest are rife as to its contents, that several tunnels be projected through the base. Miners from Collinsville, under an engineer familiar with tunnelling operations, would be able to do the work, and with proper timbering and inspection the proposal is quite feasible and should be carried into effect. Tunnels from the base are suggested rather than one from the apex, because in the latter event one's observations would be confined to a shaft six or seven feet in diameter, whereas lateral base tunnels would expose vastly more area. Lateral tunnels would settle more effectively the question as to the natural or artificial origin of Monks Mound than a single, narrow shaft. We are informed by Engineer Taylor that with modern engineering operations in effect, it would be quite possible to enlarge the tunnels, thus forming small rooms, or chambers, in case important discoveries were made.

It is, of course, understood that none of our expeditions attempted any exploration of Monks Mound, although we examined carefully the several deep washes at various points, and at one place put our extension auger down about twenty feet. So far as these observations—which were superficial—extended, the mound appeared of human handiwork (like all other Cahokia Mounds) and there were traces of pottery, charcoal, flint chips, etc. We might add a personal note that we have examined mounds throughout the Mississippi Valley since 1887 and comparing Monks Mound with all other large ones, we have never doubted its artificial origin.

Dr. J. F. Snyder of Virginia, Illinois, presented an interesting paper in *The Archæologist,* September, 1894, entitled "An Illinois 'Teocalli'." In this article he comments at some length on the monuments at Lebanon, which were visited by us in 1923, and are briefly referred to on pages 260-262 of this report.

It is unfortunate that no one of our early observers has left us a plan or map of the ancient Indian trails, which were to be observed nearly a hundred years ago. Dr. Snyder sheds a little light on the subject and we quote from his paper.

The distance from this system of earth-works to the great Cahokia Mound in the American Bottom, on a straight line deviating but a few degrees from east and west in direction, is fifteen miles. That the architects and builders of the two Teocallis were contemporaneous and of the same ethnic stock, admits of little doubt. The relations existing between the people clustered about each of these temple mounds must have been intimate and harmonious. When a small boy, I remember hearing the statement made by Rev. John M. Peck—a noted Baptist minister, who came from Connecticut to this part of Illinois in 1818, and afterward founded Rock Spring Seminary, three miles west of Lebanon—that, at that early day, a deeply-worn footpath, or trail, could be readily traced from Emerald Mound through the dense woods, crossing Silver Creek at a rocky shallow ford, to and down the bluffs and continuing through the Bottom directly to the mound on Cahokia Creek. This statement was corroborated by Gov. John Reynolds and other old pioneers of this region. On the top of one of the highest points of the bluffs, where this trail emerges from the uplands into the Bottom, is a large conical mound, locally known as the "Sugar Loaf," which probably served the prehistoric savages, who erected it, the purpose of a signal station. From its summit the eye sweeps over a splendid view of this portion of the great river bottom, with its beautiful groves and small prairies, its many Indian mounds and numerous lakes and creeks, reaching far beyond to the mighty Mississippi and the western border of rocky bluffs, on the crest of which were, long ago, artificial mounds similar to this one—the "Big Mound" of St. Louis, fifty feet in height, could from here be plainly seen —now replaced by the miles of masonry and smoke-clouded walls and chimneys and towers of the rapidly expanding city.

PONDS AND DEPRESSIONS

There has been not a little speculation with reference to the numerous depressions, some rather extensive, scattered throughout approximately three thousand acres of the Cahokia group. On the map, Fig. 1, most of these are shown but there are several additional ones south of Mounds Nos. 6 to 11, and two or three large ponds south of Nos. 65 and 66. Drainage operations have affected several of these and in dry seasons there is little or no water in them.

The writer has never been of the opinion that these depressions were of special significance, but rather held the view in common with Myer, Willoughby, and Cowen that the explanation is rather simple. The Indians obtained the earth for mound construction from such places, preferring to dig rather deeply in the ground than to take up the soil evenly from a larger area.

The presence of chipped objects and pottery fragments in the muck in the several ponds surrounding the Cahokia group gave rise to the suggestion that possibly (but not probably) the Indians built houses on piles over the water. Four men were put to work in October, 1921, testing the bottom of two or three of these depressions. A dredging apparatus similar to oyster tongs was made, and the workmen lowered the tongs from a flat bottomed boat, and continued dredging for about two days. Where the water was shallow, they waded and made use of ordinary garden rakes. The result of the test was not satisfactory. The bottom is rather smooth, not irregular, and slippery. While numbers of artifacts were brought up, the tongs slipped over others. Our investigation did not extend to all the ponds. There is not sufficient material to indicate that Indians had built dwellings over the water, and furthermore, in dry seasons, such as frequently occur, there would not be sufficient water to afford protection to dwellers in cabins of the Swiss lake dweller type. Two of the large depressions were dry, and the survey was able to test them with augers and shovels. Little material was secured.

The Ramey brothers claim that when they were boys, two of these ponds contained water throughout the year, were deeper, and such fish as crappie, bass, and buffalo were frequently taken. A more careful search, extending over a greater length of time, might give different results, but at the present writing we are of the opinion that artifacts were either lost or thrown in the ponds by the Indians. Quite likely in early times some of these ponds drained into Canteen or Cahokia creeks and the fish came up during freshets.

THE VILLAGE SITE

The approximate extent of this has already been given. The ancient habitations, cabins or wigwams, appear to have been placed on either side of Cahokia Creek, and for a considerable distance up Canteen Creek (a small stream tributary to Cahokia Creek). The width of the village appears to have varied from a few hundred yards to as much as a mile in breadth. That is, the main axis of the village followed the course of Cahokia Creek south, west, and then southwest. The statement as to its extent is based upon examination by several workmen under our direction at various places. On the open farm lands we experienced no trouble in tracing the village site, but within the city limits of East St. Louis it was necessary to seek out many owners and secure permit for test pits in their back yards. We were not able to test generally, but throughout the city as a whole we tested in some thirty or forty places. We depend chiefly on Dr. Rau's rather complete description of the East St. Louis area. Our work tends to verify in most particulars Rau's observations of sixty-seven years ago.

The question arises whether all of this extensive village was inhabited at one time. Were there several periods of occupation? Did the Indians make their first settlement at the mouth of Cahokia Creek on the banks of the Mississippi? Again, was the first settlement made on Cahokia Creek near the spot now occupied by Monks Mound?

It is scarcely conceivable that so large a village—verily a city in extent—existed as a unit in a given time epoch. That suggestion is contrary to Indian custom and history so far as we know it. That great quantities of corn, beans, or other foods could be grown in the fertile American Bottoms, one grants. Indians were dependent to a large extent on game, and such a population as the far-flung debris indicates could not subsist on game alone.

Is it not likely that the Cahokia folk established camps from time to time at different points along the two creeks? Was not the region inhabited for several hundred years? These questions are important. At present we cannot answer them. Aside from concentration on descriptions of Monks Mound, the early writers present little of technical interest with regard to the village life. Rau, being a scientist, has given us material of considerable value. Readers will understand that this is no reflection on the other men, for archæology, as a science, had not been established. Some later observers, such as McAdams, Patrick, and others, failed to avail themselves of remarkable or unusual opportunities afforded before the roads, factories, and other "improvements" changed the entire Indian setting. Dr. J. F. Snyder, one of the best amateur archæologists that the State of Illinois has produced, was not afforded financial support and was unable to do any considerable work in the Cahokia region. As evidence of Snyder's ability and his knowledge of Illinois cultures, readers are referred to his paper, "Prehistoric Illinois," in Nos. 2-3, Vol. I, of the *Journal of the Illinois Historical Society* (1908).

The ground occupied by the village, as previously mentioned, varies in width. The heaviest occupation appears to lie in an area bounded by Mounds Nos. 4 and 73 to the east, 44 and 80 to the west. At a rough estimate this is some five hundred acres. In short, the thickest deposit and numerous ash pits center east and south of Monks Mound.

The pits dug in the stockyard district of East St. Louis, five miles westward from Monks Mound, would indicate an equally populous village at that point, the pottery fragments exhibiting characteristic Cahokia decorations, and disturbed ground containing human artifacts extends downward from twenty inches to three feet.

The Ramey brothers informed us that many years ago their father had some trenches dug to drain land north of Mounds Nos. 18 to 24 into Cahokia Creek. It was found that this land had filled in, due to overflow, probably five or six feet, if not more. Testing with our eight-inch augers at several points thereabouts, we found heavy village debris at a considerable depth. We should not forget that Cahokia and Canteen creeks have probably changed their channels more than once. Dr. Cyrus Thomas in the *Twelfth Annual Report of the Bureau of Ethnology,* pp. 133-134, comments as follows:

It is worthy of note that nearly all the relics found at the Cahokia group of mounds have been taken from the low ground between the mounds. The remarkable find of pottery, implements, and shells made by Mr. McAdams in the winter of 1881 was in the low land a short distance from the northeast corner of the great mound. The articles were nearly all taken from a square rod of ground. This has been to some extent Dr. Patrick's experience in making his fine collection of pottery.

The real burial places of the builders of the Cahokia mounds probably is yet to be discovered.

The bank of Cahokia Creek during the occupation of the mounds was evidently more to the south than its present line along the eastern part of the group. The old bank is still plainly visible. The low land between this old bank and the creek is now covered with forest trees. All along this bank, which forms the edge of the plateau on which the mounds stand, are abundant evidences of occupation in remote times. In digging two or three feet at almost any point along this bank indications of fire-places are found, with numerous river shells, broken pottery, and kitchen refuse. As all the arable ground about the mound has been in cultivation many years, it is quite possible that some of the burial places, which are usually quite shallow, have been destroyed, as pieces of human bones are very common in the plowed fields.

Since Thomas's visit the drainage commission has had one or two deep canals dug through swamp lands north of Monks Mound. These are indicated on our map, but there have been some extensive developments since this map was drawn. The result is the gradual filling up of most of Cahokia Creek and the lower portion of Canteen Creek. Trees and bushes are in evidence in the old channels and on the banks, and observations rendered difficult. In order to make careful study of the village and its relation to the first creek bed, it is suggested that at some future time a trench some three hundred feet in width be carried for a distance of one thousand feet. There is no immediate need of such an operation, the undertaking would be expensive and it may be well deferred to the future, but the plan should certainly be put into effect some years hence.

There were two extensive explorations of the village site during the years 1921 and 1922, and some testing, rather than trench digging, done during the season of 1923. In this report we include the observations published in Vol. XXI, No. 6, University of Illinois Bulletin, October 8, 1923, with some changes and additions.

We had read William McAdams's volume, *Ancient Races of the Mississippi Valley* (1877) and observed that on page 57 he says:

In excavating near the base of the great temple mound of Cahokia, whose towering height of over one hundred feet gave a grateful shade for our labors, we found in a crumbling tomb of earth and stone a great number of burial vases, over one hundred of which were quite perfect. It was a most singular collection, as if the mound-builder, with patient and skillful hand, united with artistic taste in shaping the vessels, had endeavored to make a representation of the natural history of the country in ceramics. Some of these were painted, and there were also the paint-pots and dishes holding the colors, together with the little bone paddle for mixing, and other implements of the aboriginal artist. Some of these are figured in our "Antiquities of Cahokia."

This discovery was made in the village site. Both of Mr. Mc-Adams's sons, as well as W. J. Seever, Esq., visited the scene of our operations and indicated where they thought Mr. Mc-Adams had excavated. During that season (1921) we had a crew of twenty-one men at work and we examined the ground some six hundred feet northeast of Monks Mound where the witnesses thought McAdams made the discovery. We also extended operations, working rather intensively here and there for a radius of three hundred yards. Some of the trenches were fifty feet in length. Broken human skeletons were found scattered here and there, probably where Mr. McAdams had made finds. We recovered one flexed burial accompanied by half of a bowl. There was another partial burial a few feet to the west. The ground about it was much disturbed. Above both burials was a layer of hard baked red earth some two feet from the surface. The disturbed earth extended from three to as much as five feet in depth. During the course of operations in the village site, numbers of fragments of galena,[1] portions of Busycon shells, arrowheads, hammerstones, and other material in common use among the Indians were discovered.

It is most unfortunate that McAdams did not preserve intact so interesting and unusual a deposit. Apparently the skeletal material was carelessly handled. The bones we found indicate perfectly good skeletons which might have been easily saved for study, measurement, and tabulation.

When excavating by means of test pits, with a view of studying the character and extent of the village site, we found a number of level, burnt clay floors varying from twenty to thirty feet in diameter. Three or four of these had been disturbed by the plow, others, somewhat deeper, were in fair condition. One near the shore of the lake, a quarter of a mile south of Monks Mound, was composed of ordinary clay, burned quite hard and some twenty by twenty-five feet in diameter. Whether these are the floors of wigwams or houses, we do not know. They seem rather small for dance floors or assembly places. There may be

---

[1] Lumps of this ore occurred in several mounds. It probably served as paint. Surfaces of galena masses are often flattened, indicating rubbing. The material may have been secured by the Indians from galena deposits in Missouri or Illinois.

more of them revealed by future exploration. No more refuse occurred on these floors than elsewhere in the village site.

Just north of Mound 31 are three mounds which have been cultivated until the edges overlap. About the bases of these the village site material seems to be most numerous. We are of the opinion that this part of the site should be quite thoroughly examined, since we dug up several pottery heads of birds, etc., all of exceptional form and finish.

The following is quoted from a study made by Dr. Charles Rau of the pottery found in the Cahokia village site.[2]

That the fabrication of earthenware was once carried to a great extent among the Indians, is shown by the great number of sherds which lie scattered over the sites of their former villages and on their camping places; but they are, perhaps, nowhere in this country more numerous than in the "American Bottom," a strip of land which extends about one hundred miles along the Mississippi, in Illinois, and is bounded by the present bank of the river and its former eastern confine, indicated by a range of picturesque wooded hills and ridges, commonly called "the Bluffs." This bottom, which is on an average six miles wide and very fertile, was formerly the seat of a numerous indigenous population, and abounds in tumular works, cemeteries, and other memorials of the subdued race. Among the lesser relics left by the former occupants may be counted the remnants of broken vessels, which occur very abundantly in various places of this region. These fragments are, however, mostly small; and, according to my experience, entire vessels are not found on the surface, but frequently in the ancient mounds and cemeteries, where they have been deposited with the dead as receptacles for food, to serve on their journey to the happy land of spirits.

About six years ago, while living in the west, I was much gratified by the discovery of a place in the American Bottom where the manufacture of earthenware was evidently carried on by the Indians. The locality to which I allude is the left bank of the Cahokia Creek[3] at the northern extremity of Illinoistown, opposite to St. Louis. At the point just mentioned the bank of the creek is somewhat high and steep, leaving only a small space for a path along the water. When I passed there for the first time, I noticed, scattered over the slope or protruding from the ground, a great many pieces of pottery of much larger size than I had ever seen before, some being of the size of a man's hand, and others considerably larger; and, upon examination, I found that they consisted of a grayish clay mixed with pounded shells. A great number of old shells of the unio, a bivalve which inhabits the creek, was lying about, and their position induced me to believe that they had been brought there by human agency rather than by the overflowing of the creek. My curiosity being excited, I continued my investigation, and discovered at the upper part of the

---

[2]Smithsonian Report for 1866. Published 1872, pp. 346-352.
[3]This creek runs in a southwardly direction through Madison County and a part of St. Clair County, and empties into the Mississippi, four miles below St. Louis, near the old French village of Cahokia.

bank an old fosse, or digging, of some length or depth, and overgrown with stramonium or jimson weed; and upon entering this excavation, I saw near its bottom a layer of clay, identical in appearance with that which composed the fragments of pottery. The excavation had unmistakably been dug for the purpose of obtaining the clay, and I became now convinced beyond doubt that the fabrication of earthen vessels had been carried on by the aborigines at this very spot. All the requisites for manufacturing vessels were on hand; the layer of clay furnished the chief ingredient, and the creek not only supplied the water for moistening the clay, but harbored also the mollusks whose valves were used in tempering it. Wood abounded in the neighborhood. All these facts being ascertained, it was easy to account for the occurrence of the large fragments. Whenever pottery is made, some of the articles will crack during the process of burning, and this will happen more frequently when the method employed in that operation is of a rude and primitive character, as it doubtless was in the present case. The sherds found at this place may, therefore, with safety be considered as the remnants of vessels that were spoiled while in the fire, and thrown aside as objects unfit for use.

I did not succeed in finding the traces of a kiln or fireplace, and it is probable that the vessels were merely baked in an open fire, of which all vestiges have been swept away long ago. The occurrence of the broken pottery was confined to a comparatively small area along the bank, a space not exceeding fifty paces in length, as far as I can recollect. They were most numerous in the proximity of the old digging, and at that place quite a number of them were taken out of the creek into which they had fallen from the bank. Farther up the creek I saw another excavation in the bank, of much smaller dimensions, and likewise dug for obtaining clay. Among the shells and sherds I noticed many flints which had obviously been fashioned to serve as cutting implements; they were perhaps, used in tracing the ornamental lines on the vessels or in smoothing their surfaces.

I did not find a single complete vessel at this place, but a great variety of fragments, the shape of which enabled me to determine the outline of the utensils of which they originally formed parts. This was not a very difficult matter, especially in cases when portions of the rims remained. The rim, it will be seen, is formed into a lip and turned over, in order to facilitate suspension; sometimes, however, it is cut off abruptly. Some of the vessels—more especially the smaller ones—were provided with ears, others had the outer rim set with conical projections or studs, both for convenience and ornament; and a few of the fragments exhibit very neatly indented or notched rims. In size these vessels varied considerably; some measured only a few inches through the middle, while the largest ones, to judge from the curvature of the rims, must have exceeded two feet in diameter. The bottom of the vessels mostly seems to have been rounded or convex. I found not a single flat bottom-piece. This, however, may be merely accidental, considering that flat-bottomed vessels were made by the Indians. The appearance of the fragments indicates that the earthenware was originally tolerably well burned, and the fracture exhibits in many instances a reddish color. But, as the art of glazing was unknown to the manufacturers, it is no wonder that the sherds, after having been imbedded for many years in the humid ground, or exposed to rain and the alternate action of a burning sun and a severe cold, are now somewhat brittle and fragile; yet, even when new, this aboriginal earthenware must have been much inferior in compactness and hardness to the ordinary kind or European or American crockery.

The thickness of the fragments varies from one-eighth to three-eighths of an inch, according to the size of the vessels, the largest being also the strongest in material. But in each piece the thickness is uniform in a remarkable degree; the rims are perfectly circular, and the general regularity displayed in the workmanship of these vessels renders it almost difficult to believe that the manufacturers were unacquainted with the use of the potter's wheel. Such, however, was the case. I have already mentioned that the clay used in the fabrication of this earthenware is mixed with coarsely pulverized unio-shells from the creek; only a few of the smaller bowls or vases seem to consist of pure clay. The vessels were covered on the outside, and some even on both sides, with a thick coating of paint, either of a black, dark brown, or beautiful red color, and in some fragments the latter still retains its original brightness. Only one color, however, was used in the painting of each article. It is evident that the coloring preceded the process of baking, and the surfaces thus coated are smooth and shining, the paint replacing to a certain extent the enamel produced by glazing.

The land lying west of Sand Prairie Road belongs to George Merrell, Esq., and for nearly half a mile, until Mr. Recklein's property is reached, is leased by Mr. Stolle. Throughout this land, from 1500 to 2500 feet west of Monks Mound, we found indications of a heavily populated village. Varying from twelve inches to four feet in depth, the soil was disturbed, and the usual pottery fragments, bones of animals, ashes, Unio shells, hammer stones, spalls, etc., were present. The Stolle land was tested in October, 1922. We again examined properties to the south, owned by Mrs. Tippetts, Mr. Wells, and Mr. Cole. Beyond Stolle's land, to the west of the Recklein land, the village site continued for more than a quarter of a mile, and is said to extend through the property owned by Mrs. Thomas. She was the only person in the Cahokia region who would not permit us to excavate. Her workmen, however, said that pottery vessels and bones were found when they dug post holes. Just how far north of Cahokia Creek at this point the village existed, we do not know, but we presume about a quarter of a mile.

Across the National Highway from Monks Mound are the estates of Mr. Cole, Mrs. Tippetts, and Mr. Wells. We did considerable work on Mr. Wells's land in the vicinity of Mounds Nos. 50, 52, and 53. We discovered the usual village site debris to be quite as heavy as at any point on Ramey lands to the north. Mound No. 52, a low structure, appeared to be a house site, and during excavation we observed many lumps of hard burnt clay in which were impressions of reeds and sticks. These gave us information with reference to the walls or methods of construction of the dwellings. Cane, the favorite material used in clay or mud in building wigwam walls in the South, does not occur on Cahokia Creek, so other growths more or less cane-like in character were employed by the Indians.

EXPLORATION OF CERTAIN MOUNDS DURING THE VARIOUS SEASONS

Examination of the ground on which was located the village of the Cahokia people is necessary to an understanding of their mode of life. However, since nearly every tribe of Indians living in the Mississippi Valley placed with the dead objects illustrative of their arts, occupations, religious beliefs, etc., it is equally essential that the burial places of the ancient Cahokians be discovered. To this end the various surveys worked intensively and tested numerous mounds. More than that, opinions were sought from Mr. Willoughby, director of the Peabody Museum, Mr. Bushnell, who is familiar with Cahokia, the late Mr. Myer (previously referred to), Mr. Seever, Dr. Whelpley, and many others. Frequently these, or other archæologists visiting our headquarters, would go over the map with us and give their opinions as to what tumuli should be selected for observation. The net result of all digging and conferences is to the effect that up to the present time there is no positive evidence as to the location of the great burial place at Cahokia—that repository which all agree exists, and the discovery of which would enable us to answer many questions concerning the Cahokians. These matters are mentioned in some detail for the reason that those who do not visualize the extent of the territory and the numbers of mounds, both large and small, and the amount of labor and money necessary to proper examination, have sometimes been prone to criticize. We have steadfastly kept in view the primary purpose of the Cahokia exploration, which is to shed light on this most interesting and ancient culture. According to our experience we are justified in the conclusion that only by intensive spade work in the future, testing mound after mound, will we achieve the desired result. There is no such thing as an "archæological divining rod." One of our old workmen in the State of Maine, who served on many expeditions between 1910 and 1920, in his simple way uttered a great truth: "Nobody can look into the ground." We think this rather commonplace expression covers the Cahokia situation. Without objects of aboriginal origin, no one can study aboriginal art and concept.

Southwest of Monks Mound (No. 38) is No. 48, on which in 1921 stood a farmhouse in a fairly good state of repair. This was used as headquarters during that season. Mr. Bushnell gives the elevation as twenty-five feet. Our measurements did not agree with those of either Mr. Bushnell or Mr. Ramey. The question of wash, or feather edge, at the base probably accounts for the differences. We might remark in passing that the proposed new survey will present accurate measurements of all these mounds, hence, throughout this report they might well be omitted. On reflection, it seems to us that Mound No. 48, although of pyramid form, may contain a large number of interments. This is merely a matter of opinion, but certainly there is much village site debris on or near the surface, and the earth appears to be much disturbed. An auger hole or two indicated very dark earth—not gumbo—that similar to Etowah, Hopewell, or other burial mounds.

THE KUNNEMANN MOUND[1]

On the estate of George Merrell, Esq., half a mile north of Monks Mound, is No. 11, a large structure which we named in honor of Mr. Merrell's tenant, Mr. A. Kunnemann, who has resided on the tract for over twenty-five years.

Originally the tumulus was about four hundred feet diameter and conical—not a pyramid as has been recorded on one of the maps. Twenty years ago fifteen to sixteen feet of the summit was removed, and a trench run in from the north side some ninety feet, in order that earth to build a dike along Cahokia Creek might be obtained. Thus the mound had been seriously damaged. We wished to test one of the larger structures, and as this one offered unusual facilities, we began work September 16, 1921. Witnesses present during the previous work were questioned and all agreed that the mound was conical, or "pointed" as Mr. Kunnemann expressed it. The present diameter of the top is seventy-five by fifty-six feet. The sides are about twenty-five degrees slope. Restoring this same ratio of slope to the top would give fifteen to sixteen feet more elevation, as stated. We found the base near the center to be thirty-five feet below the present flattened summit. Therefore, the tumulus was originally not below fifty, or more than fifty-one feet in altitude. This would make it the third mound of the whole group in height, but not in cubic contents.

---

[1]See Plates I and VII.

Some three weeks were spent upon Kunnemann Mound. When we stopped work we were near the center and had excavated some eighty feet beyond the point reached by the dike builders. (Plate VII, Figs. 2 and 3). No skeletons were discovered, but in the earth were great quantities of flint chips, broken pottery, animal bones, and other refuse scooped up by the natives when they took the earth from about their cabins to build the mound.

As we had before us a nearly straight wall thirty-five feet in height, we were afforded an excellent opportunity to study mound construction.

It was found that the mound (that is, the portion we excavated) rested on a heavy layer of clear sand. Test pits sunk in this sand indicated that it was natural, had not been deposited by man. The lowest part of the mound is ordinary mixed earth and not stratified. About eight feet above the sand, or base, is dark earth in which are many broken artifacts; above this, some five or six feet of yellowish loam, then a rather distinct decayed vegetation layer running across the face of our fifty-foot trench. This is rather thin and even; then several feet of darker soil, but not gumbo, and above this the heaviest layer of decayed vegetation, in some spots about half an inch in thickness. Yellow loam containing some sand extends fully ten feet above. In this and the layer below the "dumps" or basketfuls of earth are noted. That is, natives carried the earth in loads varying from a trifle over a peck to a half bushel or more. Just below the summit is a four to five foot layer of heavy, compact gumbo. These layers or stratification are presented in Plate I.

All these lines and strata are more or less even—that is, level —indicating that the people did not first build a small conical mound and gradually increase the size. Apparently they decided to construct a large tumulus, built up layers of somewhat different soil, and placed the heavy gumbo some distance from the apex. It is assumed they continue through the whole mound, but as mounds are sometimes irregular in construction, subsequent exploration of the remaining half may present differences in stratification.

After the work had progressed some days and when we were at a point north of the center, and where the mound was originally about forty-one feet high, we found a heavy layer of burned earth. This was almost floor-like in character. It was followed for a distance of thirty-five feet east and west, but was considerably narrower north and south. In the northern edge of this floor, eighteen feet above the base and eight feet below the present summit, we uncovered a circular, altar-like burned basin. It is shown in Plate VIII. Half of this had been broken off, whether by the Indians or the dike builders, we do not know. The latter state that they observed no burned basin. It was empty, but consisted of ordinary clay, hard burned. It was about a yard in diameter, ten or twelve inches deep and surrounded by a well defined, broad rim somewhat elevated. Extending in all directions beyond (save north) was the level, burned floor referred to. Why this altar should be nearly halfway above the base, we are unable to state. Altars are often found in Ohio mounds, but they lie on the base line.

When we had approached near the center of the mound we observed a burned area extending most of the distance across the face of our wall. It was sometimes nearly two feet thick. There was also a light sand stratum, some twenty feet above the base line, which extended some thirty-eight feet east and west.

Near the center and twenty-seven feet from the base, Mr. Eldridge found the head of a frog effigy pipe and numerous fragments of fine pottery. Various large flat, shell beads were also discovered from time to time. Pottery fragments were quite common.

Why no burials were found in the north half of the Kunnemann Mound, we do not know. Possibly, they will be found in the southern or eastern portions of the structure. Examination of the mound should be completed, but we did not feel justified in continuing operations. Some fragments of human bones were mingled with the village-site debris, but they were not burials. Broken human bones are frequently found in ash pits and in mounds.

SCHMIDT'S MOUND

Just back of Mr. Schmidt's hotel are Mounds Nos. 31 and 30. Both are flattened pyramids, the large one, No. 31, is twenty-two and one-half feet high, although originally it must have been much higher. No. 30, although entered on the Patrick-Seever survey as a pyramid, at present appears as an extensive platform. While to the eye it does not appear to be over five feet in altitude, yet on examination we found burnt stone, pottery sherds, and refuse extending to a depth of over seven feet. There was a level floor of burnt earth in the base—possibly a dance floor. Our measurements of No. 30 indicate the following—one hundred eighty feet east and west and one hundred eighty feet north and south. Fourteen men excavated a trench fifty-five feet in length. Test pits were sunk in this trench to the depth of ten feet five inches, but no human artifacts were discovered at any point below seven feet eight inches. About half a bushel of broken implements, pottery fragments of superior workmanship, and many lumps of burnt clay were taken from the excavation. Some of the burnt masses contain impressions of reeds and rushes. No. 31 was not tested, but in the north end Dr. Higgins of St. Louis had excavated a mushroom cellar. He found broken pottery and objects, also soft, dark "mound earth," not gumbo.

The Edwards Mounds

Ranging from one-quarter to one-third of a mile east of Mr. Schmidt's Mounds are several tumuli on the land of Mr. Edwards. In No. 24, a rather small mound, was found the skeleton shown in Plate IX. This was at a depth of four feet, was extended, and all the bones were present and in position. There were some flint chips and two or three flint knives near the head, also some large fragments of broken pottery. The base of the mound was about a foot below the present surface. A trench some sixty feet in length and twenty feet wide was run through the structure. Throughout the soil was scattered broken pottery.

East of this, distant about four hundred feet, is another mound, No. 25, about seven feet in height. We dug a trench through the center and sunk eight or ten test pits, finding no burials but discovered scales of copper on the base line. About one-third of this mound remains to be explored.

Since the above was written, much of the Edwards tract has been taken over by a commercial corporation and a large horse-racing track built and various structures erected. We have not seen the mounds, but are informed they have been much damaged.

No. 56. Jesse Ramey Mound

This is about twenty feet in height at the present time, the base diameter some three hundred feet. It is the second mound directly south of Monks. It is not quite clear whether this was originally an oblong mound or of the pyramid type since it has been cultivated for many years. Some twenty-five men were employed in the work and a trench sixty-five feet in length and ten feet deep was extended from near the base on the south side to a line some distance from the center. Then test pits were sunk and post augers used. Five or six feet farther down (a total depth of fourteen to sixteen feet) we came upon rather soft, dark earth quite different from the clay and gumbo of which most of the mounds are composed. It resembled the earth found about burials in the several mounds of the Hopewell group. There were a few scales of copper, and some fragments of highly finished pottery. That is, the fragments recovered indicate the finer pottery such as accompanies burials. This mound was tested during our first season. At a subsequent visit the Ramey family did not care to have it explored. Now that it is State property, it is recommended that thorough exploration be undertaken.

Mound No. 64

This lies to the extreme south of the group, fully a mile from Monks Mound, and many years ago was considerably damaged by the construction of the Baltimore & Ohio and Pennsylvania Railroads which pass on either side. Some of the earth was utilized in grading tracks. It is stated by older residents that the Baltimore & Ohio construction crew removed some two-thirds of the structure, and found a stone pipe, said to represent an eagle, about twenty inches in length. Diligent inquiry fails to indicate the present location of this specimen. The structure is composed of very heavy, dark gumbo and although eight or ten test pits six to ten feet in depth were dug by our crew, no pipes, skeletons, or other objects were uncovered.

Several mounds south of the National Highway were tested somewhat superficially with our eight-inch augers. Most of them are composed of very hard gumbo and there was no indication of burials, although our tests should not be considered as final.

The Sawmill Mound, No. 39

Reference to Fig. 1, our map will indicate that on Rameys' land (northwest from the barn) is Mound No. 39, which is designated by local people as the Sawmill Mound. It is, as near as we could determine without actual survey, two hundred forty feet by two hundred forty feet in extent, a square mound, with level summit. South oɪ it six hundred feet is a large oval mound, No. 41, twenty-five feet high. The original form may have been either pyramidal or oval. No one knows. We think a long, low platform existed between the Sawmill Mound and the first one to the south, No. 77. On the north side of the Sawmill Mound (No. 39) is the old bed of Cahokia Creek, and on that side the mound appears to be eighteen or nineteen feet

Design on a fragment of pottery

high, whereas to the south there is a more gradual slope. To the eye the mound does not appear to be over seven or eight feet high when one looks northward.

The name was given long ago, since sometime between 1850 and 1860 a mill boiler exploded, killing twelve to fifteen men, who were buried in a small mound south of the turnpike, probably Mound No. 73, or possibly No. 47. This circumstance should be remembered in case some future explorers find well preserved skeletons with traces of wooden coffins about them.

It is not necessary to present a map of the burials along the southern slope of the Sawmill Mound (No. 39). Extending in a somewhat irregular row, or line, for about thirty feet east and west, eight were found, and numbered four to eleven. The first four of these burials were headed north, the next three south, and No. 11, northeast. Nos. 4, 5, and 6 lay in black soil at a depth of about thirty inches. The surrounding area for a distance of several hundred feet was tested carefully and disturbed ground extended down for a depth of as much as three feet, indicating an extensive village site. Black pottery predominated, and a few red fragments were observed.

Just south of No. 39 is a small mound (No. 77), on the slope of which, down two feet, was discovered a small bowl-like mass of hard, burnt clay. Although broken somewhat, it appeared to be circular in form, about twenty inches in diameter, or sixty inches around the curvature. No complete measurement could be made, yet the rim was well defined. In the cavity, where the base should have been, was a large lump of galena blackened by fire, also some pulverized galena. The lump weighed fully eight pounds and the powdered galena was about a quart in quantity. There was a pottery bowl, seven or eight inches in diameter and three inches high, with this deposit, and a shallow dish very flat, like a plate, of rather thick clay, also an oval stone on which were distinct markings or lines (Plate XVIII, Fig. 5). There were several ordinary hammer stones, and a small jar, almost crucible-like. This is dark brown, well made, stands about four inches in height, and the base is unusually thick and heavy. The jar is shown in Fig. 5, Plate XVII.

The work continued along the southern slope of Mound No. 39, and with skeleton No. 9, a young person, was a small toy vessel, about two inches in diameter, near the head (Plate XVII, Fig 4). At the right of skeleton No. 8 was a blackened bone object, probably an awl; also an entire deer jaw bone, in the point of which had been cut a groove, thus forming a small chisel or gouge. On the east side of this mound we ran a trench thirty-five feet in length, and five feet deep, but no burials were encountered. A pit was sunk in the center, fourteen by fifteen feet. This was dug down sixteen feet, then the post augers put down three and one-half to four feet farther. In the extreme base was found a heavy wet clay. The mound was stratified as follows:

Mixed earth	4 feet	Dark streak	3 inches
Dark earth	10 inches	Yellow earth	1 foot
Yellow earth	2 feet	Mixed earth	2 feet
Dark streak	4 inches	Dark earth	3 feet
Yellow earth	18 inches		

The layers in the Sawmill Mound were not even; in the northwest corner they radiated from a cone formation—dipping to the southeast or east. Yet when we were down about ten feet they appeared to be more horizontal. On the south side of the trench was a heavy black layer.

Some fragments of pottery (Plate XXVII, Fig. 1) also chips and spalls were found scattered throughout the structure. A peculiar clay effigy of a mammal head (Plate XXIII, Fig. 7), an awl cut from the lower jaw of a deer (Plate XXV, Fig. 13), and a rare shell effigy cut from a river mussel (Plate XXIII, Fig. 2), were also found in this mound. The auger borings in the south side of the pit showed heavy blue clay, along with the gray.

While some workmen sank the pit, others continued searching for burials. They found a number of disturbed burials, or rather fragmentary ones, much broken. These were scattered throughout the soil two and one-half to four and one-half feet in depth and without regularity. Probably Dr. Patrick or Mr. McAdams had dug here, since the soil seemed soft and disturbed. Below all the burials we sank test pits several feet in depth.

Skeleton No. 11 lay extended head northeast (Plate XXIX, Fig. 2). It was quite well preserved. An ordinary jar lay near the right hand, and a bowl near the left knee (Plate XVII, Fig. 6). A shell gorget and a bone knife were also found with this skeleton (Plate XXIII, Fig. 1; Plate XXV, Fig. 8).

While part of the men were working under the writer's direction, Mr. Seever took a crew and prospected two low mounds west of No. 48. In Mound No. 80 he ran a trench about six feet in width, and fifty in length, finding a large number of potsherds, bones, and burnt clay, and village site material. He also went more than a mile up Canteen Creek and prospected both sides of the stream for a distance of half a mile. The drainage canal system inaugurated by the County Commissioners sometime ago has so changed conditions that it was impossible for him to make further observations. He says, "I find that the old bottom lands of Cahokia and Canteen creeks have been filled in by wash in flood time from five to ten feet, thus obliterating some low mounds that were in existence, and covered up the deposits mentioned as having been seen by Charles Rau in the 1860's."

MOUNDS NOS. 19, 20, AND 21

Probing the lesser mounds indicated burials north of Mound No. 33, and reference to the large map will indicate that there are seven mounds in a line east and west. Three of these, Nos. 19, 20, and 21, are so near together that the edges overlap. This is probably due to cultivation of the soil. The **original** heights of these structures are unknown, but we assume **that** No. 20 was the largest. No. 19 is at present about five **feet in** height, No. 20 about four feet, and No. 21 is about **three feet** in altitude. Most of the burials were in No. 20, or **on** the slope of it. Skeleton No. 12 was found on the southern slope of No. 20 at a depth of about three feet, and was fairly well preserved. The right leg had been much elevated and we found the tibia and femur at least a foot above the rest of the body; yet it had not been disturbed by the plow, and this curious form of burial must have been intentional.

At the head of this skeleton were **four pots shown** in Plate XXX, Fig. 1: first the bowl, next **the jar, then** a dish in which a fine, dipper-like object was placed. This is decorated with sun symbols and has a long, slender, projecting handle. The right arm of the skeleton was in normal position to the elbow, but the ulna and radius lay across the abdomen, and the left leg was bent at the knee. All of this pottery was perfect, but there was nothing else in the grave (Plate XVII, Figs. 1-3). Skeleton No. 33 was doubled up, the knees being drawn up to the abdomen. There was disturbed earth just east of it, and a detached skull two feet north. Numerous test pits showed several fragmentary human skeletons, and much village site debris.

About one hundred fifty feet from the west end of our trench, at the depth of three feet, were many fragments of spades and hoes, or digging tools of reddish chert. Why these were all broken we do not know. There were enough fragments to comprise fifteen or twenty of the tools, and about them were ashes and burnt earth. Fifteen feet beyond was a mass of pulverized galena lying in ashes.

Our total trench was extended a distance of over two hundred fifty feet from the center of Mound No. 19 well into No. 21. Much village site material occurred through the soil and extended in places as deep as seven feet. Naturally, the greatest depths at which village site debris occurred were near the highest parts of the mounds. Plate XXXI, Fig. 2, shows the position of two skeletons. The burial in the foreground had a vessel at the head; the skull rested upon a small sea shell and there were traces of pigment (in small lumps) near the face. Between burials 21 and 22 was found an ordinary cooking pot, lying five feet from the nearest skeleton. With three or four of the other skeletons we found ordinary clay dishes or bowls usually placed by the head. None of the skeletons were well preserved although two or three were taken out fairly entire and lent to Dr. A. J. Terry of the Medical Department of Washington University. It is not necessary to record all the depths of the skeletons; they varied from two and one-half feet to six and one-half feet, and save one or two were all extended. Eight of them lay with the heads to the north, three with the heads to the east, two with the heads west, five with the heads south, and others northwest and southeast (Text Fig. 2). Whether pottery originally placed by the natives had been re-

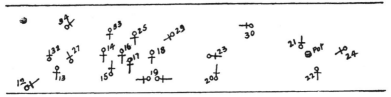

FIG. 2—Position of skeletons in trench cut through Mounds Nos. 19, 20, 21.

moved by McAdams, Patrick, or others, we do not know. It is possible that no pottery was placed with these interments, except such as we recovered. Assuming that such statement is correct, about one-third of the burials were accompanied by vessels or pottery. Two-thirds were without pottery. The exception is with No. 12 which was accompanied by four vessels as has been stated. A fine needle was found with skeleton No. 30 (Plate XXVIII, Fig. 2) and an awl made from the tibia of a deer with skeleton No. 18 (Plate XXV, Fig. 10).

Dr. F. S. Smith, of Nevada, Iowa, was present during the removal of these skeletons, and attempted to make some observations on the remains, as they lay in the ground. He made no measurements and his notes are mere field suggestions.

No. 16. Female.

No. 18. Probably female, decayed, and therefore sex uncertain.

No. 20. Young woman eighteen to twenty-five years.

No. 21. Female; pelvis very light, the brim typical form. Anteroposterior diameter about four and one-half inches. The iliac crest very thin and the roughened crest for attachment of muscles not well developed. All long bones small and delicate. The femora typical form and meeting of the lower leg at the usual angle for women.

"It is impossible to make any accurate measurements but the thin light bones, and typical size and form of the clavicles all point to the above numbered skeletons as being females."

All the interments appear to be on the same level or base line, and were probably village rather than mound burials. That most of them appear to be women is interesting, as usually both sexes are found in the cemeteries.

THE JAMES RAMEY MOUND, NO. 33

Spring Operations, 1922.—It was decided to select a large tumulus and examine as much of it as possible. This structure adjoined a pyramid or "temple mound" and both seemed to occupy a central position in ancient Cahokia times.

There was originally a deep depression between Mounds Nos. 33 and 34, so the Rameys informed me, which had been filled in by dragging the earth from the summit of the mound down the steep slopes into this depression. The mound was conical originally, and according to all witnesses probably fifteen feet higher than at the time of our exploration. This would give it a height of thirty-eight feet. The adjoining mound to the west, No. 32, is a temple or pyramid structure with flattened summit, and is so shown in the maps and old records. No. 33 was supposed to be a burial structure, since it came to a "point," and local tradition is persistent in so describing this tumulus.

Testing elsewhere was deferred and fourteen men were put to work on the north side at the lowest slope. We began at a point which appeared to the eye to be four or five feet above the general surface, yet we had gone down over seven feet before we found the base line. Our trench extended to the south.

When Curator F. C. Baker of the University of Illinois came to visit our survey, on April 3, we had run the trench thirty feet south in the mound. The face of the trench, or south wall, was twelve feet high. The width of the pit was twenty-seven feet east and west. A number of marine shells, a few bone awls, and the usual broken pottery and animal bones were found. While Curator Baker was present we sank a number of pits with the post augers and brought up bones from the lower layers or bottom. These bones were observed to be of brownish green color. Later, during the research in this mound, the same peculiarity was observed, and all bones below the eighteen-foot level were coated and discolored. Chemical analysis will determine the nature of this action, which has seldom been observed in other mounds. On the seventh of April the trench wall, being nearly fifteen feet in height, became dangerous and the earth caved in frequently. It was therefore sloped down by the men and four teams were put to work scraping the earth out and depositing it on the slopes to the north and south. Teams and scrapers were continued at work until about the twenty-second of April when we again resorted to hand work to complete the trench.

Our total area excavated was about one hundred feet north and south, and thirty-five feet east and west. Some area was lost since it became necessary to slope the walls (twenty-three feet high) to prevent injury to our men. East and west, on top, the opening was about forty-five feet—the base line narrower, as stated. In Text Fig. 12, Part II, is shown a cross section made by Dr. Leighton. The scale indicates the thickness of the strata.

For some two weeks the men dug until the base line was exposed. On the west side of the trench opposite stakes 110 to 130 were a number of post holes three to five inches in diameter. The posts had decayed but traces of wood remained. There had been no fire at this point. The holes appeared to be part of a large circular edifice or wigwam, and were found at a depth of about fourteen feet from the summit. Lying near one of them was a long double-pointed flint knife which is shown in Plate XXVI, Fig. 1. In the center of the cut was found the circular trench, and the circular post holes, and the altars or basins shown in Text Figs. 3 and 4. These lay upon the base line about twenty-three feet from the summit.

Nothing just like these circles and basins have been previously found in mounds so far as we are aware. That is, there have been more perfect altars, and post holes arranged in circular form but not all of them in one place. Plate XXXI, Fig. 1 shows the excavation, the circles being in the foreground; Plate XXXI, Fig. 3 the two circles and depressions to the right; and Plate XXX, Fig. 2 a close view of the depressions or altars and the two circles. As the holes would not show clearly in a negative, corn stalk stubs were inserted to bring into sharper relief the holes. The men carefully hand troweled the entire space for a distance of twenty-five feet. In the center were two burnt basins or depressions which were filled with ashes.

Mr. Cowen has called them altars in his drawing, and they may be such. They vary from seventeen to twenty-six inches in diameter and the depressions were four to seven inches in depth. They were not burned hard as are the Ohio altars. The one south of the circle contained nothing. North of the circle were two shown near the top in Text Fig. 3, and these were of different form, rather shallow, and three-fourths circular. Instead of the circle being complete, the depression in one was extended to the east and in the other to the north. When uncovered, they were not unlike crude pans in appearance, the handles being rather short and the cavity in them not as deep as in the main body of the depression.

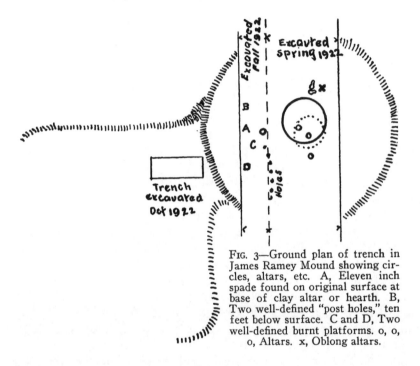

Fig. 3—Ground plan of trench in James Ramey Mound showing circles, altars, etc. A, Eleven inch spade found on original surface at base of clay altar or hearth. B, Two well-defined "post holes," ten feet below surface. C and D, Two well-defined burnt platforms. o, o, o, Altars. x, Oblong altars.

The trench was about three inches wide and twenty feet in diameter. It was nearly a true circle (Text Fig. 4). To form it the Indians dug out the earth to a depth of several inches and then filled it with dark soil so that the contrast was unmistakable. There was nothing in this trench—not even ashes or charcoal. From the center of the sun symbol and extending south was a circle of post holes two to three inches in diameter. Probably saplings had been inserted and then the primitive wigwam burned, as there were great quantities of charred stubs and charcoal. In the center of this wigwam circle was a burnt basin and to the northwest lay another. Ashes from these two depressions were taken by Mr. Alfred C. Carr and analyzed for Mr. V. C. Turner of the Scullin Steel Company by Mr. L. Z. Slater.

I enclose herewith complete qualitative and quantitative analysis of the samples you gave me. You will note there is a large quantity of silica.

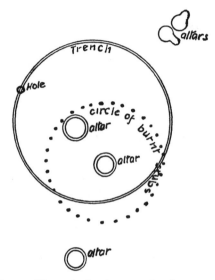

Fig. 4—Plan of circular trench, altars,
etc., in James Ramey Mound.

We could not account for this until the specimens were examined under a microscope and then it was found that small quantities of clay or sand had been washed down into and between the fibres of the specimens. It was impossible to take these off and therefore we have assumed that the silica was the particles which adhered to the fibre, together with part of the iron and alumina. The phosphoric acid, calcium carbonate, and magnesium carbonate, together with some of the alumina led us to assume that specimen must have been bone at one time, at least it could not have been wood-ash or charcoal.

There was also another interesting discovery and that is that under fire test there is a trace of lithium. This leads us to believe that there was tobacco present among the bones and clay, as this lithium is always present in tobacco and it is hardly possible that it would be in any other substance that was placed in the receptacle where the samples were found.

V. C. TURNER

Following is the analysis of sample taken from James Ramey Mound:

Silica (Si)..62.10
Iron and alumina (Fe & Al)...............................25.15
 mostly oil 203
Phosphoric acid (P205)....................................... .49
Calcium carbonate (CaCO₃)..............................10.55
Magnesium carbonate (MgCO₃).......................... 1.66

$$\overline{}$$
99.95

Fire test shows trace of Lithium.

L. Z. SLATER

Through an area of twenty-five feet, having as a center the altars, was a floor not very hard burnt, and yet beyond question a level surface on which fires had been built.

Sections of gas pipe were screwed together and with these the men were able to test to a depth of fifteen or twenty feet with the augers. They thoroughly tested the mound to the east and south of these circles. It was then thought that possibly there might be burials in the structure and that the altars and sun symbols occupied the center portion of the mound area. However, no burials could be discovered.

The various artifacts found during the course of exploration were kept in cigar boxes according to the levels at which they occurred. There was no particular difference in material to be noted except, possibly, the best pottery—that is, the red ware and the sherds indicating thin, well-made vessels—was found from fifteen to twenty feet below the surface. Near the bottom there appeared to be more village site material, and at about ten feet from the summit the preponderance of fragments indicating ordinary cooking vessels. Types of pottery fragments are shown on Plates XXI and XXII.

Numerous photographs were taken at various stages of the work. About the first of May the walls were thrown in, and with the consent of the owners the mound was abandoned until fall. When we left, the excavation had the appearance of a crater about one hundred feet in length, sixty feet in width, and twelve feet deep in the center.

September-October Operations, 1922.—On arrival at the James Ramey Mound in the fall of 1922, although but four months had elapsed since the abandonment of the work in the spring, we noted that vegetation had sprung up in the depression. Visitors had attempted to dig, but fortunately we had left the mound in such shape that they could do no damage.

It was decided to work toward the west and extend the trench in that direction. Text Fig. 3 presents the total work done on the mound. When we completed operations the latter part of October, the total area excavated was one hundred twenty feet north and south and about fifty-five feet east and west. As the Temple Mound, No. 32, adjoined this structure, a deep pit was sunk to the bottom of that mound. The pit was about twenty-five feet from the western edge of our trench and was fourteen by eight feet in diameter at the bottom. This is shown in Text Fig. 3. While the teams lowered the mound to the bottom, the men sank the pit mentioned, and found the base line down about seventeen feet. It was not thought necessary to excavate the space between the west wall of No. 33 and this pit, although the augers were put down at many points. The usual village sites debris extended clear to the bottom, but on the base line was a very heavy deposit of dark soil and ashes a few inches in thickness and here we observed much more village site material than in the other mound. It would appear that the Temple Mound was erected over a site occupied by a wigwam, for the mound was built directly on this part of the village site and none of the refuse had been cleaned up. Some thirty-seven-inch auger holes were put to the bottom of No. 32, and decayed bones, burnt earth, etc., were found at several points. It might be advisable to trench this mound at some future time.

On October 12 but one team was retained and a party of sixteen men dug out the remainder of Mound No. 33 by hand. Another of these burnt basins was found near stake 130. This was about twenty inches in diameter and about five or six inches deep and was filled with charcoal. The west side of our trench, being somewhat beyond the center of the mound, was not over nineteen feet in depth. Stratification was not as well marked as observed last spring. There was a good deal of gumbo in the west wall and it was not necessary to slope the bank very much. A thin layer of pure sand about half an inch in thickness, which we had traced continuously from the north side of the old trench, extended in the mound but seemed to disappear a little south of the center.

The large post holes observed last spring in the west side of our trench did not continue regularly. Several more were observed but there was no special regularity and we therefore concluded that they did not represent a circular dwelling.

During the course of sinking the trench, part of a human femur some six inches in length, a vertebra, and two teeth were found, but there were no burials. Near stake 120, at a depth of seventeen feet, was found a large flint spade about a foot in length. This is shown in Fig. 5, on Plate XXVI. Nothing very important was found during the course of exploration save that a heavy layer of charcoal, in which was bark, extended to the south and southwest between stakes 130 and 140. When we ceased operations this layer continued in the walls, but as we had already spent a great deal of money on this mound the pit was not enlarged.

There was an even, burnt floor, and covered by a thin layer of white ash and above that large pieces of charcoal and charred wood. We estimated this layer to be some three feet above the base of the mound. At several points on the burnt floor were small, flat stones, irregularly shaped and apparently limestone, which had been subjected to heat. There were also many calcareous clay concretions. This platform or burnt floor with accompanying ashes and charcoal, we hand troweled for a distance of nearly twenty feet. It still continued in the wall of our trench toward the southwest when we ceased work.

Conclusions on James Ramey Mound.—The circles have been called sun symbols, though they may not be such, but that is our opinion. What led the Indians to construct such a mound, we do not know. It is often difficult for us to appreciate the aboriginal point of view. That certain ceremonies were here enacted we may believe, but the nature of these still remains a mystery.

A few notable objects found in the James Ramey Mound are shown on the plates. Two clay discs on Plate XXVII, Figs. 2, 4. Peculiar pottery designs on Plate XXIII, Figs. 8, 9. Two bird head effigies on same plate, Figs. 5, 6. Two good bone awls on Plate XXV, Figs. 3, 7. A peculiarly cut leg bone of Wapiti or American elk is shown in Fig. 12, on same Plate. A very finely-cut and decorated gorget shell of the Spike River mussel *(Elliptio dilatatus)*, with evenly notched edges, probably used as a nose or ear ornament, is shown in Fig. 3, on Plate XXIII. It was found at a depth of twenty feet, near stake 110. Broken projectile points and arrow heads are shown in Figs. 1, 6-8, 11, on Plate XXVIII. Marine mollusks, beads, and ornaments are shown on Plate XXIV. Most of the Cahokia beads are flat and not cylindrical.

THE JONDRO MOUND, No. 86

This was not put on the map which we inserted in our previous report (Vol. 19, No. 35, University of Illinois publications). In fact, Patrick, Van Court, and the other surveyors seem to have left out a number of small mounds. It lies nearly a mile and a half west of Monks, and is almost circular, being one hundred forty by one hundred thirty feet. A diagram is shown of it in Text Fig. 5. The surface is rather irregular and we supposed

Fig. 5—Cross section of Tusant Jondro Mound. Sec. 34, Twp. Edgemont, St. Clair Co. Position of burials is indicated, the first burial being seventy-five feet from north edge of mound.

originally the mound was conical and that it had been worked down during cultivation in the field, but the owner, Mr. Tusant Jondro, informs us that while his father had a garden on one side and he set out an orchard, the eastern half had never been cultivated. Therefore the structure, which now varies from four to six feet in elevation, could not have been much higher than at present. It might have served a double purpose, that is, for burials and later as an elevation on which wigwams were set.

Mr. William J. Seever had charge of the work, and spent some time running a trench north and south through the entire mound, and another trench from the south end of the mound, northwest for twenty feet. He found twenty-four burials, and enough detached burials, or rather bodies so decayed that only a portion of skeletons were observed, to account for sixteen or seventeen more. In the north half of the mound there are probably many more burials. Mr. Jondro states that his father uncovered burials during the operations incident to tree planting or gardening. The cross section in Fig. 5 shows that at the north end there was an original mound four feet high, composed of buckshot gumbo. This was extremely hard digging, and nothing was found therein. In fact, in our excavations,

survey members never found burials or much village site debris
in gumbo soil, except the Chucallo Mound and this was not all
gumbo.

The skeletons were headed in various directions, and no uniformity as to points of the compass was observed by the Indians. Excepting one skeleton noted on the map, no objects accompanied any of the burials (Text Fig. 6). Not enough pot-

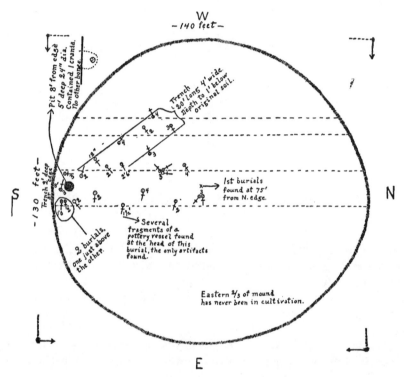

Fɪɢ. 6—Field plan of the Jondro Mound.

tery fragments were found with this burial to enable restoration. Every skeleton was badly decayed; in many instances it
was impossible to remove even one-third of a femur or tibia.

About two hundred feet north of the mound is a depression
from which earth and gumbo were taken for this mound; a
similar one lies one hundred seventy-five feet south of the
mound.

SAM CHUCALLO MOUND

This is the last of the several tumuli in the corporate limits of East St. Louis and is not on our map. It lies on the edge of a deep depression where the earth has been removed by the Pennsylvania Railroad to make a filling. Cahokia Creek is one hundred yards to the north. The distance from Sam's Mound to Monks Mound is something over three miles. The Pennsylvania excavation removed the western edge of the mound, up to where it was about four feet in height. The owner did not wish a large group of men to be put to work so he and another man were employed to dig a trench some seventy feet in length, ten feet deep, and eight feet in width (March-April, 1922). The mound was of very heavy gumbo, and unpromising. Very little village site material occurred save now and then a hammer stone and animal bones. A large flint spade was taken from the seven-foot level, somewhat east of the center of the mound. At the nine-foot level, near the center, Sam discovered a skeleton surrounded by a dome-shaped mass of very black gumbo. The soil on either side and above this mass was somewhat lighter. Dr. M. M. Leighton of the University of Illinois was present when part of this skeleton was uncovered. After Dr. Leighton departed, the workmen uncovered seven other skeletons lying on a little burnt bench about a foot above the bottom of the mound, or nine feet from the surface. This find was made just west of the skeleton mentioned. Above the burials one could clearly observe a small mound of tough gumbo perhaps four feet in height. Apparently the burials were covered by this, and the rest of the mound added afterwards. A brick building (the residence of the owner) to the south somewhat disturbed the southern edge of the mound. In making the street a little of the east edge was removed, and the trolley tracks are flanked by a low bank on the north side of the mound. It is, therefore, difficult to give accurate measurements but we judge the mound to have been about one hundred fifty by one hundred twenty feet in diameter.

The seven skeletons referred to were bunched burials, all crushed by the heavy gumbo and many of the bones powdered so that they appeared like sawdust. This form of decay had not previously been observed, and several boxes full of disintegrated bones were taken for preservation. There were no objects with the burials. Undermining the bank to the south

brought into view the feet of two more skeletons—better preserved and not bunched burials. Although badly broken, as
stated, the bones seemed unusually heavy.

Work on this mound was abandoned until the next season
when the owner was again employed, and he and another
workman excavated an area approximately thirty by forty feet
and some eleven feet in depth. Near the center of the tumulus
they found six skeletons, placed in a row, side by side, heads
to the south. Each body was extended, arms at the sides, feet
not crossed. Just below this was a heavy layer of slightly burned
earth on which there were traces of bark or matting very much
decayed. It was impossible to save much of it although parafin
and white shellac were applied. Some small samples were secured and sent to Urbana. None of the crania or long bones
could be removed for study. There were no objects with the
deposit. The distance from these bodies to the surface was ten
feet.

PITTSBURG LAKE CEMETERY

On the shores of Pittsburg Lake, about six miles southeast of
Cahokia, a large cemetery was discovered when a new automobile road, known as the Louisiana Boulevard, was constructed a few years ago. Mr. H. Braun was present when the
teams and scrapers at work on the boulevard uncovered the remains. He states there were thirty or forty burials and he secured some fifty-one pottery vessels.

To ascertain whether this cemetery was of the Cahokia culture, we visited the site, paid the owner for two acres of wheat
and began testing. We found a total of thirteen skeletons in a
space some twenty by twenty-five feet. With them were eleven
pottery vessels, six of which were whole. The cemetery was
thoroughly trenched by us for several days, six workmen being employed, but we could discover no other interments.

The skeletons (save one) were badly decayed, due to the
character of the soil, and most of them were near the surface.
Our field notes are as follows:

Skeleton 38. Head south. Extended. Depth three feet.
Skeleton 39. Bowl, set with rim upwards.
Skeleton 40. Two pots. A detached skull. Three awls were laid across
a wide dish. Head south. Dish against the jar two inches from jar. One
foot from surface. Well preserved. Body extended on back. Bone arrow
point on face.

Skeleton 40A. Depth three feet. Head east, and badly crushed.

Skeleton 41. Skeleton south. Decayed and broken, twenty-four inches from surface.

Skeleton 42. Red pot with decayed skeleton. Pot in dish. Effigy head broken off. Some red paint. Twenty inches down.

Skeleton 43. Small pot by head of a child. Very badly decayed. Eighteen inches down.

Skeleton 44. Young person, two pots. Head north. Badly decayed. Down eighteen inches.

Skeleton 46. Five feet deep. Legs drawn up. Two photos. No objects.

In several instances, near the head of the body was a large flat stone set in the grave. There were several of these, and they were smaller than the stone slabs forming the well known box graves of the middle South. Mr. Braun stated that this peculiarity was observed in many of the burials destroyed by the road construction crew. All pottery found was typical of the middle South, and did not exhibit any of the Cahokia decorations. A bone awl found with skeleton No. 39 is shown in Fig. 4 on Plate XXV.

MOUNDS NOS. 14 AND 79

Except the Kunnemann Mound, none lying north of Cahokia Creek had been examined by us. Therefore, in April, we trenched two of them.

Number 14.—The field notes state, "About one-third mile north of Monks is a mound lying between old Cahokia and the present drainage canal. Years ago a road through the swamp passed along the crest of this structure. There is a depression in the center of this mound from end to end. Dimensions, north and south one hundred eighty feet, east and west one hundred ten feet. About five feet high. Composed of heavy gumbo. Very hard digging. Put eight men to work. Sunk ten pits each four feet deep; also used post augers for three and one-half feet. A few pieces of stone, no pottery; some broken bones."

Mackie Mound, No. 79.—This is about one and one-fourth miles west of Monks Mound and is on the bank of old Cahokia Creek. It is covered by a heavy oak grove, has never been plowed, and is about one hundred thirty feet north and south and ten feet high. It is surrounded on three sides by a swamp and there is a long low platform, or apron, extending about one hundred fifty feet to the east. This platform varies from three to five feet high. A trench was extended a distance of about thirty feet in the mound down to within a few feet of the base line, then the post augers were brought into service. Numbers of pits were sunk three or four feet in depth. With the exception of a few scales of flint or chert and one pottery fragment, absolutely nothing was found. The mound was composed of the hardest kind of buckshot gumbo, with no sign of stratification. It is clear that no village existed at the point from whence the earth was taken to build this mound, as there are no broken artifacts to be observed in the soil.

Sullivan's Mounds

Persons frequently called our attention to two mounds on Signal Hill. These command a view of the American Bottoms and in an air line are some four miles south of the largest tumulus— Monks. We secured permission to excavate from Judge J. D. Sullivan, both structures being in his yard. The largest one when viewed and measured from its base, is a low conical mound, ten feet in height, some ninety feet in diameter, nearly circular at the base line, very symmetrical in the contour line, not differing, when viewed from the slope on which it is erected, from similar ones in the Cahokia Mound region (Text Fig. 7). Excavations of a trench some six feet wide through the east and west axis, carried down to and below its base, revealed, however, a very unusual mound construction or building. Instead of beginning upon the original surface and upbuilding from there, as they usually did, the builders of this tumulus reversed the procedure, by excavating a bowl-like depression apparently the diameter or size of the structure afterwards to be erected. This excavation, rather uneven on the floor line, a few inches in depth at its outer edges, increasing in depth until at or near the center, it attained a maximum depth of eighteen inches. Into this bowl-like depression, numerous oval and circular pits were dug, in depth from two or three to eighteen inches; in diameter from twelve inches, to the largest encountered, of five feet two inches. Nine of these pits were located in the floor of the trench (with traces of others on outer sides of the trench); these were thoroughly "cleaned out," and accompanied clearly definite strata of white or gray ashes, mixed with charcoal, in very dark and loose loamy soil, numerous pieces of broken pottery or earthenware, some animal and bird bones, quantities of small irregular broken stones showing discoloration from heat, one battered and broken grooved granite axe, several defective celts, hammer stones, and Unio shells mingled with the dark colored earth of the pits.

From one pit were taken two highly specialized bone implements some four inches long (Plate XXV, Figs. 5, 6). From another, two perforated bone beads, and from another a fragment of quartz crystal, and a small specimen of worked hematite.

Apparently, the entire floor or bowl-like depression of this

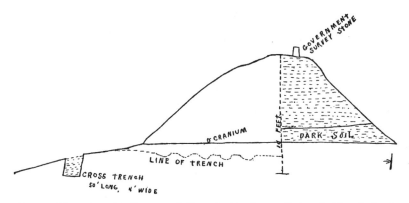

Fig. 7—Mound on bluffs east of East St. Louis, on Judge Sullivan's land. Excavated Oct. 5, 6, 9, 10, 1922.

structure contains similar pits or depressions, since edges of others were noted in the trench.

The loess formation, of which these uplands largely consist, being of an almost bright yellow color, the least discoloration or excavation therein, and subsequent filling in of foreign material is instantly and plainly discernable and easily followed.

Seemingly these pits had been used either as hearths, or for purposes of cremation. Then the bowl-like depression was filled in with a dark soil or earth to the original surface and on top of this the mound was erected, the latter being a mixture of light and dark colored earths.

Directly east of this mound some two hundred fifty feet was a smaller tumulus removed some years since during the erection of a residence. Numerous pottery fragments were taken therefrom, and an entire pot or vase; it could not be ascertained if there were any human remains.

THE KRUGER BONE BANK

At the point marked burial and village site on the map near the lower left hand corner, is a long low ridge flanking a depression in which, in former times, there was considerable water. Old residents state that before the present drainage system was inaugurated, there were many fish in this depression, and that it was connected with the pond to the east.

Along the sandy ridge burials had been made by Indians, and both Mr. Kruger and the owner who preceded him had dug up skeletons. He permitted excavations and about a dozen men sank test pits here for two days. None of the burials were more than three feet in depth, and most of them within twenty inches of the surface. There were fragmentary skeletons indicating disturbances. Dr. James Terry of Washington University took one or two of the best ones to the medical school for observation. The rest were left in the ground. We did not excavate the entire area as the burials were accompanied by no objects and did not appear to be of special importance. Some sixteen bodies were found.

It is well to remark in passing that these scattered burials and little cemeteries are found throughout the entire Cahokia area.

MRS. TIPPETTS' MOUND, No. 61

This is an oval mound located between the two ponds on land owned by Mrs. William Tippetts. Externally it is rather promising, and as it is shaped not unlike altar mounds of the Ohio Valley, the survey decided to test it. Much to our surprise we found it composed of exceedingly heavy, black gumbo. Two pits were sunk and by means of the augers we tested to the base, a distance of twenty feet. Very little in the way of material was encountered. The mound appeared to be unstratified. The ground was so hard it required the united efforts of six strong workmen to put down six auger holes in three days time. Whether stratification or burials are to be found is problematical. We would suggest February to April as more favorable months for work in gumbo since winter rains have a tendency to soften the material.

THE COLLINSVILLE-EDGEMONT BLUFFS

Flanking the east side of the American Bottoms are the high bluffs frequently referred to. McAdams, Patrick, and others seem to have secured most of their better specimen (pipes, bicaves,[2] and long chipped objects) from graves, small mounds, or sites on these promontories. Local collectors affirm that the entire range of high land flanking the river from Alton to Cairo is one vast, ancient cemetery. Mr. E. W. Payne, whose agents have collected extensively in that region, estimate that thousands of various implements, ornaments, and utensils have here been gathered. Skeletons are plowed up every spring and fall. A thorough investigation of the remains on these bluffs should be made at some future time. Our work included an inspection of the bluffs for ten miles, but we attempted no excavations.

THE MITCHELL MOUNDS

March 15, 1923, Hon. W. E. Myer, Mr. Cowen, Mr. Seever, and myself went to Mitchell, Madison County, Illinois, to examine the group of mounds described in several publications, notably Volume 3, Bulletin No. 5, of the Buffalo Society of Natural Sciences in 1877, and D. I. Bushnell, Jr., in Volume 3, No. 1, Peabody Museum of American Archæology and Ethnology, Harvard University, May, 1904. Since remarkable discoveries had been made in the Mitchell Mounds at the time of both railroad and highway construction many years ago, and as these mounds are but eight miles north of Monks Mound, it was necessary that we make an inspection. The builders of the Mitchell Mounds may or may not have been of the same tribe as that responsible for Cahokia, and we desired to ascertain the facts.

Although a large crew was employed, for sometime we were unable to discover burials or any objects of consequence, and we were, therefore, dependent upon Dr. Howland's description of the finds of long ago. Before quoting him (p. 90), it is well that our field notes of the work at Mitchell be condensed and presented in this report.

The area occupied by the mounds is something like one-half mile in extent, and there were several heirs to the property, one or two of the ladies being abroad. However, through the kindness of Mr. Treckler, superintendent of the estate, we secured permission.

It has always been of interest to us to observe the variations in testimony regarding evidence of discovery given by several

---

[2]Often called discoidals.

people. We questioned a number of persons as to the finds. An elderly lady stated that she was a small girl when the country road was widened, and during the demolition of one of the mounds skeletons and numbers of chipped objects were discovered. Another observer stated that a very large number of bones were found both by the railroad crew and the road builders, that these were loaded on a flat car with the earth and general debris, and dumped into the outlet of Long Lake. Mr. McAdams's son states that his father secured some very fine specimens in flint, stone, and copper at the time two or three of the mounds were destroyed. We shall use Mr. Bushnell's map to refer to mounds, adopting his letters to designate them.

The survey, having read Dr. Howland's interesting description of the finds and having listened to various witnesses, entered upon the exploration the following day with great zest. First was dug Mound C, a small structure about six hundred feet north of Long Lake. Our exploration revealed no special stratification although there was a dark, irregular layer two or three feet from the surface and extending across the mound. Four hammerstones occurred near the surface but there were neither traces of burials, nor ashes, nor animal bones. The earth constituting the structure was probably taken from the adjacent surface, but at a time when there was no considerable village site as we did not find broken pottery, chips of chert, or other objects which are common at Cahokia.

Having secured permission from the Chicago & Alton, Wabash, and Big Four Railway Companies, we began the exploration of what remained of Mound A. So far as can be determined, the original structure was about two hundred sixty feet north and south and some twenty-five feet high. The results were disappointing. In fact, the exploration was carried on with difficulty as trains were continually passing and the space between the tracks was rather narrow. Yet a large crew of men was employed and spent an entire week excavating what remained of this famous mound. The elevations vary from one to about seven feet in height at the present time. Our observations were confined to two long narrow strips about six or seven feet in width, east and west, and about one hundred feet in length, north and south. Our total finds consisted of two decayed skeletons placed near each other on the base line, and distant but a few yards from the ends of the ties of the Big Four and Wabash tracks. None of the bones could be removed.

There were six triangular arrow points lying alongside one of the skeletons—no other objects. What little remained of this mound gave us some slight clue as to the method of construction. Apparently a layer of sand about two inches in thickness was laid down by the Indians, and the interments placed upon this. One hundred and fifty miles to the north a similar construction was followed by the Indians in certain of the mounds near Liverpool.

Mound G is drawn on Mr. Bushnell's plan as a square mound. These structures at Cahokia are known as temple mounds. The height is given by him as five feet, the length one hundred fifty feet and the width one hundred twenty-five feet. Continuous cultivation has altered the form so that the outline has been marred. We decided to excavate this mound carefully, and ran a trench from the south side northward to a distance of fifteen feet beyond the center. Our trench was thirty-five feet in width and we continued for some fifty-five feet. In places this mound appeared to be nearly six feet high, and for some distance on each side of the center we discovered a disturbed layer of some three feet below the surface, and varying from a few to ten inches in thickness. Under that was a heavy layer of black gumbo from eight to twelve inches thick which appeared to rest on the base. There were a few fragments of pottery scattered through the mound, some ashes and charcoal, but no burials, no animal bones, and no burned basin or altar.

On the completion of Mound G we held a consultation. We had now opened three of the Mitchell Mounds at considerable expense. We decided to test with our large augers three or four more mounds, concluding that if our augers were put down forty times in each mound, since they took up a seven-inch section of core, we would be able to secure information as to the construction, and in case there were burials in any one of the mounds, probably some of our test holes would encounter skeletons.

Mound E, a large one, is given on the map as ten and four-tenths feet high, circular, and two hundred sixty-seven feet diameter. In one of the pits, two feet from the surface, we found a flint spade about eight inches long. The augers brought up from other pits a few fragments of pottery. This mound did not appear to be stratified.

We crossed Long Lake and sunk pits and thirty auger holes in the long, low mound just north of the group. It is about ten feet high at the present time. The testing resulted in no evidence of stratification and no burials.

Mound J was probably the largest of the group, and is given as sixteen and four-tenths feet in height, and the augers showed the base line to be down about eighteen feet. Thirty tests were made which required three days work on the part of five or eight men. Eighteen feet down, in the center, was a stone object of unknown character, and apparently rather large. Auger holes were put down all around this stone but we could not bring it up. It could have been removed had we dug a large pit eighteen feet in depth, but since nothing had been found in the other structures, it was thought inadvisable to trench Mound J. We are of the opinion that it was a stone spade. No special stratification was noted, and very little village site debris in this structure.

Mound D was tested somewhat superficially, the augers being put down twenty times with negligible results. This completed the exploration of the Mitchell group. It had been confidently predicted that copper and other objects would be found in these tumuli. Such flint objects and sherds of pottery as were found indicated prevailing Cahokia culture. The fields lying along Long Lake show few traces of occupation as a village site.

We may assume that the Mitchell Mounds, from the examination of the pottery fragments, are a part of the Cahokia culture. This brings up the question of the use of copper, and we, therefore, present a portion of Dr. Howland's paper (pp. 90-93).

WOOD RIVER MOUNDS

After testing at Mitchell, we decided to examine several mounds which lie on the crest of a ridge paralleling the old channel of the Mississippi River. This ridge varies from fifteen to twenty feet above the water, and the abandoned channel is now choked with vegetation. At the time the mounds were built, it is possible that the river flowed along the east side of the Bottoms for a mile or more from its present channel.

We began at the southern end of the group and worked northward. The first mound is four feet high, and eighty feet in length, with a diameter of about fifty feet. The property is owned by Dr. Poague. The trench was extended for a distance of about thirty feet to the base line. We found a few arrowheads and chips of flint near the surface, but nothing in the mound itself. Apparently, it had been disturbed.

Four hundred feet north, on the same ridge, is a mound owned by Messrs. Gerke and Lusk of Edwardsville. This mound is about six feet in height, ninety feet in length, north and south, and some fifty feet wide, and was tested by means of numerous pits. The base appears to rest on a level surface, and it would appear that the natives built fires and burned the ground for a space of some forty or fifty feet, over which area they heaped the mound, extending it for a considerable distance on either side. No burials and no objects were found. There was no stratification.

Mr. Frank Smith owns the property adjoining that of Messrs. Gerke and Lusk. There is a small elevation two hundred fifty feet north of the mound just described. This is all that remains of the mound, the earth of which was hauled away a few years ago. During the process of demolition the workmen discovered about twenty-five skeletons, but no objects. One hundred fifty feet farther north, and in Mr. Smith's garden, is a conical mound sixty feet in diameter and about six feet high. The base of the mound is slightly elevated toward Grassy Lake, the local name of the old Mississippi channel. There was no stratification to be observed, and no definite periods of occupancy. In this mound were three badly decayed skeletons, all on the base line, and two of them a little west of the center. The heads of all of these were toward the south. Near the head of skeleton No. 108 was a peculiar pottery vessel, somewhat basin-shaped. The natives had purposely made it very thick, the diameter from the interior to the exterior exceeding an inch in places. At the time it was excavated, it was green in color, and yet showed no contact with copper. The form suggests a crucible of some sort. We have never observed a pottery vessel of similar character. Directly beneath the crucible was considerable charcoal and ashes. There were also fragments of a large pot.

The two skeletons to the west of No. 108 lay under a hard pan of burnt clay. Near them was some broken pottery which did not appear to be fragments of an entire vessel. Near the hand of No. 110 was a spearhead five inches long, and two small projectile points.

The fourth mound examined by us lay four hundred feet due north of Mr. Smith's garden. Its dimensions were sixty by fifty-five feet in extent, and three and one-half to four feet high. There is one decayed skeleton near the center, No. 111, but nothing with it.

Mound No. 5.—This was four hundred feet due north of No. 4 on land owned by Mr. Henry Smith. Local people persist in the statement that this mound was originally nine or ten feet in height, but due to cultivation has been reduced to eighty feet in diameter and five or six feet in elevation. Three skeletons were discovered, all of them so decayed that only a trace of the bones remains. They were numbered 112, 113, and 114. They lay on the base line not far from the center. Near the head of No. 113 was a stone pipe, four inches in length along the base, and two and one-half inches in height. There was some broken pottery, about ten arrowheads, and three or four knives scattered throughout the mound in the earth. There were no animal bones.

A large trench, some forty feet in diameter, was extended through this mound for a distance of nearly sixty feet. The interesting feature noted in the structure was the rather even base line. Extending downward from this were four depressions, or ash pits, at different points. In these there was much charcoal, black earth and quite a number of pottery fragments and a few chipped objects. Each of these pits extended some two feet below the base of the mound but they appeared to be no other than ordinary fire pits, common in many of our mounds.

Contrary to the evidence of Mitchell, we were informed by officials of the Roxanna Oil Company Corporation, which owns extensive tracts just north of the Smith property, that when their oil tanks were constructed they found a number of burials in graves, several pipes, a great deal of broken pottery, bones, etc., indicating that the village of these people lay beyond where we worked. An effigy pipe in the form of an owl and several fine pottery vessels are owned by some of the members of the Corporation.

Mounds at Lebanon, Illinois

Dr. J. F. Snyder of Virginia, Illinois, in the Smithsonian Report for 1876, describes some interesting tumuli at this place.

We desired to examine the region and took a large party to Lebanon and worked for several days in mounds owned by Messrs. A. M. Stock and E. J. Schmidt. It is not necessary to go into any detail of our explorations. We found very little in the mounds and came to the conclusion that they were elevations probably on which Indian cabins had been placed. Many interesting objects have been found in the neighborhood.

EXAMINATION OF HARDING MOUND, No. 66

It will be seen by preceding pages that we have examined not only numbers of the Cahokia Mounds, but also tumuli and village sites within a radius of twenty-five miles of Monks Mound. However, we made no observations on the Missouri side of the river.

It was thought best to make a rather thorough examination of one of the large structures. The Baltimore & Ohio Railway purchased considerable land lying south of its right-of-way. This included Mounds Nos. 66, 65, and some lesser mounds not on our map. As these were all to be removed by steam shovels in the near future, Mr. Taylor and his men were assigned the task of examining No. 66. The writer consulted with some of the leading archæologists and as this mound is long and narrow, and there is scarcely room on its summit for cabins of any size, we supposed that it must be a mortuary tumulus. The perusal of Mr. Taylor's report will indicate that there were many burials, all of which have disappeared except traces of larger bones and the enamel of the teeth. It is rather unusual that in so large a mound all of these were near the surface. It has been thought best to present complete details of the mound construction and its peculiar character, although we are quite aware that no persons except technical students will find much of interest in these succeeding pages. Mr. Taylor's report here follows.

Field Notes of Engineer J. L. B. Taylor
April 28 to August 1, 1927

Because of the surrounding flood waters, it seemed advisable to establish a bench mark, or datum point, somewhere on the mound rather than elsewhere, and an examination of the mound by the crew, all of whom have worked on surveys with me in the Ozark Mountains for the past several years and who are experienced in such matters, showed that the point shown as Stn. 27, or B M, on my map captioned "Contours," was the highest point on the mound. This was accordingly selected as datum point for all of our elevations, and it should be borne in mind that such readings have been computed downward from B M rather than upward from a point or points at the base line of the mound. It is also well to call attention at this point to the scale of measurements used in compiling all maps submitted: Horizontal measurements are laid off on a scale of ten feet to the inch; vertical measurements, two feet to the inch. This gives the maps a distortion of five to one, and may be misleading to persons not familiar with cross section or profile maps. However, it is a practical method of graphic illustration and is always used in some such relation on maps of this kind.

Setting up the transit over B M, and working away from this point in various directions, we were surprised to find that instead of being an irregular mass of earth thrown together without regard for symmetry, No. 66 seemed to have been very carefully built up, a conviction that grew on us as the work of laying out axes and other lines progressed.

For example: The flagman, Mosier, set a temporary station at either end of the summit where he judged the end slopes proper really began. Careful measurement of the distance from B M to the temporary station at the east end of the crest showed this to be one hundred thirty feet, and from B M to the one at the west end, one hundred forty feet. Having clamped the transit with the telescope trained on the temporary station at the east end of the mound, the telescope was reversed and then showed the temporary station at the west end in perfect alignment with B M and the temporary station to the east.

Investigating relative elevations, the temporary station to the east was found to be two and four-tenths feet below B M, and the one to the west two and three-tenths feet below, a difference in elevation of one-tenth foot in a horizontal distance of two hundred seventy feet.

B M, then, as established, is five feet east of what might be designated as the exact center of the summit, but since a substantial post had already been planted, and since there was little if any difference in elevation between one point and the other, no change was made. Permanent Stn. 1 was established at the former temporary station at the east end, and the temporary station to the west became permanent Stn. 55. The distance between these two points was staked at five-foot intervals and this line, established as the major axis of the mound, was produced through them to what was considered safe points to use as base, or to Stn. 85, west, and Stn. 105, east, making a total major axial distance of five hundred twenty feet. It is apparent, however, that fifteen or twenty feet should be deducted from the west end of this where modern excavation for a building site has disturbed the original contour of the mound so that exact relocation of the original base line is no longer possible. In these circumstances the major axial length of No. 66 may be fixed at five hundred feet, with a drop at the west end, Stn. 81, of approximately twenty-nine feet, and at the east end, Stn. 105, of twenty-six and fifteen-hundredths feet below B M.

Adopting B M as the center of the mound, through which the original plan was to cut a fifty-foot trench to base, B M also marked the north end of the center line of the proposed trench, which center line, in turn, became the southern portion of the minor axis of No. 66. In establishing this axis, trouble was had again in relocating the original base line on the slight but continued slope of the flood plain southward, and in order to be sure that the trench should begin at base the southern extremity of this axis was fixed at one hundred sixty feet south of B M, or at Stn. 0, elevation −29.3 feet. Turning on B M, the northern portion of this axis was projected one hundred ten feet to Stn. 27/11, elevation −26 feet. Here we found a striking example of uniformity of outline: Stn. 27/1, ten feet north of B M, is nine-tenths of a foot below B M, while Stn. 30, ten feet south, is seven-tenths of a foot below; Stn. 27/2, twenty feet north, is three and four-tenths feet below B M, and Stn. 28, twenty feet south, three and six-tenths feet below; Stn. 27/3, thirty feet north, is six and four-tenths feet below B M and Stn. 26, thirty feet south, is six and seven-tenths feet below, uniformity of construction that might well be credited to present day engineers using modern equipment. Even greater regularity of construction marks the lines of levels run at right angles to the major axis through its Stns. 19 and 35. On the other hand, level lines laid off transversely through Stns. 1 and 55 of this axis, or at the east and west extremities, respectively, of the summit, show a decided variation in elevations at corresponding horizontal distances from the axis, but probably this may be accounted for by comparatively recent excavations for building sites. An old barn foundation, eighty feet long, was uncovered at the south end of the line through Stn. 1, and quantities of glass, wire, old irons, and harness buckles, were found.

Further evidence of uniformity of construction appears when the following data concerning elevations at the ends of the two axes and the north-south lines through the extremities of the summit are considered:

West end, major axis, Stn.   85......................29.3' below B M
East end,   "   " ,   "   105......................26.15' "   "
South end, minor " ,   "   0......................29.3' "   "
North end,   "   " ,   "27/11......................26.0' "   "
South end, line through Stn. 55, Stn. 55/20...........25.9' "   "
North end,   "   "   " 55, " 55/10...........26.2' "   "
South end,   "   "   "   1, "   1/21...........26.1' "   "
North end,   "   "   "   1, "   1/11...........26.2' "   "

Allowance must be made here for the fact that the west end of the major axis, elevation −29.3 feet, and the south end of the minor axis, elevation −29.3 feet, as these were laid out were purposely prolonged, and that the corresponding elevations given here cover points well beyond the foot of the mound proper. Incidentally attention is called to the fact that taking Stns. 68 and 98, major axis, as foci, the mound's peripheral outline is almost a perfect ellipse. Such a plan might have been carefully worked out before the mound was erected, but it would seem that in such deliberations as these the builders would have chosen more prominent or important points as foci.

Continued cloudy weather prohibited observations of Polaris, so a magnetic declination of 5° 30' E., previously ascertained and used by the county engineer in his surveys in this locality, was also used in our survey of No. 66, and the major axis was found to run S. 84° 30' E. (Stn. 85, major axis, bears S. 85° E., two hundred sixty-nine feet from the quarter-corner of Secs. 2 and 11, T. 2 N., R. 9 W., St. Clair County, Illinois).

The basal area of the mound measured about two acres, and its body content approximately forty thousand cubic yards.

Trench Operations at Base.—In accordance with your instructions of April 22, plans were made to begin at or somewhat below base at the south side of No. 66 and run a fifty-foot trench northward to a point well beyond the major axis. This work was started on May 2 after the surface of the area to be trenched was staked off in five-foot squares, the center line of the proposed trench coinciding with the minor axis of the mound, but projecting southward beyond it to a point one hundred sixty feet from B M, the common center of the two axes.

The minor axis appeared to be about two hundred twenty feet in length, but close relocation of the southern limit of the mound had been made impossible through farming operations carried well up on the slope, so it was thought best to begin the trench well back from the mound rather than too far within it.

Stakes were lettered A, B, C, D, E, F, G, H, I, and K transversely to the center line to indicate the east lines of trench sections, while successive numbers on center and side line stakes showed the north sides of given sections. By means of a thirty-inch steel probe, the first transverse five-foot section of the proposed trench was thoroughly sounded but appeared to contain no remains. Nevertheless, it was cut away to a depth of three and one-tenth feet, which exposed a very stiff, dark yellow gumbo that appeared to be original flood plain material. This is known locally as "blue" gumbo, but on my field map captioned "Tests on Minor Axis" is designated as "bluish" gumbo. It was adopted as the lower limit for all our work, and throughout the mound proved barren of archæological material.

The three and one-tenth feet of earth so removed consisted chiefly of heavy black gumbo, the upper eight inches, however, being more in the nature of coarse black loam carrying a noticeable amount of humus originating probably from agricultural operations of the past several years. My field notes show that no remains were found in this section.

By May 4, the crew had reached section 5, and at quitting time that afternoon were well into section 7, having encountered no perceptible change of formation except occasional small masses or pellets of yellow clay or gumbo that gradually became more frequent as trenching progressed northward. A few very small sherds and unworked flakes of flint were found. Auger tests from here backward to Stn. o showed the blue gumbo extending downward to thirty-six and four-tenths feet below B M. Beneath this was no less than eight feet of yellow water-bearing sand, so fine in texture that deeper tests would have been impossible without the use of casing.

Continued rains made the gumbo extremely difficult to handle and work progressed very slowly, especially as frequent showers forced the crew to find shelter in the tents, a condition that prevailed day after day until late in June.

On May 6, working between showers, we unearthed a number of very small fragments of pottery three and four-tenths feet below the surface (twenty-six and two-tenths feet) in section 10-B. These were not confined in a small area as might have been expected had they all been pieces of the same vessel, but were recovered one at a time from different parts of the section, and all were too small to be of any practical archæological value. The next day, at from three and four-tenths to five and seven-tenths feet below the surface of section 10, we encountered a distinct stratum of small sherds, bits of charcoal and unworked flint spalls. A test hole in section 10-K went through four feet of blue gumbo, seven and one-half feet of water-bearing sand, and about three feet deep into what appeared to be fire clay. Our trench face now measured something more than six feet in height, and a heavy rain that night caused the whole fifty feet to slide in on our working floor, an unexpected interruption that necessitated the removal of several tons of heavy muck before trenching could be resumed. Incidentally, the American Bottoms, in which these mounds are situated, were so completely inundated that numbers of blue racers and rattlesnakes sought refuge on the mound where they finally became so annoying that we postponed work in the trench long enough to mow and burn all the vegetation on such parts of the mound as we were camped on or working over.

A violent storm drove the crew out of the trench at 2 P. M. At 3 P. M. our supply tent and all our provisions and cooking utensils were blown off the mound, and the office tent, in which all our instruments and records were stored, was held in place through a driving rain and wind only by the united efforts of the crew who quit the shelter of their own tents and mounted the south end of the frame. But by five o'clock we had salvaged practically all of our equipment and supplies.

Section 11 was cut down to blue gumbo the next day, May 10, leaving a new trench face seven feet high, the work being materially, though by no means satisfactorily, hastened by a local resident who had been persuaded to bring a slip and a span of mules to keep the loose dirt out of the crew's way.

Section 12 was opened May 11, but except for some pieces of sandstone no larger than small marbles and none of them showing evidences of having been worked, we found nothing more than a few scattered bits of flint, charcoal, and pottery.

Section 12 was cleaned out and section 13 opened on May 12, but the ground was so wet that trenching operations were temporarily suspended, with a trench face seven and four-tenths feet high. A test hole four hundred feet south of the mound showed blue gumbo appearing at a depth of one foot below its level at the center line of the trench. Levels run across ground west and southwest of No. 66 showed one mound three and one-half feet high and one hundred fifty feet in diameter, the approximate apex of which lies S. 25° E., two hundred feet from the quarter-corner of Secs. 2 and 11, T. 2 N., R. 9 W., St. Clair County, Illinois. Another, of the same dimensions bears S. 85° E., ninety-four feet from the same corner. Sounding these with thirty-inch steel probes failed to indicate the presence of any remains within them.

Resuming work in the trench the next morning, we were forced out at 8 A. M. by a rain that lasted an hour and drenched everything in the tents. By quitting time on the afternoon of May 14, however, we were down three feet in section 14, and although the fifteenth was Sunday we took advantage of the cold, windy weather and carried section 14 down to blue gumbo. This left a clean cut trench face of eight and six-tenths feet and afforded the best opportunity we had had to secure definite data on the cross section composition of the trench. At three and four-tenths feet above blue gumbo (−29.0′ B M) appeared a scant half-inch stratum of yellowish gray sand that extended entirely across the fifty-foot face, overlaid for the west forty feet with a twelve-inch stratum of sandy black gumbo. In the east edge of the trench, from two feet above blue gumbo (−30.4′ B M) a yellow clay stratum gradually ascended to section 14-I, then dipped sharply and finally pinched out at the two-foot level at the center line, whence a stratum of yellow and irregularly shaped clay pellets, ranging in size from that of a walnut to a base ball, extended to the west edge of the trench, grew gradually thicker downward, and merged with a similar formation beginning at the one-foot level in the east edge of the trench. The few sherds and spalls taken from this section all came from below the one-foot level and were mixed in with the clay pellets. This is the face you inspected on May 16.

On May 18, at three feet below the surface (−26.0′ B M) in section 15-C, we uncovered a human skull. This was badly decayed, as were also the humeri and femora that accompanied it, and all were so firmly bonded in the gumbo that none could be preserved for measurement. In reality the bones themselves had completely disintegrated and left only their shape and color as a portion of the soil in which they originally lay. Soon after this discovery was made, a bundle of three other skulls likewise accompanied by the heavier limb bones was found in the same section. In this case, however, a red sienitic granite discoidal, three inches in diameter and one inch thick, almost as perfectly fashioned as if it had been turned out on a lathe, lay at the point of the lower jaw of one skull. This, and a flint scraper, constituted the sole artifacts recovered from No. 66, and though the first assumption was that it had been buried with the skull, there seems to be reasonable ground now to doubt this. On the contrary, the total absence of other material with the comparatively large number of similar burials subsequently discovered might lead to the conclusion that this discoidal had accidently found its way to where it was uncovered.

Careful examination of the surrounding soil immediately after these burials were discovered and before the rain softened it failed to disclose any visible evidence that it had ever been disturbed. So far as could be ascertained, the earth in which these bones lay did not in any wise differ in color, texture, or formation from that in the immediate vicinity, and if a trench or individual pits had been dug to receive the burials, all evidence of such outlines had been obliterated.

The next day, May 19, an almost continuous bed of human skulls, humeri, ulnæ, radii, femora, tibiæ, and fibulæ was cut into, but no other bones appeared. These lay at from three to four feet below the surface of the west half of the trench. Burials appeared to have been deposited in bundles of from two to six skulls with their corresponding limb bones, and teeth were so irregularly mingled with the mass that except for an occasional somewhat better preserved skull or bundle of skulls, identification of individual burials was impossible. However, not less than fifteen, and probably twenty or more individuals were unearthed.

By noon, May 20, we estimated our burials at fifty, all of which had been found in the usual bundle-like groups. The first and only piece of flint that showed unquestionable signs of having been fashioned by the hand of man, a very crudely-made scraper, was found in section 16-D that morning, but not close to any human remains. What might have been a sort of altar appeared at a depth of one foot below the surface in section 16-B. This was a circular, disc-like formation of orange-yellow earth, of somewhat denser texture than the surrounding soil, and was one foot thick and five feet in diameter. Close inspection did not reveal the presence of ashes, charcoal, flints, sherds or other similar material in it, and no bones or other remains were found above or beneath it. There was no visible evidence that it had been burned. Approximately fifteen more burials were unearthed that afternoon, and three fragmentary and badly crushed crania from sections 16-A and 16-D were carried to the office tent in their original gumbo blocks to be preserved for shipment. But at best, these crania, or so much of them as were recognizable as having once been such, were little more than shapeless masses of gumbo, and although they were shipped to the museum at Urbana they could have had little if any archæological value.

The only skull complete enough to show the eye sockets came from section 16-A. This faced N. 40° W., and was tilted slightly to the right. The occipital, temporals, malars, both maxillaries and lachrymals, and the right parietal were missing, the nasals were badly decayed, the frontal was crushed almost flat, and the left parietal was broken. No teeth were found.

Femora and other limb bones accompanying skulls usually lay parallel with the minor axis of the mound, although a few bundles were found lying almost at right angles to this.

Sunday, May 22, a heavy rain began falling at 2 A. M. and continued throughout most of the day, so saturating the mound ahead of the trench face that practically the entire face slid into the trench. This made more extra work, but the next day we cut out section 16. Here we found the blue gumbo floor eight inches deeper than at the north edge of section 14, which was our first intimation that this formation had other than a plane surface. An immediate examination was made to see whether we had overlooked an abrupt break or trench face cut into this material. Nothing of the sort appeared, however, and we found the work thus far had been carried over a comparatively level stretch of this formation, a physical feature which subsequent soundings showed to be unusual rather than typical.

The stratum of sand that showed in section 14 no longer appeared, but four distinct strata of clay pellets, dipping westward, had become dominant features of the trench face. No remains were found below four feet under the surface or under the burials.

Burials still appeared in the west half of the trench, though in less distinct bundles, but nothing appeared in the east half. A steady downpour of rain throughout the whole of that afternoon put six feet of water in the trench, and sometime during the night of May 24 the entire face, more than fourteen feet high, slid off. An attempt was made to remove the resultant muck, but neither men nor teams could work in it, so further trenching operations there were abandoned, and plans were made to open the trench at the summit of the mound.

As nearly as could be estimated, the remains of at least one hundred fifty burials had been found, but none of this material except the crowns of about two hundred teeth was fit for shipment, and these were mailed to Dr. Henry W. Gillett at New York. A narrow trench and several auger holes, sunk immediately to the west of the burial area later, did not disclose any further remains.

Trench Operations at the Summit.—According to the original plans, a fifty-foot trench, starting at base, was to be cut through No. 66 along the minor axis, and allowing for a 1–1 slope of the side walls, which would have made these quite safe, even though the natural angle of repose would have been much steeper, and for a trench depth of thirty feet, the opening through the summit would have extended fifty-five feet on either side of the center line. But preliminary operations in opening such a cut would have called for removal of the office tent which, although all four tents had been crowded against each other, was nevertheless close against Stn. 16, major axis. Consequently, having been forced to change some of the original plans, further changes now seemed justifiable, so it was decided to shift the original location of the trench some fifteen or twenty feet to the west. Hence, what was to have been the final west edge of the cut through the summit was started at Stn. 43, major axis, instead of at Stn. 39, and a vertical section was taken down at Stn. 34+ instead of at Stn. 32, the plan being to keep a vertical face near the original trench limit proper and to break this down with squib shots for quicker removal.

About 3 P. M., May 27, the slip team uncovered the knees of a human skeleton at a depth of three feet immediately under Stn. 35, major axis, and was then moved to the opposite edge of the cut in order not to interfere with the work of laying this skeleton bare by means of trowels. When the bones had all been cleaned off, they were given a coat of wet Spanish whiting to bring them into relief, were then photographed, and left in place.

Dr. Judd of the Smithsonian Institution and Dr. Terry of Washington University were present when this skeleton and another one were found. As there were traces of wooden coffins and numbers of nails and metal buttons and buckles found with these, we concluded that the burials were, probably, those of Frenchmen or early settlers.

They were reburied west of the mound, each accompanied by a bottle containing a note from myself telling where and under what circumstances they had been found.

June 1 brought another flood, and by 3 P. M. the waters covering the American Bottoms around No. 66 had risen three inches. On June 2, rain forced us off the job at 3 : 15 P. M. and kept falling steadily till 9 A. M. the next day. But we worked until six o'clock that afternoon and when we quit, had a six-foot trench face. The upper nine inches of this was loam, the next nine inches was buckshot gumbo, and the lower four and one-half feet was a stiff yellow clay or gumbo carrying numerous pockets of less than a cubic foot of yellow sand. No remains were found. Another heavy rain, beginning at eleven o'clock that night and continuing until daylight the next morning, left the mound so muddy and slippery that neither the men nor teams could work on it. Examination of the trench face on June 6 showed the dirt still too mucky to be handled with shovels. Powder was used without effect, so we returned to the west cut in the summit, where by quitting time that afternoon we had a nine-foot face. Concentric strata of black gumbo, yellow clay, and sand seemed to indicate that the mound had been brought up to this point in its present form rather than built up with a flat top and gradually drawn in.

On June 8 our face was ten and four-tenths feet, and such a variety of material showed in this and was so irregular in composition that a photograph of the cross section seemed to be the best means of recording it. Accordingly, a heavy mixture of lime and water was used to bring out contrasts, after which photographic exposures were made at a distance of fourteen feet and at intervals of ten feet in a line parallel with the face of the cut, the intention being of course to match and mount the resultant pictures as one. In a general way this was a weirdly duplicated background. But as the sun and wind dried out the face of the cut, textures and formations seemed to change, and specific designations shown in the picture no longer seemed applicable. Consequently, so far as geological classification is concerned, this built-up picture should not be too seriously considered.

On June 9, we had a fourteen-foot face, measured downward from Stn. 34, major axis, with a base one hundred feet long. Slight traces of charcoal appeared at the bottom of this face, under the axis, and one very small unworked flint spall, and a fragment of sandstone no larger than a pea, were taken out during the day. The central portion of the mound showed black and gray sand in gumbo, the two being plainly separate, and each shot through with yellow gumbo pellets. At thirteen feet below the summit, a broken two-inch stratum of multicolored buckshot gumbo seemed at first glance to be a deposit of disintegrated pottery, but closer examination showed that coloration (orange, red, yellow, blue, purple, and vermillion) appeared only on the fracture planes, that the material bore no traces whatever of pulverized shell or other stiffening matter for earthenware, and that not the slightest bit of pottery was present. It was assumed, therefore, that coloring probably originated from chemical action on the original vegetable or mineral content of the soil.

Weather conditions had improved slightly and although nothing of value had yet been found in the cut, the work was progressing satisfactorily.

Further use of teams and slides on Harding Mound No. 66 was impossible due to an unusual circumstance. A land owner, knowing that but two teams were available, forbade his neighbor to drive these teams across his land. Therefore, June 9, we ended trenching operations in No. 66 and depended on auger tests.

Auger Tests.—Tests on No. 65 were completed by June 20, weather conditions had improved, and tests of No. 66 with augers were begun. Of ten holes bored to water in the trench under Stn. 34+, major axis, one produced two badly disintegrated sherds not more than a quarter of an inch in diameter.

Still trying to take advantage of every hour of good weather, we worked an hour over time that afternoon, but were driven off the job by rain at 5 P. M. Further tests the next day showed water at twenty-three feet at B M as compared with thirty-six and four-tenths feet at Stn. o, twenty-three and three-tenths feet at Stn. 31, and twenty-three and one-half feet at Stn. 30, all on the minor axis. Barely audible grating sounds at eleven feet under B M seemed to indicate stone there, but no such material was recovered. The hole at Stn. 30 was put down to thirty-four and two-tenths feet, but to thirty-three feet produced only a black gumbo muck under which was a blue muck having a decidedly offensive odor and bearing numerous fine roots. At eleven feet under Stn. 26, major axis, the same depth as under B M, a very small fragment of pottery was found, and in connection with whatever was encountered at that depth under B M might indicate a slight stratum of refuse at this level. However, these discoveries were not considered of sufficient importance to justify sinking a pit at these stations.

In test holes bored on June 23, water was found at various levels, none of which was as low as our first work in the trench on the minor axis. The offensive smelling blue muck was in evidence near the base, and was overlaid in most cases by a bluish black soil full of minute white specks which changed in color to a brilliant blue soon after exposure to sun and air. From the twenty-four foot level under Stn. 27/4 to thirty-two and three-tenths feet under Stn. 29, minor axis, there appeared a six-inch deposit of fine matted roots carrying with them occasional short lengths of what resembled jointed reed stems. These joints averaged one-sixteenth inch in length and fitted into each other telescope-fashion. Repeated examinations of such vegetation failed to show conclusively whether it was living or dead matter.

The first thoroughly dry soil found in No. 66 appeared at the eighteen-foot level under Stn. 26, and at about twenty-one feet under Stn. 25, minor axis. When first encountered, beneath a moist black and yellow gumbo mixture under Stn. 26, this was plainly black gumbo, so dry and hard that the cuttings came out as fine dust that could hardly be held in the augers. At slightly below twenty feet it had changed to about equal parts of black and yellow, then a thin darker stratum appeared, and under this again, just above twenty-four feet, was dry black and yellow. Here a six-inch stratum of distinctly reddish mixture intervened, after which, slightly past twenty-five feet, the dry black and yellow prevailed. The next two feet showed moderately dry black gumbo, then came about two and one-half feet of moist black gumbo, another two feet of black muck, and finally yellow gumbo to the bottom of the hole at about thirty-three feet. Under Stns. 24 and 25 the formation was similar except that the thin dark stratum was missing.

From twenty-nine and eight-tenths feet under Stn. 19, major axis, which, it should be noted, is somewhat below base as this was finally determined, small but well preserved fragments of bone and shell were brought up. Most of the fractures in the former were undoubtedly old, which led to the conclusion that probably they were food remains. The shell was badly shattered, apparently by the auger, and was so light and so fragile in texture that it was assumed to be of fresh water rather than of marine origin. Audible grating and grinding sounds for the next four or six inches under these remains indicated the presence of stone, but no such material could be recovered. Minute fragments of charcoal and pottery and what strongly resembled bone dust were found at nine feet, Stn. 2, major axis.

On June 28, further trenching operations were resumed at the western extremity of the area of bundle burials previously encountered, but no further remains of this nature were discovered.

Returning to Stn. 19, major axis, a test hole was sunk at a point five feet to the north. Water appeared at twenty feet and the test was discontinued at about thirty-two feet with no remains having been found. Another hole was bored five feet west of Stn. 19, and at twelve feet in this the auger struck more hard material, apparently stone, but this could not be recovered. This test was inadvertently overlooked in compiling the cross-section of Mound No. 66 at major axis, Fig. 9. A grating sound was also heard at thirty feet in a hole five feet south of Stn. 19, but nothing could be brought up and the test was stopped at thirty-three feet, or four feet below base.. Curiously enough this was a dry hole, even though it was a foot deeper than the one ten feet to the north where water appeared at twenty feet. Another test made ten feet north of Stn. 19 showed fragments of shell (apparently fresh water) at twenty-nine and six-tenths feet. It appears, therefore, that there is at least a slight stratum of camp refuse at or probably below the base of the mound at this point, but a pit at this particular location would require the use of a windlass and cribbing and would be rather an expensive undertaking with extremely problematical results.

Under Stn. 45, major axis, at a depth of nine and eight-tenths feet, we found our first pure, dry, yellow sand in a stratum two inches thick. Under this was a two-inch stratum of black and yellow earth, equal parts, then came a twelve-inch stratum of what appeared to be the same yellow sand.

At Stn. 44, five feet east of Stn. 45, the twelve-inch stratum of sand appeared at eleven feet and a mixture of yellow sand and black gumbo, with the former predominant, appeared at eleven feet under Stn. 44/1, five feet north of Stn. 44. Other tests were made at intervals of five feet around Stn. 45 but no more of this sand was encountered. No remains were found in any of these tests.

What appeared to be the same variety of sand was also found in tests along the minor axis as shown on the map covering these, but in all of these tests such sand was water-bearing.

On July 25, Mr. J. E. Lamar, representing the Illinois State Geological Survey, called in response to our request and took soil samples from test holes along our trench under Stn. 34+ for identification. Results of his investigations reached us too late to be of any use in compiling maps of the cross sections that had already been tested, so our own previously established terminology, which did not appear materially unsuited, was retained.

All told, two hundred thirty-one of the eight-inch test holes were bored in No. 66 to depths ranging from three and two-tenths feet to thirty-three and three-tenths feet, and aggregating a vertical test of 4174 feet applied as follows:

Line of Tests	Number of Tests	Minimum Depth	Maximum Depth	Aggregate Depth	Average Depth
Major axis.............	65	3.2'	33.3'	1410.5'	21.7'
Minor axis.............	25	6.0'	33.0'	522.5'	20.9'
Transversely through Stn.					
1, Major axis........	22	5.5'	28.4'	345.4'	15.7'
Through 35, Major axis	30	4.5'	19.5'	486.0'	16.2'
" 19, " "	53	5.6'	29.0'	848.0'	16.0'
" 55, " "	21	6.6'	27.0'	348.0'	16.6'
Other tests.............	15	6.5'	32.1'	213.0'	14.2'
Totals..................	231	37.9'	202.3'	4174.0'	121.3'
General average........		5.41'	28.9'	18.1'	17.3'

It might seem that an average of the mean depths, Col. 6 above, should agree with the average depth shown under Col. 5, but this does not apply unless the depth or the number of holes is a constant. The true average depth is therefore eighteen and one-tenth feet.

Allowing an eight-inch test hole a cross-sectional area of 0.35 square feet, it will be seen from this table that a volume of fifty-four and one-tenth cubic yards of No. 66 was actually tested in this manner, every augerful that was taken out having been carefully examined for remains of any kind. But this is only 0.0013525 of the mound's entire content. Wholly disregarding the volume examined by trench, the remaining percentage allowed for test by auger is slightly raised but still fails to approach anything like a satisfactory volume exposed for examination.

Personally, I doubt whether a mound can be explored in this manner with even a moderate degree of reliability. However, in this particular case, ideal facilities for checking our auger tests will be afforded when the B. & O. steam shovel goes into the mound. Casual examination of the vicinity where the new yards are to be laid indicates that at least two feet and possibly three feet or more of the base of the mound will be left in place, this amount of filling being required over quite an acreage. This will afford no opportunity, of course, to check the borings to lower levels, and will no doubt permanently bury any remains that are now at or below base, but it is earnestly recommended that the University of Illinois, or other authorities, have a competent observer in attendance while steam shovel operations are being carried on.

Such an observer would be able not only to recognize and save any remains that are thrown out, but could check the actual cuttings against the cross section maps I have prepared. By this means he could report definitely as to the reliability or unreliability of such tests and thereby supply valuable data upon which to base similar future explorations.

Note by W. K. M.—While I agree with Mr. Taylor's observations on percentage of mound tested, it is no more than right to state that the auger tests are for the purpose of determining strata, burials, and general character of a mound. They have been extensively employed elsewhere and mortuary structures differentiated from domicilary mounds by their use. A sufficient number of holes were put down to the base to have brought to our attention burials had there been any considerable number in the mound. Furthermore, when the Baltimore & Ohio Railway Company removes the mound, it will be interesting to know whether skeletons are to be found in the spaces not penetrated by our augers. Theoretically, it is my opinion that none, or very few, will be discovered.

There is a complete series of thirty-five or more maps of Mounds Nos. 65, 66, and other mounds, on file in the Museum of Natural History of the University of Illinois. Particular attention is called to the great detail set forth in Mr. Taylor's excellent maps of Mound No. 66.

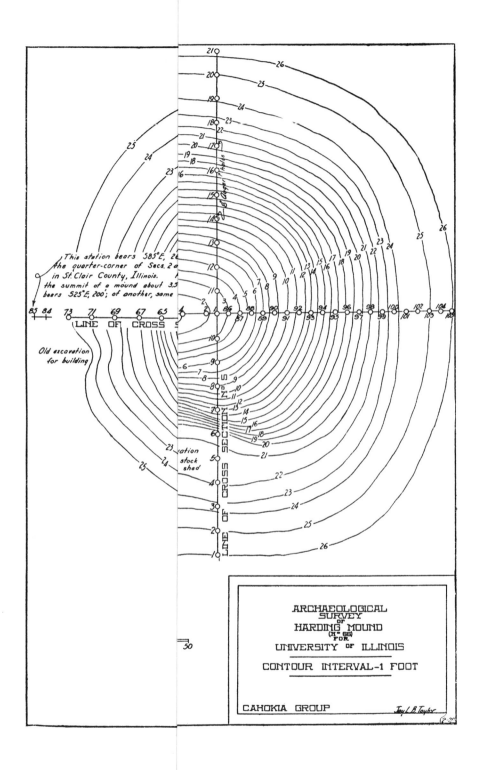

This station bears S85°E, 2...
the quarter-corner of Secs. 2 a...
in St. Clair County, Illinois. ...
the summit of a mound about 3.5...
bears S25°E, 200'; of another, same

Old excavation
for building

LINE OF CROSS S...

ARCHAEOLOGICAL
SURVEY
of
HARDING MOUND
(H-66)
FOR
UNIVERSITY of ILLINOIS

CONTOUR INTERVAL—1 FOOT

CAHOKIA GROUP

by L. B. Taylor

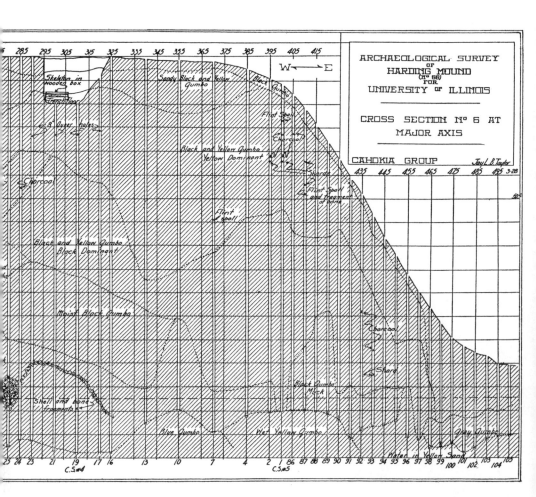

6 at major axis.

MOUND No. 65

My field notes for June 13 show that Stn. 12, major axis of Mound No. 65 bears N. 84° 30′ E., 1635 feet from a stone set on the line of Secs. 2 and 11 at a point nine hundred eighty-seven and four-tenths feet east of the common corner of Secs. 2, 3, 10, and 11, T. 2 N., R. 9 W., in St. Clair County, Illinois, and the tie point is so shown on the map of contours of this mound. In the absence of definite official notes covering the original survey of this locality, I am of the opinion, however, that this stone is on the line of Secs. 2 and 11, nine hundred eighty-seven and four-tenths feet east of the common quarter-corner of these two sections rather than that distance east of the common corner of Secs. 2, 3, 10, and 11. At the time No. 65 was surveyed the immediate vicinity was under water, 1200 feet of this tie line itself having to be measured through water from two to twelve inches deep, and no attempt was made to check up on neighboring corners.

But from Stn. 12, the major axis runs N. 84° 30′ E., two hundred thirty feet; the minor axis, through B M, runs N. 5° 30′ W., and is two hundred feet long.

The ground plan appears to be almost a circle, but at a point approximately half-way up the slope the outline becomes noticeably rectilinear, and from there to the summit the mound might be described as prismoidal in form or, loosely, as a truncated pyramid of four sides or, but for the unequal axial dimensions, as a truncated cone. But farming operations have disturbed the original perimeter, a drainage canal bank has been thrown up against the southeast slope, and the contents of at least two rather extensive pits, presumably test holes sunk within the last few years, have doubtless altered the original outlines of the summit, so that at this time the mound may for all practical purposes be considered the frustum of a cone.

Here again, surrounding flood waters forced us to establish a datum point or bench mark at the summit, hence all elevations referred to are computed downward from the highest point on the summit. In connection with this subject it is interesting to note the regularity of outline of the upper portions of the mound. For example: Stn. 2, major axis, twenty feet west of B M, and Stn. 16, twenty feet east of B M, are each one and one-tenth feet below B M; Stn. 3, thirty feet west, has an elevation of −2.5 feet, while that of Stn. 17, thirty feet east, is two and seven-tenths feet; Stn. 4, forty feet west is four and one-half feet lower than B M, and Stn. 18, forty feet east, is four and six-tenths feet lower; Stn. 5, fifty feet west, drops to six and nine-tenths feet, and Stn. 19, fifty feet east, to seven feet; and Stn. 12, on the western extremity of the major axis, one hundred twenty feet west of B M, stands at nineteen and nine-tenths feet, while Stn. 25, the eastern extremity of this axis, one hundred ten feet east of B M, has an elevation of −20.6 feet. Corresponding elevations on other lines surveyed as shown on the map of contours follow practically the same degree of regularity, and base was established at −20 feet.

A test hole at B M showed water at twenty-five and eight-tenths feet which is at the same level as the surface of the water in the drainage canal to the south of the mound. In this respect there appears a marked difference between this mound and No. 66, for in the latter water was struck at various depths (usually above base along the central portions or at points removed from the perimeter) while here it always occurred at twenty-five and eight-tenths feet and always in yellow sand. This sand was entered at from twenty-three to twenty-five feet and although it did not appear to be of uniform depth was found in every one of the forty-four test holes put down. It was found to be deepest under Stn. 28, minor axis, but some disturbance may have resulted here from construction of the nearby drainage canal. Above this stratum of sand was found a deposit of stiff multicolored gumbo or clay in which red and yellow and their various shades predominated, and which for want of a better name, has been indicated on the cross section maps of this mound under its local name of "shale." This stratum reached a maximum thickness of two feet under the central portions of the mound, but pinched out and disappeared altogether within from ten to twenty or twenty-five feet of the mound's perimeter. This might lead to some speculation as to whether No. 65 was built on a low natural mound, speculation that is rather encouraged by examination of stratum immediately above the shale. This is a deposit of gray sandy gumbo, averaging less than twelve inches in depth, and always decreasing in every direction toward the perimeter of the mound. At a point within three feet from the east end of the major axis it disappears completely, only to reappear in increased depth two feet higher and twenty feet further east whence it sloped eastward under something more than a foot of pure gray sand.

Extending the entire length of the major axis and across at least the south half of the mound's base, we found a sharply marked deposit of black gumbo, so dry and hard along the minor axis, where we sunk a line of test holes, that it was difficult to cut and so loose after being cut that it could hardly be kept in the augers for removal. At twenty feet under Stn. 7, minor axis, the augers went through a foot of hard dry sand, an entirely new formation to us but which was encountered later at eighteen feet under Stn. 6, where it was nearly four feet deep, and at about twenty and six-tenths feet under Stn. 18, also minor axis, where it was about two feet deep. In every case, this sand appeared under extremely dry and very hard black gumbo. It seems reasonable to attach some significance to the existence of these sand deposits, but since they lie at or below base and since preparation of the vicinity of the mound for yards by the B. & O. will probably not require removal of the sand it can be examined only by means of pits sunk before the steam shovel is brought in.

The central portions of No. 65 appeared to be a mixed mass of black and yellow gumbo of about equal parts, and the whole was capped with a layer of black gumbo ranging from about one and one-half feet in thickness on the south slope to a maximum thickness of nearly six feet under B M.

No remains of any kind were found within the mound, but twenty feet beyond Stn. D, in the field southwest of the mound, one very small sherd was taken from a depth of three and two-tenths feet below the surface.

Mound No. 64

This appears to have been originally a long, narrow, and comparatively low mound, the major axis running N. 87° W., and from the highest point on which, taken as B M, base appears at eleven and three-tenths feet. Northward from B M, the minor axis extends sixty feet; southward, the center line of the B. & O. track lies at thirty feet, and the cutting operations necessary to laying this have seriously marred the entire south half of the mound. No tests were made.

From Stn. 24, major axis, B M of Mound No. 65 bears S. 9° E., nine hundred ninety-four feet; a small low mound bears N. 35° E., about five hundred feet; another small mound, between the Pennsylvania and the B. & O. tracks, bears N. 78° E. about three hundred feet, and what may have once been a small mound lies south of Stn. D, beyond the B. & O. track.

Casual observation shows the summits of Mounds Nos. 64 and 65 in a nearly direct line with the eastern shoulder of Monks Mound, which is as the Patrick map of 1880 shows them.

The Powell Mound

A survey of this mound (which I have not been able to identify positively by number on the Patrick map) shows a major axis three hundred ten feet long and running S. 89° E., a minor axis of approximately one hundred seventy feet, and a height of forty feet. (See Plate XXXIX.)

From the southwest corner of Sec. 34, T. 3 N., R. 9 W., Madison County, Illinois, Stn. 15, minor axis, bears N. 79° 30′ E., three hundred four feet, thence North 25° E., six hundred seventy-five feet.

Several smaller mounds lie near by and the surfaces of these, as well as of the Powell Mound, yield considerable quantities of sherds and flint spalls.

In my opinion, the Powell Mound is the most imposing member of the Cahokia group, Monks Mound being so large and so heavily timbered as to pass for a natural feature of the landscape, and No. 66 being too low and long and too obscure in location to attract special attention.

Mr. Powell, on whose property the mound is located, informs me that he will give all archæological material found in the mound to any individual or institution that will completely level it and transfer it to the low overflow land to the west of it. At first thought, this might appear as a very liberal offer, but loses much of its attraction when the apparent barrenness of No. 66 is considered. Moreover, the mound is so regular in outline and stands out so clearly as an artificial structure that it should by all means be preserved.

The Two Low Mounds West of No. 66

By written permission dated July 26, 1927, from Mr. H. Mewes, lessee of the B. & O. property on which these mounds are located, a single north-south trench was cut through both and across the narrow neck of low land lying between them. This trench was approximately four feet wide, and was sunk to the yellowish water-bearing gumbo below the mounds, with a maximum depth of five and one-half feet at the apecis of the mounds and slightly more than two feet through the strip of ground between them. Midway between them, however, the trench was put down to a depth of four feet in order to examine any changes in formation that might appear, but the yellowish gumbo persisted and water prohibited deeper work.

The upper twelve inches of both mounds was a loose, dark, and very sandy loam in which, on the north mound, three very small fragments of pottery were found. Under this, heavy black gumbo prevailed, changing in color as greater depths were reached and blending gradually into the yellowish and extremely wet formation already mentioned. No evidences of stratification or disturbed earth were found.

Two small sherds and half a dozen unworked flint spalls were picked up on the northeast slope of the south mound, but no remains whatever were found in the trench. Prior to trenching, both mounds were thoroughly sounded with thirty-inch steel probes.

From previous experience, Mr. H. M. Braun, of East St. Louis, who has spent much time exploring the Cahokia Mounds, expressed the opinion that these two mounds were much more likely repositories for archæological material than No. 66, and in support of such a theory cited several instances in his own and others' investigations when such attendant mounds had actually yielded greater returns than had ever been found in the adjacent dominant structures. It may be possible, however, to attribute this fact to the greater ease and cheapness with which the smaller structures may be explored as compared with the larger ones. Further examination might bear out his belief in this case, but these two mounds will be completely buried under the new B. & O. yards, after which they will no doubt be closed to further archæological examination.

ORIENTATION OF THE CAHOKIA MOUNDS

Observing in reports of previous explorations of the Cahokia Mounds that the major axes of the dominant structures lay in an approximately east-west direction, and inferring from such reports and other information that this feature of construction was now considered intentional rather than accidental on the part of the Mound Builders, it occurred to me to ascertain if possible whether, as in the erection of the Egyptian pyramids, any consideration had been given a pole star when the mounds were built.

The very first observations of No. 66 seemed to encourage such investigations, for there it was found that the major axis, running S. 84° 30' E. lay at a right angle to the magnetic meridian when a magnetic declination of 5° 30' E., as ascertained by local surveyors, was used. It appeared only reasonable to assume, however, that in all probability the Mound Builders had no conceptions of magnetic variation, but it also seemed just as reasonable to assume that if the Egyptians oriented their structures with reference to the stars, which is, I believe, generally conceded, then the Mound Builders might have followed, or at any rate attempted to follow, a similar plan. Pursuing such a line of reasoning further, it appeared that if backward calculations covering successive so-called pole stars that might have been used by the ancients would lead eventually to identification of a star that might have served as a guide for the Mound Builders (assuming all the time, of course, that they did recognize such a star, and that they did orient their structures accordingly) then fairly definite conclusions as to the age of the mounds might be reached.

But, investigating this problem, the precession of equinoxes demands consideration, for the outstanding visible effect of this is the apparent tendency of some stars to approach the pole while others recede. For example: Although Polaris is now used as our pole star, there was a period when it was not so used, and there will come another period when it will be discarded. At the time the first catalog of the stars was compiled this star lay about twelve degrees from the true pole, but since that time has approached to within approximately a degree and a quarter of the pole. It will yet approach still closer, but in time will recede, so that in about 12,000 years from now Alpha

Lyræ, which is the brightest northern star and which will then lie within five degrees of the pole, will probably succeed Polaris as the pole star. When the pyramids were erected 4,000 years ago, the longitudes of the stars were 55° 45' less than they are now, and Thuban (Alpha Draconis) lay within 3° 44' 25" of the pole, and, since it was then the most conspicuous star in the immediate vicinity of the pole, no doubt served the Egyptians as their pole star. At any rate, viewed from Gizeh, Egypt, the latitude of which is 30° north, the pole star's altitude was likewise 30°, and its lower culmination 26° 15' 35". It is interesting to note that the downward slope of the passageways in the nine largest pyramids in the Nile Valley is at a mean angle of 26° 47', which made the pole star of that age, at lower culmination, visible at the extreme foot of such entrances. Possibly the construction of these passages at such an angle was a mere coincidence, but it was followed with such regularity in all the dominant structures that there can be little doubt that it was intentional and worked out only after careful observation of the stars.

But I found no evidence that the Mound Builders had so used this star.

Lying as it does, between Alpha Draconis and Polaris, and being brighter than the one and little dimmer than the other, Beta Ursæ Minoris must have been for a considerable period of time preferable to either of these as a pole star, and an assumption that it might have been so used does not appear unreasonable. Yet, so far as I have been able to learn, no ancient monuments have yet been found that appear to have been oriented by this star.

Likewise it may reasonably be assumed that one other star in Ursæ Minoris, lying nearer the path of the pole than does Beta, might have served as a pole star even though it is of but the fifth magnitude, but here again I do not know of the existence of any prehistoric monuments that might have been oriented by such means.

Beta Ursæ Minoris and Polaris lay the same distance from the pole about 400 A. D., at which time either may have been used as the pole star by civilized peoples, but I can not see that the Mound Builders recognized them in the orientation of their mounds.

Other computations failed to indicate satisfactorily what star might have served the Mound Builders as a pole star or even whether any star was so used, and the only recourse left was to examine the astronomical history of Polaris as shown below where the azimuth at elongation is given as seen from the latitude of the Cahokia Mounds:

Year	Distance from Pole	Azimuth at Elongation
1000 B. C.	17°.2	22°.4
500	14°.5	18°.8
0	11°.8	15°.2
500 A. D.	9°.0	11°.6
1000	6°.2	8°.1
1500	3°.4	4°.4

This table offers little encouragement to any theory of close observation of Polaris, at least, in connection with the construction of No. 66.

Later, when our camp organization and working plans had been better perfected, I felt at liberty to pursue this question further so I turned the work on No. 66 over to a part of the crew and took some of the others to help me survey other prominent mounds, viz., No. 65, 1,700 feet east of 66, No. 64, about nine hundred feet north of No. 65, and the Powell Mound, a mile or so to the northwest of No. 66, the chief end in view being always to find evidence for or against a theory of astronomical predetermination of the mounds' axes.

The major axis of No. 66 was already known to lie S. 84° 30' E. (N. 84° 30' W.) but in the very next mound examined was found to run N. 84° 30' E. (No. 65). The major axis of No. 64 lay N. 87° W., and of the Powell Mound N. 89° W.

Obviously, a small per cent of the entire Cahokia group, which includes probably one hundred fifty mounds, were thus examined, and if all of these one hundred fifty structures were still well enough preserved to leave their axes recognizable, then any conclusions based on examination of the few mounds mentioned above would be subject to severe criticism. But, with the exception of the Kunnemann Mound, which lies northwest of the great Monks Mound, and which I had no opportunity to examine, Nos. 64, 65, and 66 and the Powell Mound, because of their magnitude and the uniformity of their construction, unquestionably rank next to Monks Mound as physically dominant individuals of the Cahokia group. By analogous reasoning, their original construction must have had a significance not attached to minor structures of the group; the direction of their axes, even at this late day, is not a matter of doubt but may be determined with no difficulty whatever so long as such determination is based on the theory of axial coincidence with maximum elevations in regular lines; few if any of the lesser structures retain sufficient physical evidences to indicate whether in their original form they were markedly elliptical, ovate, or rectangular or to leave the direction of their original axes determinable, the prevailing forms apparently having been either circular, quadrangular, or irregularly pyramidal in plan and probably though not certainly truncated in elevation.

Moreover, careful surveys of the mounds mentioned show the direction of their major axes varying through an arc of 11° which, curiously enough, is bisected by a true east-west line predicted on a magnetic declination of 5° 30′ E., or exactly one half of that arc. If axial lines were determined by astronomical observation, then this wide variation would seem to indicate that the mounds were built in distinctly different eras, and that the total elapsed time intervening between the erection of the first and the last ones covered a period so great that an extremely wide range of development should mark such remains as are found.

Further investigation may, but probably will not, reveal a significant relation between these variations, and while the Mound Builders doubtless had a fair working knowledge of the equinoxes and the solstices, my own very brief examination of their work at Cahokia disclosed no evidence that led me to believe their monuments were astronomically oriented.

Nevertheless, intensive investigation of the subject, particularly with reference to Monks Mound, would not be amiss, nor would a close survey and platted location with dimensions of each mound in the group be a bad investment from a scientific viewpoint, especially since succeeding years bring certain destruction to the smaller mounds and serious injury to the larger ones.

THE USE OF COPPER IN THE
CAHOKIA REGION

During all our explorations we found no evidence as to the use of copper in ornamentation or for tools on the part of the Cahokia people. It is therefore necessary to republish the article on copper from the Mitchell Mounds written by Dr. Howland many years ago. A copper serpent was found by a boy on the surface not far from Mound No. 76 in the summer of 1922. The serpent effigy was some four or five inches long, composed of thin sheet copper with no filigree work. We were unable to secure this object for the University collection.

Dr. Howland's paper follows:

Prior to the destruction of the St. Louis "Big Mound," in 1870, no articles of copper had been found in the vicinity; in leveling that mound two "spoon-shaped" copper implements were discovered, and in the possession of Dr. J. J. R. Patrick of Belleville, Illinois, is a nugget of native copper, which was found in a large mound at East St. Louis.[1] The mound from which the articles now under consideration were taken was one of that second group of the American Bottom system to which I have alluded. Some twelve miles north of East St. Louis, a sluggish creek or slough with high banks, called Long Lake, joins Cahokia Creek, and on its banks, near the point of junction, stands a group of some thirteen or fourteen mounds, circled around a square temple mound of moderate height. At the western border of this group, and close to Mitchell Station, stood originally three conical mounds of considerable size, which were first cut into some years since in laying the tracks of the Chicago & Alton Railroad. On the twentieth of January, 1876, acting upon a chance intimation in a St. Louis morning paper, I visited this group, and found that the largest of these three mounds was being removed to furnish material for building a road dike across Long Lake, replacing an old bridge. The work was already far advanced, but in its progress some singular discoveries had been made. The mound was originally about twenty-seven feet high, and measured one hundred and twenty feet in diameter at the base, but the various assaults which from time to time had been made upon it for similar purposes had materially altered its proportions, the surface workings having reduced its height some ten feet, although I could not learn that in these early openings anything of especial interest had been discovered.

During the present excavations, however, the workmen found, at a height of four or five feet above the base of the mound, a deposit of human bones from six to eight feet in width, and averaging some eight inches in thickness, which stretched across the mound from east to west as though the remains had been gathered together and buried in a trench.

[1] From Bulletin of the Buffalo Society of Natural Science. *Recent Archæological Discoveries in the American Bottom* by Henry R. Howland—March 2, 1877.

On this level, scattered about within an area of six to eight feet square, and perhaps twenty feet from the south-easterly side of the mound, were discovered a number of valuable relics, together with a large quantity of matting in which many of them had been enveloped. The archæological zeal of the Celtic mind, was, however, not adequate to the preservation of this matting, and, unfortunately most of it, together with the bones, had been carted off and re-interred in the ditch. I was able to secure several small fragments which show a coarse, vegetable cane-like fibre, simply woven without twisting, the flat strands measuring about one-eighth of an inch in width.

Among the many curious articles carefully wrapped in these mattings and here buried, were found a number of small tortoise shells formed of copper, which being unique, are worthy of special attention. Of these I obtained three specimens, the rest having been scattered.

They are made of beaten copper scarcely more than one sixty-fourth of an inch thickness, the larger and more perfect one measuring two and one-eighth inches in length and thirteen-sixteenths inch in height. Their shape is remarkably true and perfect, showing a central ridge from end to end, produced by pressure from the under surface. A narrow flange or rim, five-twelfths inch in width, is neatly turned at the base, and over the entire outer surface the curious markings peculiar to the tortoise shell are carefully produced by indentation—the entire workmanship evincing a delicate skill, of which we have never before found trace in any discovered remains of the arts of the Mound Builders. Each of these tortoise shells would seem to have originally been covered with several wrappings of a very singular character, and one still adheres to its original envelope, presenting a peculiar mummified appearance. Closely fitting over the outer surface of the copper shell is, first, a woven cloth of vegetable fibre, similar in its general character to the outer matting above described, but of a stronger and better preserved fibre, apparently more like that which forms the woven coating of the Davenport axes.[2] This is covered in turn with a softer, finer fabric, now of a dark brown color, formed of twisted strands, laid or matted closely together, though apparently not woven. The material of which these strands are formed proves, under microscopic examination, to be animal hair. The fact is of singular interest, as it is believed that this is the only instance in which any such fabric has been discovered in connection with relics of the Mound Builders. A careful examination would seem to show the material to be rabbit's hair, in a perfect state of preservation, though none but short hairs are found and most of these are without either tip or base, though occasionally, as shown in the plate, the tips are found, as also the parts towards the base of the hairs, showing several rows of cells.

Overlying this singular fabric and adhering closely to it is a dark colored layer, which under the microscope is shown to consist of a membranous substance with numerous pores and distinct cellular structure (nuclei not visible) and would seem unquestionably to be an animal cuticle, a conclusion which is confirmed by the opinion of the eminent botanist, Sir Josep Hooker, who has examined the specimen. The pores

[2]Prof. Asa Gray, on a hurried examination of this matting, expresses the opinion that it is made of a bark fibre (not bast), possibly from the fibrous bark of Thuja.

are apparently gland openings, and the dark line shows a rent in the cuticle.

This layer seems also very carefully and smoothly shaped, and is covered in turn with a final coating of small, dark, iridescent scales which probably owe their color to carbonization, as they show in the spectroscope traces of carbon. They appear on the microscopic examination to be the remains of a layer of non-striated muscular fibre with connecting tissue, possibly from the intestines or bladder of some animal, this having originally served as an outer wrapping for these carefully treasured objects.

Next in point of interest are two specimens (also believed to be unique in their character) of the lower jaw of the deer in both of which the forward part or that containing the teeth is encased in a thin covering of copper, which extends over the teeth, and over this copper sheathing are the same mummy-like wrappings which I have already described, though in one specimen the coarse vegetable fibre cloth is lacking, and the case is primarily formed of the fine, soft, matted fabric of animal hair which in the others forms the second coating. In both, these wrappings are skillfully made to form a close-fitting and symmetrical case. They measure about two and a half inches from the end of the teeth to the point where the bone is cut off, and the copper sheathing reaches to within half an inch of this, while a hole is bored from side to side through the back of each jaw, as though the articles had been worn suspended from the neck for totems or as badges of authority.

Three curious implements which were found were in the shape of two flat circular discs of uniform size, two and three-sixteenths inches in diameter, united by a central shaft, and in general appearance not unlike a narrow spool or thread reel, each having a circular hole through the center three-fourths inch in diameter. These were made of bone and having been polished very smoothly were neatly coated with beaten copper. This is also true of a slender pointed rod of wood eight and three-fourths inches long, which was skillfully covered with a thin copper sheathing extending over its entire length. A number of pieces of very thin wood (of which I secured eight specimens) were also found, which were about three inches long, probably about two and one-fourth inches across at the widest point and very carefully shaped, being rounded at the base and running to a point at the top where they were perforated for convenience in stringing or fastening them together. The striking peculiarity of these thin plates of wood, as of the other objects just mentioned, is that they show evidence of having once been coated with thin copper, many fragments of which still adhere to their surfaces. It is as difficult to conjecture the use of these articles as of a series of five flat copper rods, measuring three and one-eighth inches in length and pointed at one end, placed edge to edge and fastened together with flat bands probably of the same material.

Close at hand were one or two rude weapons of stone. Of one a fragment only was preserved, the other was a double-pointed spear head, a foot long made of light colored chert and precisely similar to those made by the North American Indians. With them was found a bundle of eight copper rods or needles from fourteen to eighteen inches in length, all in one bundle and wrapped together with matting. In addition to these several awls, and needles of various sizes made of bone were discovered, and with them a considerable quantity of beads made from the column of Busycon shells; two of those which I obtained measured respectively two and one-eighth and four inches in length, are slightly curved in shape and perforated from end to end. Not less curious is a necklace or circlet of twenty flat crescent-shaped ornaments of shell, each some three inches long and pierced at one end for the cord or thong which fastened them together.

A day or two later, in digging on the northwest side of the mound, the workmen found near its base a mass of bones indicating another trench burial, but the only relics found with these remains were numerous sea shells of the species *Busycon perversum,* which must have been brought from the Gulf of Mexico, concerning which it is worthy of note that the crowns or tops of the shells are missing, having apparently been cut off in each instance at about the same angle, indicating that one part or the other was made to serve some useful purpose in the economy of this strange people. In one very large specimen which I secured the whorl or column of the shell had been cut away and the edges smoothly ground forming a scoop-shaped implement about a foot in length.

NOTES ON CAHOKIA SKELETONS

By DR. R. J. TERRY, Washington University, St. Louis

Skeleton No. 28. Cemetery in Mounds Nos. 19, 20, 21. Skull, most of the vertebræ and ribs, parts of the sternum, fragments of scapulæ, clavicles, right humerus, parts of both radii and ulnæ, some hand bones, fragments of hip bones, both femora and right tibia, parts of both fibulæ, some bones of the feet. Skeleton was found two feet beneath the surface; extended, head to the east, face upward. A univalve shell was found beneath the chin; five rough flints around the neck; a piece of sandstone marked with two straight grooves on opposite surfaces, a small bone spatula, pieces of ochre, and soft red hematite upon the chest. The bones are fragile, very dry, and porous. The cranium lacks the basioccipital and sphenoid; is symmetrical, broad, and high. Marked occipital taurus, tendency toward kneeling of vertex; beginning closure of sagittal suture. Teeth much worn; incisors lost; lower molars all shed. Glabello-occipital length 16.8 cm.; greatest breadth 14.2 cm.; height 12.3 cm.; bigoniac breadth of mandible 9.8 cm. Clavicles slender, curved, right measures 14.7 cm.; right humerus, maximum length 30.7 cm.; right radius 24.1 cm.; right femur, maximum length 42.6 cm. Shape of shaft prismatic: platymeria marked. Right tibia presents shape of shaft No. 5 (Hrdlicka) length 34.5 cm. (medial malleolus lost); platycnæmy marked; retroversion of head slight.

Skeleton No. 29. Cranium large, broad and high; not well enough preserved to give trustworthy measurements. Marked asymmetry apparently post-mortem; vertex reaches highest point at obelion; sagittal suture closed. Slight keeling of vertex. Occipital taurus prominent. Bigoniac breadth 10.8 cm.; teeth much worn; shovel-shaped incisors; left lower canine, three ridged. Right clavicle slender, curved, length 15.8 cm. Humeri perforated; left large, right medium. Left humerus maximum length 32.1 cm. Femora moderately platymeric; shape cylindrical to prismatic. Right bone maximum length 45.8 cm.; tibiæ show pathological enlargement in diameters of shafts; head of left bone roughened, marked retroversion in right and obscure facet at lower anterior margin. All of the bones are very brittle and dry. A male skeleton.

Skeleton No. 1 consists of only a cranial fragment including face and frontal bone, left parietal and temporal. Very dry and fragile. Apparently a high cranium. Slight tendency to keeling. Dental alveoli all present; wisdom teeth not erupted: incisors and canines present lateral ridges.

Skeleton No. 100. Skull only, taken from cemetery at Pittsburg Lake. Well preserved. Glabello-occipital length 17.4 cm.; greatest breadth 13.6 cm.; height 19.4 cm. No tendency to keeling. No occipital taurus. Sagittal suture open; coronal obliterated inferiorly. Chin pointed, bigoniac breadth 8.8 cm.; teeth much worn. Evidently the skull of a woman.

The skulls excepting No. 100 have the highest point of the vertex about the obelion with a steep slant to the glabella. This head form is also strikingly marked in an endocranial cast that was obtained by lifting away the fragile bones of the cranium from the hard mass of gumbo which completely filled the cranial cavity. A plaster replica of this earth cast has been made and will be the subject of future study.

PREVIOUS WORK AND COLLECTIONS RELATING
TO THE CAHOKIA GROUP

Dr. Patrick

Dr. A. J. R. Patrick, Belleville, Illinois, was one of the pioneers in Cahokia work. The survey called on his widow, who is now Mrs. John Bauman. She showed us some field notes written by Dr. Patrick, in 1877. On November 18, of that year, he visited Monks Mound, and did some exploring in the vicinity. Again, on April 7, 1878, April 6, 1879, and May 11 and 12, 1879, Dr. Patrick dug in a number of places along Cahokia Creek, and in the low mounds. His observations, for the most part, were confined to burials, within four feet of the surface, since he used a slender, steel rod, by means of which he sounded for bones, pottery, or stone. This method of testing has been employed for many years by collectors, and others, and is possible when soil is free from stone. The rods will not penetrate hard gumbo, but in the late winter, or early spring, the rods penetrate easily to a depth of four feet. One is able to distinguish by feeling with these rods stone from pottery, bone or decayed wood from layers or sections of hard earth. The use of the rod in the Mississippi Valley burial places, (where the soil is favorable) has been so extensive that a large percentage of all burials near the surface have been reached. Most of the large collections of pottery vessels were secured in the manner described.

Dr. Patrick, in the field notes, states that in a small mound east of Monks, he found a floor of clay. In the center there was a depression, or basin. On the slopes of mounds and in one or two low mounds he found some effigy pottery, portraying frog, deer, bear, fish, and duck, but unfortunately, he does not give us the numbers and we cannot identify the mounds he explored. In one of his notes, he does not think the large mounds were used for burial places. He suggests the theory that they were made in order that dwellings might be elevated above the plain. He considered the ponds as artificial. On April 6, 1879, he found a skeleton and pottery, also a skull, which he calls No. 3, accompanied by a copper plate. Mrs. John Bauman says this plate was sent to the Smithsonian Institution. A letter from Dr. Neil M. Judd, Curator of Archæology, informs the writer that he cannot locate the copper specimen in the Smithsonian collections.

Mrs. Bauman has in her possession several field maps, and a profile survey of the group. She says that the first survey was executed November 5, 1876, and that the profile survey was made July 5, 1879, and that Louis Gainer Kahn, a surveyor, either made this survey, or assisted on it. She thinks there were several surveys, more or less thorough, made of the Cahokia Mounds in the period between 1870 and 1888.

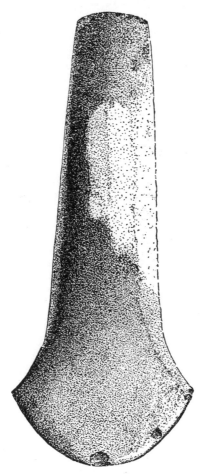

FIG. 10—Large polished celt or hatchet in Peabody Museum. Half natural size.

After considerable investigation we were able to trace the location of a number of Cahokia objects. Most of these were found many years ago and the exact circumstances of discovery are not available. The interesting local collection on exhibition in the museum of Monticello Seminary, Godfrey, Illinois, was made by William McAdams probably twenty-five to as far back as forty years ago. Some of the objects in this collection appear to have been in the hands of other owners for some time. The largest private collection of material from Indiana, Illinois, Kentucky, and Missouri is that owned by E. W. Paine of Springfield, Illinois. Mr. Payne has many objects from mounds, graves, and the surface of the Cahokia district and a radius of ten miles about it. His collection is packed away and it is impossible to secure photographs or descriptions.

In the Peabody Museum is a large polished celt, or hatchet. This is shown in Text Fig. 10. This was chipped from very fine, highly colored flint—dark brown and yellow, with a suggestion of pink in the coloring. The specimen was then carefully ground and polished until all depressions made by flaking were removed. Mr. Charles C. Willoughby, Director, called my attention to this specimen. The catalog stated that it was secured from Monks Mound about 1873. This was six years prior to Professor Putnam's visit to the mounds.

Figure 8, Plate XXXII, shows a very large axe, twelve by seventeen inches, weight seventeen pounds. It was found near the Kunnemann Mound. There is a low mound just west of the Kunnemann, No. 12, from which a great number of large unfinished celts have been secured. Mr. Seever obtained a number of these for the Missouri Historical Society collection years ago. The small hematite axe (Fig. 7) was also found near the Kunnemann Mound, on the surface. (Plate XXXVII.)

Plate XXXIII, Figs. 1-5, show five pipes, three of which are effigies. No. 1 is a large frog effigy pipe from a grave on the bluffs east of Cahokia. No. 2 is a human effigy pipe found near Cahokia. No. 5 is a pipe of sandstone, from the region, exact locality not given. No. 3, a clay pipe from a grave near Cahokia. No. 4 is probably a bird effigy, although the workmanship is not very good. Figure 8 is a sandstone effigy pipe, large. Shown one-third size. Found with a burial in the cemetery on the bluffs between the two sugar loaf mounds, known as Group 3, Madison County, Illinois. William J. Seever collection.

Figures 6, 7, Plate XXXIII, show two stone idols from the Monticello Seminary collection. Number 7 is of fluorspar and about twelve inches high. It was found on the bluffs directly east of Cahokia. Number 6 is of red material, almost pipestone, is about eighteen inches high, exceedingly well made and came from a small mound, one of the Cahokia group, on the Caseyville Road, St. Clair County, Illinois. Unfortunately the number of the mound is not given.

Plate XXXIV. Two sea shells and a string of shell beads. The string of shell beads (Fig. 1) and the shell vessel (Fig. 2) were taken from the Mitchell Mound at the time it was destroyed by the Chicago & Alton Railroad in the winter of 1876. The shell (Fig. 3) shown for comparison, was found in a mound in Jersey County. They are shown one-fourth size.

Plate XXXII, Figs. 2-6 show shell spoons and bone awls (Fig. 1) from cemeteries south and west of Cahokia. Collection of William J. Seever. Broken Unio shells with scalloped edges have frequently been found by the survey and were identical with those shown in this picture.

Plate XXXIV, Fig. 4. Attention is called to this remarkable art-object. It portrays the height of efficiency in flint-chipping. Found by Mr. Barth, a tenant of the Rameys, south of Monks Mound, in December, 1921, on the surface. Shown full size.

CAHOKIA POTTERY

Some thousands of pottery fragments, both plain and decorated, have been placed in stacks and on exhibition in the Natural History Museum by Professor Baker. No attempt at either classification or study has been attempted by the writer. Inspection of the fragments shown in plates presented in the rear of this report will indicate the great range in form, design, or motif. Ceramic art at Cahokia was highly developed and there is a wealth of material available for comparative studies with other portions of the Mississippi Valley. Dr. Carl Guthe has established for the National Research Council a pottery repository at the University of Michigan Museum. Dr. Guthe has had considerable experience in ceramic studies in the Southwest, and his volume on art in pottery at Pecos Pueblo is most thorough and scholarly. It has been suggested that he devote time to a general classification of pottery forms and concepts of the central, southern, and eastern United States. Such research will indicate relationships and differences to be obtained in no other way. While many Cahokia forms are common throughout the whole great Mississippi basin, yet one need not be an expert in ceramic art to sense that which might be termed Madisonville, Etowah, Cahokia, Moundville, or St. Francis. There is a persistent Cahokia concept, just as there appears a positive Etowah concept. The field of pottery distribution east of the Pueblo-Cliff country offers abundant and far-reaching possibilities of great interest and importance to archæological science. These multitudinous designs made by Indian women on clay vessels are imperishable records preserved these many years. A careful and far-reaching study of them may solve some of our migration and origin problems.

GENERAL OBSERVATIONS ON THE
CAHOKIA GROUP

In this report we expand, or change, the brief conclusions offered in previous bulletins. Subsequent and more thorough explorations will doubtless enable us to solve the Cahokia mystery. Notwithstanding rather extensive research through several seasons, we are unable to go as far as we would like in the matter of definite conclusions.

The surveys of Phillips Academy have spent portions of six winters in researches in certain sections of Georgia, Mississippi, and Tennessee. The Director of the Cahokia explorations served on all these surveys and the knowledge obtained of distinctly Southern cultures presents us with a firm basis of comparison. We, therefore, now state that Cahokia represented the farthest northward push of a strictly Southern culture. It is true that many of the art forms, common to Tennessee, Georgia, Alabama, and elsewhere are not present at Cahokia. At least they have not been discovered the past eight years, yet the mounds themselves, the pottery, and game stones are Southern in character. In brief, Cahokia bears a closer relationship to Tennessee and Georgia mound groups and cultures than to the tumuli of the Illinois valley to the north, and is quite different from those of Ohio.

In March of this year our survey began work again in the Illinois valley and we continued explorations until the end of December. Our observations on the region between Lewistown and Alton will be set forth in a future bulletin.

Frequently during the past few years has arisen the question, "What is the relationship between Cahokia culture and that of the Illinois valley?"

Such query has occurred to many observers and we recall that during the preliminary inspection of Cahokia years ago, Mr. W. J. Seever made a positive statement that we would find in the Illinois valley proper a totally different archæological setting from that apparent at Cahokia. He based his statement on artifacts and utensils, and subsequent explorations have confirmed the view expressed.

Between 1860 and 1900, there was a great deal of indiscriminate digging throughout the Illinois valley. Search through the literature reveals that aside from papers by Dr. J. F. Snyder (see bibliography) and the observations of both Dr. Howland and Dr. Rau, previously referred to, little of scientific value has been produced. The several books or pamphlets written by state archæologist, MacAdams, are not helpful in the broad sense, yet they contain a few paragraphs worthy of preservation. Mr. George Langford, Joliet, Illinois, published in *The Anthropologist* for July-September, 1927, a most excellent paper on explorations of Indian sites of that region. Dr. Fay-Cooper Cole and his able assistants have also carried on mound explorations above Joliet and in northern Illinois, the results of which will be published in due time.

Hence, our preliminary conclusions are based on recent explorations, the few published papers, and archæologic material in public and private collections.

Toward the end of 1926, Dr. Don F. Dickson of Lewistown began the excavation of a large cemetery on his father's farm. At present writing there are one hundred eighty skeletons and accompanying objects preserved in the ground as found and enclosed in a museum. A careful study of this exhibit enables us to visualize one of the middle Illinois cultures, one hundred seventy miles northward of Monks Mound.

In answer to our question as to relationships between the interesting region of the Illinois and Cahokia proper, it is necessary to enter into some detail.

As observed, the pottery of Cahokia for the most part is distinctly Southern, whereas the ceramic art between the mouth of the river at Alton and the city of Peoria far to the north, presents certain variations. Some of the types are Southern, as one would naturally expect, whereas other forms seem local and not unlike those of Madisonville cemetery, Ohio. The exact differences and correlations will be worked out by Dr. Guthe, and those in charge of the study and classification of ceramic art of the United States east of the Rocky Mountains.

Aside from differences in the pottery, there is to be observed in the large private collection of Mr. George Waters of Godfrey, Illinois, and museum exhibits of the Missouri Historical Society, the Smithsonian, New York, and other museums, marked differences in the stone artifacts of the Cahokia site and those of the Illinois valley proper. Godfrey, being but twenty-five miles from Cahokia, presents several well known Cahokia forms. The peculiar small arrow points, notched at the base, and shown in Plates XIII and XIV, occur in great numbers on the American Bottoms near the mounds, but are not found to any considerable extent beyond Alton. Large flint objects, such as spades and hoes, numerous about Cahokia, almost entirely disappear when we reach Peoria. One of the chief differences in the artifacts is observed in beads, which at Cahokia are large, thin, and flat. They are usually disc form, from two-thirds to one and a half inches diameter. The special types referred to are shown in Figs. 7-12 in Plate XXIV. They are manifestly distinct and indicate a local development. Such forms of ornamentation in shell occur elsewhere, but seldom in profusion as at Cahokia. In the mounds along the Illinois River, particularly in the vicinity of Beardstown, Havana, and Lewistown, are great quantities of small shell and bone beads as well as fresh water pearls, which were perforated and strung.

We might be justified, in view of the evidence, in assuming that there are two, and possibly three, cultures in the Illinois valley between Alton and Joliet, which are not closely related to Cahokia. After a cursory inspection of objects found between Joliet and Lake Michigan, one might suggest that intensive study will probably prove the presence of a different tribe (rather than a general culture) in that region. The types discovered by Mr. Langford at Joliet and described in his excellent article (referred to) indicate that his site lies within the borderland between the Illinois proper and the Lake. Let us be a trifle more explicit. Mr. Langford finds a world of material which does not differ essentially from artifacts or utensils, etc., common to all stone-age Indians within two hundred miles south or three hundred miles east of the Joliet region. At present writing it would seem that the term Fort Ancient Culture might well apply. Certainly it is not high, and little stone-age art is in evidence. Copper has been found, yet so far there is not much indication of aboriginal trade.

Something over a year ago commercial diggers in the Havana region discovered two "log tombs" or cribs in which burials were made. These we shall describe later, but it is well to remark here that they indicate a specialized and rather "Hopewell" form of culture. In the same region another band of Indians appears to have buried in mounds, yet they did not employ cists of either logs or stone.

During October-November, 1927, and March-December, 1928, we were unable to find log structures in any of thirty or forty mounds tested. All of which suggests that the normal form of burial in mounds predominated, and these lob cribs are not characteristic of the entire region, but present departure from established mortuary custom, just as in certain of the lower Scioto tumuli. Readers are requested to compare forms presented in Plates XL to XLIX of this bulletin with Mr. Langford's figures in *The Anthropologist,* July-September, 1927.

Coming back to Cahokia itself, one's most lasting impression, after years of research, is the immensity of the place. Added together, all the earth of all tumuli between Peoria and Alton would not equal in bulk the central Cahokia group. Writers have frequently speculated on the real purpose of this prodigious mound construction. Our excavations were extensive. What significant facts could be deduced from these labors? One is that some of the mounds contain a great deal of refuse material (pottery, animal bones, and arrow heads) distributed through the earth from the surface down to the base line.

Our pits in other mounds of size indicated a surprising scarcity of village debris. To these simple observations should be added the surface inspections and village site trenches. We come to the conclusion that certain sections of the 2,000-acre tract were always favorable cabin or wigwam sites. Others were not. Cabins may have been moved. Obviously, we have no knowledge as to the exact changes which took place, but we may safely conclude that there are, today, two types of mound body or material. Those in which gumbo predominates, such as Nos. 65 and 66, and the loam sandy soil, or stratified tumuli of which Nos. 10-11 and 35 are outstanding examples.

Naturally, in mound construction, Indians would remove earth from convenient or near-by spots. Variegated layers, especially in colors, sometimes found may be composed of soil brought from a distance. Yet the greater bulk of mound contents was carried up by Indians in baskets from the immediate vicinity. Tumuli of gumbo contain a minimum of cabin or camp-fire refuse, whereas the loam mounds contain much. The reason? Wigwams, with some exceptions, were located on sandy or loam soil. There is some village-site material south of the Pennsylvania and Baltimore & Ohio railways. Yet here gumbo predominates and there are indications of no large village site. All field evidence tends to prove that the Cahokians erected their cabins on the more favorable surface. Gumbo is sticky, damp, and disagreeable.

Since the natives scooped up earth from near their houses, we naturally have a preponderance of pottery fragments, bones, and flint chips in all but the gumbo mounds.

Sometimes it is a short distance from such a setting to one more conducive to comfort in living. Indians wore moccasins and the wetness of gumbo soil from November to mid-April is a factor to be taken into account at Cahokia.

The soil around Mrs. Tippetts' Mound (No. 61) is mostly gumbo; the village-site indications are not heavy, but several hundred yards north, where there is less gumbo, the village was thickly populated. It does not seem likely that the Indians would go any distance to secure the earth for the construction of No. 61. It would be more convenient to obtain it from points nearby and the two depressions marked "Lakes" on the map probably represent the places from which earth was taken for Nos. 61 and 62, and probably for other mounds.

Why were so many mounds built of gumbo? It was difficult to handle—even our own men using modern steel shovels find it heavy and wearisome to remove. Possessed of naught but stone and shell hoes, digging sticks, and baskets or skin bags, the removal and transportation of sufficient gumbo to erect Mound No. 66 was a herculean task.

And the purpose of No. 66? It is too narrow on top for large wigwams or temples. The auger tests—nearly two hundred to the base—did not indicate the level or burnt floor common in mortuary tumuli. Beyond No. 66 towards the north is an elevation flanked by two ponds or depressions. Old observers used to call this a causeway leading to other mounds. There being no village-site worthy of the name around No. 66, why the causeway? The burials found by Engineer Taylor a few feet below the surface, down the southern slope were made after the mound had been constructed. There appear to be no burials, altars, or distinct stratigraphy in the body of the mound. It must remain one of the outstanding mysteries of Cahokia and we may be pardoned again for referring finally to the series of complete and detailed maps drawn by Mr. Taylor, which cover every possible fact or circumstance of mound construction of this remarkable tumulus.

The age of Cahokia? We cannot answer this question. We have always believed that it was long before 1660. In distant Quebec, La Salle, Hennepin, and other explorers heard of the main Illinois village located on the present site of Utica. Now, the surface debris at Utica is far less than that of Cahokia.

Had Cahokia been inhabited, certainly the early French explorers would have visited the site. We find the Cahokia Indians mentioned, but they lived to the southward and we have never been able to positively identify them as builders of the famous group. Peradventure, one might estimate that Cahokia was occupied between the years 1200 to 1500. Why? This is a matter of opinion after seasons of exploration and study. As yet the statement cannot be positively proven.

We have never believed that all these structures were erected within a short space of time, individually or as a group. No. 66 seems to show completion within limited dates, there being no sod-lines.

In all of the larger mound groups, with scarce an exception, there has been found one or more mortuary tumuli in which the ranking personages were interred. Future exploration doubtless will result in such discovery at Cahokia. Then we shall be able to study the art and life of the builders more comprehensively, since in such a structure would be placed objects illustrating all phases of aboriginal life of the Cahokians.

THE CAHOKIA MOUNDS

PART II
THE GEOLOGICAL ASPECTS OF SOME OF THE CAHOKIA (ILLINOIS) MOUNDS

BY

MORRIS M. LEIGHTON
Chief, Illinois Geological Survey

State Geological Survey Division
March 1, 1923

Dr. David Kinley

President, University of Illinois

Dear President Kinley:

The accompanying report on a geological investigation of Cahokia Mounds by Dr. M. M. Leighton, undertaken at your suggestion, is transmitted for your information and for publication if desired.

The interest attaching to the mounds, and particularly the movement to include them in a State Park, made it desirable to supplement the archæological investigations of Dr. W. K. Moorehead with those of a specialist in surficial geology, in order that all possible light might be thrown on the origin of the mounds. While there has been a decided difference of opinion, and casual consideration of the problem would lead a geologist to assume, tentatively, that the mounds are natural remnants of an alluvial terrace which has been mostly removed by erosion, the careful scrutiny of the excavations, supplemented by systematic auger borings and study of the oxidation and leaching of the materials in the mounds and under the surrounding flood plain, makes it clear that the mounds so far investigated are artificial rather than natural. Others which have not been studied may prove to be natural, but I am not justified in expressing an opinion in advance.

The careful observations and deductions by Dr. Leighton supplemented by my own less extensive studies may lead to a conclusion harmonious with that of Dr. Moorehead. I am glad to transmit the results of Dr. Leighton's efforts and to express the hope that the State may acquire and preserve these interesting and significant relics of a settlement and civilization in Illinois far back of anything recorded in the history of man.

Very respectfully yours,

F. W. DeWolf, *Chief*
State Geological Survey

INTRODUCTION

THE PROBLEM

For many years there has been a difference of opinion as to whether the group of mounds northeast of East St. Louis, on the American Bottom of the Mississippi River, has had a natural mode of origin, or whether they represent the work of Mound Builders. Monks Mound has been pointed out by some as being the largest Indian mound in North America, if not in the world, while others have insisted that it is natural.

In September, 1921, excavations were started in the smaller mounds by Professor Warren K. Moorehead, Archæologist, of Andover, Massachusetts, and continued for two months under the joint auspices of the University of Illinois and the Illinois State Museum Division. The following spring and fall of 1922, the exploratory work was assumed entirely by the University. The excavations afforded an excellent opportunity for a geologic examination of the materials composing the mounds, and in this work the State Geological Survey Division cooperated. The writer was requested to undertake the geological work. Five visits of about two days each were made at advantageous times for inspection, and the data for the following report were collected.

ACKNOWLEDGMENTS

The writer wishes to express his sincere thanks to the Ramey family, owners of Monks Mound and other mounds; to Mr. Schmidt, owner of the Schmidt Mound, and to Mr. Kunnemann, owner of the Kunnemann Mound, for the privileges they extended and their hearty spirit of cooperation; to Professor Warren K. Moorehead for his contribution of men for certain manual labor necessary to the study; to Curator Frank C. Baker, of the Museum of Natural History of the University of Illinois, for his identification of fossil shells found in the mounds and the east bluffs; and to Professor W. S. Bayley of the Department of Geology of the University of Illinois, for his identification of certain rock materials. The writer also acknowledges his indebtedness and gratitude to F. W. DeWolf, Chief of the Illinois Geological Survey, who by his discussions and suggestions contributed scientifically to the success of the study.

FORMER OPINIONS OF GEOLOGISTS REGARDING THE ORIGIN OF THE MOUNDS

In searching the literature for opinions regarding the origin of the mounds, the writer has been careful to select those of geologists, rather than those of archæologists, inasmuch as the supreme motive of the former is to critically study and properly interpret land forms and the materials of the earth, while the archæologists are interested primarily in the physical, mental, and social characteristics and activities of pre-historic man.

The Views of G. W. Featherstonhaugh, F.R.S., F.G.S.— During his travels in 1834 and 1835 from Washington, D. C., to the frontier of Mexico, the English geologist, G. W. Featherstonhaugh, visited the Cahokia Mounds, and gave his account in his book, *Excursions in the Slave States,* Vol. I, 1844, pp. 266-270. Featherstonhaugh evidently did not doubt the human origin of the mounds, for he offered no suggestions to the contrary and definitely states that "the soil of which the mound consists is the rich black mould taken from the surface below. ..." (p. 268).

The Views of Professor A. H. Worthen.—As early as 1866, the natural theory of the origin of the mounds received the support of a no less reputable geologist than Professor A. H. Worthen, Director of the Geological Survey of Illinois. Professor Worthen, in Vol. I of the Geological Survey of Illinois, p. 314, considered the mounds as "proof" that the Mississippi Valley had been filled to a height of fifty or sixty feet above its present level and that this was "in part removed by subsequent erosion during the period of elevation and drainage that succeeded the drift epoch." Artificial exposures in the large mound in the upper part of the city of St. Louis, now destroyed, were examined by him, and these showed about fifteen feet of common chocolate brown drift clay at the base, overlaid by thirty feet or more of "the ash colored marly sands of the loess, the line of separation between the two deposits remaining as distinct and well defined as they usually are in good artificial sections in the railroad cuts through these deposits."

From this he inferred that the "mounds are not artificial elevations . . . . but, on the contrary, they are simply outliers of loess and drift, that have remained as originally deposited, while the surrounding contemporaneous strata are swept away by denuding forces."

It seems pertinent to call attention to the fact that the science of Glacial Geology was scarcely beyond its embryonic state at this time, and but little more could be claimed for the sciences of Physiography and Sedimentation.

The Views of William McAdams.—William McAdams, a teacher and careful observer of natural science, including geological phenomena, regarded Monks Mound (called by him Cahokia Mound) as of artificial origin. In his pamphlet, "Antiquities of Cahokia, or Monk's Mound in Madison County, Illinois," Edwardsville, Illinois, 1883, pp. 2-3, he says:

Since some doubts have been expressed as to the artificial origin of this structure we were much interested to ascertain what could be learned in this respect by examination. On the top of the pyramid are the remains of a house, said to have been commenced by the monks, but afterwards added to and finished as a comfortable residence for the family of a man named Hill, an enterprising settler who owned the mound and a large body of land adjoining. Beneath this house is a deep unwalled cellar. A section down the side of the cellar to the depth of ten feet very plainly revealed a deposit of various kinds of earth without stratification. The principal part of this deposit was the black humus or mould, so common in the bottom and forming the principal soil, very sticky when wet and breaking into cubical blocks when dry. Here and there, as if thrown promiscuously among the black mould, is a bunch of yellow clay, or sand, or marly loess, these bunches being about such size as a man could easily carry.

Similar sections can be seen up the old road made by Hill to ascend to his residence.

About midway, on the north side, or face of the pyramid, and elevated twenty-five or thirty feet above the base, in a small depression, stands a pine tree, singularly enough, since this tree is not found in the forests in this locality. There was a story rife among the early settlers that this tree stood at the mouth of an opening or gallery into the interior of the mounds. To ascertain the truth of this matter, Mr. Thomas Ramey, the present owner of the mound, commenced a tunnel at this tree and excavated about ninety (90) feet towards the center of the mound. When fifteen feet from the entrance to the tunnel a piece of lead ore was discovered, but no other object of interest was found. The deposits penetrated by the tunnel are very plainly shown to be the same as seen in the cellar mentioned above.

Mr. McAdams republished a paragraph from Edmund Flagg's book on *The Far West,* 1838, p. 167, regarding an old well on the mound. Flagg's description reads:

Upon the western side of Monks Mound, at a distance of several yards from the summit, is a well some eighty or ninety feet in depth; the water of which would be agreeable enough were not the presence of sulfur, in some of its modifications, so palpable. This well penetrates the heart of the mound, yet, from its depth, cannot reach lower than the level of

the surrounding plain. I learned, upon inquiry, that when this well was
excavated, several fragments of pottery, of decayed ears of corn, and
other articles, were thrown up from a depth of sixty-five feet; proof
incontestible of the artificial structure of the mound.

The Views of Dr. N. M. Fenneman.—Dr. N. M. Fenneman
of the University of Cincinnati believes that the valley was
much aggraded in the Wisconsin epoch, but that this filling has
not been entirely removed, there being remnants left within the
cut-offs of the meanders which were later eroded, dissected, and
narrowed "by the meander of the main stream and its tributaries until mounds were produced.[1] Among those," he continues, "was the great natural hill which was subsequently
modified by man and is now the partly artificial Monks Mound.

The partly artificial character of Monks Mound is evident from its
form. That it is in part a natural feature, is seen by its structure. Sand
is found neatly inter-stratified with loam at an altitude of about four
hundred fifty-five feet, or thirty-five feet above its base. To this height,
at least, the mound is natural and as there is sufficient other evidence that
the valley was filled in the Wisconsin epoch to at least that height, the
original mound may be regarded as a remnant of the alluvial formation
of that time. Its base was probably narrowed artificially by the removal
of material which was carried to the top. In this way also the conspicuous
abruptness of its slopes was probably produced. No natural stratification
has yet been found more than thirty-five feet above its base and therefore, for aught that is now known, more than half its height may be
artificial. There is therefore no reason at present to deny to Monks
Mound the distinction claimed for it of being the largest artificial mound
of its kind in the world. The time of its building and the people by whom
it was built are unknown.

The many other mounds within a mile or two of Monks Mound had
the same origin. Several of the larger ones have been similarly altered
artificially. The low ones of gentle slope and less definite outline are believed to be in their natural forms.

A later statement[2] reads:

To a height of thirty-five feet above its base the material of Monks
Mound shows assortment and stratification, which is evidently natural.
Above that height it affords no structural evidence bearing on the question
whether it is of natural or artificial origin; but the form plainly indicates
the work of man, and not of geologic processes. It is highly probable that
the mound in its natural condition was much lower and broader than at
present, and was of rounded, almost drumloidal form, similar to the
smaller ones of the group which now surround it. By cutting down its
margin to the level of the surrounding plain its builders obtained ma-

---

[1] *Physiography of the St. Louis Area,* Ill. State Geol. Survey Bull. 12, 1909, pp.
62, 63.
[2] *Geology and Mineral Resources of the St. Louis Quadrangle,* U. S. Geological
Survey Bull. 438, 1911, p. 12.

terial to raise the mound to perhaps two or three times its former height without making excavations beneath the level of the plain and without carrying material from the bluffs, two and one-half miles distant. There is no evidence that material was obtained by either of these latter means.

The Views of Dr. A. R. Crook.—At the Philadelphia meeting of the Geological Society of America, December 29-31, 1914, Dr. A. R. Crook, Chief of the State Museum Division, presented a paper on the "Origin of Monks Mound," based on twenty-five borings made in the north face of the mound, and upon an examination of the surrounding mounds and the valley bluffs two miles away. Quoting from an abstract of this paper which appears in Vol. XXVI, 1915, of the Society, pp. 74, 75, he says:

Twenty-five borings were made in the north and most abrupt side. 1. They showed different strata at different elevations. 2. These strata agree with similar elevations in the other mounds and with soil from the bluff two miles away. 3. Fossil hackberry seeds *(Celtis occidentalis)* and such gastropods as *Pyramidula, Succinea, Helicina,* and *Physa* are found in beds. 4. A study of the physiography of the mounds makes clear that they occur along the divide between streams, and that their arrangement and individual forms are characteristic of the remnants of stream cutting.

Chemical and mineralogical study of the soil, as well as paleontological and physiographical investigations, indicate that the mounds are the remnants of the glacial and alluvial deposits which at one time filled the valley of the Mississippi River in this region.

It may be well to inquire if all so-called mounds in the Mississippi Valley are not natural topographic forms.

Dr. Crook held to the same view in subsequent papers[3] until May, 1922, when he published a bulletin on *The Origin of the Cahokia Mounds* under the auspices of the Illinois State Museum. In this bulletin, which was written following a field conference between him and the present writer when several of the mounds were excellently exposed for study, he inclines strongly towards the artificial theory of origin and has since definitely expressed himself in favor of that theory.[4]

---

[3]"The Composition and Origin of Monks Mound," *Trans. Ill. Acad. of Sci.,* Vol. 9, 1916, pp. 82-84; Additional Note on Monks Mound, *Bull. Geol. Soc. Amer.,* Vol. 29, 1918, pp. 80, 81.
[4]Remarks before the Section of Geology and Geography, Illinois Academy of Science, Galesburg meeting, 1923.

GENERAL DESCRIPTION OF THE MOUNDS

Our chief concern in this connection will be to fix our attention upon those points which are of significance in the question of the origin of the mounds. The reader whose interest carries him into archæological questions and interpretations is referred to (1) Part I of the present volume, (2) a preliminary paper on the Cahokia Mounds by Warren K. Moorehead, and (3) the bibliography (p. 171). If, on the other hand, the reader is interested in a brief summary of the geologic evidences and conclusions he is referred to the summary statement at the close of this paper. The discussion which now follows is a rather detailed treatment of the geologic aspects of the mounds so far as they have been examined.

Number, Size, and Shape

Some eighty-five mounds have been mapped within a radius of about one and one-half miles, and more widely scattered mounds are to be found in adjacent territory. Monks Mound dominates them all. It stands about one hundred feet high above the plain, and the longer side of its rectangular base is about 1,000 feet and its shorter side about seven hundred feet. An inspection of the map, Fig. 1, will show approximately the comparative sizes in ground plan of the rest of the important mounds. The smallest mounds are mere swells of the surface and are not shown on the map. In shape the mounds range from pyramidal forms, with nearly rectangular bases, to elongate ovoid and conical forms. Rain-wash and farming have modified some of the pyramidal mounds and given them sub-rectangular to sub-oval basal outlines. Some are flat-topped and, as in No. 48, have sufficient summit area for a residence site. Practically all of the mounds which are large enough to attract attention have a distinct artificiality in their regularity of form and steepness of slope (Plates V, VI). They lack the irregularity in ground plan and the wide range in summit area so characteristic of erosional remnants and they show no meander scars at their bases or on their slopes. They are but little sculptured by slope-wash—Monks Mound the most of all—which speaks for their recency geologically, although they may be rather ancient historically. Some of the larger mounds, those about thirty or thirty-five feet high in the vicinity of Monks Mound, show some accordance of level.

Monks Mound

Monks Mound has some peculiarities of form worth noting, which were faithfully described by McAdams:[1]

On the southern end, some thirty feet above the base is a terrace or apron, containing nearly two acres of ground. On the western side, and some thirty feet above the first terrace, is a second one of somewhat less extent. The top of the mound is flat and divided into two parts, the northern end being some four or five feet higher than the southern portion. The summit contains about an acre and a half. Near the middle of the first terrace, at the base of the mound, is a projecting point, apparently the remains of a graded pathway to ascend from the plain to the terrace. The west side of the mound below the second terrace is very irregular, and forms projecting knobs, separated by deep ravines, probably the result of rain-storms. . . . The remaining sides of the structure are quite straight and but little defaced by the hand of time.

It should be added that on the north side, there are projecting spurs, fifty to one hundred feet long and thirty to fifty feet high. Some have horizontal summits, while others are sloping and have the form of approaches. This is the most abrupt side and some gullying has no doubt taken place. On the east side there is some evidence of creep of considerable masses of material, and deposition at the base of the mound of material washed down from above.

The present writer's impression of the form of this huge mound with its platforms and approaches is in harmony with that of Dr. Fenneman, that it "plainly indicates the work of man and not of geologic processes."[2]

Arrangement of the Mounds

There are certain significant points regarding the arrangement of the mounds. (1) The elongate mounds are, in most instances, oriented with respect to the cardinal points of the compass, either north-south or east-west. (2) Some have a striking alignment, as for example, Nos. 19 to 26 and 6 to 11 (see

[1]*Records of Ancient Races in the Mississippi Valley*, St. Louis, 1887.
[2]*Geology and Mineral Resources of the St. Louis Quadrangle*, U. S. Geological Survey Bull. 348, 1911, p. 12.

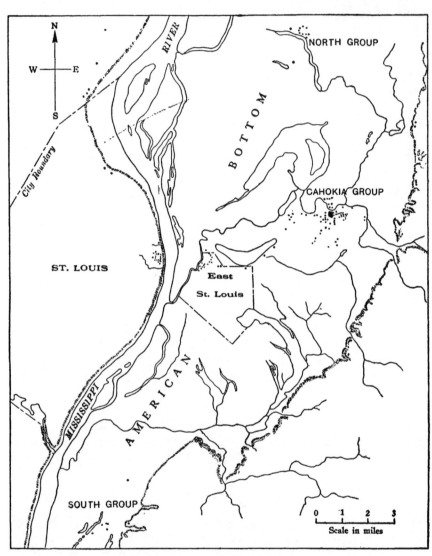

Fig. 11—Map showing the location of the Cahokia group. (After David I. Bushnell, Jr., Smithsonian Institution)

Fig. 1), and this alignment as well as their orientation carries the aspect much more of the human mode of origin than by ordinary physiographic processes. (3) The grouping of the mounds on the American Bottom is shown in Fig. 11. This grouping, as well as the alignment and elongation, is not in harmony with the theory of terrace remnants or any other physiographic origin to which they can tenably be referred.

THE GEOLOGICAL SETTING OF THE MOUNDS

TOPOGRAPHIC POSITION

The American Bottom.—The Cahokia Mounds are situated on the great flood-plain of the Mississippi River, known as the great American Bottom, some four miles northeast of the center of East St. Louis (Fig. 11). The mounds offer the only relief possessed by this extensive flat except the valley bluffs which bound it. Before the artificial levees were built, large portions of the flood-plain were subject to the highest floods, but so far as the writer could learn there has been no time in the history of the settlement by white man when all of it was under flood-waters. Even today, with the artificial levees, the flood-waters back up into some of the abandoned channels previously occupied by the Mississippi River, as for example the old channel now followed by Cahokia Creek, in its wanderings across the plain.

The highest known flood-level of the Mississippi River at St. Louis was in 1844,[1] when the waters rose 7.58 feet above the city directrix, reaching an altitude of 420.31 feet above sea-level. According to the topographic map of the St. Louis quadrangle, published by the U. S. Geological Survey, involving the site of the Cahokia Mounds, there are considerable areas above the four hundred twenty-foot level along the foot of the east valley wall and in the vicinity of Granite City. Monks Mound and a few others nearby are on a slight swell a little above four hundred twenty feet, but the surface surrounding most of the others appears to be somewhat under that level. Hence, it is thought that many of the mounds were surrounded by this flood. The flood of 1903, two or three feet below that of 1844, reached and covered the low sags in the vicinity of the mounds.

The valley has a maximum width of about twelve miles just north of Granite City and a minimum of three and three-fourths miles south of the village of Cahokia. In the latitude of the mounds it is about nine and one-half miles wide. The valley flat is traversed by many old channels—former courses of the Mississippi River—showing that many shiftings have taken place in recent geological times, and the existence of ox-bow lakes in several of these indicate an occupancy so recent geologically

---

[1]Woodward's *The St. Louis Bridge,* G. C. Jones and Co., Publishers, St. Louis, 1881, p. 2.

that they have not yet been filled. Besides the distinct abandoned channels, faint sags apparently represent earlier channels.

The East Valley Wall.—The east valley wall rises from one hundred fifty to two hundred feet above the valley flat. It is generally a distinct bluff, notably steep in spite of the weak resistance of the Coal Measures shale and Pleistocene clays of which it is chiefly composed, and surprisingly steep when the width of the valley is considered. This has an important bearing upon the activity of the Mississippi River, making it clear that this great stream frequently shifts its course, geologically speaking, striking the valley wall here and there and preventing weathering, slope-wash, and creep from making the slope gentle.

THE ALLUVIAL FILLING

Thickness and Characteristics.—The filling of the valley is considerable; the bedrock floor lies deep. The upper ten to twelve feet is mud and clay, beneath which is fifty to one hundred feet of sand with subordinate beds or lenses of clay and gravel, and gravel and boulders at the base.[2] The position of the bouldery material at the base has a special significance. Great changes in the volume of the stream take place in response to heavy rainfall or rapid melting of snow over the large basin which the river drains, and this greatly modifies the velocity and the stream's transporting power. At St. Louis, the velocity of the Mississippi River has been known to vary from two and three-fourths miles per hour at low water to eight and one-half miles per hour at high water, or three-fold. In time of high flood, therefore, the stream scours deeply, probably reaching and abrading the bedrock, making it necessary for the piers of the bridges at St. Louis to be sunk into the rock. When the excavations were made by the engineers for the St. Louis bridge, and the bed-rock was laid bare, the rock surface was found to be smooth and water-worn and to be overlain by the heavier debris of river floods.[3] There have been known instances of scour reaching nearly one hundred feet. The larger materials are moved at a slower rate than the smaller, and are the first to be deposited, upon the slackening of the current during the

[2]Fenneman, N. M., *The Physiography of the St. Louis Area,* Ill. State Geol. Survey Bull. 12, p. 6, 1909.
[3]Woodward, *op. cit.,* p. 5.

ebb of the flood. Although the scouring is probably local in the bed of the channel during any one flood, yet in successive floods all points along the channel may become affected.

The Age of the Alluvial Filling.—In view of (1) the scouring action of this great stream along its present channel and the alternate play of scour and fill; (2) the abundant evidence that in the past the stream has had almost every conceivable position on the valley-flat; (3) the lateral shifting of the meanders, cutting on the outside of the curves and filling on the inside; (4) the length of post-glacial time having probably been sufficiently long for this great stream working in loose and fine materials to plane the full width of the valley several times, and (5) the gradation from bottom to top of coarse to fine, it would appear that the larger part if not all of the present alluvial filling of the American Bottom has been worked over and repeatedly shifted down-stream and that its present position is due to the action of the stream in the Recent epoch. Therefore, it seems proper to regard the filling, exclusive of terraces, as chiefly post-glacial in age.

REMNANTS OF THE ORIGINAL GLACIAL FILLING

Inasmuch as this portion of the Mississippi River received glacial drainage from more than 2,000 miles of ice front of the Wisconsin Glacier—from the basin of Illinois River to the Rocky Mountains—it would be expected that the valley here would show evidence of fill, provided it was given more load than it could carry; and since this locality was far from the ice edge, that such a filling would be composed dominantly of fine material; and further, that since the volume of the glacial waters varied greatly between the winter and summer seasons, the glacial Mississippi behaved much as the modern Mississippi, only on a much larger scale; and moreover, that since the suspended load and bed-load were probably greater, the amount of filling during the recession of floods would average greater and the average level of the flood-plain would be higher.

Evidence of such a condition appears to exist chiefly in the mouths of some of the tributaries,—Canteen Creek and Prairie du Pont Creek, where alluvial terraces are found, some of them rising forty to sixty feet above the Mississippi Valley flat. The material of these terraces, however, is probably not so much that brought down by the Mississippi River as that washed down from the uplands and deposited in the back-water of the tributaries due to filling in the main valley. But in either case they seem to record a former higher filling in the main valley than now exists, which is the significant point in this connection.

This period of aggradation was brought to a close by the melting back of the ice into the basins of the Great Lakes and Lake Agassiz. From these bodies of water three great streams of relatively clear water combined and formed a Mississippi of more constant volume than before. Just how the amount of this water would compare with the maximum summer floods which had been coming down the valley from the glacier before the lakes came into existence is problematical, for, on the one hand the length of the ice front was now much less, and on the other the climate was becoming warmer and the rate of melting greater. An important point to keep in mind though is this. The waters from Lake Chicago and its contributary area to the east, the waters from Lake Superior, and the waters from Lake Agassiz formed a stream of very large volume, with less fluctuation than when the drainage came direct from the ice, and since most of the sediment had been dropped in the lakes, the outflowing waters were much less loaded.

This condition of flow lasted during the building of several recessional moraines and a corresponding number of periods of ice recession,[4] probably resulting in a lowering of the former glacial flood-plain, and probably to a level considerably below the present plain. Indeed, the previous fill may have been entirely swept away and the rock-floor subjected to abrasion, but this cannot be affirmed.

POST-GLACIAL CONDITIONS

With (1) the melting away of the ice from the basin of Mississippi River, (2) the establishment of the outlet of the Great Lakes by way of St. Lawrence River, (3) the disappearance of Lake Agassiz, and (4) the melting of most of the contributing Alpine glaciers of the Rocky Mountains, the drainage conditions of the Mississippi River assumed approximately their present proportions and variations. Inheriting the low gradient of the preceding epoch, the Mississippi of smaller volume must have built up its flood-plain to its present level.

[4]Some of the recessional moraines are known to have been built after a readvance of the ice following an unknown amount of melting back, but the volume of water was doubtless less during the advance of the ice than during the retreat.

The widespread distribution of abandoned channels and the absence of any tendency on the part of the present stream to break up into distributaries indicate that the present flood-plain is essentially at grade or some of it is slightly above grade because of the present fairly straight course of the stream. Before the stream assumed its present course, it meandered widely, as the abandoned channels and ox-bow lakes indicate. Under those conditions much of the present flood-plain was formed. With the stream subsequently assuming the present nearly straight course, probably at a time of widespread overflow, its gradient became higher and its transporting power greater, enabling it to develop a narrow flood-plain adjacent to the channel slightly below the rest of the valley flat, thereby reducing for the present the chances and the frequency of widespread flooding other than in the old abandoned channels and adjacent low areas.

Bearing Upon the Age and Origin of the Cahokia Mounds

(1) The enormous scour and fill of the Mississippi during the rise and ebb of floods; (2) the fact that the stream has shifted to many different positions over the valley flat; (3) the fact that this shifting has been so frequent that abandoned channels of the second or third stages back are not entirely filled before another shift takes place; (4) the absence of any remnants of filling which clearly correspond to the terraces in the mouths of some of the tributaries; and (5) the fact that the mounds do not show the scars of meander curves on their slopes or at their base as they would if they were remnants of a former higher fill,—when we consider these things, it appears that the mounds are neither natural nor as old as the present valley flat.

If this conclusion is correct, the mounds themselves should reveal this in their constitution; should have no nuclei of natural origin, and should rest upon alluvial materials as a foundation. We may well give our attention to this phase of the question.

CONSTITUTION OF THE MOUNDS

There was opportunity to study the character and structure of the material in four mounds, and as a matter of record, these will be discussed separately. These mounds were: the James Ramey Mound, No. 33; the Albert Kunnemann Mound, No. 16; the Sam Chucallo Mound; and the Sawmill Mound, No. 39. As will be seen from Fig. 1, these mounds are widely spaced and are fairly representative of the mounds which range in height from twelve to thirty-five feet. The James Ramey Mound, No. 33, situated a quarter mile east of Monks Mound, was the most thoroughly opened and examined in the greatest detail.

The James Ramey Mound, No. 33

This mound was trenched through its center in a north-south direction, nearly to the level of the surrounding valley flat and a fine opportunity was presented for ascertaining the composition, degree of assortment, arrangement of the materials and their relations to the materials of the valley flat.

General Description of the West Face.—In the west face (Fig. 12), Formation 1 is made up chiefly of yellowish sand with balls and irregularly shaped inclusions of dark silt scattered through it. It is unstratified and has the spotted and lumpy appearance of man-made fills. It is cut off abruptly at the south end. Formation 2 is a mixed gray and yellowish silt and sand with scattered charcoal fragments. The upper surface is strongly undulating. At (a) is a reddish brown horizon having every appearance of having been the site of a bonfire. Charcoal fragments occur in the material. Formation 3 is a mixed gray and yellowish silt and sand with included masses such as is shown in the figure. In the north end is a peculiar mixed mass, (c), and a filling in a well-defined cut-out, (b). At (a) is another apparently burned horizon with charcoal fragments associated with it. Formation 4 is a yellowish sand with an abundance of charcoal fragments up to one and one-half inches in diameter. Formation 5 is finely stratified sand about eight inches thick—the only clear case of water stratification in the section. It ends bluntly at its northern end and pinches out at its southern. Formation 6 is a fine yellowish sand with bits of charcoal. Formation 7 is a well-defined horizon with an ap-

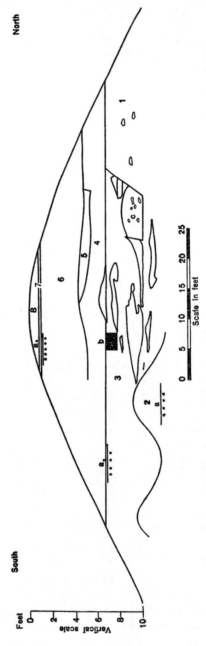

FIG. 12—Diagrammatic sketch of the west face of the trench, James Ramey Mound. Subsequent excavation extended the section to a depth of about twenty feet.

parent burned horizon at its south end. Formation 8 is a fine grayish yellow sand with some small lumps. Throughout the whole section bones and pottery, artifacts of flint, and angular fragments of travertine and charcoal were found, varyingly oriented. Near the center of the cut a boring was put down with a post-hole digger, and at a depth of about twenty feet from the top of the mound, a fairly large piece of charcoal and a piece of pottery were found. Another boring yielded bones and pottery at a depth of eighteen to nineteen feet. Regarding the occurrence of human skeletal remains in this and other mounds, the reader is referred to Part I of this publication.

Detailed Description of a Vertical Section in two Dimensions. —A chimney-like section, three feet square, was dug in the west face of the main trench and a detailed sketch and description were made at the south and west sides of this section. (Fig. 13.) The description follows:

	Thickness Feet
7. Fine grayish yellow sand, with lumps of gray clay which give a spotted effect; a few small fragments of charcoal up to one-fourth inch in diameter; the material effervesces to the surface although it is dark in the upper three to four inches	2 to 3
6. Interlayered dark and light fine sand and sandy silt, the lower portion with many charcoal fragments, a scattering in the upper part; layers discontinuous and horizontal in the south face, dipping southward in the west face; a few fragments of bones (one a bone of a bird); some fragments of pottery	2¼
5. Mottled fine silty sand in indefinite layers; a heterogeneous mixture of highly calcareous and slightly calcareous material with no indication of secondary concentration or differential solution; no assorting; a few tiny particles of charcoal..	3¾
4. Dark clay layer, something like gumbo, with fragments of pottery and charcoal; thickness...........................	¾
3. Mostly dark fine sandy silt with light mottling, some brownish clay; irregular lenses and balls of the light colored silt in a dark matrix, and lenses and balls of the dark in the light; the light parts are more calcareous than the dark; a few charcoal and pottery fragments.......................	5¼
2. Fine stratified silty sand, yellowish gray; calcareous; charcoal fragments mostly minute but two fragments up to one inch; layers of sediment thin, numbering three or four to the inch. These beds fade out to the east, changing upward to mixed material as if the stratified portion were deposited in a local pool in the mound............................	1
1. Massive dark gray silt, no stratification, scattered specks of charcoal, non-calcareous................................	1¾

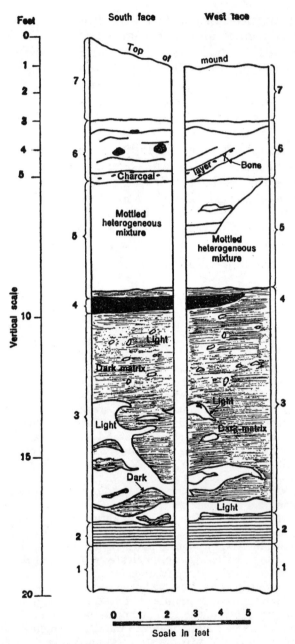

FIG. 13—Diagrammatic sketch of a chimney section made in the west face of trench, James Ramey Mound.

Special Features of the West Face.—Bones and fragments of pottery were found throughout the vertical section of the mound. In the west face of the trench was found a linear series of holes, about thirty in number in a distance of twenty-three feet, most of them less than six inches in diameter and about two feet in depth. Although they had been completely covered over by at least nine feet of earth, the holes were only partly filled with dirt. In the bottom of many of them occurred brown decayed bone; a small leg bone of a bird was still preserved. It appeared that originally the holes had been filled with bones before the overlying earth was put on and later the bones decomposed leaving the holes unfilled and a residue of bone material in the bottom. The series trended nearly due north-south and while most of the holes were vertical, a few slanted ten degrees from the vertical. The full series was not entirely uncovered, for the north end curved slightly west of north into the west face. Such features must be human in their origin.

General Description of the East Face.—A section of the east face is shown in Fig. 14. A-A' is a well defined horizontal horizon marked by burned lenses (b) and short stretches of coarse sand (c). The burned lenses are two and one-half inches in maximum thickness and up to three feet long. They are reddest in the center with charcoal fragments immediately beneath and at the ends. The materials, including the sands, effervesce with acid. Below the sharp horizon is Formation 1, a dark, fairly compact silt, irregularly layered and with greenish lenses and some yellow sand layers. In this case the dark is distinctly less calcareous than the light, and charcoal is generally scattered through them. Above the sharp horizon, is Formation 2, a fine sandy silt mottled dark and light, arranged without order in irregular lenses, balls and masses up to four inches in diameter. Both the light and the dark are calcareous, and charcoal fragments are scattered through them promiscuously. Bones and fragments of pottery were found from bottom to top of the section. A large marine shell was uncovered near the west end three or four feet below the surface. Similar shells were found in other parts of the mound, one at a depth of seventeen feet.

The mound was about twenty-three feet high. At a depth of nineteen and one-half feet, pottery, bones, and flint were found, some of them on end. The containing matrix was a fine, sandy silt, gray with brownish tinge and slightly calcareous. A fragment of calcareous tufa and a one-inch fragment of charcoal,

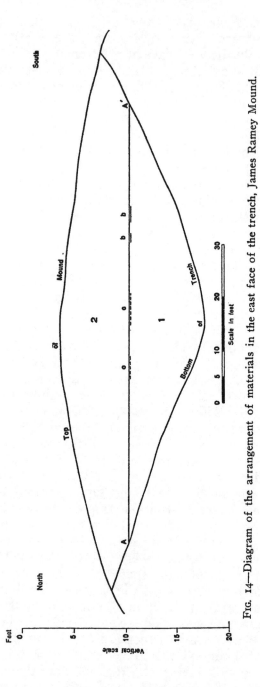

FIG. 14—Diagram of the arrangement of materials in the east face of the trench, James Ramey Mound.

which clearly exhibited the structure of the original wood were found at the eighteen-foot level. All of the material, save for a thin lens of finely stratified sand, had the appearance of having been dumped, mixed, and spread by human agencies. It was indeed a motley mixture.

Significant Features Common to Both Sides of the Trench.— (1) The materials are not stratified or assorted like waterlaid sediments, except as above mentioned, though they have a stratiform arrangement.

(2) The contacts of the various layers are quite irregular in detail, (Fig. 15), sharp projections of one fitting into the sharp indentations of another. This shows that the surface upon which each layer was spread was irregular in detail although nearly level, and could not be due to deposition in quiet or slack-water. They are such as would develop from human hands spreading silts and fine sands over a surface previously smoothed artificially but retaining minute irregularities. This is also in harmony with the mixed aspect of the materials.

(3) Some horizons in the mound are reddish brown, with charcoal fragments closely associated. The reddish color does not appear to be due to natural processes of oxidation in view of the presence of the charcoal, which is reducing in its chemical reaction, and of the promiscuous and limited occurrence of material of reddish color. Its association with charcoal would seem, on the other hand, to point to bonfire oxidation.

(4) Both sides of the trench show a content of bones of several forms of life; shells of gastropods whose habitats vary from terrestrial, fluviatile, and lacustrine of local occurrence to the large ornate marine shells from the Gulf of Mexico; shells which have been shaped or perforated as ornaments of utility and dress; artifacts of various sorts; flint chips which are at least in part refuse of the Indian stone arts; and travertine fragments apparently derived from local spring deposits. Many of these lack the orientation with the stratiform character of the layers which would be expected if they were alluvial in origin. Such an assemblage of "fossils," such a promiscuous arrangement, and such a complete absence of signs of water attrition is decidedly in agreement with the conception of an artificial mode of origin for this mound.

(5) Both sides of the trench show planes of separation which run clear through the mound, thus revealing that the mound

was built by stages to platform summits, each of which was used for a time before the mound was built to another level.

The Basal Contact of the Mound.—An important question bearing on the origin of the mounds is whether or not the materials of the surrounding plain pass under them. When the trench through Mound No. 33 reached approximately the level of the surface outside of the mound, the writer hoped to ascertain the exact situation by having three pits dug, two of them in the bottom of the trench, near the center of the mound, each three and one-half feet square and four feet deep, the

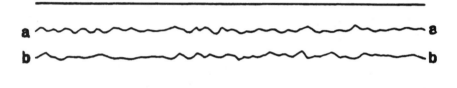

FIG. 15—Diagrammatic sketch of the minutely irregular contacts between the layers of fine material in the mounds.

third outside of the mound, one hundred ninety feet east and one hundred thirty-seven feet south of the center of the mound, on the valley flat, this pit being three and one-half feet square and three and one-half feet deep.

The pit outside of the mound exposed:

		Thickness Feet
4.	Black soil, no pebbles............................	½ to 1⅓
	grades into	
3.	Non-calcareous silt, dirty buff.....................	½
	grades into	
2.	Non-calcareous silt, yellowish, somewhat mottled, one band somewhat rusty colored, three-fourths to one inch wide...	1½
1.	Sandy silt, non-calcareous, yellowish, watery.............	1

All of the latter section looked natural. There was found no pottery, charcoal, bones, flints, shells, lumps, or other material of human derivation, and neither was there any mixing of materials.

The pit nearest the center of the mound showed:

		Thickness Feet
3.	Dark gray, sandy silt, slightly effervescent with acid, containing an occasional charcoal fragment..................	¼ to ¾

2. Brownish yellow silt, containing old rootlet channels stained rusty, non-calcareous, limonite, and pellets of $CaCO_3$ up to three-fourths inch; no distinct stratification, no charcoal or artifacts here; no sign of disturbance; has every appearance of being a former sub-soil.............................. 1
1. Fine silty sand, calcareous, scattering of small shells of gastropods, grayish yellow color, some iron oxide spots and streaks, no sign of disturbance.......................... 2

The second pit beneath the mound, dug eight feet south and fifteen feet west of the center, starting twenty feet below the top, showed:

Thickness Feet

2. Grayish yellow, fine sandy silt with old root canals stained rusty, very slight effervescence with acid, apparently an old sub-soil.. 1½
1. Yellowish gray, fine sand, calcareous, after striking water the sand behaved like quicksand........................... 2½

These materials were all undisturbed and had every aspect of being natural. They seem to be without question the materials of the flood-plain passing under the mound.

THE ALBERT KUNNEMANN MOUND, No. 11

About three-fourths of a mile north of Monks Mound, on the north side of Cahokia Creek, is a large mound known as the Albert Kunnemann Mound. Along a part of the north side of this mound, an excavation was made giving a fairly abrupt face sixty feet long and thirty feet high, the lower ten to fifteen feet being covered. The arrangement of the materials is shown in Fig. 16. Upon cursory inspection they appear to constitute a stratified deposit, but inasmuch as a detailed examination revealed the structure to merely simulate stratification, the details are deserving of some attention. The appearance of stratification is due to two thin horizontal layers, 1 and 3 in the diagram, about four feet apart, the upper one having a position about fourteen feet below the top. Layer No. 1 is a dark sandy silt, No. 3 a black soil-like material. No. 3 was clearly not a soil in place, however, for the contact with the underlying materials is sharp. At this horizon a large bowl and a burned "altar" were found by Mr. Moorehead in the course of the excavations. Between these layers is No. 2 which is a sand containing broken shells, the spots being due to dark lumps of incoherent sandy silt, which could hardly have been handled by water. Near the east end are oblique black mixed streaks. The sharp irregular contacts of the thin fine layers show that they were not deposited in quiet water but were spread over a level surface, having minute irregularities, by some such agency as man. Horizon (4) is a spotted sand with scattered charcoal, small shells,[1] pot-

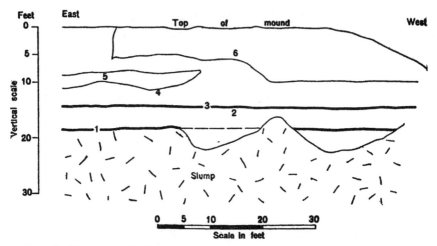

Fig. 16—Diagrammatic sketch showing the arrangement of the materials in the Albert Kunnemann Mound.

tery, bones, and chips of flint. Horizon (5) is a lens in horizon (4) of mixed gray and dark gumbo with charcoal. Its exposed length was about twenty-four feet, and thickness two to three feet. Horizon (6) is a mixed dark and gray gumbo-like material showing no stratification. The top of the mound is now flat but it is reported to have originally been some fifteen feet higher and to have consummated in a point, the removed material having been scattered over the adjoining fields.

The materials of this mound in their lack of assortment, absence of water stratification, presence of man-made features, mixed materials, and scattering of artifacts are against the natural theory of origin and strongly favor the artificial theory.

---

[1]The following were identified by Curator F. C. Baker: Gastropods: *Physa gyrina* (Say.) (a common fresh-water shell living in summer-dry ponds), *Vivipara contectoides* (W. G. B.) (fragments); Pelecypod; *Anodonta grandis* (Say.) (fragment); miscellaneous: shell head of marine conch *(Busycon),* vertebra of small fish.

THE SAM CHUCALLO MOUND

The Sam Chucallo Mound is situated about three miles south-west of Monks Mound and one-fourth mile north of Lansdowne Heights at the brink of an old channel.

It is about one hundred feet in diameter and ten to twelve feet high above the surface to the east.

As the result of digging an east-west trench through the mound, eight feet deep at the maximum, and forty feet long, it was possible to examine the materials to advantage. The north face of the trench showed a structure as in Fig. 17. Most of the material is Formation 2, a dark silty clay, the color apparently being due to humus, and mixed in the silty clay are irregular lumps and streaks of gray to dark gumbo which show minute rusty, ramifying canals and imprints of rootlets. The rootlets are almost gone, but such as are found are in these minute canals. Apparently the oxidation of ferrous compounds was favored along these minute canals by the ready access of oxidating ground water. Intimately mixed with the gumbo is some fine sand.

At the base of this motley arrangement of materials is Formation 1, a yellow to grayish-yellow fine sand, the contact being nearly level for most of the distance but sloping and passing beneath the trench at the east and west ends. Mixed with this sand in heterogeneous fashion are lumps of black soil, and the sand itself is a mixture of calcareous and non-calcareous materials. It contains snail shells,[2] some in fragments, some soft, and some mashed. All of the aspects of this sand layer are unlike those of deposits made by natural agencies and like those made by man.

The south face shows the same sequence and mixing, but the sand layer, No. 1, at the bottom is a little lower than in the north face, and near the center the sand layer is interrupted sharply by gumbo and black silty clay. (See Fig. 18.) A human skeleton was found just below, at about eight feet below the summit of the mound. Clearly, after the sand was accumulated there by man, the sand was cut into for burial purposes, and it

---

[2]The following species were identified by Curator F. C. Baker: Gastropods: *Planorbis trivolvis* (Say.), *Lymnæa palustris* (Müller). *Segmentina armigera* (Say.). *Helicodiscus parallelus* (Say.). The first three snails live in small ponds which may become wholly or partially dry in summer; the fourth one is a land snail living near water.

appears that the overlying material was brought there and dumped, thereby increasing the height of the mound.

This mound had two stages of building. First a low conical mound was built, then a burial was made, and finally it was covered over, making the sides steeper and the summit rounded. It is to be noted that this is in contrast to the platform-type of mound as represented by the James Ramey Mound No. 33.

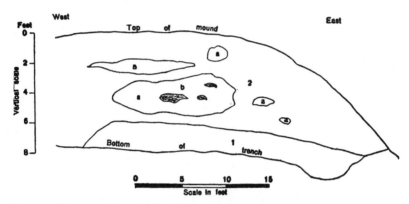

Fig. 17—Diagrammatic sketch of the structure of the materials in the north face of the trench, Sam Chucallo Mound.

The Sawmill Mound, No. 39

A low mound about 1,000 feet northwest of Monks Mound, on the south side of Cahokia Creek, was opened for a depth somewhat below the ground-water level for wet seasons. About thirteen feet was exposed. The upper three to five feet consist of gumbo material with a few small fragments of charcoal and pottery, and lumps of yellow sandy silt. Below this are yellowish stratified sandy silts, the layers having very irregular contacts, dipping to the east, and showing lumps of dark incoherent silt up to one and one-half inches. The materials are somewhat calcareous in spots, but at no particular horizon. The arrangement of the materials has every aspect of being due to human dumping.

Auger Borings on Monks Mound

The size of Monks Mound forbade any extensive exploratory work and hence no decisive evidence was obtained regarding its constitution. Its artificial form, however, invited some investigation to determine the trend of the evidence, and although it is realized that borings are not conclusive, yet it was felt that they would show something. Three borings were made on the summit and two on the east slope, by means of an auger one and one-fourth inches in diameter, attached to sections which permitted penetration to a depth of seventeen and one-half feet.

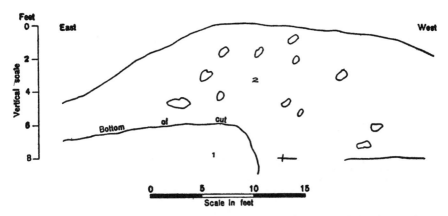

Fig. 18—Diagrammatic sketch of the structure of the materials in the south face of the trench, Sam Chucallo Mound.

By digging pits three feet deep, the total depth penetrated on the summit was twenty and one-half feet. Samples were laid out in succession and carefully examined and described.

Boring No. 1.—A pit three feet deep was dug on the summit near the north end, which showed black soil with charcoal and fragments of pottery at the bottom. The boring was started in the bottom of this pit, and the following materials were revealed:

	Thickness Feet
3. Sandy silt, dark, with one- to two-inch streaks of fine sand, light gray in color, some of the dark shows mixing with the light,[3] resembling the exposed materials in the smaller mounds..	8
Changes to	
2. Fine sand, dirty buff, loose; a little ochre-sand.............	3

[3]The writer satisfied himself after careful inspection that the mixing was not due to the auger. The relationships of the materials are markedly similar to those found in the exposed mounds.

1. Grayish yellow sand, showing a little admixture of dark silt and some thin streaks of light ochre sand, strongly effervescent at seventeen feet but not effervescent at the bottom except in spots.................................   6½

Boring No. 2.—About fifty feet south of Boring No. 1 a pit three feet deep was dug, all of it being in black soil which contained a few pieces of charcoal. The boring in the bottom of this showed:

	Thickness Feet
6. Fine sandy silt, dirty gray, non-calcareous.................	9
5. Black clay with a thin streak of fine sand, a piece of charcoal at a depth of thirteen and one-half feet from the surface	2
4. Fine sand, somewhat silty, moderately calcareous...........	4
3. Dark sandy silt, ochre pellets............................	¼
2. Fine sand, silty...	½
1. Dark clay, like gumbo, with streaks of fine sand............	1¾

Boring No. 3.—This boring was made in the bottom of a pit three feet deep, about fifty feet south of Boring No. 2, the pit showing dark soil with small chips of brick in the top and charcoal fragments below, changing to dirty silty sand in the bottom. The boring revealed:

	Thickness Feet
3. Fine silty sand, some pellets of limonite and rusty streaks, some trace of charcoal and some evidence of mixing, slightly calcareous at the base...............................	10½
2. Intermixture of dark clay and fine yellow sand, a fragment of charcoal one-half inch in length about sixteen feet below the original surface, non-calcareous....................	5
1. Dark clay, like gumbo; trace of charcoal at depth of nineteen feet below the original surface, non-calcareous...........	2

The dark clay and the mixture of materials are similar to that seen in the various human mounds previously described. The presence of charcoal in the lower part of the section as well as in the upper is also indicative that this material has had human associations.

Boring No. 4.—On the east slope due east of Boring No. 1, a pit was dug to a level of sixteen feet below the top of the mound at Boring No. 1, and the back edge of the pit was cut back about four and one-half feet horizontally from the slope, developing a vertical face four feet high. The back face showed a mixture of materials, but whether or not they were in place could not be definitely ascertained. A boring was put down about three feet from the natural slope, which showed:

2. Mottled gray and ochre and grayish yellow and black silt, calcareous in spots at a depth of one to three feet from the top of the boring, non-calcareous below................. 12½
1. Black, tenacious, humus clay, like gumbo, with some suggestion of a gray mixture, non-calcareous.............. 5

The mixture of materials, the rather anomalous relation of non-calcareous beneath calcareous without the usual additional evidence of an interval of weathering, and the gumbo-like clay at the base, are indicative of a human mode of origin. The end of the auger reached a level thirty-three and one-half feet below the top of the mound. It is of course not possible, without trenching or tunneling, to demonstrate that these materials pass into the mound. Even though the upper part of the boring may be in slump material, the lower part is believed to be deep enough to pass through the slump.

Boring No. 5.—A pit was dug eleven feet lower vertically than the preceding, or twenty-seven feet below the summit of the mound, and a boring was made three feet from the outer edge and three feet vertically below the slope. The materials found by boring were sixteen feet of blue-black clay with thin layers of light gray and ochre-mottled clay, all non-calcareous and without pebbles.

Statement of Conclusions.—Such chance as these borings afford for ascertaining the nature and arrangement of the materials, indicates that they are man-laid. They are at least in line with the evidence offered years ago from the dug well on the west side of the mound and described by Flagg. (See p. 16.) Repeating a previous remark, these borings, while made carefully, cannot be regarded as the equivalent in scientific value of open trenches, but it is to be noted that the results are consistent with the artificial form of the mound.

COMPARISON WITH THE MATERIALS OF THE EAST VALLEY BLUFF

Inasmuch as it has been asserted that the materials of the mounds are similar to the materials of the valley bluffs, the writer made a careful examination of the excellent road-cut exposures recently made along the National Highway where it ascends the bluffs directly east of Monks Mound. The deepest cut is at least twenty-five feet deep and reveals only loess from the foot of the bluff to the top. Judging from the adjacent localities, the loess is a thick mantle concealing the underlying glacial drift and bed-rock, the present grade of the road nowhere being down to the level of the underlying materials.

The loess is loose and friable, floury, gritty, and easily blown. It contains a rather prolific mollusca fauna, the following having been collected, the large species occurring mostly in the lower part:

Polygyra appressa (Say.)	*Pupoides marginatus* (Say.)
Pyramidula alternata (Say.)	*Succinea retusa* (Lea.)
Pyramidula shimekii (Pilsbry)	*Succinea vermeta* (Say.)
Gastrocopta contracta (Say.)	*Helicina occulta* (Say.)

From a grayish color in the lower part, the loess grades through yellowish and buff to brownish in the upper part. In places it presents a slight pinkish cast. On the slope it is rarely leached of calcium carbonate more than four or five feet, and generally less, but below this leached zone it is highly calcareous. Save for a few places where there is a semblance of bedding, stratification is generally lacking. Some sub-spherical concretions are scattered through it, and along horizontal or gently inclined fracture planes there is a limy concentration, the product of the dissolving action of ground water above and precipitation below.

In all of the cuts, there was no such mixture of materials as occur in the excavated mounds; no sign of human disturbance; no content of human implements, flint chips, sea shells, pottery, charcoal fragments, specimens of travertine, burned horizons, bones of animals nor any other evidence of human activity; no content of gumbo lenses or balls or irregular masses; no promiscuous mixing of calcareous and non-calcareous materials. In short, there is no possibility whatsoever of correlating the materials of the bluffs with the layers of the mounds. Some loess may have been secured from the bluff and used with various materials of the Mississippi flood-plain in the building of the mounds, thus accounting for some of the loess fossils reported from the mounds, but the quantity of such material found in the mounds is very small.

In the mouth of Canteen Creek Valley, are terrace remnants with a summit reaching the four hundred eighty-foot level on the point of a spur where an Indian Mound, twenty feet or more in height, is situated. Many flint chips occur in the soil but no exposure of old alluvial materials could be found. A gulley wash on the south side exposes seven to eight feet of fossiliferous buff loess. The terrace has a maximum width of about three hundred yards. About one-fourth mile farther up the valley is another terrace remnant. On the south side of the creek a thirty-five-foot exposure in the valley wall shows only loess, yellowish in color, with a mottling of gray and buff. Another road-cut, twenty to twenty-five feet deep, on the north side of Schoenberger Creek, near the interurban tracks, exposes only loess. A new highway cut at Edgemont just north of the crossroads shows reddish loess with large, sub-spiral snail shells, beneath buff loess.

About one mile southwest of Caseyville, the Pennsylvanian strata make up a considerable portion of the bluff.

SUMMARY OF THE EVIDENCE AND CONCLUSIONS

The present study of the external characteristics and geological setting of the mounds, and of the exposures made in four of them, has yielded the following lines of evidence bearing upon their mode of origin:

1. The summit area of all of the mounds is so limited that this fact alone minimizes the force of the suggestion that they are terrace remnants of a former higher filling of the Mississippi River Valley.

2. Their pyramidal, ovate, and conoid shapes are not in keeping with the usual irregular outlines of erosion remnants and this, together with their steep uniform slopes, carries the aspect of an artificial mode of origin. They are clearly not sand dunes, kames, eskers, or natural, constructional forms of any sort.

3. The dominant orientation of the elongate mounds with the cardinal points of the compass, and the striking alignment of many of the mounds, are difficult to explain on the basis of the natural theory, and point strongly to their being man-arranged and man-made.

4. The absence of meander scars on the slopes of the mounds or at their base is out of harmony with the idea that they are terrace remnants.

5. A critical consideration of the history of the alluvial filling of the Mississippi River Valley and of the behavior and capacity for work of that master stream, together with the evidences of its great activity and shifting, makes it appear doubtful if any of the original fill is present in the valley, although such a possibility can hardly be precluded. According to this view, the glacial filling was probably removed by the voluminous waters of Lake Chicago, Lake Duluth, and Lake Agassiz, and the present filling is the result of the "scour and fill" and "cut and fill" processes of the present shifting and oscillatory stream.

6. If the mounds are terrace remnants of a former higher filling, the materials of which they are composed should show the stratification and assortment of that type of filling. If the filling was glacial till, the materials should be of that character; if eolian, they should be limited in texture to that size which wind can carry; if lacustrine, they should be characteristic of quiet water deposition except near the short line; if fluvial they

should show the texture and structure of materials deposited by running water. The materials of all four mounds examined do not show the characteristics of any of these physiographic agencies. They are stratiform but not stratified; they are mainly of fine materials—silts, fine sands and gumbo—but unassorted, lumps and masses of one kind being intercalated with materials of another kind, and bones, artifacts, flints, travertine fragments, charcoal and pottery being scattered throughout without any suggestion of a mechanical separation or orientation; the contacts of the layers are minutely jagged and not smooth; calcareous materials are mixed heterogeneously with non-calcareous materials; salt-water shells from the Gulf of Mexico occur indiscriminately with local fresh-water shells; burned layers occur at various horizons; and a long series of holes with bone refuse in their bottoms was found in one mound. Such mixture, such an arrangement, such a complex association of unusual materials, are characteristic only of man-made mounds.

7. In the mound which was opened down to its base, undisturbed material, characteristic of an old sub-soil zone and similar to natural flood-plain materials was found to underlie the mound. In this case the mound possessed no original nucleus, and if any is present in the other three mounds, which were opened almost to their base, they must be trivial.

In the face of these evidences it is difficult to conclude other than that the mounds which have been thus far exposed are of human origin, and in view of the external features of the others, it seems probable that they are also the product of human activity, the case being less clear for Monks Mound than for any other because of its large size and the possibility of it possessing a considerable nucleus. But it seems fair to say that its artificial form and the evidence derived from auger borings is consistent with the view that a large part of it at least is the work of the Mound Builders. Further exploratory work on these mounds will be observed with interest by both the geologist and archæologist.

8. The two smaller mounds herein described appear to have always been sub-conical in the various stages of building, whereas the two larger mounds had platform summits at various stages.

APPENDICES A, B, C, D

———

A. THE USE OF MOLLUSCAN SHELLS BY THE CAHOKIA
MOUND BUILDERS

———

B. SOME RESEARCHES IN THE ILLINOIS RIVER VALLEY
NEAR HAVANA, ILLINOIS

———

C. THE DICKSON MOUND AND THE LOG TOMB
BURIALS AT LIVERPOOL

———

D. CAHOKIA BIBLIOGRAPHY

THE USE OF MOLLUSCAN SHELLS BY THE CAHOKIA MOUND BUILDERS[1]

Frank Collins Baker,

Museum of Natural History, University of Illinois

The use of the Mollusca by aboriginal man has received scant attention from students of the Mollusca. Stearns,[2] many years ago, published a very able paper on the use of molluscan shells as primitive money, but the wide use of shells for many purposes has been noted almost exclusively by ethnologists. Figures and descriptions of these are scattered through the reports and bulletins of the Bureau of American Ethnology and in papers and reports by archæologists. One of the best summaries of the use of molluscan shells may be found in Moorehead's *Stone Age in America,* pp. 117-133.

The excavation and study of the Cahokia group of mounds near East St. Louis, Illinois, carried on by Professor W. K. Moorehead under the auspices of the University of Illinois, has given unusual opportunity to study the use of the Mollusca by the ancient Mound Builders, at least in this region.

The molluscan shells may be divided into two groups: those of marine origin and those gathered from near-by streams and ponds—fresh water shells. The latter may be considered first.

FRESH WATER MOLLUSCA

An examination of the region about the Cahokia Mounds indicates that there were numerous bodies of water as well as creeks (and the Mississippi River) from which mollusks could be obtained. The collection contains specimens from both creek and river, as well as a few from ponds and swales.

MUSSEL SHELLS PROBABLY OBTAINED MAINLY FROM THE MISSISSIPPI RIVER

Elliptio dilatatus (Raf.) Spike or Lady-finger. Common. A fine specimen of this shell, which had been made into a nose or

---

[1]Contribution from the Museum of Natural History, University of Illinois, No. 31.
[2]Ethno-Conchology: *A Study of Primitive Money.* By R. E. C. Stearns. An. Rep. Smithsonian Institute, 1887, Part II, p. 297.

ear ornament, was found at a depth of 20 feet in the James Ramey Mound. The purple nacre of the interior was beautifully preserved.

Proptera alata megaptera (Raf.) Pink Heel-splitter. An effigy representing a human head was found in the Sawmill Mound (a burial structure) made from a piece of this shell. A gorget or ornament of peculiar design made from this species was found in burial mounds 19, 20, 21 (overlapping mounds). This species was not common.

Megalonaias gigantea (Barnes) Washboard. A medium sized specimen from the James Ramey Mound had been made into a shell hoe. Very rare. Fragments believed to be of this species were found mixed with deer bones.

Amblema costata (Raf.) Three-ridge. Found in all mounds, common. One specimen from James Ramey Mound made into a hoe.

Amblema peruviana (Lam.) Blue-point. Rare.

Quadrula quadrula (Raf.) Maple-leaf. Common.

Quadrula cylindrica (Say.) Rabbit's-foot. Rare.

Cyclonaias tuberculata (Raf.) A specimen (broken) from mounds 19, 20, 21, had been used as a hoe. Rare.

Truncilla truncata (Raf.) Deer-toe. Rare. Found at depth of twenty-one feet in James Ramey Mound near the bottom of the structure.

Lampsilis fallaciosa (Smith) Simpson. Slough sand shell. Rare.

Lampsilis anondontoides (Lea.) Yellow sand shell. Not common.

Lampsilis siliquoidea (Barnes) Fat mucket. Not common.

Lampsilis ovata (Say.) Pocket-book mussel. Rare. A specimen from the cemetery at Pittsburg Lake, south of the Cahokia group, had been used as an ornament, several holes being drilled in the side.

Lampsilis ventricosa (Barnes) Pocket-book mussel. Specimens of this mussel were common in all mounds and fragments occurred in village site debris. Two specimens from Pittsburg Lake cemetery had been variously cut along the anterior margin. It is thought that these were used as scoops or spoons.

Ligumia recta latissima (Raf.) Black sand shell. Rare.

Snail Shells

Anculosa praerosa (Say.) River snail. This snail was used largely for beads. The side was ground until a perforation was made into the cavity of the body whorl and the shells could then be strung on threads or cords through this hole and the natural opening at the aperture. Shells thus prepared were common in the James Ramey Mound at various depths and also in other mounds.

Campeloma subsolidum (Anthony) Large river snail. This shell, which in life has a beautiful green epidermis, was also esteemed by the Mound Builders and used as beads in the same manner as *Anculosa* described above. These shells occurred in the mounds and in the village site material.

Campeloma ponderosum (Say.) Heavy river snail. Rare. Two specimens were found in the James Ramey Mound.

Pleurocera acuta (Raf.) A few specimens of these slender river snails were found in the James Ramey Mound. Their practical use is not indicated by marks on the shells.

Near the bottom (twenty-one feet deep) of the James Ramey Mound, as well as in other mounds, a number of fresh water shells were found which evidently were not used by the aborigines for ornamentation or domestic use but were included when the mound was built. If the material from which the mounds were built was in part taken from the border or bottom of ponds which were dry in summer but contained water in the winter and spring, such mollusks as here indicated would be included. They occur abundantly in such locations in all parts of Illinois. It is possible also that this depth (twenty-one feet) marked the base of the mound and these shells may have lived in a swale on the original site of the mound. Three species were found, as follows: *Physa gyrina* (Say.), *Planorbis trivolvis* (Say.), *Lymnæa reflexa* (Say.). One specimen of *Planorbis trivolvis* was found in the upper eight feet of the mound. This must have been contained in the material used in erecting the mound.

Professor M. M. Leighton collected several shells from other mounds during his geological examination of this region. These are noted below. *Planorbis trivolvis* (Say.), *Segmentina armi-*

gera (Say.), *Lymnæa* palustris (Müll.) (fresh water shells): *Helicodiscus parallelus* (Say.), land shell. From Sam Chiucallo's Mound, on outskirts of East St. Louis, Illinois. These probably were included in building material.

Physa gyrina (Say.), *Vivipara contectoides* (W.G.B.), *Anodonta grandis* (Say.) Fresh water snails and paper shell clam from the Kunnemann Mound. These probably were included in building material.

Nineteen species of fresh water shells are listed above as occurring in the mounds and as being used by the Indians for some purpose. Seven additional species probably were included in building material. The first mentioned species doubtless were used largely as food, for the ancient aboriginee, like his more modern descendant, probably esteemed this bivalve as a valuable part of his menu. The curious and brightly colored shells of the clams and the form of the snails doubtless attracted his attention and suggested ways in which they could be used for practical use as well as for bodily ornamentation. The shell gorgets and effigies also indicate that the large flat surface of some of the mussels created an art impulse which is reflected in these curious objects.

Marine Mollusca

That the Mound Builders and other aboriginal inhabitants of America were traders is evidenced by the presence of many marine shells which evidently came from the west coast of Florida or from the Gulf coast of the southern states. That certain of these mollusks were highly esteemed is shown by the number of fragments and finished objects made from at least one of these marine snails. It is probable that the canoes of the more southern tribes ascended the Mississippi River and barter was carried on between them and the Cahokia Indians.

Busycon perversa (Linn.) Marine conch. This mollusk, so common on the Gulf and Atlantic coasts of the United States, is the most abundant snail in the Cahokia Mounds. Hundreds of specimens of the heavy axis occurred in the James Ramey Mound from top to bottom. This part evidently was used to make a drill, and it may also have been used for ornamental purposes. Beads, nose and ear ornaments, and gorgets were made from parts of this shell. A dipper made from the body whorl of this species was found in burial Mounds 19, 20, 21. A gorget made from the side of the body whorl was found in the Sawmill Mound with skeleton No. 10.

Busycon carica (Gmelin) Marine conch. Two specimens of this species were found in the James Ramey Mound.

Busycon pyrum (Dillwyn) Marine conch. One specimen of this small conch was found in the James Ramey Mound.

Strombus pugilis alatus (Gmelin) Stromb conch. One perfect specimen and a fragment of this species were found in the James Ramey Mound. Used as nose or ear ornament.

Fasciolaria gigantea (Kiener) A portion of the axis of this largest of American marine snails was found in the James Ramey Mound.

Fasciolaria distans (Lamarck) A single specimen of this Banded Snail occurred in the James Ramey Mound. Its probable use was not indicated.

Oliva litterata (Lamarck) Olive shell. The spire of this specimen had been removed and it might have been used as a bead or as a pendant from a string of beads. From the James Ramey Mound.

Littorina irrorata (Say.) Periwinkle. A single perfect specimen was found in the James Ramey Mound. Its use was not indicated.

Rangia cuneata (Gray) Marine clam. Left valve of a medium sized specimen found at a depth of twelve feet in James Ramey Mound. Also found with surface material.

Marginella apicina (Menke) This small marine snail occurred in abundance, especially in the James Ramey Mound. This species was used largely for the purpose of making beads, the side of the shell being ground down to the natural cavity, as in the case of the fresh water shells *Anculosa* and *Campeloma*. The number of specimens found indicates that this shell was a favorite for this purpose. A singular fact, though perhaps without significance, is that these shells were found only in the James Ramey Mound, none occurring in any of the burial mounds thus far examined. In the mound mentioned they were found at several levels between one and twelve feet below the summit, and from twenty feet deep to the base of the mound, twenty-three feet below the summit.

Ten species of marine shells have been found in these mounds, all but one being gastropods. Three of these species were used definitely for ornamentation, either as beads, nose ornaments, or gorgets. It is possible that these other species will be found to have been used for the same purposes when other mounds are examined.

COMPARISON WITH HOPEWELL MOUNDS OF OHIO

It is of interest to compare the mollusks found in the Cahokia group with those preserved in the Hopewell group of mounds in Ohio (Moorehead, Publication 211, Field Museum of Natural History, 1922). An examination of the collection on exhibition in the Field Museum shows that apparently only four species are common to both mound groups, *Busycon perversa, Fasciolaria gigantea, Cyclonaias tuberculata* and *Amblema costata,* the last two fresh water mussels.

Two large and characteristic species of Mollusca occur in the Hopewell group that are absent from the Cahokia group, *Cassis madagascariensis,* and *Cypraea exanthema.* This may indicate a different trade route, perhaps with different tribes, because these shells would appeal to the aboriginal mind on account of their size and striking appearance as well as attractive colors, and would have been sought eagerly by the Cahokia people. These shells are found on both sides of the Floridan peninsula, their distribution including the east coast of Texas. The finest specimens, however, occur in southern Florida and in the West Indies.

The Hopewell people used these large shells (some of which are larger than any recent specimens the author has seen) for dippers and perhaps for drinking vessels. The interior whorls are usually removed, leaving only the large outer or body whorl. *Busycon perversa* is also of large size and seems to have been used as a dipper. Of these large shells, several were found with skeletons. The following were noted:

Cassis madagascariensis with skeleton 241 in Mound 8; skeleton 192, in Mound 4; as ear ornaments eight inches long with skeleton 281 in Mound 25. *Cypraea exanthema* with skeleton 191 in Mound 4. *Amblema costata* with skeleton 173 in Mound 20. A fragment of *Cyclonaias tuberculata* was observed with other mussel fragments.

It is noteworthy that in mounds in Calhoun County, Illinois, the large *Cassis madagascariensis* occurs and is the same form as found in the Hopewell Mounds. This might indicate a different route of barter from that of the Cahokia group, possibly overland from Indiana and Ohio. That this large shell should be absent from the Cahokia Mounds is significant. Beads of *Anculosa praerosa* are more abundant in the Calhoun County mounds than in the Cahokia group.

The builders of the Hopewell Mounds used shell beads, made of both marine and fresh water shells, to a marked degree, thousands of these being in the collection. Barouque pearls were also in demand, judging by the number of these in the collection which had been made into beads. It is probable that valuable free pearls were used also. None of these have as yet been found in the Cahokia Mounds.

It would be of interest to both malacologists and ethnologists if the shells found in various tumuli left by aboriginal people could be listed accurately and the uses of the shells indicated. The present paper is a contribution toward that end. All of the material listed from the Cahokia Mounds is in the Museum of Natural History of the University of Illinois.

FRESH WATER MUSSELS FROM MOUND No. 5

The kitchen midden material found in Mound No. 5 of the Havana is of great interest, indicating that the people who built the mound used large quantities of these mussels for both food, and raw material for implements or ornaments. So great is the extent of this material that without a geological examination serious doubt would be entertained as to its artificial intrusion. A careful examination by Dr. H. R. Wanless, for the Illinois State Geological Survey, proved conclusively that it was deposited by the aborigines and was in no sense a natural deposit of Pleistocene age. Eleven species are represented, of which the first three are common to abundant. It will be noted that all are of the sold shell forms. All species now live in the Illinois River near by and the mound material does not differ from the species as now living in the river. The common and scientific names of the species represented are listed below:

Elliptio dilatatus (Rafinesque), Lady finger; spike.
Elliptio crassidens (Lamarck), Elephant's ear.

Amblema rariplicata (Lamarck), Blue point.
Quadrula pustulosa (Lea), Pimple-back.
Tritogonia tuberculata (Rafinesque), Buckhorn.
Cyclonaias tuberculata (Raf.), Purple warty-back.
Plethobasus cyphyus (Raf.), Bullhead.
Plagiola lineolata (Raf.), Butterfly.
Pleurobema solida (Lea), Small niggerhead.
Lampsilis fallaciosa (Smith-Simpson), Slough sand shell.
Lampsilis ventricosa (Barnes), Pocketbook.

SOME RESEARCHES IN THE ILLINOIS RIVER VALLEY NEAR HAVANA

It was thought advisable to study the relationship—if any—between the Cahokia people and those of the Illinois River Valley to the northward. McAdams and other observers had found many objects such as effigy pipes, copper hatchets, and pottery vessels in various tumuli between the mouth of the river at Alton and Peoria, yet there had been no complete published report. Furthermore, the remarkable discoveries made by Dr. Don Dickson in a burial place, near Lewistown, prompted us to visit the region.

We located on the farm of Mrs. Anna Neteler, near Havana, and are much indebted to the kindness of this lady and her family for permitting exploration.

The mounds of the region are described in the accompanying report written by Mr. Taylor. It is well to remark that one structure, which has aroused considerable speculation, is known by local persons as the "Man Mound," or the "Bird Mound." It has been somewhat damaged by the elements, or possibly by excavations. Mr. Taylor's presentation of local traditions is an illustration of how old residents differ in their views and opinions with reference to the same subject. Mr. Taylor's observations follow.

THE HAVANA TUMULI

Survey of October to December 5, 1927

By JAY L. B. TAYLOR, *Engineer*

Magnetic Variations: In all instances where compass readings are referred to, a declination of 5° 15′ east, has been adopted, unless otherwise indicated.

Mr. Chris Kreiling, County Engineer of Mason County, Illinois, states that practically all of his surveys in this locality are based on such a variation, and because of limited operations carried on in Fulton County, lying immediately across the Illinois River, the same variation was adopted in locating Mounds Nos. 1, 2, and 3 of the Liverpool group. Topographical notes have been computed downward from the bench marks (B M) established on respective summits. Various horizontal scales have been adopted but in all cases the unit of measure is five or a multiple of five. Vertical scales also vary to suit conditions, but the unit is either one or two. Such scales will be shown clearly in final map.

Mound No. 1. This is located immediately on the left bank of the same bayou and the western extremity may have been slightly cut away by river action. Its B M lies north 68° west, 160.0 feet from B M, Mound No. 2, and 58.0 feet from and 22.4 feet above water line (October 18, 1927). Opened.

Mound No. 2. This is referred to in the field notes as the "Bird Mound," and as shown by the survey is in the form of what may be designated as a flying bird. B M lies 2043.0 feet west and 305.0 feet north of the southeast corner of Section 11, Township 21 north, Range 9 west, third P. M. in Mason County, Illinois. It is also south 68° east, 216.0 feet (through B M Mound No. 1), from and 25.4 feet above water level at the left bank of a bayou of the Illinois River (October 18, 1927).

Mound No. 3. Height, 1.5 feet; diameter 60.0 feet; ovate; opened. Center lies 2326.0 feet west and 116.0 feet north of the southeast corner of Section 11, supra.

Mound No. 4. Height, 1.5 feet; diameter 30.0 feet; circular; B M lies 2320.0 feet west and 35.0 feet north of southeast corner Section 11, supra. Opened.

Mound No. 5. B M lies south 66° east, 422.0 feet from the southeast corner of Riverside Park (NE¼ SE¼ Sec. 11, supra). Opened.

Mound No. 6. B M lies 198.0 feet east of and 29.3 feet above water line at left bank of Illinois River (November 11, 1927) and bears south 82° west, 213.0 feet from the southeast corner of Riverside Park, supra. Opened.

Mound No. 7. B M lies 210.0 feet from and 42.3 feet above water line at the left bank of the Illinois River (November 2, 1927) and bears south 52° 30' west, 450.0 feet from the southeast corner of Riverside Park, supra. Tested with augers and two pits.

Mound No. 8. Height, 4.0 feet; diameter, 100.0 feet; circular; not opened. B M bears south 23° east, 310.0 feet from southeast corner of Riverside Park, supra.

Mound No. 9. Station 14 (B M) bears north 19° west, 187.0 feet from southeast corner of Riverside Park, supra. Tested with augers. B M lies in the major axis 220.0 feet from and 52.9 feet above water line at the left bank of the Illinois River (November 8, 1927). Recent excavation (apparently for a building) appears at the western extremity and here, also, river action may have cut away a portion of the mound.

Mound No. 10. Height, 2.0 feet; major diameter 100.0 feet; minor diameter, 60.0 feet; B M lies 1640.0 feet west and 265.0 feet north of the southeast corner of Section 11, supra. Tested with augers but not opened.

Mound No. 11. This lies in Chautauqua Park, about 1½ miles north of Havana, Illinois. Station 21, which lies north 44° east, 50.0 feet from B M, at the extremity of Line No. 2, bears south 28° 20' east, 184.0 feet from the northwest corner of Section 31, Township 22 north, Range 8 west, third P. M., Mason County, Illinois.

Mound No. 12. Height estimated at 6.0 feet and diameter at 75.0 feet; circular. An angle of 42° 40' left, from a line to Station 21, Line 2, Mound No. 11, shows B M 270.0 feet distant from Station 21, supra. Not opened.

Mound No. 13. Height estimated at 7.0 feet and diameter at 120.0 feet. An angle of 76° 20', left, from line from center of Mound No. 12 to Station 21, Line 2, Mound No. 11, shows iron flagpole at center of No. 13, 131.0 feet distant and across the road from center of Mound No. 12. Not opened.

THE LIVERPOOL GROUP

Consultation with the county authorities at Lewistown, Illinois, seemed to indicate that these mounds lay in the southeast quarter of the southwest quarter, Section 21, Township 5 north, Range 4 east, fourth P. M., Fulton County, Illinois, and notes were compiled accordingly. Later, however, an examination of the sheet covering the Havana Quadrangle, State Geological Survey, Edition of 1925, led to the conclusion that they are located a short distance southwest of the center of this same section, 21, hence a note has been added to the field records calling attention to this uncertainty of location.

Mound No. 1. This mound is 3.0 feet high and 80.0 feet in diameter, and lies 65.0 feet west and 100.0 feet north of what is assumed to be the common quarter-corner of Sections 21 and 28, Township 5 north, Range 4 east, fourth P. M. in Fulton County, Illinois. Attention was first directed to it on November 6, 1927, by Mr. Charles Harris, a local collector. Mr. Harris had started to open it the day before but had sunk a pit only a few inches when he encountered numerous slabs of stone. He assumed that these indicated the presence of a stone tomb, and not being familiar with the means usually employed in removing such remains immediately suspended operations and asked that the mound be examined by the University Field Crew. This crew began work on November 7, and soon uncovered an irregularly circular arrangement of what appeared to be sand stone slabs, varying in size from 6" x 8" to 12" x 18" and in thickness from 2" to 4". This circle was uncovered at a depth of about 12", and was broken at the northeast side by about a 3' 6" gap in which slight traces of charcoal and ash appeared in black gumbo earth. A trench cut down to a depth of from 2' to 3' and extending entirely around the outer circumference of the circle showed a yellow clay formation, barren of archæological material and apparently constituting the original and undisturbed basal structure. The same formation appeared at about the same depth within the circle, but lay in the form of a low rounded ridge running from southwest to northeast through the mound. Only one layer of slabs, very irregularly placed, was found, and there were no indications whatever that a wall had ever been laid up. Aside from the fragments of charcoal mentioned, the only evidence of human occupancy of the mound was the head of a femur, recently cut through as if with a shovel or spade, and found directly on the surface of the dirt thrown back into his pit of the day before, presumably by Mr. Harris. There has been no opportunity to ascertain whether he carried it there with him and either intentionally or accidentally left it there, or whether he found it in the mound.

Similar slabs of sandstone appear in numbers just across the road east and southeast of this mound in Mr. Whitnah's field, but these appear to have been carried there by man and are not in the nature of original outcropping. An extensive outcrop of the same material does appear how-ever, on the left bank of Sister Creek, less than one-fourth mile to the west, at the junction of the Sister Creek and Lewistown-Liverpool roads, and possibly these slabs originally came from there. No time was avail-able for tracing the formation further.

Inquiries among local residents indicate that the slabs found in Mound No. 1 may have been carried there several years ago as foundation ma-terial for a small building, but no remains of such a structure were found.

Mound No. 2. This is 3 feet high and 80 feet in diameter and lies 50 feet north of the Lewistown-Liverpool road and 130 feet west of No. 1. It was tested with augers and several fragments of sandstone were found but no archæological remains appeared. Basal formation was apparently the same as that of Mound No. 1.

Mound No. 3. Lies 100 feet north of the Lewistown-Liverpool road and 435 feet west of Mound No. 2. Its height was estimated at 2 feet and its diameter at 60.0 feet. No tests were made.

OTHER MOUNDS

About 200 yards north of Mounds 1, 2, and 3, is a long high ridge upon the point of which another mound-like formation appears. East-ward from this so-called mound, slightly river-ward from the summit of the ridge, evidences of old testholes remain and about these pits numerous human and animal bones, sherds, shells, et cetera, appear. It seems rea-sonable, to judge from such remains, that here may be an extensive burial ground, probably of modern Indians. Mrs. Grigsby, present owner of this land, has agreed to let the ridge be examined provided proper care be taken to leave the ground in such condition that it will not wash.

About 200.0 feet northeast of Mound No. 1, across the Lewistown-Liverpool road, lies a rather extensive mound upon which the Whitnah residence stands. Mrs. Grigsby, former owner of this property, and per-sonally acquainted with operations there for the past fifty years, states that when the basement for this building was dug no archæological ma-terial whatever was found. No examination of this basement as to depth or of the mound as to height was made, but it is doubtful if the floor of the basement is as low as the base of the mound.

Further northeast, beyond the residence, lies another extensive mound upon which a barn stands. This mound is not as high but has a much greater diameter than the other. The Whitnah property is occupied by a tenant, and it was not practicable to hunt up and interview the owner as to permission to test.

EXAMINATION OF MOUNDS

(1) Havana Group

Mound. No. 1. Extensive trenching and cross-trenching through this mound, which lies a short distance from the main body of the Illinois River on the left bank of a slough (possibly an old channel) revealed merely a pile of sand bearing numerous small sherds, fragments of shell,

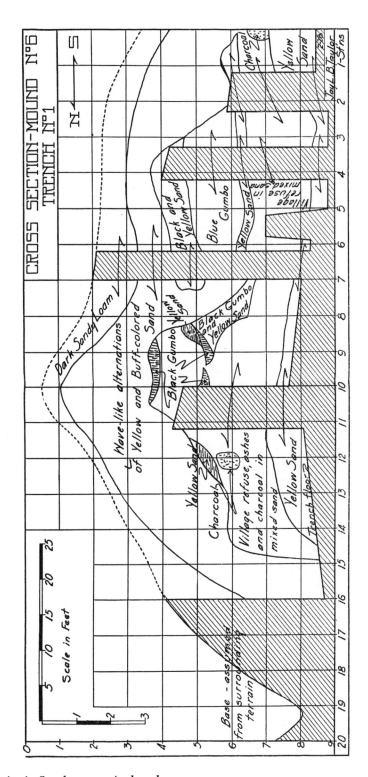

Fig. 19—Cross section of Mound No. 1, Havana group, on land of Mrs. Anna Neteler.

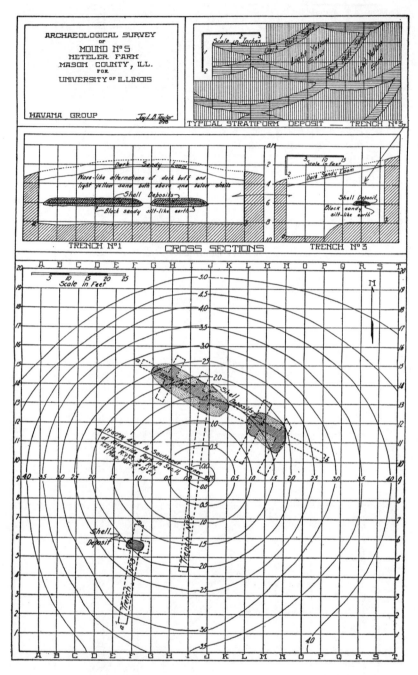

Fig. 20—Ground plan and cross section of Mound No. 5, Mrs. Anna
Neteler's farm, Havana, Illinois.

a few small pieces of broken stone (probably creek gravel) and one flint spearhead 5.3″ long and 1.7″ wide. The trench through the minor axis was extended across the narrow flat and through

Mound No. 2. This mound, locally known as the "Man Mound" but referred to in the field notes as the "Bird Mound," lies further back and was thoroughly trenched and examined for human remains. Nothing of this nature was unearthed however, although a few sherds, spalls, and broken gravel were found. Sherds appeared at from 12″ below the surface of the mound to hardpan which was found at from 3.0 feet to 4.0 feet, and in Section S-7 two small fragments of pottery were found 2″ below the surface of the hardpan. The latter, curiously enough, appears at a practically uniform depth below the mound's surface except at the north side and near the edge next to the river where it disappears completely, which leads to speculation as to whether it originated during or after construction of the mound or whether it originally existed as it now appears and was covered with mound material. Examination by Dr. Wanless, of the University of Illinois, failed to solve this problem.

An old resident of Havana, whose identity could not be determined, told a member of the field crew that within his memory this mound was ovate in plan but that one Diffenbacher, operating some fifty years ago, and trenching into the mound from either side, failed to fill up his trenches, with the result that the dumps he left formed the ridges that are now supposed to represent the wings of the bird. A careful study of the underlying hardpan, as shown by cross-sections measured to tenths of a foot and which will be indicated on the final cross-section map, both as to depth below the surface of the mound and as to thickness, might seem to corroborate such a statement. On the other hand, careful examination of the timber growing on the mound and on the wings, on the extreme tip of either of which now stands a mature hickory (hickoria ovata?) undoubtedly more than fifty years old, shows that no dirt has been piled about the roots of any of the trees.

Another local story is that this same Diffenbacher dug into and obliterated a small mound-like structure located where the bird's head might have been shown. Close examination by means of trenches shows no signs of such a structure ever having been here.

A persistent and extremely interesting feature of the remains that were found here was the number of broken gravel appearing at all depths down to but not in the hardpan. Evidently these were originally ellipsoidal in form, from the river, and varied in size from the dimensions of an egg to a third as large as a football. One such broken stone may have been a fragment of an ax. Flint spalls, artifacts, and shells were conspicuous by their absence.

Mound No. 3. This is a low, ovate mound overlooking the left bank of the same slough or bayou of the Illinois River, and when trenched through yielded only broken gravel, sherds, and a few fragments of fresh water shells. Local residents state that a few years ago extensive beds of burned shell appeared on and in this mound but no such material was found by the field crew.

Mound No. 4. A low circular mound on the left bank of this bayou. This was trenched but yielded only broken gravel, shell fragments and a few small sherds. It too was examined for beds of burned shell but none was found.

Mound No. 5. This mound is located in the Neteler wheatfield about ⅛-mile from the left bank of the Illinois River and was first tested with augers. Fresh water shells appeared at a depth of about 4.0 feet and when the mound was trenched were found in distinct deposits under a black silt-like soil at three different points. Most of them had been opened, and frequently they appeared closely nested together. Charcoal and ash accompanied them. Several unopened shells were shipped to the University Museum at Urbana, but Dr. Wanless states that Curator Baker informed him that no ash was found in these. The dominant structure of No. 5 is of yellow sand showing darker wave-like layers as if laid down by wind action. Basal structure is of unmixed yellow sand.

Mound No. 6. This is a low conical mound lying between the two longest and highest mounds of the Havana group, viz: Nos. 7 and 9, thrown up parallel to each other and almost at right angles to the left bank of the Illinois. It proved to be rich in village refuse, which was found from the surface to a depth of about 8.0 feet, at which point yellow sand, barren of archæological material, appeared as the original basal formation. As in No. 5, the upper portions, particularly in the north slope, showed undulating layers of dark brown sand in lighter yellow sand, suggesting wind formation, but nothing definite in this respect was determined. After trenching had continued for several days, local residents asserted that years ago a considerable portion of the top of this mound had been removed to facilitate building but when they were informed that its present structure showed no evidence of such disturbance, admitted that possibly they were mistaken and that such grading operations might have been confined to nearby grounds.

The first human remains found were uncovered near base and consisted merely of a badly broken human lower jaw which was assumed to be more in the nature of refuse than of a burial, and which was not, therefore, recorded as a burial. Later, in the southwest quarter of the mound, at a depth of about 2.0 feet, portions of sixteen human skeletons were unearthed.

Field notes taken November 19 show: "Skeleton No. 1: extended on back; head southeast in northwest part of Sec. 1-8; right arm, lower legs and feet missing; about twenty poorly preserved shell beads at neck; eight split bear teeth and both sides of a cut and perforated human lower jaw at front of pelvis; torso, humeri and partial cranium of Skeleton No. 2 on shins of No. 1, head to northeast; torso only of No. 3, head northeast, beside No. 2; 15 roughly triangular but nicely chipped flints about 5″ x 7″ x ½″ to 1″ arranged irregularly in two parallel lines begin in southwest part of Sec. 1-7, pass through southeast corner of Sec. H-7 and end near center of Sec. H-6; 3-inch spearhead under a buffalo shoulder blade, 6.0 feet deep in northeast corner of Sec. 1-8; numerous sherds, bone awls and needles, 2 long flat perforated bone objects, pieces of antler, fresh water shells, and flint spalls.

For November 20: "Head, torso and upper legs of Skeleton No. 5, 2.0 feet deep on bed of 37 flints similar to those found yesterday, with ten more set vertically beyond head which is to the southwest in west part of Sec. H-7; between top of skull and vertically placed flint, a copper implement 6" long, flat sides, square edges and poll, double-convex single bit badly battered and at left side of head; crushed pot beyond vertical flints; bear teeth and shell beads at neck and waist, those at neck well preserved, but of greenish color originating probably through chemical action on copper; cut and dressed animal jaws at front of pelvis.

"Skeleton No. 6: head and torso only; 2.0 feet deep; head to southeast in corner of Sec. G-7; parallel with No. 5; on bed of 27 horizontal flints with 3 other flints set vertically beyond head; between head and vertical flints, one 8" and one 9" copper instrument, similar in form to that in No. 5 but with bits of both to right of head; the shorter lay on its side, with the longer on edge beside it; 3 crushed pots beyond vertical flints; shell beads and bear teeth at neck and waist; those at neck fairly well preserved but of greenish color.

"Skeleton No. 8: head and torso only; 2.0 feet deep; on bed of 26 flints; lower portions of torso somewhat nearer No. 6 than are the upper portions; 3 flints inclined upward and away from head at angle of about 45°; 3 small flat copper implements, each with flat sides, square edges and poll, double bevelled or double-convex single bit slightly wider than poll, 1 small hammer stone, 1 medium size spearhead, 1 copper band, and a crushed pot in the southwest corner of Sec. H-6 at considerably greater distance from head than was apparent in Nos. 5 and 6, may or may not have been significantly related to this burial; bear teeth and shell beads at neck and waist.

"Skeleton No. 4: partial cranium and a few teeth only; 4.0 feet deep near center of Sec. 1-8, southeast of head of No. 1.

"Skeleton No. 9: partial cranium south of center of Sec. G-8 and northeast of No. 10.

"Skelton No. 7; on bed of 16 flints; 2.0 feet deep; at feet of and almost at right angle to Nos. 5, 6, and 8; flint superimposed on human bones.

"Total of 134 flints to date; bear teeth estimated at 200, practically all split, a few ornamented with grooves and pits in geometrical designs; probably 100 shell beads ranging from 1/8" to 3/4" in diameter and from 1/4" to 1" in length."

For November 21: Uncovered Skeleton No. 10; partial cranium; torso and arms missing; extended on back; head southeast in corner of Sec. H-8; femora only of Skeleton No. 11, head southwest, across legs of No. 10, in northwest corner of Sec. H-8; femora and lower torso only of No. 12, head southeast beneath edge of bed of flints under No. 7, in northeast corner of Sec. F-7; femora only of No. 13, head northwest, below edge of bed of flints under No. 7, in southwest corner of Sec. G-8; No. 14, torso, cranium and arms only, face downward, near center of Sec. F-8, 1.8 feet deep; No. 15, skull cap only, 1.8 feet deep, at right side of skull, No. 14; No. 16, femora only, heads south, over torso of No. 14 in southwest corner of Sec. F-8.

What appeared to be an ornament fashioned from an unknown, light-colored material, was found with one skeleton, but the notes on this are not complete. It was so labelled for shipment, however, that its location can be established.

On first examination, which was rather hurried and attended by more or less confusion created by an excited crowd of onlookers, skeletons No. 5, No. 6, No. 7, No. 8, No. 12, and No. 13, were recorded as of children but subsequent investigation of the teeth and femora of these skeletons leave some doubt as to the correctness of this classification. This uncertainty will be cleared up by examination at the museum.

All remains were platted in place and final maps will show relative positions of burials.

All bones were in a poor state of preservation, and the skulls were too badly crushed to permit accurate measurements.

Partial skeletons and superimposed burials were noticeably the rule rather than the exception, the significance of which needs no comment here.

Of eight earthen-ware pots recovered, only one was found unbroken. This was unaccompanied by a burial and was full of what appeared to be the same material as the sandy earth that surrounded it. This was not removed from the vessel but was shipped with it.

A particularly interesting discovery was that of a complete but crushed vessel, 1½" high and 1¾" in diameter, 8.0 feet deep and unaccompanied by any other remains.

Each of the five beds of flint was so platted as to show the actual position of individual flints, which will make possible accurate restoration of these beds in the museum cases if this is desirable.

These remains appeared in an area that comprised only 16 of the 400 five-foot square sections into which the mound was divided, but local conditions seemed to justify suspension of further operations and closure of trenches and pits already opened although there was good reason to believe that the mound contained much more material similar to that removed. Owing to certain complications that arose after these discoveries were made, however, further exploration of Mound No. 6 is not recommended.

Mound No. 7. This is the second largest mound of the Havana group thus far examined, is ovate in plan, located directly on the left bank of the Illinois River, and lies with the major axis almost at right angles to the river's course. The field notes show that it was tested extensively with augers and yielded numbers of shells, a few sherds, an occasional flint spall and, in one instance, a few human teeth. A pit sunk to a depth of 11.0 feet or 12.0 feet where these teeth were found, revealed no other remains. Another pit was put down at the summit, on the major axis, some 20.0 feet to the east of B M. Careful measurements of cross-sections were taken and will be shown on the final map. Very fine, light, gray sand, too dry and loose to be removed with augers, was encountered immediately east and southeast of B M. This appeared at 18.0 feet, extended to well below base, and might be well worth further examination. It lies at such a depth, however, that its removal will require the use of cribbing and a bucket, at expense not considered justifiable, at the time these tests were made. This variety of sand was not found in any other mound of the Havana group.

Mound No. 8. This lies a few hundred feet directly east of No. 7, on a high ridge in the Neteler wheatfield, and was neither surveyed nor examined, but was accurately located with respect to the southeast corner of Riverside Park, a common tie-point for Mounds Nos. 5, 6, 7, and 9, and previously described.

Mound No. 9. Is the largest mound in the Havana group, is elliptical, lies almost parallel to Mound No. 7, and directly on the left bank of the Illinois River. An excavation in the end next to the river, evidently intended for a building site, destroys the uniformity of profile there but except for a few shell fragments discloses no evidence of prehistoric habitation. Test holes sunk at intervals of ten feet along both axes show a heavy shell content and a greater percent of fine gravel than was found in any other mound. A few small sherds and flint spalls were also taken out. Sherds appear in considerable numbers on the surface along the south base but these may have been turned out by farming operations which have extended well up on the slope. The present owner, Mr. L. A. England, of Havana, Illinois, has issued a written permit for exploration to continue through 1928 but states that he intends to remove the upper 8 feet or 10 feet for filling to be used on low ground to the north. This work, which he expects to begin next spring, should be watched by a competent observer.

Mound No. 10. Is a low ovate mound near No. 2, and was tested with augers but yielded nothing. A few very small fragments of pottery were found on its surface, and others appeared on the surface of adjacent territory.

Mound No. 11. Located in Chautauqua Park, about 1½ miles north of Havana, and was opened on December 5 by written permission (holding good through 1928) from Mr. O. F. Pfetzing, Chairman of the Grounds Committee of the Chautauqua organization, and yielded eight fragmentary skeletons. The teeth of Skeleton No. 1 were discovered by auger test at a depth of 6.5 feet near Station 10 of Line No. 1 which will be shown on the final map. Other tests showed stone at 7.0 feet under Station 10, Line No. 2; at 6.5 feet under Station 9, and at 6.0 feet under Station 8, same line. Further tests were discontinued and a pit was sunk over Skeleton No. 1. This lay extended on its back, in Sec. K-12, head north, and was complete except for the lower portion of the left arm and a few of the smaller bones. The bones were poorly preserved, lay in very dry, compact, light gray earth resembling hardpan, and were so firmly bonded in this that removal without breakage was impossible. The skull was badly crushed, and the auger had disturbed the jaws and teeth, but nearly all of the latter were eventually recovered. A horizontal layer of eight small slabs of sandstone, irregularly placed, formed a rude semicircle around the upper part of the skull. Careful examination revealed no shells, teeth or other ornaments, or implements at neck, waist, wrists, or ankles, but a marine shell about a foot long and six inches in diameter lay, opening upward, at the right shoulder. It was full of a slightly darker variety of earth than surrounded the skeleton but this was not disturbed and no attempt was made to ascertain if the columnella had been removed, the shell and contents being shipped intact as found.

In making room for removal of this skeleton, Skeleton No. 2 was found lying at No. 1's right side and parallel to it. The legs were missing. The skull was badly crushed and the right side of the frontal and the right parietal appeared to be fire- or smoke-blackened. Two humeri, apparently from different bodies, lay parallel with each other, diagonally across the torso, with their upper ends to the southeast. The easternmost of these was recorded as Skeleton No. 7, and the other as No. 6. Lying between them, also on the torso of No. 2, was a calcanum, and this was recorded as Skeleton No. 8. Five small slabs of sandstone lay under the upper edge of the crushed skull.

Operations involved in removing No. 2 disclosed the presence of a child's skeleton, No. 5, to the right of and parallel with No. 2. Frontal portions of the skull were fairly complete but could not be held intact upon removal. The lower right arm lay diagonally across the lower torso, and the legs from the knees down were missing. Three small slabs of sandstone lay beyond the head and with those at the heads of No. 2 and No. 1 formed a rough semi-circle about the three crania. None of these lay completely under the skulls. They varied from 2″ to 8″ wide or long and were from ½″ to 1″ thick. In the opinion of Dr. Wanless, who examined them, and who states that no such material appears in Mason County, they were probably brought from the outcrops at the mouth of Sister Creek across the river in Fulton County.

A bone implement 4½″ long, about ¼″ wide, and ⅛″ thick, blunt at one end, rounded at the other, and bearing a small hole or eye about an inch from the rounded end, lay at the left side of the skull.

A copper implement, 4¼″ long, 2″ wide at one end and 3″ at the other, about ½″ thick, with a concave-convex bit at either end, all heavily encrusted, lay under the right hip. (See Plate XLII.)

Nos. 1, 2, and 5, lay at the same level.

Skeleton No. 3, partial cranium only, appeared at a depth of 3.3′ under the foot contour line in the northeast corner of Sec. 1-8, or at practically the same level as Nos. 1, 2, and 5.

Skeleton No. 4, femora only, heads southwest, lay at a slightly higher level near the center of Sec. 1-9, and about 3.0 feet northwest of No. 3. There is no probability that this was a part of No. 3, unless the body was dismembered before burial or disturbed later, and the surrounding earth showed no evidence of such disturbance.

Weather conditions suddenly became so unfavorable during the work of uncovering these remains that canvas had to be stretched over the pit to protect the workmen, and the shadow cast by this and by the walls of the pit, together with extremely cloudy weather, made photography impossible. Careful sketches and measurements of the remains in place were accordingly made and added to the field record, and these will be shown in detail on the final map. Parts of other skeletons were also found and will likewise be shown on the map. There is good reason to believe that the mound contains more similar material, and it is urgently recommended that its exploration be resumed as soon as the weather will permit in 1928.

Mound No. 12. This constitutes the second member of a triangular group of three mounds in this Park, is high and narrow in comparison to its base, and seems to be a likely place for exploration.

Mound No. 13. This is much flatter in comparison to its greater base than either No. 11 or No. 12 and is not as impressive as either of these but should be examined if operations are resumed in No. 11. Permit from Mr. Pfetzing covering Mounds 11, 12, and 13, holds good through 1928.

Other Mounds. Prominent in the Havana group are at least two, and probably three, structures lying in Mr. George Ermerling's alfalfa field on the left bank of the Illinois River at the outskirts of Havana and immediately north of Riverside Park. Lateness of the season prevented examination of these mounds but Mr. Ermerling has agreed to allow exploration next year. What appears to be a series of small mounds, located immediately on the left bank of the Illinois, with perceptibly lower ground back of them, lie along this bank from above Mound No. 2 to the bayou at the north side of Riverside Park.

South and west of Chautauqua Park, along the left bank of the river, in the adjoining section, on property belonging to a Mr. Hahn of Havana, four other mounds stand out quite prominently, and examination of the surrounding grounds revealed the presence of flint spalls and numerous fragments of pottery. When approached in the matter of allowing exploration, Mr. Hahn was non-committal, but there is good reason to believe that his final reply will be favorable. In that event examination of this group may be carried on from the same camp in connection with the work in Nos. 11, 12, and 13.

Some 18 miles below Havana, near Bath, other mounds appear on property owned by Mr. L. H. Kramer who did not hesitate to grant permission to explore. These also lie on the left bank of and near to the river. One, which he says has never been disturbed, may be described as an inverted mound without drainage facilities, and lying near the mouth of a ravine. Sherds appear in numbers on the surface of adjoining fields.

Other mounds lying across the river from Havana are available for exploration through the influence of Dr. Charles M. Atkinson and Mr. P. D. Diffenbacher, both of Havana, and permits may be had to examine many more, so that in event such a course seems justified, probably two years or more can well be spent in the Havana group.

GENERAL CONCLUSIONS

I can, of course, lay no claims to technical archæological training but it seems to me the remains recovered from Mound No. 6 are of comparatively modern Indians, a conclusion based chiefly on the high grade of workmanship displayed in fashioning the flint discs referred to and on the fact that pottery appeared in such profusion and in such variety and detail of design. Moreover, save for the miniature pot, practically all of the material from this mound was found at a comparatively high level.

This consideration may be affected, however, by the possibility that the crown of the mound may have been removed. Personally, I doubt this story.

On the other hand, the general appearance and location of the remains found in No. 11 lead me to believe that they are much older than those recovered from No. 6, and that they may, therefore, really represent the true Mound Builders. Furthermore, while the copper axes taken from No. 6 had square polls and sides and flat or slightly double convex single bits which, in the heavier ones at least, were badly nicked and battered as from rough usage, the one copper object found in No. 11 had a concave-convex bit at either end and neither of these showed evidences of wear. I assume therefore, that save for the so-called head band in No. 6, the copper objects found there were designed primarily for utilitarian purposes, while the one in No. 11 was probably for ornamental or ceremonial use. So far as I know, it is not common to the Havana group.

The most striking contrast in remains taken from the two mounds, and one that might seem to strengthen the conclusion that those in No. 11 were older than in No. 6, is in the matter of pottery. In No. 6 from the very surface to as deep as we trenched, this appeared in profusion, both as sherds and as whole vessels, and as before mentioned, showed such a wealth of variety and detail in design that it seems to indicate a long period of development. Not the least fragment of pottery was found in No. 11.

The one bone implement found in No. 11, a slender, pointed bone, perforated near the pointed end, might well appear to be a primitive form of needle. Two similarly shaped, though larger, bone objects were taken from No. 6, but in addition to having one perforation well back from the rounded end, both of these bore what appeared to have been a second perforation, through which the wide end of the bone had been broken. These may or may not have been fashioned for use as needles, but if they were so intended, then their complication of design would seem to indicate considerable advance in form over the cruder so-called needle from No. 11.

Great quantities of unworked fresh-water shells but no marine shells appeared in No. 6, but only one shell was found in No. 11 and this was of marine origin. Judging from its location between the shoulders of two skeletons it probably bore some religious or ceremonial relation to one or both of these burials.

Several pieces of worked flint indicating more or less expertness in shaping such material, were taken from No. 6, but not one such piece was found in No. 11.

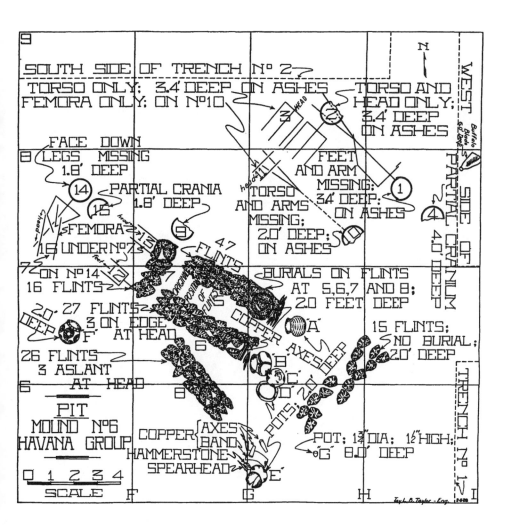

Fig. 21—Ground plan of interments and objects in Mound No. 6, Havana group. Land of Mrs. Anna Neteler.

THE DICKSON MOUND AND THE LOG TOMB BURIALS AT LIVERPOOL

Upon a ridge flanking the Illinois River, and distant five miles from Lewistown, lies the Dickson Mound. Early settlers discovered the site and removed many skeletons and various objects. We questioned both Dr. Dickson and his father and these observations are condensed from their statements. According to testimony of witnesses, the original was in the form of a crescent approximately six hundred feet or more in length. The surface of this crescent has been considerably altered by the building of a hen house with brick foundation and various other excavations, so that today it appears mound-like, but the crescent feature is absent. Dr. Dickson states that his father, Thomas M. Dickson, bought the property about thirty years ago. When the contour of the crescent was changed through digging for building foundations or grading in order to obtain more even surface, many skeletons were found. It is claimed that nearly one thousand burials have thus far been in evidence.

Mr. Thomas Dickson personally dug out a large number (included in this total) some of which were accompanied by objects similar to those found by his son. The work by Mr. Thomas Dickson was the top of the mound, and it is not known how many feet of the mound have been removed.

Objects obtained by Thomas Dickson, especially the pottery, according to an old photograph appear to be more decorative and of higher art than those found by the son. Also there was a profusion of beads. It is claimed that effigy pottery, pearl beads, and several stone pipes accompanied the top burials.

About the end of March, 1927, Dr. Don F. Dickson began his excavations, finding many skeletons at different depths and various angles, but practically all extended. He worked carefully and brought a number of these into relief by means of proper hand trowel methods and technique. Plates XLVI and XLVII show a portion of the cemetery. He found most of the skeletons placed on a slightly burned base. This would not apply to all, especially those in the lower level. He left a bench around each, and the skeletons stand out clearly and distinctly. As he proceeded downward he found other skeletons at right angles, or diagonal to upper burials and developed these. No majority of the one hundred eighty bodies are headed in the same direction.

Sixty or seventy feet distant, he found a group burial of six or eight persons and erected a small temporary structure over them for protection.

We have not sufficient exact data to prove that the interments in the upper layers removed by Mr. Dickson senior, represent a different tribe from that indicated by Dr. Don Dickson's finds lower down. Mr. Marion Dickson states that about twelve years ago they found copper ear bobs on each side of several crania and also a bird's-head effigy pipe.

Inspection of the groups in Plates XLVI and XLVII will present readers with prevailing types, or ceramic characteristics. Our conclusion is, naturally, subject to change when Dr. Dickson's complete report is available. Yet so far, the indications are that we have here at his field museum what remains of a large cemetery of the Illinois Indians such as La Salle found at Utica to the north, and which the Iroquois from Onondaga destroyed more than two hundred fifty years ago. A careful study and comparison between the pottery common at Utica and that of Dickson's farm will undoubtedly solve the question.

The "Log Tomb" Mounds at Liverpool

The mounds at Liverpool were about four and one-half miles northeast, but occupied low land lying very near the river. Originally they were on an island, and differ decidedly from the bluff and high terrace tumuli. Those at Havana lie on a well defined terrace some twenty feet above ordinary water stage.

In the Liverpool group were three mounds. One farthest up the river, some nine hundred or one thousand feet distant from the other two, was said to have been nearly fifteen feet high and seventy-five feet base diameter. Down river from this one, a small house is located on the larger of two mounds which are joined together. The total base line of these is over two hundred fifty feet and the height of the larger mound about twenty-one feet.

Although we carefully interviewed the owners and other interested persons, and particularly a Mr. Solomon, who did the actual digging, we were unable to secure a satisfactory account of the so-called log tombs and the stone tomb. The objects themselves, having been lent to Dr. Don F. Dickson, were available for study and some of them are shown in Plates XLVIII and XLIX.

It would appear that in the mound up-river Solomon discovered some forty skeletons which were surrounded by what he called a wall composed of small stones. Mr. Marion Dickson visited the site while work was in progress and it is his opinion that these stones were laid in whitish clay which was almost, but not quite, sufficiently hard to be considered cement. We observed some of the stones scattered about the surface and also traces of the clay. The wall was said to be about four feet high. Indians had spread a layer of pure white sand an inch or two in thickness on the base inside. Upon this were laid the bodies accompanied by various objects. The witnesses do not agree as to the size of the tomb, one stating that it was twenty feet long and ten feet wide, another that the tomb was about ten feet in length. Solomon declares that the earth within was very loose, indicating that it was arched over, or roofed with timbers or slabs which have decayed.

In the double mound were larger tombs composed of logs fifteen or sixteen inches in diameter. All witnesses agree that these were laid up to a height of about five feet, but the statements vary as to whether three or four logs were employed for each wall.

In these was a similar layer of white sand on the bottom and long bone daggers, or pointed instruments, shown in Plate XLVIII were stuck in the ground, points downward. About seventy of these were found grouped about the heads of certain burials. One Indian had six at his head, and others three to four.

Although the field data itself is rather unsatisfactory, the objects themselves indicate a modification of Hopewell culture. While the full seventeen Hopewell characteristics are not present, it is safe to assume that some seven or eight of them are in evidence.

Indeed, the artifacts themselves clearly stamp the "Log Tomb" tribe as essentially Hopewell. A significant feature is the absence of pottery—little of which occurs in Ohio Hopewell mounds and none in most of the lower Scioto mound groups.

From all accounts, the logs when uncovered were sufficiently sound to have been parafined, wrapped with twine and removed. Had our force made such a discovery we could have removed the tomb and contents and set it up in the University museum as a permanent exhibit. That a burial of such unusual character and importance was found by ignorant men seems the irony of fate. Up to present writing, December 25, we have been unable to discover an undisturbed log or stone mortuary structure. Diligent search last season as well as this year and our failure in this direction would seem to indicate that the so-called log-tomb people occupied a restricted area in the middle Illinois valley.

There may be several remaining in unexplored mounds of the Liverpool district, or even farther up the river. Due to the commercial spirit now manifest on the part of several land owners, it was not possible for us to secure permits to excavate.

Under other circumstances it might not be advisable to seek legislative aid, but in view of the high importance to science of careful examination of this "Hopewell-like" culture, it would appear proper that some kind of control be established. If there is to be general "digging" on the part of enthusiastic but untrained persons, irreparable damage will result. It would appear to us that while the State of Illinois would not seek to interfere with owners' disposition of ancient remains, yet the Survey suggests that a bill be passed through the Legislature to the effect that all archæological explorations be under the supervision of either the University of Illinois, The State Museum, the University of Chicago, The Field Museum, Academy of Science or some other competent institution. A trained observer should be sent by one of these institutions to see that the work is properly and intelligently carried out and the usual maps, field notes, photographs and other accurate data obtained.

APPENDIX D

CAHOKIA BIBLIOGRAPHY

We are indebted to Dr. Thomas English, of Emory University, Atlanta, Georgia, for revision of our bibliography together with additions.

CHARLEVOIX
  1761. *Journal of a Voyage to North America.* Vol. II, p. 256. London, 1761.

BRACKENRIDGE, H. M.
  1813. "Notes on the Antiquities of the Mississippi Valley." *Transactions of the American Philosophical Society.* Philadelphia, 1813.
  1814. *Views of Louisiana; Together with a Journal of a Voyage up the Missouri River, in 1811.* pp. 181-95, 287-91. Pittsburgh, 1814. Second edition, Baltimore, 1817.
  1818. "Brief Report on the Cahokia Mounds." *Analectic Magazine,* p. 328. Philadelphia, 1818.

BECK, LEWIS C.
  1823. *A Gazetteer of the States of Illinois and Missouri.* Albany, 1823.

LONG, STEPHEN H.
  1823. *Account of an Expedition from Pittsburgh to the Rocky Mountains, Performed in the Years 1819, 1820.* By order of the Hon. J. C. Calhoun, Secretary of War, under the command of Maj. S. H. Long, of the U. S. Top. Engineers. Compiled from the notes of Maj. Long, etc., by Edwin James, botanist and geologist to the expedition. Vol. I, Chap. III. Philadelphia (2v.) and London (3v.), 1823.

SCHOOLCRAFT, HENRY R.
  1825. *Travels in the Central Portions of the Mississippi Valley: comprising observations on its mineral geography, internal resources, and aboriginal population.* Performed under the sanction of government, in the year 1821. pp. 224, 293. New York, 1825.

FLINT, TIMOTHY
  1826. *Recollections of the Last Ten Years, Passed in Occasional Residences and Journeyings in the Valley of the Mississippi . . . in a Series of Letters to the Rev. James Flint, of Salem, Massachusetts.* pp. 164-74. *Lines* (by Micah Flint) *on the Mounds in the Cahokia Prairie, Illinois.* pp. 167-9. Boston, 1826.

PRIEST, JOSIAH
  1833. *American Antiquities and Discoveries in the West. Traits of Ancient Cities on the Mississippi.* pp. 193-4. Albany, 1833.

PECK, JOHN M.
  1834. *A Gazetteer of Illinois.* Jacksonville, 1834. 2nd ed. rev. Philadelphia, 1837.

LATROBE, CHARLES JASPER
  1835. *The Rambler in North America.* Vol. II, pp. 175-182. London and New York, 1835.

FLAGG, EDMUND
  1838. *The Far West.* pp. 166-167. New York, 1838.

PARKER, SAMUEL
    1838. Journal of an Exploring Tour Beyond the Rocky Mountains.
        p. 39. Ithaca, N. Y., 1838.
MORRISON, ANNA R.
    1840. "Diary of a Journey from New York to Jacksonville, Novem-
        ber-December, 1840." *Journal of the Illinois State Historical Society.*
        Vol. 7, No. 1. pp. 34-50. April, 1914.
THOMAS, LEWIS FOULK, and
WILD, J. C.
    1841. *The Valley of the Mississippi Illustrated in a Series of Views.*
        Edited by Lewis Foulk Thomas. Painted and Lithographed by J. C.
        Wild. Accompanied with Historical Descriptions. pp. 52-6, and
        Plate X. St. Louis, 1841.
DICKENS, CHARLES
    1842. *American Notes.* Chapter XIII. London, 1842.
MAXIMILIAN, PRINCE OF WIED-NEUWIED
    1843. *Travels in the Interior of North America.* Translated from the
        German. pp. 475-6. London, 1843.
FEATHERSTONHAUGH, G. W.
    1844. *Excursion Through the Slave States.* Vol. I, pp. 264-272. Lon-
        don and New York, 1844.
SQUIER, E. G. and
DAVIS, E. H.
    1848. "Ancient Monuments of the Mississippi Valley." *Smithsonian
        Contributions to Knowledge,* Vol. I, Chap. VIII, p. 174, Fig. 60.
        Washington, 1848.
LEWIS, HENRY and
DOUGLAS, GEORGE B.
    1857. Das illustrirte Mississippi thal, dargestellt in 80 nach der Natur
        aufgenommenen Ansichten . . . von H. Lewis . . . Nebst einer his-
        torischen und geographischen Beschreibung der den Fluss Begrän-
        zenden Länder. pp. 331-6. Düsseldorf, 1857.
RAU, CHARLES
    1867. "Indian Pottery." *Annual Report of the Smithsonian Institu-
        tion,* 1866. pp. 346-55. Washington, 1867.
DEHASS, W.
    1869. "Archæology of the Mississippi Valley." *Proceedings of the
        American Association for the Advancement of Science.* 17th Meet-
        ing, held at Chicago, Illinois, Aug., 1868. pp. 288-302. Cambridge,
        1869.
LUBBOCK, JOHN
    1869. 1st Baron Avebury. *Pre-Historic Times, as Illustrated by
        Ancient Remains, and the Manners and Customs of Modern Savages.*
        2nd ed., London, 1869. 6th ed., pp. 253, 260. New York, 1900.
RAU, CHARLES
    1872. "A Deposit of Agricultural Flint Implements in Southern Ill-
        inois." *Annual Report of the Smithsonian Institution,* 1868. pp. 401-
        7. Washington, 1872.

FOSTER, J. W.
 1873. *Pre-Historic Races of the United States of America.* pp. 106-7. Chicago, 1873.
HOWLAND, HENRY R.
 1877. "Recent Archæological Discoveries in the American Bottom." *Bulletin of the Buffalo Society of Natural Sciences,* Vol. III, No. 5, p. 204. Buffalo, 1877.
MACLEAN, J. P.
 1879. *The Mound Builders.* pp. 42-3. Cincinnati, 1879.
CONANT, A. J.
 1879. *Foot-Prints of Vanished Races in the Mississippi Valley.* pp. 53-61. St. Louis, 1879.
PUTNAM, F. W. and
PATRICK, DR.
 1879. *Twelfth Annual Report of the Peabody Museum.* p. 472. Cambridge, 1879.
SHORT, JOHN T.
 1880. *The North Americans of Antiquity.* pp. 40-3. New York, 1880.
MCADAMS, WILLIAM
 1881. "Ancient Mounds of Illinois." *Proceedings of the American Association for the Advancement of Science.* 29th Meeting, held at Boston, Mass., August, 1880. pp. 710-18. Salem, 1881.
THWING, C. F.
 1881. "The Peabody Museum of Archæology and Ethnology." *Harper's New Monthly Magazine,* Vol. LXIII, pp. 670-7. New York, October, 1881.
MCADAMS, WILLIAM
 1882. *Antiquities [of Madison County] History of Madison County, Illinois.* pp. 58-64. Edwardsville, 1882.
NADAILLAC, MARQUISDE
 1884. *Pre-Historic America.* Translated by N. D'Anvers. Edited by W. H. Dall. p. 103. New York and London, 1884.
MCADAMS, WILLIAM
 1887. *Records of Ancient Races in the Mississippi Valley.* pp. 98-109. St. Louis, 1887.
PATRICK, J. R.
 1888. Article on Monks Mound. *St. Louis Globe-Democrat.* Feb. 5, 1888.
SNYDER, J. F.
 1894. "An Illinois 'Teocalli'." *The Archæologist,* Vol. II, No. 9, pp. 259-264. Waterloo, Indiana.
THOMAS, CYRUS
 1894. "Report on the Mound Explorations of the Bureau of Ethnology." *12th Annual Report of the Bureau of Ethnology, 1890-91,* pp. 131-4. Washington, 1894.
SHIPP, BERNARD
 1897. *Indian Antiquities of America.* pp. 251-4. Philadelphia, 1897.

BATEMAN, NEWTON and
SELBY, PAUL
    1900. *Historical Encyclopedia of Illinois.* Edited by Newton Bateman
    and Paul Selby. pp. 388-91. Chicago, 1900.
SNYDER, JOHN F.
    1900. "The Field for Archæological Research in Illinois." *Transactions
    of the Illinois State Historical Society for 1900,* pp. 21-9. Spring-
    field, 1900.
SMITH, HARLAN INGERSOLL
    1902. "The Great American Pyramid." *Harper's Monthly Magazine,*
    Vol. 104, pp. 199-204. New York, January, 1902.
PETERSON, C. A.
    1902. "The Mound Building Age in North America." Read Feb. 15,
    1902, before Missouri State Historical Society.
BUSHNELL, DAVID I., JR.
    1904. "The Cahokia and Surrounding Mound Groups." *Papers of the
    Peabody Museum of American Archæology and Ethnology,* Harvard
    University, Vol. III, No. 1. Cambridge, May, 1904.
PARRISH, RANDALL
    1905. *Historic Illinois: The Romance of the Earlier Days.* pp. 15-26.
    Chicago, 1905.
HODGE, FREDERICK WEBB
    1907. *Handbook of American Indians North of Mexico.* Edited by
    Frederick Webb Hodge. Smithsonian Institution, Bureau of Ameri-
    can Ethnology, Bulletin 30, Vol. 1, pp. 186, 949-51. Washington,
    1907.
MCADAMS, CLARK
    1907. "The Archæology of Illinois." *Transactions of the Illinois State
    Historical Society for 1907,* pp. 35-47. Springfield, 1907.
RANDALL, E. O.
    1908. *The Masterpieces of the Ohio Mound Builders.* pp. 1-13. Co-
    lumbus, 1908.
SNYDER, JOHN F.
    1909. "Prehistoric Illinois. Certain Indian Mounds Technically Con-
    sidered." *Journal of the Illinois State Historical Society.* Vols. 1 and
    2, pp. 31-40, 47-65, 71-92. Springfield, 1909.
FOWKE, GERARD
    1910. *Antiquities of Central and South-Eastern Missouri.* Smithsonian
    Institution, Bureau of American Ethnology, Bulletin 37, pp. 5-7.
    Washington, 1910.
FENNEMAN, N. M.
    1911. *Geology and Mineral Resources of the St. Louis Quadrangle
    Missouri-Illinois.* U. S. G. S. Bulletin 438, Dept. of the Interior,
    p. 12. Washington, 1911.
SNYDER, JOHN F.
    1911. "Prehistoric Illinois. Its Psychozoic Problems." *Journal of the
    Illinois State Historical Society,* Vol. 4, pp. 288-302. Springfield,
    1911-12.

1912. "The Kaskaskia Indians. A Tentative Hypothesis." *Journal of the Illinois State Historical Society*, Vol. 5, pp. 231-45. Springfield, 1912-13.

1913 (?). *A Booklet on the Prehistoric Mounds of Illinois*. 8 pp. Prepared by the "Monks of Cahokia." "This booklet is respectfully submitted to call to the attention of the public a project, now before the General Assembly of Illinois, to make of these prehistoric mounds a State Park."

BUSHNELL, DAVID I., JR.

1915. "The Origin and Various Types of Mounds in Eastern United States." *Proceedings Nineteenth International Congress of Americanists*, Washington, 1915. pp. 43-7. Washington, 1917.

RAMEY FAMILY

1916. *The Mound Builders. The Greatest Monument of Prehistoric Man, Cahokia or Monks Mound*. 28 pp. Excerpts from McAdams and others. Prepared by the Ramey family about 1916.

JESSUP, THEODORE

1916. "Illinois State Parks." A paper read before the Chicago Literary Club. April 10, 1916. pp. 9-10.

SNYDER, JOHN F.

1917. "The Great Cahokia Mound." *Journal of the Illinois State Historical Society*, Vol. 10, pp. 256-9. Springfield, 1917-18.

CAHOKIA MOUND ASSOCIATION

1917 (?). "Save the Mounds." Collinsville, 1917 (?). 32 pp. Testimonials, petitions, etc., gathered by the Cahokia Mound Association.

ALVORD, CLARENCE WALWORTH

1920. *The Illinois Country 1673-1818*. The Centennial History of Illinois, Vol. I, Chap. II. Springfield, 1920.

ENGLISH, THOMAS H.

1921. "The Cahokia Indian Mounds: A Plea for their Preservation." *The Geographical Review*, Vol. XI, pp. 207-11. New York, April, 1921.

MOOREHEAD, WARREN K.

1921. "Help Save the Cahokia Mounds." Circular, 4 pp. Andover, Mass., August, 1921. Reprinted in part in the *Literary Digest* for September 10, 1921, pp. 22-3.

1922. "Preservation of the Cahokia Mounds." *The Wisconsin Archæologist*, n. s. Vol. 1, No. 1, p. 25, Jan., 1922. Milwaukee.

1922. "The Cahokia Mounds: a preliminary paper." *University of Illinois Bulletin*, Vol. XIX, No. 35. April 24, 1922. Urbana.

1922. "The Hopewell Mound Group of Ohio." *Field Museum of Natural History, Publication 211, Anthropological Series*, Vol. VI, p. 177. Chicago, 1922.

CROOK, A. R.

1922. "The Origin of the Cahokia Mounds." *Bulletin of the Illinois State Museum*. 26 pp. Springfield, May, 1922.

BUSHNELL, DAVID I., JR.

1922. "Archæological Reconnaissance of the Cahokia and Related Mound Groups. Explorations and Field-Work of the Smithsonian Institution in 1921." *Smithsonian Miscellaneous Collections*, Vol. 72, No. 15, pp. 92-105, Washington, 1922.

WISSLER, CLARK

1922. *The American Indian.* An Introduction to the Anthropology of the New World. 2nd ed., pp. 105, 116, 268. New York, 1922.

MOULTON, ROBERT H.

1923. "Save our American Pyramids." *The Outlook*, Vol. 133, pp. 83-5. New York, Jan. 10, 1923.

1923. "Movement is Launched to Preserve Prehistoric Mounds in Illinois." *America To-day* combined with *Fort Dearborn Magazine,* Vol. IV, No. 4, July, 1923. Published by American Bond & Mortgage Company, Inc. Chicago, New York, etc.

MOOREHEAD, WARREN K.

1923. "The Cahokia Mounds." *University of Illinois Bulletin*, Vol. XXI, Oct. 8, 1923, No. 6, Urbana, 97 pp. Pt. I. "A Report of Progress on the Exploration of the Cahokia Group," by Warren K. Moorehead, pp. 7-50. Pt. II. "The Geological Aspects of Some of the Cahokia Mounds," by Morris M. Leighton, *Illinois Geological Survey*. Notes on Cahokia Skeletons, by Dr. R. J. Terry, pp. 51-2.

BAKER, FRANK COLLINS

1924. "The Use of Molluscan Shells by the Cahokia Mound Builders." *Transactions of the Illinois State Academy of Science*, Vol. 16. pp. 328-334. 1924.

GARDNER, FRED

1926. "Mysterious Old Monks Mound is to become a State Park and Tourist Camp." *The Globe-Democrat Magazine.* St. Louis, September 5, 1926.

TOWNLEY, E. C.

1927. *Some Mound Builders in Illinois. Art and Archæology.* Vol. XXIV, No. 6, pp. 234-8, Washington, December, 1927.

THROOP, ADDISON J.

The Mound Builders of Illinois. Call Printing Company, East St. Louis, Illinois, 1928.

Plates

Key to Plates and Figure Numbers

The illustrations on the following pages use the plate numbers and captions from the 1929 edition.

The captions have been reset but retain the original spellings and capitalization. Within the captions, the figure numbers from the 1922 volume are added in brackets. The figure numbers from the 1923 volume are the same as the figure numbers shown in the 1929 captions.

The illustrations are printed in the order shown in the 1929 column.

1922 Figures	1923 Plates	1929 Plates
1	-	- [Plate I in 1922 vol.]
2	-	I
3, 4	-	II, Figs. 1, 2
5, 6	-	III, Figs. 1, 2
7	-	IV
8	XIX	V
9	XX	VI
10–12	-	VII, Figs. 1–3
13	-	VIII
14	-	IX
-	-	X
15–20	-	- [Plate XI in 1922 vol.]
-	-	XI
21–28	-	- [Plate XII in 1922 vol.]
-	-	XII
29–32	-	- [Plate XIII in 1922 vol.]
33	-	XIII
34–36	-	XIV, Figs. 1–3
37, 38	-	XV, Figs. 1, 2
39–46	-	XVI, Figs. 1–8
-	I	XVII, Figs. 1–6
-	II	XVIII, Figs. 1–5
-	III	XIX, Fig. 1–6
-	IV	XX, Fig. 1–10
-	XXI	- [Plate XXI in 1923 vol.]
-	V	XXI, Fig. 1–8
-	XXII	- [Plate XXII in 1923 vol.]
-	VI	XXII, Figs. 1–7

-	VII	XXIII, Figs. 1–9
-	VIII	XXIV, Figs. 1–20
-	IX	XXV, Figs. 1–13
-	X	XXVI, Figs. 1–5
-	XI	XXVII, Figs. 1–6
-	XII	XXVIII, Figs. 1–11
-	XIII	XXIX, Figs. 1, 2
-	XIV	XXX, Figs. 1, 2
-	XV	XXXI, Figs. 1, 3
-	XVI	XXXII, Figs. 1–9
-	XVII	XXXIII, Figs. 1–8
-	XVIII	XXXIV, Figs. 1–4
-	-	XXXV, Figs. a–j
-	-	XXXVI
-	-	XXXVII
-	-	XXXVIII
-	-	XXXIX and XL (same page)
-	-	XLI
-	-	XLII
-	-	XLIII
-	-	XLIV
-	-	XLV and XLVI (same page)
-	-	XLVII
-	-	XLVIII
-	-	XLIX, Figs. A, B
-	-	L

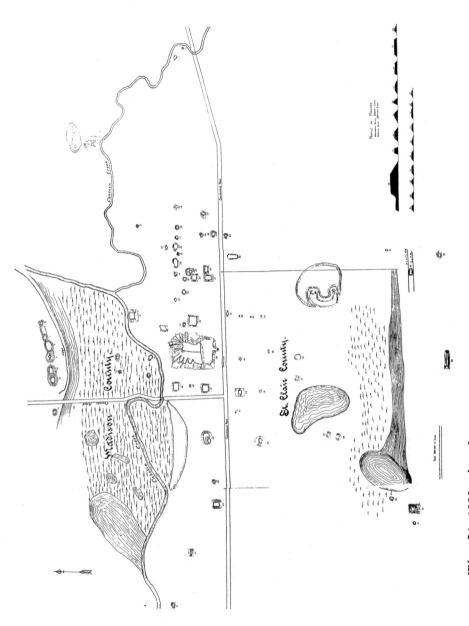

[Plate I in 1922 volume]

Fig. 1.—Reproduction of the map drawn by J. J. R. Patrick about 1880. From (apparently) an accurate survey.

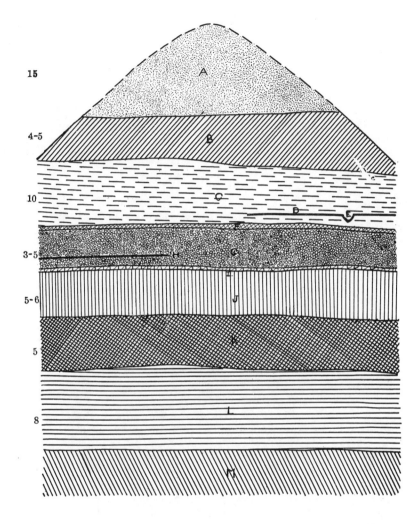

Plate I

cross section of Kunnemann Mound a short distance north of the center.
The outline is not exact, but it is approximate. Depth of strata in feet at the
left of the figure. A—Top removed. B—Dark, rather uneven gumbo layer.
C—Yellowish loam, mixed with sand. D—Burned Floor. E—Altar. F—
Vegetation. G—Dark soil, rather irregular. H—Light sand stratum. I—Thin
vegetation layer. J—Yellowish loam. K—dark earth. L—Mixed earth. M—
Clear sand base.

Plate II
Fig. 1.—East view of Monks Mound. Fig. 2.—North view of Monks Mound.
Photographs by Mr. Gordon Severant.

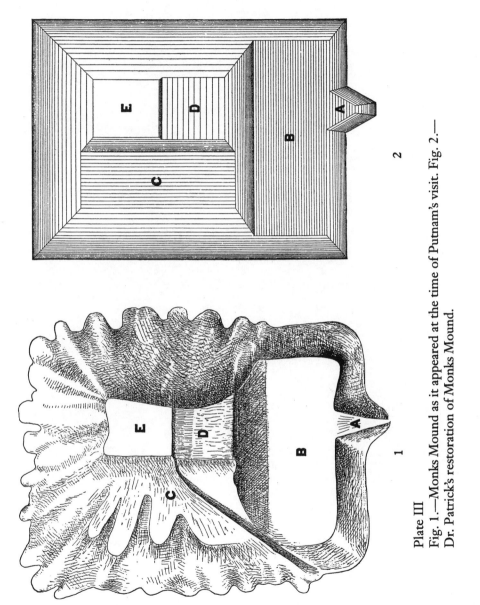

Plate III

Fig. 1.—Monks Mound as it appeared at the time of Putnam's visit. Fig. 2.—
Dr. Patrick's restoration of Monks Mound.

Plate IV
The Red Mound south of Monks Mound.

Plate V
View of the Fox Mound and another mound located about three-fourths of a mile south of Monks Mound. Photograph by Miss Ruth Wallace, Monticello Seminary.

Plate VI
One of the smaller mounds of the group, north of Monks Mound. Photograph by Mr. Gordon Severant.

Plate VII
Fig. 1.—A large pond near the Kunnemann Mound. Fig. 2—The face of the trench of the Kunnemann Mound at a height of 25 feet. Fig. 3.—Trench in the Kunnemann Mound.

Plate VIII
The altar of baked clay in the Kunnemann Mound.

Plate IX
Skeleton of Cahokia Indian in the Edwards Mound.

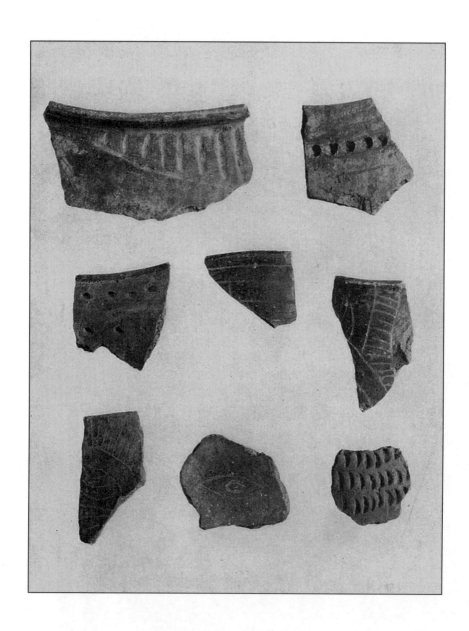

Plate X
Fragments of pottery obtained during excavation of the James Ramey
Mound, No. 33.

[Plate XI in 1922 volume; not in 1929 volume]

Fragments of pottery from the Cahokia mounds. These were collected by Dr. George Higgins many years ago. Fig. 15.—Forearm and hand. Fig. 16.—Red and white ware. Fig. 17.—Handle to vessel. Fig. 18.—Red ware with depressed squares in which were probably inserted small squares of shell. Fig. 19.—Ornament made of pottery. Fig. 20.—Typical Cahokia design.

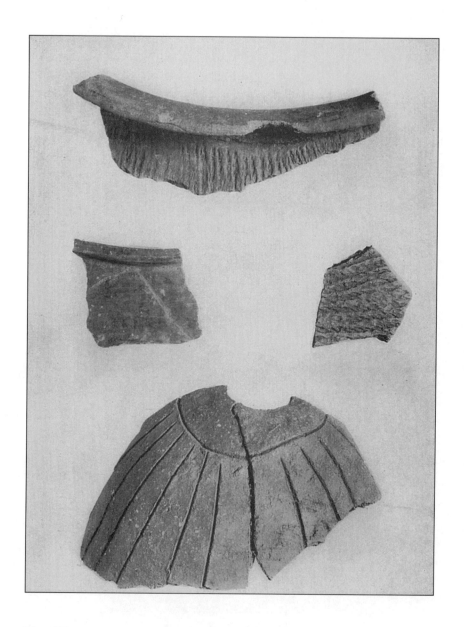

Plate XI
Fragments of pottery from the village site located on the Wells and Tippetts
farms.

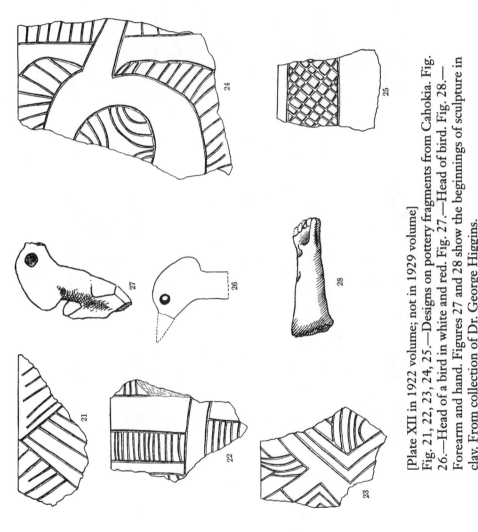

[Plate XII in 1922 volume; not in 1929 volume]

Fig. 21, 22, 23, 24, 25.—Designs on pottery fragments from Cahokia. Fig. 26.—Head of a bird in white and red. Fig. 27.—Head of bird. Fig. 28.—Forearm and hand. Figures 27 and 28 show the beginnings of sculpture in clay. From collection of Dr. George Higgins.

Plate XII
Fragments of pottery from village site on the Ramey, Wells, and Tippetts farms.

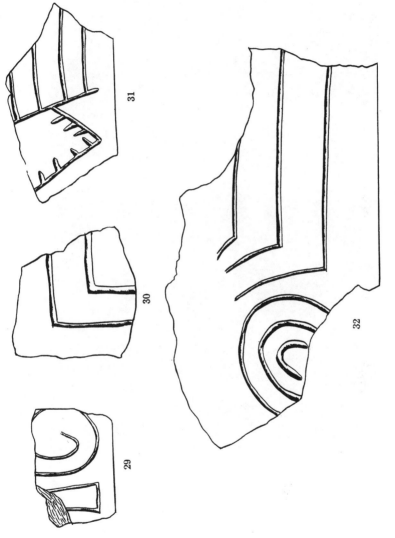

[Plate XIII in 1922 volume; not in 1929 volume]
Figs. 29, 30, 31, 32.—Designs on pottery fragments from Cahokia. From Collection of Mr. Fred Ramey.

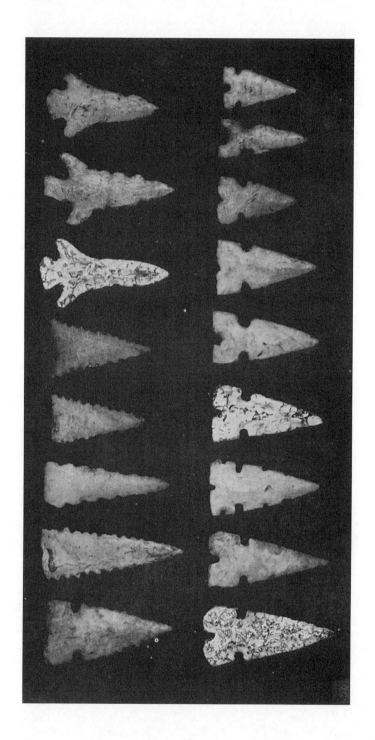

Plate XIII
The Cahokia type of arrowheads. From collection of Dr. George Higgins.

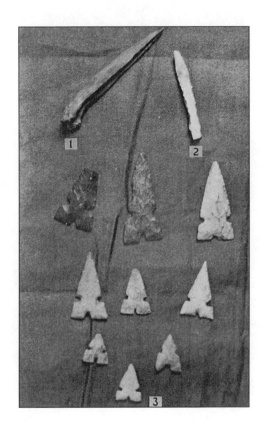

Plate XIV
Fig. 1.—The hollowed bone awl referred to on page 102. Fig. 2.—A slender, broken drill. Fig. 3.—Cahokia type arrowheads. All found in the field opposite Monks Mound. From Ramey collection.

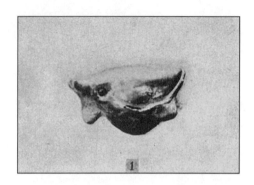

Plate XV
Fig. 1.—Pottery bird effigy. Found by Mr. M. A. Wertheimer, south of Monks Mound. Fig. 2.—Agricultural implements found by Mr. Seeling north of the Merrell Mound. ($^1/_6$ natural size.)

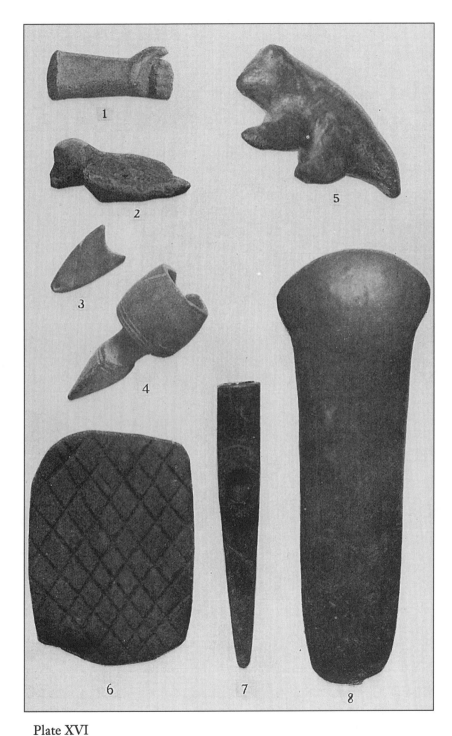

Plate XVI
Fig. 1.—Hand and forearm in clay. Fig. 2.—Effigy in clay. Fig. 3.—Orna
ment in red stone. Fig. 4.—Stone pipe. Fig. 5.—Effigy in clay. Fig. 6.—
Engraved stone. Fig. 7.—Stone pipe. Fig. 8.—Cutting tool (hatchet). Fr(
the Ramey collection. (²/₃ natural size.)

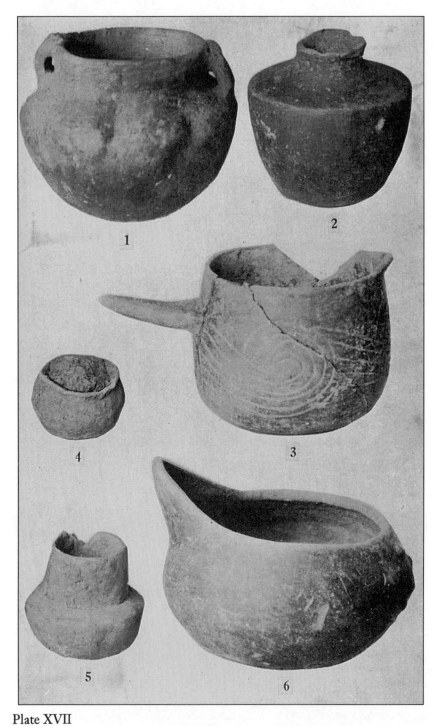

Plate XVII
Figs. 1, 2, 3.—Burial pots with skeleton No. 12, Mound No. 20; 2, 3,
characteristic Cahokia forms, especially 3. (A363, a, b, c.) Fig. 4.—Small pot
with skeleton No. 9, a child (A304). Fig. 5.—Small crucible-like pot from
burned basin, Sawmill Mound (A305). Fig. 6.—Burial pot with skeleton No.
11, Sawmill Mound (A306). ($^2/_5$ natural size.)

PLATE XVIII
Fig. 1.—A vessel of considerable size, probably a salt pan, Wells-Tippetts
Village Site (A355). Figs. 2–4.—Grooved stones of quartzite-like sandstone,
possibly sinew stones (A356), Ramey Village Site. Fig. 5.—Grooved stone of
quartzite-like sandstone, from burned basin 100 yards south of Sawmill
Mound (A357). (About $\frac{1}{2}$ natural size.)

Plate XIX
Figs. 1–6.—Types of decorated pottery. Wells-Tippetts Village Site (A313).
($^3/_4$ natural size.)

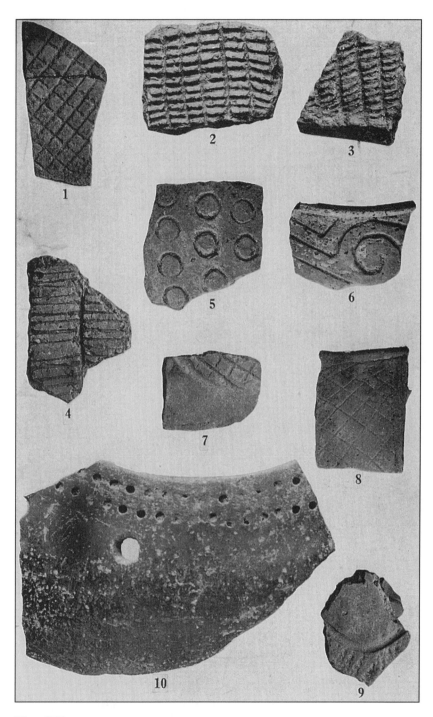

Plate XX
Figs. 1–9.—Fragments of pottery. Wells-Tippetts Village Site, 1 to 3 ¹/₂ ft. below surface (A313). Fig. 10.—Peculiarly decorated pottery fragment, Ramey Village Site (A314). Figs. 5, 6 are common Cahokia designs. (³/₄ natural size.)

[Plate XXI in 1923 volume; not in 1929 volume]
Monk's Mound viewed from the southeast, showing the left foreground the terrace or apron. Cut loaned by Smithsonian Institution.

Plate XXI
Fig. 1.—Pottery fragment, James Ramey Mound, depth of 23 feet (A310).
Figs. 2–8.—Ramey Village Site, types of pottery design (A312). ($^3/_4$ natural size.)

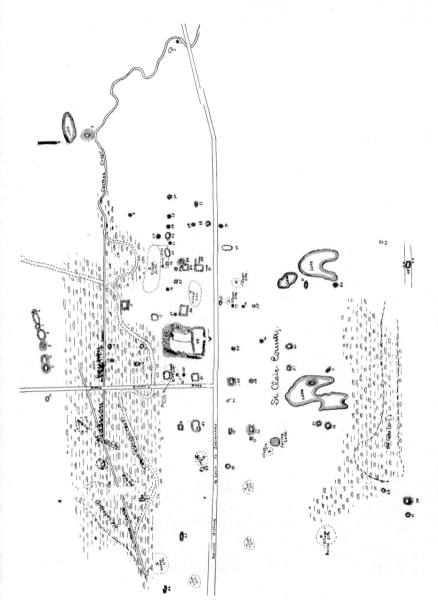

[Plate XXII in 1923 volume; not in 1929 volume]
Map of Cahokia Mound Group. Based on map of J. J. R. Patrick, 1880.
Camp sites and burial sites are indicated, showing result of 1921–22 field
work.

Plate XXII
Decorated pottery from the James Ramey Mound. Figs. 1–3.—Near surface (A307). Fig. 4.—Depth of 19ft. (A309). Figs. 5, 6.—Depth of 15 ft. (A309). Fig. 7.—Depth of 23 ft. (A310). Fig. 2.—Engraved sandstone (A311). ($^4/_5$ natural size.)

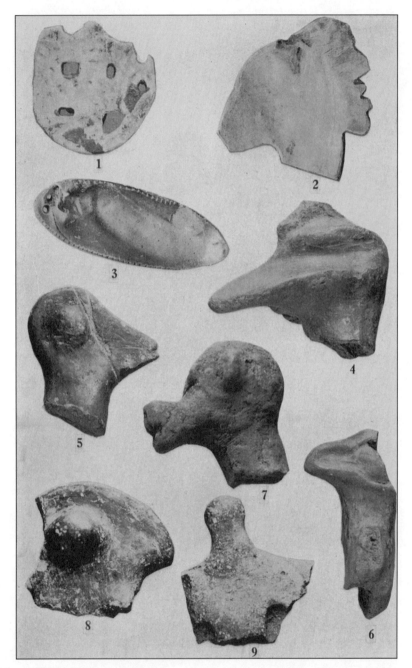

Plate XXIII
Fig. 1.—Shell gorget with skeleton No. 11, Sawmill Mound (A321). Fig.
2.—Shell effigy, Sawmill Mound, made from shell of fresh water mussel
(A322). Fig. 3.—Nose or ear ornament made from shell of fresh water
mussel (*Elliptio dilatatus*), James Ramey Mound (A323). Fig. 4.—Clay bird's-
head effigy, Wells-Tippetts Village Site, 3 ft. deep (A324). Figs. 5, 6.—Clay
bird's-head effigies, James Ramey Mound, 16–23 feet below surface (A325).
Fig. 7.—Clay mammal-head effigy, Sawmill Mound (A326). Fig. 8.—Portion
of clay pot or ornament (A327). Fig. 9.—Ornament on rim of pot (A328).
Figs. 8, 9.—From James Ramey Mound. ($^3/_4$ natural size.)

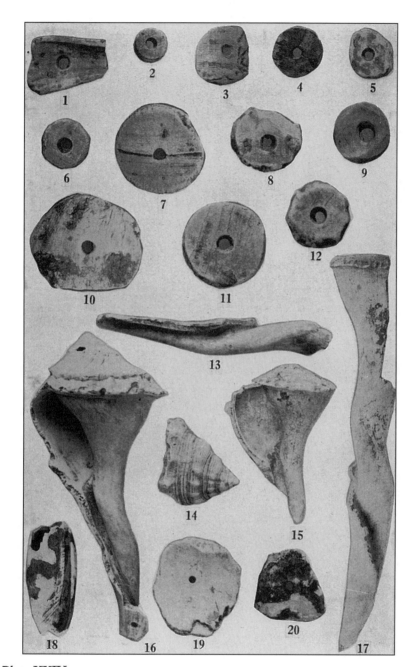

Plate XXIV

Figs. 2, 4, 9, 12.—Shell beads made from marine conch (*Busycon*) (A329). Figs. 5, 6.—Shell beads made from fresh water mussels (A330). Figs. I, II.— Shell ornaments from marine *Busycon* (A331). Figs. 7, 8, 10, 20.—Shell ornaments made from fresh water mussels (A332). Figs. 13, 15, 17.—Shells and central axis of marine conch, *Busycon perversa* (A333). Fig. 16.—Marine conch, *Busycon carica* (A442). Fig. 19.—Ornament made of side of *Busycon* shell (A334). Fig. 14.—Marine shell, *Strombus Pugilis alatus* (A334). Fig. 18.—Marine olive shell, *Oliva literata* (A336). All from James Ramey Mound, between 8 and 23 feet below surface. (Figs. 1 to 12, about natural size; 13 to 20, about $^3/_5$ natural size.)

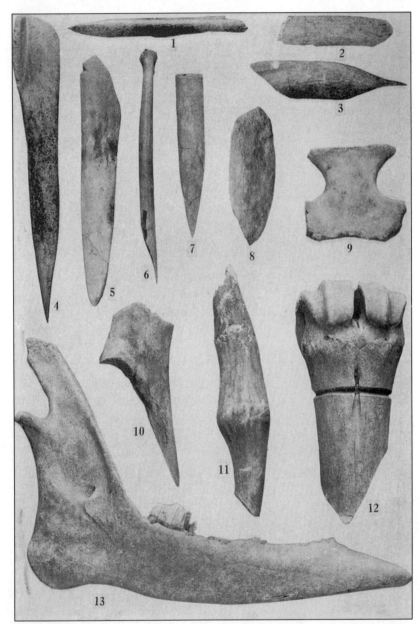

Plate XXV

Figs. 1, 2.—Awl and celt made of deer bone (A337, A338) Wells-Tippetts Village Site. Figs. 3, 7.—Deer bone awls, James Ramey Mound, 8 feet deep (A339). Fig. 4.—Bone awl with skeleton No. 39, Pittsburg Lake (A340). Figs. 5, 6.—Bone awls (A341, A342). From Judge Sullivan's Mound, 10 ft. below surface. Fig. 8.—Bone knife with skeleton No. 11, Sawmill Mound (A343). Fig. 9.—Part of breast bone of Virginia deer, Ramey Village Site (A344). Fig. 10.—Awl made from heel (calceneous bone) of deer (*Odocoileus virginianus*) found with skeleton No. 18 (Mounds 19, 20, 21) (A345). Fig. 11.—Pathologic leg bone of deer, from Ramey Village Site (A346). Fig. 12.—Foot bone of Wapiti with deeply incised lines, James Ramey Mound (A347). Fig. 13.—Lower jaw of Virginia deer used as a chisel or gouge, Sawmill Mound (A348). (About $^2/_3$ natural size.)

Plate XXVI

Fig. 1.—Flint or chert knife of fine workmanship; James Ramey Mound, 12 feet deep, near stake 125 (A358). Fig. 3.—Shouldered hoe. Figs. 2, 4.— Spades, of flint or chert, from field southwest of Monks Mound (A359, A360). Fig. 5.—Spade of flint or chert; James Ramey Mound, west side, 17 feet deep (A361). (About $\frac{1}{3}$ natural size.)

Plate XXVII

Pottery discs perforated and unperforated, are common in the mounds and on the surface. Attention is directed to the peculiar design on Fig. 3. Fragments such as Fig. 1, with a rude circle and cross lines are frequently found. Fig. 1.—Pottery fragment with oval design; Sawmill Mound, 3 feet deep (A315). Fig. 2.—Pottery disc, James Ramey Mound, 15 feet deep (A316). Fig. 3.—Fragment with peculiar design; Stockyards Village Site (A317). Fig. 4.—Pottery disc, James Ramey Mound, 12 feet deep (A318). Fig. 5.— Perforated clay disc, Wells-Tippetts Village Site (A319). Fig. 6.—Perforated disc of fine-grained sandstone, Ramey Village Site (A320). ($^3/_4$ natural size.)

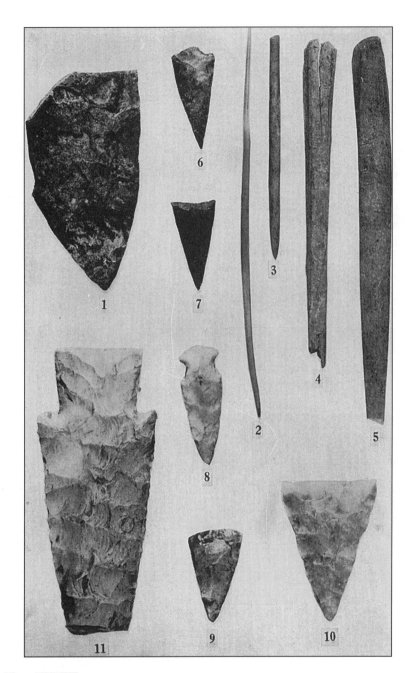

Plate XXVIII
Fig. 1.—Flint knife, broken; James Ramey Mound, 8 feet deep (A349). Fig. 2.—Fine-pointed needle of bone, with skeleton No. 30; Mounds 19, 20, 21 (A350). Figs. 3–5.—Bone awls, Wells-Tippetts Village Site (A351). Figs. 6–8.—Flint arrow points, James Ramey Mound, 17 feet deep (A352). Figs. 9, 10.—Flint war arrow points. Wells-Tippetts Village Site (A353). Fig. 11.—Flint spear head, James Ramey Mound, 17 feet deep (A354). (Figs. 2–5, ³/₄ natural size; 1, 6–11, about natural size.)

Plate XXIX
Fig. 1.—Digging trench in Sawmill Mound. Fig. 2.—Skeleton No. 11,
Sawmill Mound (A302).

Plate XXX
Fig. 1.—Skeleton No. 12, from Mound No. 20 (A485). Fig. 2.—Circle in
James Ramey Mound; also basins and circle of post holes.

Plate XXXI
Fig. 1.—Trench in James Ramey Mound (No. 33). Note altar in center foreground at trowel. Fig. 2.—Skeletons in position, Mound No. 20. Fig. 3.—General view of circles in James Ramey Mound.

Plate XXXII
Fig. 1.—Bone awls and needles. Figs. 2–6.—Mussel shells (*Lampsilis ventricosa*); W. J. Seever collection. ($^1/_4$ natural size.) Fig. 7.—Hematite axe. Fig. 8.—Grooved axe; Monticello Seminary collection. Fig. 9—Celt of porphyritic rock, Wells-Tippetts Village Site (A362). ($^1/_3$ natural size.)

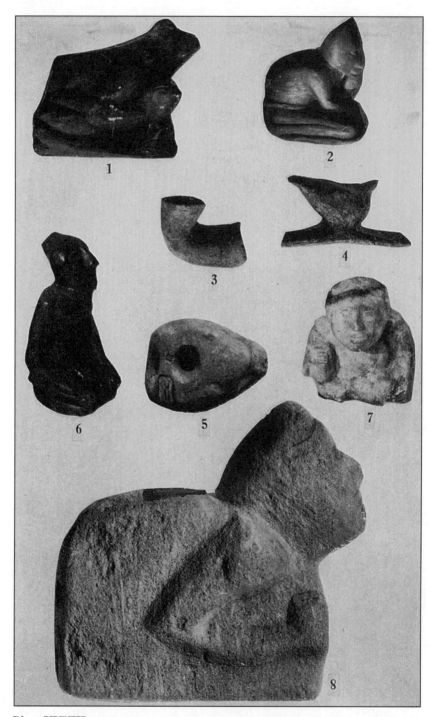

Plate XXXIII

Figs. 1–5.—Five pipes, several of them effigies, from the Monticello Seminary collection. Figs. 6, 7.—Stone effigies; Monticello Seminary collection. Fig. 8.—Large effigy pipe; W. J. Seever collection. (See p. 98 for description.)

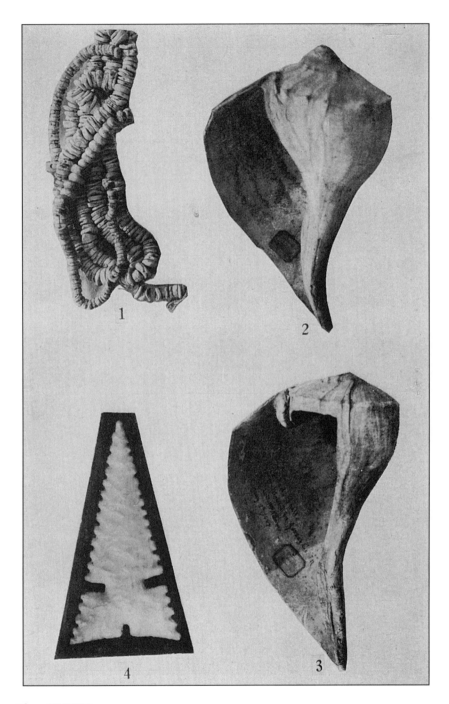

Plate XXXIV

Fig. 1.—string of shell beads cut from busycon conch. Fig. 2.—Marine conch shell, *Busycon carica*. Fig. 3.—Marine conch shell, *Busycon perversa*. ($^1/_4$ natural size.) Monticello Seminary collection. Fig. 4.—Arrowhead of quartz, unusual workmanship. (Natural size.) Found on the surface of Monks Mound.

Plate XXXV
Characteristic Cahokia motifs from the James Ramey Mound.

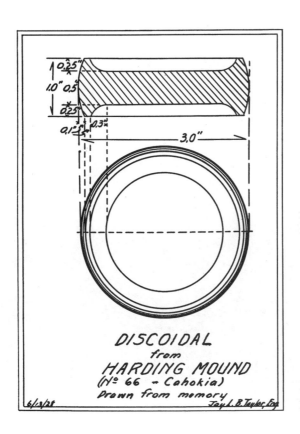

DISCOIDAL
from
HARDING MOUND
(N⁰ 66 — Cahokia)
Drawn from memory

Plate XXXVI
The discoidal, or chunkee stone, found on the face of a skeleton in Section
15-C of Mound No. 66.

Plate XXXVII
Mound No. 66. Property of the Baltimore & Ohio Railroad Company.
Camera 700 feet distant.

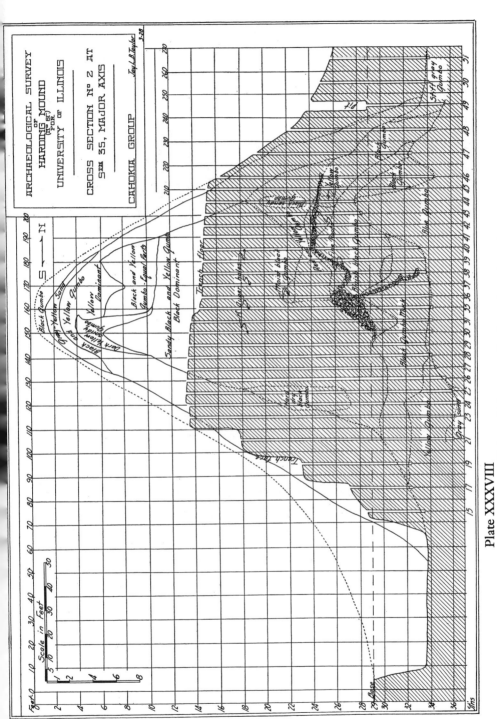

Plate XXXVIII
Cross section of Mound No. 66 at Station 35, major axis.

Plate XXXIX
The Powell Mound, from Taylor's photograph.

Plate XL
Jar with serpent motif. Mound No. 6, Neteler.

Plate XLI
Jar from the Neteler Mound, No. 6. Attention is called to the interesting decoration. The circles probably represent sun symbols.

Plate XLII
Four copper hatchets: The two upper hatchets are from Skeleton 6, Mound 6, Neteler farm, Havana; the smaller one at the extreme right is from Skeleton 5, Mound 6, Neteler farm; the one in the center, below, is from child's skeleton, No. 5, Mound No. 11, Chautauqua Park, Havana.

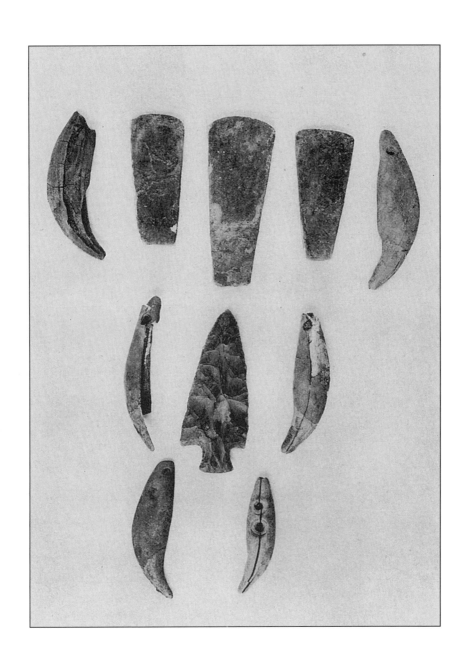

Plate XLIII
Illustrating six bear tusks, two of which are split; three small copper hatchets
and spearhead of agate-like flint from the Neteler Mound. See pp. 160, 161,
162.

Plate XLIV
Necklace of split bear tusks, Skeleton 6, Mound No. 6, Neteler. Nearly sixty
of these were found, many decayed.

Plate XLV
Copper head-band and portions of two human jaws cut into ornaments,
Mound No. 6, Neteler. The two objects at the lower right portion of the
plate are wolf jaws taken from this mound.

Plate XLVI
View of some skeletons *in situ* in the mound owned by Dr. Don F. Dickson,
Lewistown, Illinois, also accompanying objects. See pp. 167 and 168.
Photograph by Russell T. Neville, Kewanee, Ill.

Plate XLVII
Skeleton and objects in position. Dr. Don F. Dickson's Museum, Lewistown, Illinois. See pp. 167 and 168.

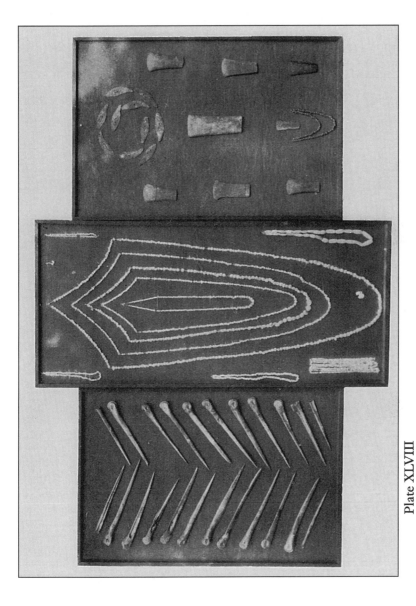

Plate XLVIII

Objects from the log tombs near Liverpool. Long bone daggers to left (12 to 16 ins.); pearl beads in center; imitation bear teeth in copper; copper axes and copper beads to the right. Dr. Don F. Dickson's collection.

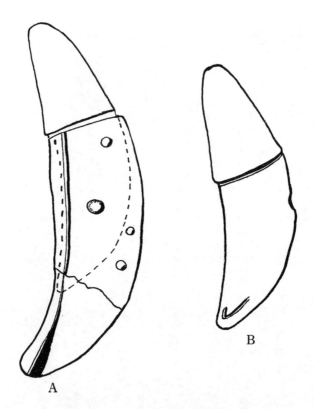

A

B

Plate XLIX
Bone knife inserted in a grizzly bear tusk. A.—The knife in sheath. B.—The knife itself. Several perforations are shown in A. The tusk is unusually large. Found in the long tomb, Liverpool, Illinois. Dr. Don F. Dickson's Museum. See p. 169.

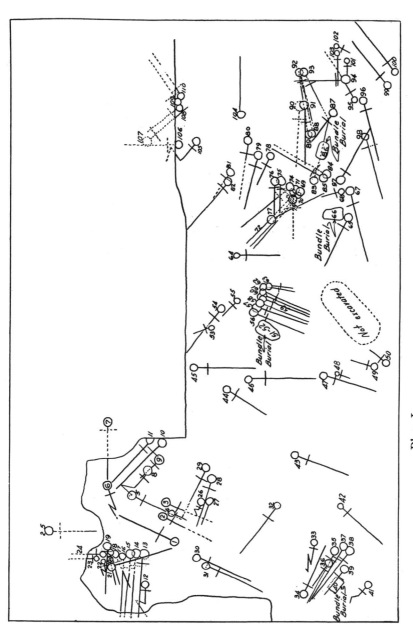

Plate L
Field map of Dickson's Cemetery.

Index

Allen, Udell, 103
Aluminum Ore Company mound, 41
American Anthropological Association, 29
American Association for the Advancement of Science, 4
American Bottom(s), 161, 197, 258, 308–9, 310
animal bones, 77, 119, 127, 252; bear teeth, 351; bird, 86; wapiti (elk), 120
Antiquities Act of the U.S. Congress, 13
arrowheads. *See* projectile points
Atkinson, Dr. Charles M., 355
auger, 135, 141, 142; borings, 110, 179, 181, 182, 303, 324–27; holes, 129, 250; post, 114, 125, 126; tests, 264–68, 293
axes: Davenport axe, 89, 279; grooved granite, 127; hematite, 139

Baker, Frank C., 1, 28, 114, 151, 191, 299
Bareis, Charles J., 44, 46
Barth, Mr., 140, 287
Bauman, Mrs. John, 137, 138, 284, 285
Bayley, Prof. W. S., 152, 299
beads, 121, 133
Benton, Thomas Hart, 8
Board of Indian Commissioners, 4
bone tools: awls, 86, 113, 114, 120, 133, 140; beads, 127; knife, 110; needles, 112, 356; spatula, 145, 282
borrow pits, 77, 92; ponds and depressions, 135–36, 211
Brackenridge, Henry Marie, 8, 65, 72, 207
Braun, H. M., 38, 124, 273
Brooks, Adele R., 104

Brown, John Nicholas, 10
burials. *See* human skeletal remains
burnt clay, 77, 109, 251
Bushnell, David I., Jr., 11, 16, 30, 63, 69, 73, 74, 200, 202, 203, 208, 249
Bushnell, David I., Sr., 11, 30
Bushnell map, 248

caches, 87, 139
Cahokia Creek, 34, 67, 134
Cahokia Fund, 21
Cahokia Indians, 70
Cahokia Mound Association, 14, 16, 19
Cahokia Mounds:
  Cahokia Mound. *See* Monks Mound, No. *38*, below
  Castle Mound. *See* Ramey Mound, No. *48*, below
  construction, 167–82, 313–27
  East Plaza, 32
  Edwards mounds, 22, 28, 31, 77–78, 225
  Harding Mound, No. *66*, 6, 35–36, 42–43, 65, 102, 103, 128, 141, 191, 253–68, 270, 272, 274, 276, 292–93
  James Ramey Mound, No. *33*, 32, 33, 34, 103, 108, 113, 141, 167, 204, 209, 313–21, 324, 336, 337, 338, 339
  Jesse Ramey Mound, 22, 31, 78, 79
  Jondro Mound, No. *83* (No. *86*), 34, 121–23, 239–41
  Kruger Bone Bank, 31, 34, 128, 246
  Kunnemann Mound, No. *11*, 22, 33, 64, 75, 79, 125, 139, 141, 151, 176, 276, 286, 299, 313, 321–22, 338

Cahokia Mounds (*continued*)

Kunnemann mound group, 27, 29
Kunnemann site, 87
Mackie Mound, No. *84*, 34, 125, 141
Merrell Mound, No. *42*, 31, 36, 142
Monks Mound, No. *38*, 10, 11, 13, 17, 33, 41, 42, 66, 69–74, 137, 139, 142, 151, 153–56, 157, 158, 179–82, 186–87, 199, 200, 201, 203–10, 272, 286, 299, 301–3, 304–5, 308, 324–27
Mound *5*, 142
Mound *14*, 34, 125, 243
Mound *19*, 31, 32, 106, 111, 112, 145, 282, 336, 339
Mound *20*, 31, 32, 106, 111, 145, 282, 336, 339
Mound *21*, 31, 32, 106, 111, 145, 282, 336, 339
Mound *23*, 31, 106
Mound *34*, 33, 113
Mound *41*, 142
Mound *43*, 31, 36, 106
Mound *47*, 32, 108
Mound *50*, 35
Mound *57*, 142
Mound *58*, 142
Mound *60*, 142
Mound *62*, 31, 106, 132, 143
Mound *64*, 22, 271–72, 276
Mound *65*, 253, 264, 268, 269–71, 272, 276, 292
Mound *73*, 32
Mound *75*, 35
Mound *76*, 141, 278
Mound *78*, 108
Mound *80*, 32
Mound *82*, 31, 32, 106
Mrs. Tippett's Mound, No. *61*, 35, 141, 143, 293
orientation, 158, 159, 274–77
Persimmon Mound, No. *51*, 31, 36
preservation, 10–21, 93–95
Ramey Mound, No. *48*, 21, 31, 74, 142, 304
Ramey Village site, 27
Sawmill Mound, No. *39*, 31, 32, 33, 39, 106, 108–11, 179, 226–29, 324, 336

Schmidt's (Smith) Mounds, Nos. *30–31*, 22, 28, 141, 151, 299
Temple Mound, No. *32*, 34, 113, 119, 141
village site, 67–68, 79–80, 132–33
Wells-Tippetts site, 31, 36, 133, 219–20
West Plaza, 32
Cahokia Mounds Museum Society, 48
Canteen Creek, 66, 164, 183, 198, 310, 328
Cantine Creek. *See* Canteen Creek
Carr, Clark E., 12
celts, 87, 127, 133, 138–39, 286
cemetery, 87, 124, 146
ceramics. *See* pottery
chert, 86, 140; knives, 86, 115; Mill Creek, 32; scrapers, 86
Chucalo, Paul, 36
Chucalo, Sam, 36
Chucalo, Zorina, 36
Cincinnati Centennial Exposition, 3, 29
Clark, George Rogers, 7–8
clay discs, 120
clay effigy head, 110
cloth, woven, 279
coffins, wooden, 263
Cole, Dr. Fay-Cooper, 45, 290
Conference on Midwestern Archaeology, 44
copper, 77, 78, 87–90, 92, 278–81, 291; axes, 356; band, 351; deer jaw with copper covering, 280; implement, 354; instrument, 351; needles or rods, 280; plates, 92, 284; serpent, 278; tortoise shells, 279
Cowen, Clinton, 21, 33, 116
Crook, A. R., 9, 16, 17, 21, 27, 29, 30, 155–56, 205, 303
cultural phases: Sponemann phase, 41; Lohmann phase, 41, 43, 46; Moorehead phase, 33, 34, 41, 46; Stirling phase, 33, 38, 43, 46; Sand Prairie phase, 32, 38, 43
cultures: Bean pot-duck effigy culture, 46; Early Woodland, 41; Emergent Mississippian, 38; Fort Ancient Culture, 156, 291, 303; Late Wood-

land, 41; Mississippian, 41; pure
village site culture, 46; Southern
culture, 289

Dartmouth College, 3
Denison College, 3, 21
Deuel, Thorne, 27, 45
Dickson, Dr. Don F., 35, 290, 359–61
Dickson, Marion, 360, 361
Dickson Mound, 359–60
Diffenbacher, 349
DuCoigne, Baptiste, 8

East St. Louis, 8, 9, 11, 38, 83–85, 93,
141
East St. Louis mound group, 9, 278;
Cemetery mound, 45; stock-yards
site, 38, 133–35, 213, 214
Emerald mound group. *See* Stock
Mound
Etowah Mounds, 5, 288

Featherstonehaugh, G. W., 152, 300
features: altars, 115, 116, 176; ash pits,
252; circular structure, 115; clay
floor, 137, 284
Fenneman, Dr. N. M., 9, 16, 154, 158,
302, 305
figurines, 139–40; fluorspar, 139; red
pipestone, 140
Fingerhut, Marie, 22
Flagg, Edmund, 66, 94, 154, 204, 301–2
Flagg, Norman G., 13, 14
flint. *See* chert
fossil shells, 85, 151
Fowke, Gerard, 29, 91, 92

galena, 32, 80, 109, 111
Goddard, Lt. G. W., 30
Grassy Lake site. *See* Wood River
mounds
Great Cahokia Mound. *See* Cahokia
Mounds, Monks Mound, No. *38*
Great Turtle Mound, The, 11
Griffin, James B., 27, 33, 44
gumbo, 122, 123, 125, 129, 249, 270,
273, 283, 284, 292, 293, 322, 323;

black, 257, 263, 265, 271, 345; blue,
257, 261; buckshot, 263, 264
Guthe, Dr. Carl, 288, 290

Hall, Robert L., 27, 44
Havana mounds, 343–45, 346–55
hematite, 86, 127, 145, 282
Henshaw, Henry W., 10
Higgins, Dr. George B., 14, 29, 69, 77,
81, 87
Hilgard, County surveyor, 69, 203
Hill, 72, 153, 204, 207, 209, 301
Hill's well, 73
hoes, 83–84, 111; limestone, 86;
notched, 86; shouldered, 133; spades,
86, 111, 120, 123, 133
Hopewell, 4, 204, 291, 361; Mound
Group, 2, 73, 78, 208, 340, 341
Howland, Dr., 87, 247, 248, 278, 290
human skeletal remains, 122, 138, 145,
169, 251, 282–83, 284; burial, 292;
burial structure, 114; burials, 87, 110,
112, 121, 124, 137, 253, 260, 262,
291, 293, 360; Frenchmen, 263;
human skull, 259, 260, 261; skeletons, 122, 138, 145, 169, 251, 282–
83, 284

idols. *See* figurines
Illinois Indians, 360
Illinois Indian village, 294
Illinois River, 191, 197, 291, 310, 341,
343, 345, 346, 349, 350, 352, 355,
359
Illinois State: Geological Survey, 299;
Historical Society, 6, 10, 12, 13, 14,
104; Museum, 16, 21, 27–28, 44, 45,
62, 80, 205, 299, 303
Indians trails, 210

Jondro, Charles, 104
Jondro, Tusant, 121
Judd, Dr. Neil M., 138, 262, 284

Kahn, Louis Gainer, 138, 285
Kaskaskia chief. *See* DuCoigne, Baptiste
Kelly, Dr. Arthur R., 43, 45
Kidder, Alfred Vincent, 6, 95

Kinley, Dr. David, 28, 41, 103, 191, 297
Kunnemann, Albert, 22, 74, 299

Langford, George, 290, 291, 292
La Salle, 91, 197, 198, 206
Leighton, Dr. Morris M., 1, 29, 33, 103,
    114, 123, 147, 192, 204, 297, 337
lithic artifacts: discoidal, 87, 260;
    hammerstones, 127; knives, 252;
    sandstone, grooved, 282; stone idols,
    139
lithic materials: diorite boulders, 85;
    greenstone, 85; limestone, 86, 120;
    sandstone, 145
Liverpool Group, 343 (mounds 1–3),
    345–46, 360–62; Bird Mound, 343,
    344, 349; Man Mound, 343, 349
log tomb burials, 291, 360–62
Lohmann site. See Aluminum Ore
    Company mound
Long Lake, 39, 248, 249, 250, 278

marine shell, 112, 114, 121, 140, 317,
    319, 338–40; Bulla, 85; Busycon
    perversum, 90; Busyconshells, 80, 87,
    204, 281; Columbella, 85; Conus, 85;
    Cruciform genre gorget, 32;
    Marginella, 85; Melampus, 85
McAdams, Clark, 11, 22
McAdams, William W., 10, 11, 21, 22,
    63, 67, 71, 79–80, 110, 112, 131, 138,
    153, 158, 200, 207, 286, 301, 305,
    343
McKinely, Ashley C., 30
Merrell, George, 14, 64, 74, 87, 103,
    132, 192, 200
minerals. See galena; hematite
Mississippi River, 161–66, 185, 197, 300,
    308–12, 330, 338
Missouri Historical Society, 29, 39, 69,
    81, 139, 203, 286, 290
Mitchell Mound group, 9, 14, 39, 87–90,
    130, 140, 202, 247–50, 278–81, 287;
    Great Mound, 14, 39; Hoefken
    Mound, 39
Mollusca, fresh water, 335–36, 341–42,
    356; gorget, 120; pearls, 291; pearls,
    baroque, 341; unio shells, 127, 140,
    204, 287; univalve shell, 282

Mollusca, marine. See marine shell
Mollusca, snail shells, 337–38; gastro-
    pods, 156, 177, 303, 319
mollusca fauna, 182
Monks of Cahokia, 13
Monticello Seminary, 138, 139, 286
Moorehead, Warren King, 46, 147, 151,
    297, 299, 304, 321, 335
Mound Builders, 8, 274, 275, 277, 279,
    299, 331, 335, 337
Mound City, 8
Mound Survey Committee, 9
Moundville, 288
Museum of Natural History. See
    University of Illinois
Museum of Ohio State University,
    curator, 5
Myer, W. E., 86, 104

National Research Council (NRC), 16,
    17, 18, 44, 93, 288
Neteler, Anna, 343
Newark earthworks, 94

ochre, 145, 282
Oglethorpe University, 3
Ohio Archaeological and Historical
    Society, 5
Omaha tradition, 91

Park Commission, 205
Patrick, Dr. John J. R., 1, 9, 21, 63, 67,
    69, 70, 83–85, 88, 121, 137, 200, 202,
    203, 206, 278, 284
Patrick-Van Court map, 104
Payne, E. W., 81, 87, 131, 139, 247, 286
Peabody, Charles, 5, 47
Peabody, Robert Singleton, 5, 6
Peabody Museum of American Archae-
    ology and Ethnology, 4, 18, 30, 69,
    139, 203, 286
Peck, John M., 210
Perino, Gregory, 43
Pershing, John J., 30
Phillips Academy, 5, 17, 22, 29, 62
pigment, 112
pipes: bird effigy, 139; clay, 139, 286;
    frog effigy, 76, 139, 286; human
    effigy, 139, 286; owl effigy, 252;

sandstone effigy, 286; sandstone, 139; stone, 78

Pittsburg Lake, 124, 146, 336

Pittsburg Lake cemetery, 38, 283, 336

Planters Hotel, St. Louis, 21

plant remains: Celtis occidentalis, 303; fossil hackberry seeds, 156, 303

Polaris, 274–76

Porter, James W., 39, 44, 46

pottery, 76, 77, 78, 86–87, 92, 109, 127, 138, 252; bird-head-eye design, 92; bowl, large, 176; designs, 86; effigy head, 125; handles, 86; heads of birds, 80, 120; human hand effigy, 260; vessel, 251; effigy, 137, 284

Powell brothers, 45

Powell Mound group, 34, 43, 45, 46, 129, 198, 272, 276

probes: Fulton County Walking Stick, 31; rod, 137

projectile points, 121, 251; arrowheads, 80, 92, 121, 133; Cahokia style arrowhead, 87; spearhead, 90, 251

Pulcher site, 9, 10; Square Mound, 10

Putnam, Frederic Ward, 4, 6, 70, 79, 139, 205, 286

R. S. Peabody Museum, 17, 18, 29

railroads: Baltimore & Ohio Railroad, 42, 191, 253, 268, 271, 272, 273; Chicago and Alton Railroad, 88, 130, 140, 248, 278, 287; Pennsylvania Railroad, 78, 123

Ramey, Lt. H. K., 30

Ramey family, 42; Fred, 21, 74, 207; James, 86; Jesse, 18; Priscilla, 10; Thomas, 10–11, 63–64, 72, 74, 154, 200, 301

Rattlesnake Mound. See Cahokia Mounds, Harding Mound, No. 66

Rau, Charles, 4, 81, 83, 111, 133

Roxanna Oil Company Corporation, 252

Russell, John, 9

Sam Chucallo mound, 33, 36, 122, 167, 177, 313, 323–24, 338

sand, 119

Schmidt, Otto L., 104

Schmidt's Mound, 13

Seever, William J., 21, 22, 31, 32, 34, 36, 39, 69, 79, 87, 104, 106, 110, 121, 209, 247, 286, 287, 289

Serant, Gordon, 105

Serpent Mound, 94

shell artifacts: beads, 76, 87, 121, 140, 338, 339, 341, 351; disc beads, 291; ear and nose ornaments, 338; effigy, 110; gorget, 32, 110, 120, 338; necklace, 90; spoons, 140; vessel, 140

shells, broken, 199

Signal Hill, 38, 126

Silver Creek, 41

skeletons. See human skeletal remains

Smith, Dr. F. S., 113

Smith's Mound. See Schmidt's Mound

Smithsonian Institution, 3–4, 5, 10, 30; Bureau of Ethnology (Bureau of American Ethnology), 10, 69; U.S. National Museum, 3–4

Snyder, Dr. John Francis, 10, 13, 130, 203, 210, 252

Snyder Groupe. See Pulcher site

soil. See gumbo; sand

Solomon, Mr., 360–61

St. Louis Academy of Science, 9, 16

St. Louis mound group, 8, 153, 300; Big Mound, 8, 9, 14, 16, 45, 88, 206, 210, 278

St. Louis World's Fair, 11, 205

State Park, 201

State Park Commission, 12

Stock Mound, 9, 41, 210

Sugar Loaf mounds, 139, 210

Sullivan, Judge J. D., 104, 126

Sullivan's Mound, 38

sun symbols, 111

Taylor, Jay L. B., 5, 42, 43, 47, 202, 209, 253, 293, 343

Tennessee Cumberland and Ohio cultures, 17

Terry, Dr. R. J., 14, 104, 112, 128, 262, 282

The Great Turtle Mound, 11

Thomas, Dr. Cyrus, 10, 67

Throop, Addison J., 42, 45, 104

Titterington, Dr. Paul F., 43, 45

Trappist monks, 69, 205
tunnels, 207, 209

UNESCO, 2
University of Illinois, 1, 22, 27–28, 36,
    38, 39, 41, 43, 45, 62, 114, 191, 200,
    268, 299, 349, 362; Board of Trust-
    ees, 21; Dept. of Geology, 152, 299;
    Museum of Natural History, 21, 31,
    28, 103, 105, 268, 288, 341; President
    David Kinley, 103, 297
University of Michigan, Museum of
    Anthropology, 43, 288
Utica, 197, 295

Van Court, B. J., 69, 72, 202, 207

Waters, George, 290
Wells, Rufus, 103
Whelpley, Dr. H. M., 87
Willoughby, Charles C., 17, 139, 286
Wilson, Thomas, 3, 4
Wissler, Clark, 16, 18
Wittry, Warren, 44, 46
Wood River mounds, 41, 250–52
World's Columbian Exposition, 4, 5
Worthen, Amos H., 9, 16, 152, 300